Genealogies
of
HADLEY FAMILIES

Embracing the Early Settlers
of the Towns of
HATFIELD, SOUTH HADLEY, AMHERST
AND GRANBY

Compiled by Lucius M. Boltwood

CLEARFIELD

Reprinted for
Clearfield Company, Inc. by
Genealogical Publishing Co., Inc.
Baltimore, Maryland
1993, 1996

International Standard Book Number: 0-8063-4652-3

Excerpted and reprinted from the 1905 edition
of Sylvester Judd's *History of Hadley*
Genealogical Publishing Co., Inc.
Baltimore, 1979
Library of Congress Catalogue Card Number 79-52942
Made in the United States of America

NOTE

Boltwood's *Genealogies of Hadley Families* was compiled, initially, from notes left by Sylvester Judd with the unfinished manuscript of his *History of Hadley*. It was first published in 1862 and appeared again the following year as the final section of Judd's *History*, which Boltwood completed and saw through press. The *History* was re-published in 1905, this time with Boltwood's *Genealogies* fully indexed. It is this edition of the *Genealogies* that we have reprinted.

GENEALOGICAL PUBLISHING CO., INC.

INTRODUCTION

THE material for the following pages has been drawn from every available source. Town, county, probate, church, and family records have been examined with the utmost care, and the moss-grown and crumbling tomb-stones of all the old burying yards within the limits of ancient Hadley, have been carefully deciphered. I may safely say, that prior to 1700, the records of but few towns were more carefully kept than those of Hadley, and although since that time, until within about twenty years, the records are less complete, it is thought that in few works of this character are so many of the families traced back to the first settlers of the town, as in this.

The plan adopted in the arrangement of the families, is so simple as to be readily understood by all familiar with genealogical tables. For the information of others, it is only necessary to explain, that the figures which precede the names of individuals denote their place in the series, and those which follow point back to the place in the series where the paternal ancestor is to be found. For example, in the family of Barnard, we read, "5. John, s. of Joseph, (4.)" The figure 5 denotes that this is the fifth family described; and the figure (4) refers back to the fourth family, on examining which we find that John was born Nov. 19, 1696. By observing this rule, it will be easy to trace any family back to the first ancestor in the town.

In justice to myself, and as an apology for the delay in putting these genealogies to press, I ought to remark, that Mr. Judd left his minutes of Hadley settlers in quite a confused state, not having taken the first step towards preparing them for the printer, and hence the labor of arranging them has been four-fold what I had anticipated. Having however, at length compared with the original records every date in regard to which I was at all in doubt, and arranged the same with care, I have the satisfaction of submitting the work to the public, with the feeling that it will be found, in the main, accurate and reliable.

L. M. BOLTWOOD.

AMHERST, June, 1862.

ABBREVIATIONS

abt.	. about.	m.	. married.
A. C.	. Amherst College.	mos.	. months.
ae.	. aged.	N. H.	. New Hampshire.
Amh.	. Amherst.	Nh.	. Northampton.
b.	. born.	North.	. Northfield.
bapt.	. baptized.	per.	. perhaps.
Capt.	. Captain.	prob.	. probably.
Ch.	. Church.	pub.	. published.
Cong.	. Congregational.	rem.	. removed.
d.	. died.	res.	. resided.
D. C.	. Dartmouth College.	s.	. son.
dau.	. daughter.	s. p.	. without issue.
Dea.	. Deacon.	So. Had.	. South Hadley.
Deer.	. Deerfield.	Spr.	. Springfield.
gr.	. graduated.	Sund.	. Sunderland.
Gr.	. Granby.	unm.	. unmarried.
Green.	. Greenfield.	Weth.	. Wethersfield.
Had.	. Hadley.	wid.	. widow.
Hart.	. Hartford.	W. C.	. Williams College.
Hat.	. Hatfield.	Wind.	. Windsor.
H. C.	. Harvard College.	Y. C.	. Yale College.

GENEALOGIES

ABBOTT, DANIEL. Children—*Phila; Achsah; Moses Graves; Lucy Willard; Ithream*, bapt. Jan. 14, 1798; *Son*, b. 1800; *Loi*, b. 1802.

ABBOTT, JACOB, Amherst, m. Mercy. Children—*Daniel*, b. July 25, 1764; *Persis*, b. Oct. 8, 1766; *Amos*, b. April 28, 1769; *Eliab*, b. Sept. 24, 1771.

1. ALEXANDER, JOSEPH, s. of Joseph of Winchester, N. H., res. for a few yrs. in North. before coming abt. 1748 to Had.; d. Sept. 30, 1761, ae. 70 or more. m. (1) 1736, Mary Mighill. m. (2) Experience. Children—*Miles*, b. 1737, d. in Sund., April 10, 1806, ae. 69; *Rachel*, b. Mch. 18, 1742, d. in North., 1775, ae. 32; *Mary*, b. 1743; *Aaron*, b. May 13, 1748; *Joseph*, b. Apr. 19, 1750; *Experience*, b. Feb. 5, 1753; *Eunice*, b. Aug. 25, 1757; *Thankful*, b. Jan. 6, 1761; *Eliakim*, b. Dec. 12, 1766.

2. JOSEPH, s. of Joseph (1) m. Sarah. Children—*Experience*, b. July 31, 1775; *Josiah*, b. Mch. 8, 1779, d. Dec. 1779; *Lydia*, b. Mch. 3, 1781, d. Sept. 30, 1781; *Thankful*. b. Dec. 30, 1783; *Polly*, bapt. Apr. 9, 1786, d. Dec. 1, 1786; *Elizabeth*, b. Jan. 11, 1794.

LEVI. Child—*Lewis Porter*, b. Mch. 5, 1837.

NATHANIEL, s. of George of Windsor, b. Dec. 29, 1652, d. Oct. 29, 1742.

EUNICE. Child—*Paul*, b. Oct. 28, 1790.

1. ALLIS, WILLIAM, freeman May 13, 1640, Braintree, rem. abt. 1661 to Hat., and d. Sept. 6, 1678. m. (1) Mary, who d. Aug. 10, 1677; m. (2) June 25, 1678, Mary, dau. of John Brownson, and wid. of John Graves, of Haddam, Ct. She m. (2) Mch. 16, 1681, Samuel Gaylord, Sen. Children—*John*, b. Mch. 5, 1642; *Samuel*, b. Feb. 24, 1647; *Josiah*, d. Oct. 15, 1651; *Josiah*, b. Oct. 20, 1651; *William*, b. Jan. 10, 1653, d. ae. 9 mos.; *William*, b. Jan. 10, 1656, slain in Falls fight, May 19, 1676; *Hannah*, m. June 28, 1670, William Scott; *Mary*, d. unm. Jan. 25, 1690.

2. JOHN, s. of William, (1) carpenter in Hat., m. Dec. 14, 1669, Mary, wid. of Nathaniel Clark of Nh., and dau. of Thomas Meekins, d. Jan. 1691. She m. (3) abt. 1691, Samuel Belden. Children—*Joseph; Abigail*, b. Feb. 25, 1672, m. Jan. 23, 1696, Ephraim Wells; *Hannah*, b. Oct. 9, 1673; *Ichabod*, b. July 10, 1675; *Eleazar*, b. July 23, 1677, m. Jemima; *Elizabeth*, b. Apr. 4, 1679, m. July 13, 1704, James Bridgman; *Lydia*, b. Aug. 15, 1680, d. Aug. 31, 1691; *John*, b. May 10, 1682, m. (1) Jan. 29, 1708, Mary Lawrence, (2) Bethiah Field; *Rebecca*, b. April 16, 1683, m. April 30, 1702, Nathl. Graves; *William*, b. May 16, 1684; *Mary*, b. Aug. 25, 1687; d. Apr. 20, 1688; *Nathaniel*, m. abt. 1705, Mercy Dudley, and rem. to East Guilford, Ct.

3. SAMUEL, s. of William, (1) d. Mch. 9, 1691. m. Alice, who m. (2) Sergt. John Hawks, and was slain in Deer. Feb. 29, 1704. Children— *Mehitable*, b. July 2, 1677, m. Dec. 13, 1698, Benoni Moore; *Samuel*, b. Feb. 20, 1679, slain Feb. 29, 1704; *William*, b. Oct. 19, 1680; *Mary*, b. July 6, 1682, m. Nathaniel Brooks; *Thomas*, b. Mch. 12, 1684, rem. to Guilford; *Sarah*, b. abt. 1685; *Rebecca*, b. Nov. 29, 1687.

4. JOSEPH, s. of John, (2) Hat., was slain by Indians, June 19, 1724. m. Naomi. Children—*Daniel*, b. Apr. 11, 1703, drowned at the mill, May 20, 1719; *Mary*, m. Sept. 26, 1723, John Smead; *Thankful*, b. Mch. 11, 1711, m. Josiah Holmes, of Deerfield; *Experience*, b. Mch. 11, 1711, m. 1736, Noah Ferry, of So. Had.

5. ICHABOD, s. of John, (2) Hat., d. July 9, 1747. m. (1) abt. 1698, Mary, dau. of Samuel Belding. She d. Sept. 9, 1724, ae. 45; (2) Nov. 25, 1726, Sarah, wid. of John Belden. Children—*Abigail*, b. Feb. 28, 1700, m. Nathaniel Smith; *Lydia*, b. Jan. 7, 1702, m. Jan. 13, 1736, Daniel Dickinson, and d. Oct. 16, 1737, ae. 35; *Martha*, b. Nov. 19, 1703, m. (1) ——— Hammond, of Hardwick; (2) Nathaniel Kellogg, of Hadley, and d. Sept. 13, 1764; *Samuel*, b. Dec. 12, 1705, grad. H. C. 1724, was a clergyman in Somers, Ct.; *Sarah*, b. Jan. 11, 1708, m. Nov. 14, 1734, Joseph Miller; *Bathsheba*, b. Jan. 12, 1710, m. 1734, Jonathan Warner; *Abel*, b. July 21, 1714, m. Dec. 14, 1735, Miriam, dau. of Joseph Scott; *Elisha*, b. Dec. 3, 1716.

1. ALVORD, JOHN. Children—*John; Gideon*, b. June 12, 1734.

2. JOHN, s. of John, (1) d. in S. H., July 8, 1758. m. July 17, 1734, Abigail White, dau. of Joseph. She d. Nov. 15, 1770, ae. 82. Children—*Moses*, b. Aug. 26, 1735; *Azariah*, b. Jan. 20, 1738, res. in Spr. and W. Spr., and d. Jan. 11, 1819, ae. 89. m. (1) Jan. 5, 1768, Abigail Nash, who died Mch. 31, 1782, ae. 42; m. (2) Mch. 5, 1789, Lucy Nash, of Gr.; *Abigail*, b. Sept. 23, 1739; *Jerusha*, b. Sept. 27, 1741; *Dorcas*, b. Nov. 4, 1743; Rachel, b. Apr. 15, 1747; *Phineas*, b. June 26, 1750; *Luther*, b. Mch. 4, 1753, d. 1784, ae. 31; *Rebecca*, b. Apr. 14, 1756.

1. AMSDEN, JOHN, rem. from Cambridge to Hat., and d. 1696. m. Elizabeth, who d. Aug. 13, 1689. Children—*John*, b. Nov. 24, 1686; *Isaac*, d. Aug. 8, 1692.

2. JOHN, s. of John, (1) Deerfield, was drowned 1742. m. Mch. 23, 1720, Mary, dau. of Samuel Cole. Children—*John*, b. Feb. 16, 1721, res. in Deerfield; *Isaac*, b. Sept. 27, 1722, Conway, 1770; *Elizabeth*, b. Sept. 27, 1724, d. unm.; *Violet*, b. Sept. 14, 1726, m. Jona. Bardwell; *Oliver*, b. 1728, slain by Indians, Aug. 26, 1746, *Elisha*, b. 1733, Conway, 1770; *Mary*, b. 1735, m. Aaron Phelps, of Belchertown; *Simeon*, b. 1737, slain by Indians, Aug. 26, 1746; *Eunice*, b. 1739, m. ——— Chamberlain of Sunderland; *Asahel*, res. in Ashfield, 1770.

ARMS, WILLIAM, rem. from Hatfield to Sund., and thence to Deerfield, and d. 1731. m. Nov. 21, 1677, Joanna Hawks. Children—*William*, b. Feb. 14, 1678, d. in Deer. 1690; *John*, b. Dec. 25, 1679, res. in Deer.; *Sarah*, b. Nov. 21, 1681, m. Zebadiah Williams; *Margaret*, b. Oct. 6, 1683, m. William Belding; *Hannah*, b. 1685, m. abt. 1704, Joseph Clesson; *Daniel*, b. Sept. 11, 1687, res. in Deer. 1729; *Ebenezer*, b. Aug. 28, 1689, d. Sept. 25, 1690; *William*, b. Oct. 26, 1692.

ARNOLD, THOMAS, was per. a trader during the Revolution. Children—
Rachel, bapt. Jan. 15, 1775; *Thomas*, bapt. Dec. 22, 1776; *Betsey*, bapt. Oct.
1778.

ATCHISON, JOHN, Hatfield, was slain by Indians, Sept. 19, 1677. M.
Deliverance. Children—*Elizabeth*, b. Apr. 22, 1672, m. 1690, Daniel Lamb;
Mary, b. Oct. 30, 1673, m. 1692, N. Rust; *John*, b. Mch. 23, 1676, m. and died
in Brimfield, 1738; *Benoni*, b. Nov. 22, 1677, d. in Springfield, 1704.

ATHERTON, Rev. HOPE, Hat., was bapt. Aug. 30, 1646, s. of Mr. Humphrey, ord. 1671, freeman 1672, d. June 8, 1677. M. 1674, Sarah Hollister,
dau. of Lt. Joseph of Wethersfield. She m. (2) Timothy Baker, of Nh.
Children—*Hope* and *Joseph*, (twins,) b. Jan. 7, 1675; *Sarah*, b. Oct. 26, 1676.

ATWELL, OLIVER, m. June 8, 1781, Jerusha Smith. Children—*Daughter*, b. Feb. 18, 1782, d. Apr. 1782; *Child*, b. Aug. 1784; *Oliver*, bapt. July
25, 1785; *John*, bapt. Sept. 25, 1785; *Pamela*, b. Sept. 27, 1785; *George
Washington*, bapt. Nov. 20, 1789; *Fanny Sanford*, bapt. Jan. 3, 1790.

AYRES, SAMUEL, b. abt. 1714, rem. in 1740 from Brookfield to Granby.
He was drowned in Conn. river, Nov. 15, 1768, ae. 54. His body was found,
Apr. 1771, below South Hadley falls, in a state of good preservation. M.
Martha Bell, who d. Oct. 25, 1765, ae. 41. Children—*John*, m. Ruth Smith,
of Granby, and d. in Greenwich, Jan. 26, 1817; *Aaron*, b. Nov. 12, 1744, m.
(1) Lois Moore of Gr., who d. Sept. 26, 1789, ae. 39; (2) Mary Hitchcock,
who d. June 22, 1830, ae. 69; *Eleazar*, b. abt. 1746, m. Sybil Clark, and d.
Mch. 2, 1832, ae. 36; *Martha*, m. Asher Alvord of So. Had., and rem. to Wilmington, Vt.; *Amos*, m. Esther Dickinson, and res. in Amherst; *Daniel*, b.
July 15, 1751, m. and rem. to the west; *Sarah*, b. May 10, 1754, d. Apr. 26,
ae. 22; *Lydia*, b. Sept. 22, 1756, m. Chilion Palmer, and rem. to Litchfield,
Ct.; *Susannа*, b. Jan. 28, 1759; *Asa*, b. June 5, 1761, m. Mary Wait, and
rem. to Ohio; *Ruth*, b. Sept. 22, 1763.

BACON, ANDREW, was in Hartford, 1639, where he was a highly useful
citizen, assistant of the Gen. Ct., 1637-8, and several times deputy of the
Gen. Ct. A first settler of Had., was there freeman in 1661, and d. s. p.,
Oct. 4, 1669. He m. Elizabeth, wid. of Timothy Stanley, of Hartford. She
came in 1634 from England. The court gave her all Mr. Bacon's lands and
buildings in Hadley. She rem. to Hartford, and d. abt. 1679.

BAKER, ELIJAH, s. of John of Northampton, settled in Amherst. M. (1)
June 16, 1757, Rebecca, dau. of Jonathan Smith of Amh.; (2) ——— ———.
Children by first wife—*Elijah*, a soldier, d. at Rhinebeck; *Hannah*, bapt.
Dec. 9, 1759, m. Wm. Hubbard, of Leverett; *Enos*, bapt. May 20, 1764;
Sarah, bapt. May 4, 1766; *Enos*, bapt. May 15, 1768, d. in Amh. 1845, ae. 77;
Martin, bapt. Oct. 7, 1770, m. July 16, 1797, Mary Smith. Child by second
wife—*Martha*, m. June 22, 1797, Moses Gaylord.

1. BALDWIN, JOSEPH, Milford, 1639, rem. abt. 1663 to Had., was freeman
1666, and d. Dec. 8, 1676. M. (1) Hannah; m. (2) wid. Isabel Northam,
who as widow Catlin, had come with s. John from Newark, N. J.; m. (3)
Elizabeth, wid. of William Warriner. She had before been the wife of Luke

8 BALDWIN—BARNARD.

Hitchcock, of Wethersfield. She d. in Spr. Apr. 25, 1696. Children—*Joseph;*
Benjamin, res. in Milford; *Hannah*, m. Jeremiah Hull, of New Haven; *Mary*,
m. John Catlin, of Arthur Kill., N. J.; *Elizabeth*, bapt. 1645; *Martha*, b.
1647, m. Dec. 26, 1667, John Hawks of Hat.; *Jonathan*, bapt. 1650, res. in
Milford; *David*, b. 1651, m. Nov. 11, 1674, Mary Stream, d. in Milford,
1689; *Sarah*, bapt. 1653, m. Samuel Bartlett of Nh.

2. JOSEPH, s. of Joseph, (1) d. Nov. 21, 1681. M. (1) Elizabeth; m. (2)
Sarah Cooley of Milford, bapt. 1648, dau. of Benjamin. She d. in Spr. 1689.
Children—*Joseph*, b. 1663, rem. to Malden; *James; Mary*, d. Dec. 17, 1674;
Mehitable, b. June 1670, d. July 11, 1670; *Hannah*, b. Apr. 13, 1673; *Mercy*,
b. Nov. 10, 1674. She or Mary m. Samuel Allen, Jr., of Nh.; *Hannah*, b.
Mch. 9, 1675, d. Oct. 31, 1676; *Samuel*, b. Apr. 7, 1679; *Hannah*, b. Apr. 27,
1681.

BALLARD, JOSHUA, saddler, s. of Jeremiah, of New Salem, m. Dec. 27,
1757, Ruth Kellogg, who d. May 3, 1776. Children—*Ruth*, b. Dec. 27, 1758,
m. Waitstill Cook; *Lovisa*, b. Feb. 25, 1761; *Polly*, b. Jan. 16, 1764; *Jerusha*,
b. Dec. 26, 1765; *William*, b. Nov. 1, 1768.

BARDWELL, ROBERT, Hatfield, d. Jan. 9, 1726. M. Nov. 29, 1676,
Mary, dau. of William Gull. She d. Nov. 12, 1726. Children—*Ebenezer*, b.
Oct. 19, 1679; *Mary*, b. Oct. 15, 1681; *John*, b. Sept. 16, 1683, d. 1685;
Samuel, b. Sept. 26, 1685; *John*, b. Aug. 18 or 28, 1687; *Elizabeth*, b. July
30, 1689; *Thomas*, b. Dec. 8, 1691; *Hester*, b. Aug. 8, 1693, m. Oct. 23, 1717,
Joseph Belding; *Sarah*, m. May 19, 1713, Jona. Barrett, of Hartford; *Thank-
ful*, m. May 23, 1717, Abram Graves; *Abigail*, b. abt. 1699, m. June 6, 1720,
David Graves, and died 1786, ae. 87.

1. BARNARD, FRANCIS, b. abt. 1617, Hartford, 1644, maltster, a first
settler of Had., freeman 1666, d. Feb. 3, 1698, ae. 81. M. (1) Aug. 15, 1644,
Hannah Merrill, or Meruil, or Marvin; m. (2) 1677, Frances, wid. of John
Dickinson, and dau. of Nathaniel Foote. Children—*Thomas; Samuel;*
Joseph; Hannah, m. (1) Oct. 17, 1667, Doct. John Westcarr; m. (2)
Oct. 9, 1680, Simon Beaman, of Deer., and d. 1739; *John*, slain with Capt.
Lathrop, Sept. 18, 1675; and prob. *Sarah*, who d. 1676.

2. THOMAS, s. of Francis, (1) grad. H. C. 1679, ord. Jan. 1682, pastor of
1st. Chh. Andover, and d. Oct. 13, 1718, in 62 yr. M. (1) Dec. 14, 1686,
Elizabeth Price, dau. of Theodore. She d. Oct. 10, 1693; m. (2) May 28,
1696, Abigail Bull, who d. 1702; m. (3) July 20, 1704, Lydia Goffe. Children—*Thomas*, b. Oct. 20, 1688; *John*, b. Feb. or Mch. 26, 1690, grad. H. C.
1709, pastor of 1st Chh. Andover, d. June 14, 1758; *Theodore*, b. Feb. 6, 1692,
d. Feb. 16, 1725, ae. 34.

3. SAMUEL, captain, s. of Francis, (1) d. Oct. 17, 1728, ae. 74. M. Nov.
5, 1678, Mary Colton, who d. Mch. 4 or 5, 1709, ae. 58. Children—*Mary*, b.
Aug. 11, 1681, m. 1698, Moses Cook; *Hannah*, b. June 8, 1684, m. 1715,
John Marsh, and d. Sept. 31, 1716, ae. 32; *Samuel*, b. Mch. 29, 1686, d. unm.,
Nov. 5, 1742, ae. 56; *John*, b. May 6, 1688; *Sarah*, b. Aug. 17, 1691.

4. JOSEPH, s. of Francis, (1) rem. to Deer., where he d. Sept. 6, 1695,
from wounds received of Indians. M. Dec. 19, 1675, Sarah, dau. of Elder
John Strong of Nh. She m. (2) Sept. 23, 1698, Jonathan Wells, and d. 1733.

Children—*John,* b. Nov. 19, 1676; *Sarah,* b. Dec. 30, 1677, m. 1700, Thomas Wells; *Joseph,* b. Oct. 13, 1679, d. Aug. 8, 1681; *Joseph,* b. June 20, 1681, rem. to Windsor; *Thomas,* b. Mch. 13, 1683, of Lebanon, 1701; *Samuel,* b. Dec. 1, 1684, of Salem, 1762; *Rebecca,* b. Dec. 25, 1686, m. 1718, Jonathan Wells, Jr.; *Hannah,* b. abt. 1688, m. 1709, Samuel Child; *Abigail,* b. Oct. 3, 1691, m. 1714, Ebenezer Sheldon; *Ebenezer,* b. Mch. 13, 1696, of Roxbury, 1717.

5. JOHN, s. of Joseph, (4) a physician, d. Mch. 6, 1726, ae. 49. M. Jan. 13, 1701, Bridget Cook. She m. (2) Sept. 24, 1730, Dea. Samuel Dickinson. Children—*Thomas,* a physician in Tolland, Ct.; *Bridget,* b. Sept. 30, 1708, m. 1729, Jonathan Burt, of Deerfield; *Sarah,* b. Feb. 2, 1710, m. Aug. 12, 1730, Thomas Temple; *Abigail,* b. Mch. 14, 1712, m. May, 1740, Aaron Cook; *John,* b. Dec. 12, 1713, rem. to Shutesbury; *Joanna,* b. Oct. 1, 1715, m. 1735, Enos Nash; *Francis,* b. Nov. 11, 1717, d. Jan. 5, 1719; *Joseph,* b. Jan. 1, 1720, rem. to Sund.; *Francis,* b. Oct. 6, 1721; *Rebecca,* b. May 18, 1724.

BARNARD, JOHN, rem. from Cambridge to Hartford, was a first settler of Had., where he was buried May 23, 1664. He left much of his property to the children of his kinsman Henry Hayward of Wethersfield, and the children of his sister, Mary Bedient. M. Mary, who d. Feb. or Mch. 1665.

BARNS, WILLIAM, m. Aug. 20, 1696, Mary Smith. Children—*Mary,* b. July 7, 1697; *William,* b. Aug. 7, 1698; *Mercy,* b. Nov. 14, 1700; *John,* b. Sept. 22, 1702.

1. BARTLETT, DANIEL, m. (1) Nov. 16, 1777, Elizabeth Smith; m. (2) Feb. 3, 1784, Deborah Ferguson. Children—*Daniel; Zebina; Jerusha; Samuel; Elizabeth; Leonard,* bapt. Oct. 24, 1790; *Lewis,* bapt. Feb. 26, 1792; *Stillman,* bapt. Dec. 22, 1793; *Roxa,* bapt. Jan. 17, 1796; *Nancy,* bapt. Oct. 29, 1797; *Charles,* bapt. Aug. 30, 1804; *Dexter,* bapt. Aug. 30, 1804.

2. DANIEL, s. of Daniel, (1.) Children—*Elijah,* b. Jan. 10, 1805; *Elatah Stockbridge,* b. Sept. 20, 1808; *Patience,* b. Apr. 13, 1810; *Miranda,* b. Mch. 13, 1812; *Adeline,* b. May 30, 1813; *Daniel Lewis,* b. Dec. 6, 1816.

3. LEONARD, s. of Daniel, (1.) Children—*Roxana,* b. Mch. 24, 1817; *Catharine Cooley,* b. Dec. 24, 1818; *Daniel James,* b. Mch. 8, 1820; *Henry Leonard,* b. Aug. 27, 1824; *Lewis Williston,* b. June 23, 1826; *David Norton,* b. May 28, 1828; *Lyman,* b. Feb. 20, 1831; *Hannah Jerusha,* b. Jan. 7, 1836.

BARTLETT, LEVI. Children—*Clarissa,* b. May 3, 1809; *Clarissa,* b. Oct. 27, 1810; *Levi Harvey,* b. Sept. 23, 1812; *Mary Ann,* b. June 3, 1814; *Elijah Henry,* b. Mch. 1, 1816; *Harriet Newell,* b. Mch. 8, 1818; *Elizabeth,* b. June 1, 1820; *John,* b. Aug. 22, 1824; *Clarissa Naomi,* b. Apr. 11, 1827.

BARTLETT, NICHOLAS, m. Nov. 14, 1771, Mary Morton of Hat. Children—*Lucy,* bapt. Oct. 11, 1772; *Mary,* bapt. Aug. 7, 1774; *Caleb,* b. Dec. 29, 1777; *Abigail,* bapt. Jan. 17, 1776.

BARTLETT, OLIVER, m. 1765, Asenath Smith of So. Had. Children— *Sarah Lane,* bapt. May 17, 1767; *Henry,* bapt. 1767; *Benjamin,* bapt. Dec. 11, 1769; *Oliver,* bapt. Jan. 30, 1773; *Warham,* bapt. Sept. 1775; *William,* bapt. Aug. 18, 1782; *Asenath,* bapt. Aug. 1784.

BASCOM, Thomas, Amherst, m. Martha. Children—*Joel*, b. Sept. 18, 1773; *Nathan*, b. June 22, 1775; *Martha*, b. Aug. 12, 1777; *Nathan*, b. Apr. 8, 1779; *David*, b. Aug. 8, 1780.

BEDIENT, Mary, widow of Morgan, of Staynes, England, with her two sons came to New England to receive estate devised by her brother, John Barnard. Children b. in England—*Morgan*, b. June 25, 1651; *Thomas*, b. July 22, 1654, rem. to Fairfield, Ct., and d. abt. 1698.

BEEBE, James, m. Oct. 24, 1667, Mary Boltwood, dau. of Robert. She d. Aug. 19, 1676, and he then perhaps rem. to Stratford, Ct., and m. Dec. 19, 1679, Sarah Benedict, dau. of Thomas of Norwalk, Ct. Children—*Mary*, b. Aug. 18, 1668; *James* b. Dec. 9, 1669, d. Jan. 3, 1670; *Rebecca*, b. Dec. 8, 1670; *Samuel*, b. June 26, 1672; *Mary*, b. 1675.

BEERS, Ephraim, Hatfield, m. Sept. 9, 1680, Mary Gardner. Child— *Elizabeth*, b. June 27, 1683, d. Oct. 19, 1684.

BELDING, Daniel, b. Nov. 20, 1648, s. of William of Wethersfield, settled as early as 1671 in Hat., whence abt. 1689 he rem. to Deer., and d. Aug. 14, 1732, ae. 85. M. (1) Nov. 10, 1670, Elizabeth Foote, dau. of Nathaniel; she was slain Sept. 16, 1696; m. (2) Feb. 17, 1699, Hepzibah, wid. of Thomas Wells of Hat., and dau. of Wm. Buell. She was b. in Windsor, Dec. 11, 1649, slain Mch. 1704; m. (3) Sarah, wid. of Phillip Mattoon. She d. Sept. 17, 1751, in 95th yr. Children—*William*, b. Dec. 26, 1671; *Richard*, b. Mch. 29, 1672; *Elizabeth*, b. Oct. 8, 1673, m. —— Brooks; *Nathaniel*, b. Jan. 26, 1675, d. Aug. 21, 1714; *Mary*, b. Nov. 17, 1677, m. —— Trowbridge; *Daniel*, b. Sept. 1, 1680, slain Sept. 16, 1696; *Sarah*, b. Mch. 15, 1682, m. —— Trowbridge; *Daniel*, b. Sept. 1, 1680, slain Sept. 16, 1696; *Sarah*, b. Mch. 15, 1682, m. Benjamin Burt; *Hester*, b. Sept. 29, 1683, m. —— Clark; *Abigail*, b. Mch. 10, 1686, d. June 15, 1686; *Samuel*, b. Apr. 10, 1687; *John*, b. June 24, 1689, d. June 25, 1689; *Abigail*, b. Aug. 18, 1690; *John*, b. Feb. 28, 1693, slain Sept. 16, 1696; *Thankful*, b. Dec. 21, 1695, slain Sept. 16, 1696.

BELDING, Joshua. Children—*Submit*, bapt. Dec. 5, 1790; *Anna*, bapt. Oct. 21, 1792; *Naomi*, bapt. March, 1796; *Content*, bapt. March, 1796.

1. BELDING, Samuel, s. of Richard, rem. from Wethersfield to Hat., and d. Jan. 3, 1713. M. (1) Mary, who was slain Sept. 19, 1677; m. (2) June 25, 1678, Mary, wid. of Thomas Wells; she d. Sept. 20, 1691; m. (3) 1691, Mary, wid. of John Allis; m. (4) Apr. 10, 1705, Sarah, wid. of John Wells. Children—*Mary*, b. July 10, 1655; *Samuel*, b. Apr. 6, 1657; *Stephen*, b. Dec. 28, 1658; *Sarah*, b. Sept. 30, 1661; *Ann*, b. Jan. 27, 1665; *Ebenezer*, b. Nov. 16, 1667, m. Martha; *John*, b. Nov. 13, 1669.

2. Samuel, s. of Samuel, (1) res. in Hat., d. abt. 1737. M. (1) Oct. 9, 1678, Sarah, wid. of Samuel Billings, and dau. of Richard Fellowes. She d. Feb. 5, 1713; m. (2) May 7, 1713, Mary, wid. of Dr. Thomas Hastings, and dau. of David Burt, of Nh., b. May 3, 1676, and d. April 13, 1734. Children —*Mary*, b. Aug. 27, 1679, m. Ichabod Allis; *Hannah*, b. Dec. 5, 1681, m. Joseph Clary; *Samuel*, b. Oct. 19, 1684, d. April 17, 1697; *Mehitabel*, b. Jan.

23, 1687, m. Samuel Hawley; *Sarah*, m. Eleazer Graves; *Thankful*, m. Dec. 5, 1739, John Belding, Jr.; *Lydia*, b. Oct. 28, 1718.

3. STEPHEN, s. of Samuel, (1) res. in Hat., and d. Oct. 6, 1720. M. Aug. 16, 1682, Mary Wells, dau. of Thomas. She m. (2) Jan. 2, 1723, Capt. Joseph Field, of Northfield, and d. 1751. Children—*Elizabeth*, b. Feb. 2, 1683, m. Richard Scott; *Mary*, b. May 20, 1685, m. John Wait; *Sarah*, b. Oct. 25, 1687; *Stephen*, b. Feb. 22, 1689, prob. m. Mindwell, dau. of Capt. Benjamin Wright, and d. in Northfield, 1735 or 1736; *Samuel*, b. Oct. 23, 1692; *Joshua*, b. abt. 1695, d. in Whately, 1738; m. Dec. 1, 1725, Sarah Field. She perhaps m. 1761, Thomas Noble of Westfield, and d. Aug. 17, 1763, in 62d yr.; *Esther*, m. 1724, Nathaniel Gunn; *Lydia*, d. July 24, 1714.

4. JOHN, s. of Samuel, (1) res. in Hat., and was killed at a raising, Oct. 18, 1725, ae. 56. M. Sarah, perhaps Wait, dau. of Benjamin. She m. (2) Nov. 25, 1726, —— Allis. Children—*John*, b. Sept. 22, 1694, d. abt. 1758; m. (1) Dec. 1, 1715, Deliverance Lawrence; m. (2) Dorothy; *Joseph*, b. Aug. 9, 1696, d. in Whately, Oct. 1788, ae. 88; m. (1) Oct. 23, 1717, Esther Bardwell; m. (2) July 13, 1727, Margaret Gillett; *Martha*, b. Aug. 6, 1698, m. —— Bridgman, prob. Orlando; *Sarah*, b. Feb. 10, 1701, m. Thomas Bardwell; *Hannah*, b. May 14, 1703, m. Nathaniel Hawks of Deer.; *Mary*, b. July 27, 1705, m. Obadiah Dickinson; *Ebenezer*, b. June 7, 1712; *Ebenezer*, b. July 29, 1714, m. Sept. 30, 1736, Hannah Nash; *Rhoda*, b. July 20, 1716, m. [Aaron?] Sheldon.

5. SAMUEL, s. of Stephen, (3) res. in Hat., and d. Oct. 5, 1732. M. 1717, Elizabeth, dau. of Hezekiah Dickinson of Spr. Children—*David*, b. Feb. 4, 1718, rem. to Swansey, N. H.; *Samuel*, b. Aug. 15, 1719, rem. to Swansey; *Abigail*, b. May 4, 1721, m. Noah Nash, of Hat., and d. Feb. 7, 1797, ae. 75; *Elizabeth*, b. Dec. 2, 1723, m. —— Arms of Deerfield; *Mary*, b. Oct. 23, 1725, d. before 1741; *Hezekiah*, b. July 2, 1728; *Noah*, b. May 8, 1731, rem. to Conway, and thence to State of New York; *Jonathan*, b. May 9, 1733.

6. HEZEKIAH, s. of Samuel, (5) a deacon in 2nd Chh Amh., where he d. June 22, 1813, ae. 85. M. (1) April 16, 1752, Mary, dau. of Jonathan Dickinson of Hat. and Amh.; m. (2) Abigail, dau. of John Nash of Hat.; m. (3) April 21, 1767, Martha Field of Sund.; m. (4) April 16, 1795, Martha, dau. of Windsor Smith of Had. She m. (2) July 6, 1815, Col. Asaph White, of Erving. Children—*Mary*, b. Jan. 11, 1753, m. Hezekiah Howard of Leverett; *Elizabeth*, m. Eleazar Warner of Sund.; *Submit*, bapt. Jan. 25, 1756, m. Ethan Billings of Conway; *Hepzibah*, m. Elias Graves of Sund.; *Abigail*, bapt. Dec. 5, 1762, m. Nov. 7, 1782, Ebenezer Dickinson of Amh.; *John*, b. July 4, 1764, m. Lydia Hunt, of Belchertown; *Elihu*, b. June 5, 1768, m. Sally Clapp, and d. in Amh.; *Martha*, b. July 21, 1770, m. (1) Gershom Ingram of Amh.; (2) John Kellogg of Amh., and d. May 10, 1837, ae. 67.

BELDING, STEPHEN, m. Feb. 10, 1796, Abigail Hibbard. Children— *Martha*, bapt. Feb. 5, 1797; *Abigail*, bapt. May 4, 1800; *Melinda*, bapt. March 31, 1805; *Lucinda*, bapt. Feb. 28, 1808; *Esther*, bapt. May 6, 1810.

1. BELL, REUBEN, doctor, m. Dec. 28, 1806, Alethea Smith. Children— *John Smith*, b. May 26, 1807; *Frederick* and *Samuel*, (twins,) b. Jan. 8, 1811; *Charles*, b. Oct. 28, 1814; *Ruth Maria*, b. Oct. 24, 1816; *Elizabeth*, b. March 17, 1824.

2. JOHN SMITH, s. of Reuben, (1.) Children—*Frederick*, b. June 26, 1834; *Mary Porter*, b. Nov. 11, 1836; *Charles Henry*, b. Nov. 22, 1838.

1. BILLINGS, RICHARD, Hartford, 1640, rem. 1661, to Hat., where he d. March 13, 1679. M. Margery, who d. Dec. 5, 1679. Child—*Samuel*.

2. SAMUEL, s. of Richard, (1) Hat., d. Feb. 1, 1678. M. abt. 1661, Sarah, dau. of Richard Fellowes. She m. (2) Oct. 9, 1678, Samuel Belding, Jr., of Hat., and d. Feb. 5, 1713. Children—*Samuel*, b. Jan. 8, 1665; *Ebenezer*, b. Oct. 29, 1669; *Sarah*, d. July 15, 1674; *Richard*, b. April 7, 1672; *John*, b. Oct. 11, 1674, slain July 15, 1698; *Sarah*, b. Oct. 18, 1676, m. Samuel Dickinson of Hat.

3. SAMUEL, s. of Samuel, (2) Hat., m. (1) Nov. 18, 1686, Hannah Wright, who d. Nov. 18, 1687; m. (2) 1691, wid. Rebecca Miller. Children—*Samuel*, res. in Sund. and Hardwick; *Sarah*, b. March 15, 1697, m. Jan. 16, 1724, Dea. Samuel Smith of Sund.; *Joseph*, b. Nov. 15, 1700, m. Jan. 7, 1726, Elizabeth, wid. of Joseph Kellogg, res. in Hat., and d. abt. 1783; *Zechariah*, b. Nov. 29, 1702, m. Ruth Meekins, and d. 1771; *Benjamin*, b. Jan. 18, 1705, m. Nov. 13, 1729, Mary, dau. of Joshua Hastings, res. in Belchertown, and d. 1782, ae. 78.

4. EBENEZER, s. of Samuel, (2) rem. after 1713 from Hat. to Sund., and d. Nov. 14, 1745. M. abt. 1691, Hannah Church. Children—*Samuel*, b. June 7, 1693; *Ebenezer*, b. Nov. 10, 1695; *John*, b. Nov. 26, 1698; *Mary*, b. May 24, 1701, m. Jonathan Field of Sund.; *Fellowes*, b. Feb. 15, 1704, res. in Sund. and Conway; *Edward*, b. Aug. 10, 1707, m. Aug. 12, 1741, Lucy, dau. of Rev. David Parsons of Leicester. He grad. H. C., 1731, was pastor of chhs. in Belchertown and Greenfield, and d. abt. 1757; *Jonathan*, b. June 2, 1710, m. Mary Root.

5. RICHARD, s. of Samuel, (2) Hat., d. abt. 1753. M. (1) March 18, 1703, Hannah, dau. of Samuel Marsh of Hat.; m. (2) Sarah. Children—*Sarah*, b. Jan. 9, 1704, m. Samuel Gillett; *Hannah*, b. July 14, 1706, m. Nathan Wait; *Richard*, b. Sept. 14, 1709, d. unm. in Amh., May 26, 1780, ae. 70; *Damaris*, b. Nov. 26, 1712, m. Samuel Church; *Martha*, d. Aug. 1720, ae. 2; *Thankful*, b. May 9, 1721, m. Elijah Chapin; *John*, b. July 8, 1725; *Ruth*, m. Moses Morton.

6. JOHN, s. of Richard, (5) rem. soon after marriage, from Hat. to Amh., where he was Dea. in 2nd Chh.; d. Aug. 31, 1813, ae. 88. M. (1) Jerusha, dau. of John Waite of Hat.; m. (2) Sarah, dau. of William Matthews. She d. July 2, 1829, ae. 91 yrs. and 11 mos. Children—*Joel*, b. April 1, 1747, d. Nov. 4, 1825; m. (1) Mary Field; m. (2) wid. Lombard; *Hannah*, b. Feb. 15, 1749, d. Oct. 5, 1823, m. Thomas Hastings of Amh.; *Lois*, b. Sept. 14, 1750, d. young; *Ursula Fellows*, b. Jan. 7, 1753, d. Aug. 30, 1832; m. Feb. 1782, Dea. Elisha Smith of Amh.; *John*, b. May 1, 1755, served in Rev. war, and d. Sept. 11, 1776; *Moses*, b. Aug. 5, 1757; *Lois*, b. July 28, 1759, d. Aug. 11, 1831; m. Giles Church, of Amh.; *Aaron*, b. Oct. 1, 1761, d. in Amh., Jan. 23, 1817; m. (1) Jan. 1782, Lucy Rich; m. (2) Dec. 23, 1810, Esther Ayres; *Jerusha*, b. Nov. 3, 1763, d. July 3, 1798; m. April, 1782, Elijah Hastings of Amh.; *David*, b. Dec. 31, 1765, rem. to State of N. Y.; m. (1) April 3, 1786, Hannah Eastman; m. (2) Aug. 21, 1798, Hannah Hyde;

Martha, b. Nov. 19, 1767, m. April 9, 1789, Calvin Rich, of New Lebanon, N. Y.; *Moses,* b. Nov. 7, 1769, d. in Amh. Sept. 18, 1798; m. July 3, 1798, Mary Field; *Sarah,* b. Jan. 5, 1774, m. (1) —— Hull; m. (2) Timothy Sturdevant; *Ame,* b. Aug. 24, 1777, d. Nov. 6, 1803.

BLYE, JOHN, m. Mary. Children—*John,* b. Oct. 2, 1715; *Oliver,* b. June 10, 1718.

BODMAN, JOSEPH, came from Westfield to Hat., abt. 1685, and d. July 8, 1711, ae. 56. M. (1) Hepzibah, who d. Jan. 15, 1686; (2) May 4, 1687, Naomi Church. Children—*Lydia,* b. Jan. 1686, d. ae. 2 weeks; *Manoah,* b. March 29, 1692, m. Anna, and d. s. p. 1759, in Sund.; *William,* b. Jan. 5, 1698, d. May [July?] 27, 1723, ae. 25; *Sarah,* b. April 10, 1701, m. Thomas Keet; *Mary,* b. Feb. 12, 1704, m. 1744, John Billings, and d. 1753; *Lydia,* b. July 30, 1707, m. Samuel Harvey; *Samuel.*

1. BOLTWOOD, ROBERT, sergeant, perhaps came from Essex Co., Eng., where the name existed as early as the reign of Edward I. (1273,) is first named on Conn. Records, in 1648, freeman, May 20, 1658. Before removing to Had., as one of the first settlers, he probably resided in east part of Wethersfield, now Glastenbury. An enterprising man, he was made freeman in Mass., March 26, 1661, and d. April 6, 1684. M. Mary, who d. May 14, 1687. Children—*Samuel; Sarah,* m. (1) May 31, 1666, Isaac Warner of Hat.; m. (2) Dec. 30, 1696, Dea. John Loomis of Windsor; *Lydia,* m. April 2, 1674, John Warner of Spr., and d. Jan. 26, 1683; *Martha,* m. April 1, 1674, Daniel Warner, of Hat., and d. Sept. 22, 1710; *Mary,* m. Oct. 24, 1667, James Beebe, and d. Aug. 19, 1676.

2. SAMUEL, s. of Robert, (1) sergeant, a man of remarkable strength and bravery, was stationed at Deer. at the time of the sack of that village by French and Indians, and was there slain Feb. 29, 1704. M. Sarah, dau. of Capt. William Lewis of Farmington. She was b. abt. 1652, and d. Aug. 10, 1722, ae. 70. Children—*Sarah,* b. Oct. 1, 1672, m. June 28, 1692, Nathaniel Kellogg; *Mary,* b. Aug. 7, 1675, d. young; *Samuel,* b. Oct. 12, 1679; *Elizabeth,* b. April 12, 1681, m. July 20, 1715, Dea. Eleazar Mattoon of Amh.; *Robert,* b. April 19, 1683, slain at Deer., Feb. 29, 1704, ae. 20; *Ebenezer,* b. March 20, 1685; *William,* b. Jan. 28, 1687, d. while on his return from captivity in Canada, Aug. 27, 1714, ae. 27; *Rebecca,* b. Aug. 1, 1691, m. May 7, 1724, Daniel Shattuck of Hinsdale, N. H.; *Solomon,* b. July 2, 1694; *Lydia,* b. Oct. 1696, m. June 29, 1719, John Ingram, 3d, of Amh., and d. abt. 1779.

3. SAMUEL, s. of Samuel, (2) rem. as early as 1731, to Amh., where he d. in Oct. or Nov. 1738. M. May 10, 1703, Hannah, dau. of Nathaniel Alexander. She was b. Nov. 1680. Children—*Hannah,* b. Jan. 2, 1705, m. Nov. 9, 1726, Ebenezer Smith of S. H., and d. Oct. 1733, ae. 28; *Samuel,* b. Jan. 29, 1706; *Sarah,* b. Dec. 21, 1708; *Mary,* b. Dec. 27, 1710; *Martha; Abigail,* m. July 10, 1739, John Field, of Amh.; *Jemima,* m. Sept. 29, 1742, David Nash, of Amh. and S. H.

4. EBENEZER, s. of Samuel, (2) rem. as early as 1716 to Berwick, Me., and there d. prior to 1741. M. Mary. Children—*William,* b. Sept. 27, 1715;

Elizabeth, bapt. May 1, 1720, m. Benjamin Gubtill of Berwick; *Sarah*, bapt. May 1, 1720; *Mary*, bapt. May 2, 1725; *John*, bapt. May 2, 1725, res. in Berwick; *Ebenezer*, bapt. Aug. 6, 1727, drowned in Nh., July 9, 1743.

5. SOLOMON, s. of Samuel, (2) rem. to Amh. as early as 1737, and there d. April 20, 1762, ae. 65. M. Mary, wid. of John Pantry, Jr., of Hartford, and dau. of John Norton of Farmington, Ct. She was bapt. Nov. 21, 1686, and d. May 24, 1763, ae. 76. Children—*Ruth*, b. April 25, 1722, m. Oct. 19, 1742, Charles Wright, of Amh., and Pownal, Vt., and d. April 15, 1806, ae. 85; *Sarah*, b. April 5, 1723, m. Elijah Merrill, and d. May 17, 1746, ae. 23; *William*, b. Feb. 4, 1725; *Solomon*, b. Dec. 26, 1727; *Ebenezer*, b. April 7, 1731, d. June 9, 1749, ae. 18; *Mary*, b. July 19, 1733, m. July 11, 1751, Samuel Ingram, of Amh., and d. abt. 1780.

6. WILLIAM, Lieut., s. of Solomon, (5) res. in Amh., served in the French war, and d. May 2, 1779, ae. 54. M. Dec. 10, 1750, Mary, dau. of Ebenezer Sheldon of Nh. She was b. Dec. 8, 1724, and d. May 10, 1809, ae. 84. Children—*Sarah*, bapt. Feb. 16, 1752, m. Israel Dickinson of Amh.; *Mary*, bapt. Nov. 4, 1753; *Lucy*, bapt. Jan. 3, 1757, m. Feb. 10, 1780, Stephen Hubbard of Amh., and d. Sept. 1823; *John*, bapt. Oct. 14, 1759; *Esther*, b. Feb. 14, 1762, m. Jan. 1, 1795, Abner Noble, of Pownal, Vt., and d. Jan. 1, 1820, ae. 57; *Abagail*, bapt. May 20, 1764, prob. d. Dec. 28, 1766; *William*, b. May 4, 1766.

7. SOLOMON, s. of Solomon (5) res. in Amh., and d. May 17, 1777, ae. 49. M. Aug. 29, 1751, Mary, dau. of Nehemiah Strong, of Amh. She was b. Feb. 21, 1732, and d. Aug. 1, 1814, ae. 82. Children—*Ebenezer*, b. July 23, 1752, grad. H. C. 1773, merchant in Amh., where he d. unm., July 23, 1804, ae. 52; *Samuel*, b. June 12, 1754; *Martha*, b. April 1, 1756, d. Oct. 2, 1778, ae. 22; *Mary*, b. Aug. 2, 1758, m. (1) Moses Dickinson of Amh.; m. (2) Oct. 5, 1780, Daniel Cooley, Esq., of Amh., and d. Jan. 10, 1795, ae. 36; *Solomon*, b. May 25, 1760, m. Sarah Benney, res. in Amh., and was killed at raising of Hat. Bridge, Dec. 12, 1805, ae. 45; *Hannah*, b. April 21, 1762, d. Dec. 13, 1784, ae. 22; *Jemima*, b. Dec. 18, 1763, m. Oct. 16, 1805, William Brewer of Wilbraham, and d. July 29, 1850, ae. 86; *Keziah*, b. Dec. 18, 1763, m. Doct. Abia Southworth of Pelham, and d. April 28, 1835, ae. 71; *Elijah*, b. Aug. 31, 1766, d. Feb. 3, 1776, ae. 9; *Elisha*, b. Sept. 16, 1767.

8. JOHN, s. of William, (6) Amh., served in Rev. war, and d. Feb. 5, 1803, ae. 43. M. —— Haze, of Pelham. Child—*John*, b. 1786.

9. WILLIAM, s. of William, (6) Amh., d. Aug. 15, 1845, ae. 69. M. (1) Aug. 2, 1789, Eunice, dau. of Stephen Noble of Westfield. She d. June 5, 1807, ae. 37. M. (2) Feb. 18, 1808, Irene, wid. of Asahel Clark, of Amh., and dau. of Isaac Hubbard. She d. Aug. 6, 1831; m. (3) April 20, 1833, Olive, wid. of Lucius Hastings, and dau. of Joel Smith. She m. (3) Rev. Samuel Ware, of Sund. Children—*Sarah*, b. May 19, 1790, m. 1809, Jonathan Marsh, and d. in Richmond, Va., Oct. 19, 1817, ae. 27; *Lucius*, b. Mch.16, 1792; *Mary Sheldon*, b. Feb. 20, 1794, m. Jan. 17,1813, Rufus Green, of Carroll N. Y.; *Emily*, b. May 8, 1798, d. unm., in Amh., Feb. 2, 1834, ae. 35; *Harriet*, b. Jan. 24, 1800, m. (1) Nov. 7, 1838, George Newhall of Athol; m. (2) April 17, 1844, Joseph Marsh of Had.; *William*, b. July 3, 1802; *Eunice Church*,

b. Sept. 19, 1804, d. May 27, 1808, ae. 3; *Oliver Noble*, b. June 1, 1807, m. Nov. 13, 1833, Nancy, dau. of Nathaniel Smith of Bridgewater, N. H., res. in Ionia, Mich.; *Eunice Church*, b. 1809, m. Horace Dexter of Willoughby, Ohio.

10. SAMUEL, s. of Solomon, (7) res. in Conway and Amh., and d. March 2, 1808, ae. 53. M. Judith, dau. of John Nash. She d. April 28, 1832, ae. 76. Children—*Martha*, b. Dec. 4, 1778, m. John Arms, of Conway; *Elijah*, b. Feb. 19, 1780, res. in Amh.; m. Nov. 5, 1807, Eliza, dau. of Tillinghast Almy, and d. s. p. April 13, 1855, ae. 75.

11. ELISHA, s. of Solomon, (7) res. in Amh., and d. Aug. 14, 1804, ae. 36. M. Lucinda, dau. of Gaius Brewer of Wilbraham. She m. (2) Enos Baker, of Amh., and d. Jan. 9, 1852, ae. 73. Child—*Elishaba*.

12. JOHN, s. of John, (8) settled in Windsor, Vt. and d. 1843. M. Mch. 5, 1808, Eunice, dau. of Urijah Brainerd, of Lempster, N. H. Children—*Joseph*, b. Dec. 7, 1808, went to sea in 1829, and has never since been heard from; *Frederick Pettis*, b. July 29, 1810, m. Sept. 6, 1840, Mabel E. Washburn, and res. in Troy, N. Y.; *Minerva*, b. Nov. 11, 1811, m. May 2, 1834, Nathan Walker, and d. Feb. 18, 1856; *William Mynders*, b. Nov. 8, 1813, m. Oct. 18, 1840, Mary McLean, res. in Victor, N. Y., and was for eight years Post Master at that place; *Harriet*, b. Aug. 21, 1816, m. Mch. 1845, Dwight L. Sanderson, and d. Aug. 5, 1847; *Emeline*, b. Nov. 3, 1821, d. unm. June 11, 1844, ae. 22; *Lucy*, b. Dec. 24, 1824, m. Oct. 16, 1848, Cyrus Houghton; *Abby*, b. June 16, 1827, m. (1) April 22, 1846; (2) Dec. 29, 1851, George Hosington; *Mary*, b. Oct. 13, 1829, m. Oct. 1, 1848, Joel Houghton.

13. LUCIUS, son of William, (9) Amherst, commenced his studies preparatory for college in the town school of Amh., under the instruction of William D. Williamson, afterwards Governor of Me., and completed the same at Had. Grammar school, under the instruction of ——— Lyman, entered Williams College in 1810, and graduated with distinguished honor in 1814, in the same class with Rev. Orville Dewey, D. D. of Boston, Hon. Samuel Farley Vinton of Gallipolis, O., and Washington, D. C., and Hon. Austin E. Wing of Detroit, Mich., pursued his legal studies with Hon. Samuel Fowler Dickinson of Amh., was admitted to the bar of Hampshire County, in Aug. 1817, and entered immediately into practice with his instructor. In 1820, his partnership with Mr. Dickinson having been dissolved, he opened an office of his own, and continued practice until 1836, when he retired from business. In 1828 he was appointed Secretary of Amh. College, an office which he still retains. In politics originally a Whig, he was subsequently a member of the Liberty party and in 1841 their candidate for Governor. He m. Aug. 30, 1824, Fanny Haskins, dau. of Rev. Mase Shepard, of Little Compton, R. I. Children—*Lucius Manlius*, b. June 8, 1825; *George Shepard*, b. April 29, 1827, d. July 19, 1833, ae. 6; *Fanny Shepard*, b. May 31, 1829, d. May 19, 1831, ae. 1; *Charles Shepard*, b. July 16, 1832, d. July 28, 1833, ae. 1; *George Shepard*, b. July 27, 1834, d. in Aikin, S. C., April 14, 1856, ae. 21; *Charles Upham*, b. March 28, 1837, is a clerk in Middletown, Ct.; *Edward*, b. Sept. 4, 1839, grad. Y. C. 1860, and is now a member of Cambridge Law school; *Thomas Kast*, b. Feb. 15, 1844, is a member of the class of 1864 in Y. C.; *Samuel*, b. Dec. 29, 1849.

16   BOLTWOOD—BROWN.

14. WILLIAM, s. of William, (9) Amherst, m. June 1, 1826, Electa, dau. of Jacob Stetson of Amh. Children—*Sarah*, b. Feb. 7, 1827, m. Jan. 1847, Silas Dexter Clark, of Keokuk, Iowa; *Caroline*, b. April 4, 1829, d. Aug. 15, 1830, ae. 1; *Henry Leonidas*, b. Jan. 17, 1831, grad. A. C. 1853, master of High School, Lawrence; *Solomon*, b. Jan. 29, 1833, d. June 1, 1833, ae. 4 mos.; *Caroline Amelia*, b. March 23, 1835, grad. 1860, at South Hadley Female Sem.; *William Francis*, b. April 16, 1837; *Edmund*, b. Sept. 5, 1839; *Rizpah*, b. Feb. 20, 1842; *John Emerson*, b. March 24, 1844; *Harriet Newhall*, b. June 26, 1848; *Robert*, b. Feb. 12, 1852.

15. OLIVER NOBLE, s. of William, (9) Ionia, Mich. M. Nov. 13, 1833, Nancy, dau. of Nathaniel S. Smith of Bridgewater, N. H. Children—*Emily Maria*, b. Sept. 24, 1834, m. April, 1853, J. A. Sweezey, Esq. of Hastings, Mich.; *Solomon*, b. July 10, 1837, d. in Jamestown, N. Y., Jan. 4, 1856, ae. 18.

16. HON. LUCIUS MANLIUS, s. of Lucius, (13) Amherst, pursued his studies preparatory to College, at Amh. Academy, between 1834 and 1839, under the instruction of Rev. George C. Partridge, Hon. Rodolphus B. Hubbard, Mr. Frederick A. Buel, and Rev. Nahum Gale, D. D., graduated at Amh. College in 1843, was appointed in 1852, Librarian of Amh. College, and in June, 1861, Post Master of Amherst. In politics a Republican, he was in 1859 by that party chosen State Senator for the Hampshire & Franklin District. He m. June 6, 1860, Clarinda Boardman, dau. of Hinckley Williams of Goshen. Child—*George Shepard*, b. March 2, 1861.

BONNEY, OLIVER. Children—*Son*, b. April 13, 1815; *Elijah Hayward*, b. Nov. 4, 1816, grad. A. C. 1839, Presbyterian clergyman in ———, N. Y.; *Franklin*, b. Sept. 7, 1819; *Franklin*, b. Feb. 2, 1822, physician in Had.; *Oliver Edmund*, b. Dec. 7, 1823; *George Washington*, b. Nov. 23, 1825; *Susan Jane*, b. Dec. 1, 1827; *Mary Jane*, b. June 21, 1830; *Elizabeth Harvey*, b. Aug. 29, 1832; *Cynthia*, b. March 12, 1836; *Cynthia*, b. Oct. 21, 1838.

BRACY, THOMAS, Hat., s. of Phebe Martin of Wethersfield, who was dau. of William Bisby of London. Children—*Thomas*, b. Oct. 8, 1675, d. Oct. 28, 1675; *Mary*, b. Oct. 20, 1677; *Phebe*, b. Nov. 14, 1680; *Hannah*, b. Aug. 12, 1683; *Thomas*, b. Feb. 12, 1686; *Sarah*, b. Sept. 23, 1688.

BROOKS. JOHN, m. Hannah. Children—*Abigail*, b. Dec. 1, 1779; *Lydia*, b. Aug. 19, 1782; *Sarah*, b. April 7, 1784; *Roxcelana*, b. May 30, 1787; *Roxcelana*, b. May 4, 1799.

BROOKS, JOSEPH, m. Miriam. Children—*Uri*, (son) b. July 8, 1759; *Miriam*, b. Feb. 9, 1761.

BROWN, JAMES, rem. abt. 1683, from Hat. to Deerfield, and thence to Colchester, Ct. M. Jan. 7, 1674, Remembrance Brook. Children—*Mary*, b. May 26, 1677; *Abigail*, b. Sept. 8, 1678; *Thankful*, b. June 1, 1682; *Sarah*, b. 1683; *James*, b. 1685; *Mindwell*, b. 1686; *Hannah*, b. 1688; *Mercy*, b. 1690; *Elizabeth*, b. 1693, d. ae. 5; *John*, b. 1695.

BROWN, LEMUEL, m. Oct. 2, 1798, Betsey, dau. of John Dickinson, Jr. Children—*Douglas; Abigail*.

BROWNE WILLIAM, had rem. to Leicester, 1720. M. Mary. Children—
Mary, b. Jan. 22, 1695; *Elizabeth*, b. Dec. 16, 1696; *Ann*, b. Feb. 27, 1700;
William, b. March 27, 1702; *John*, b. Nov. 3, 1703; *Zechariah*, b. Oct. 14,
1707; *Abigail*, b. Sept. 26, 1709; *Sarah*, b. Dec. 4, 1716.

BURNHAM, JAMES, came from Windsor, Ct., and rem. to Amherst and
Granby. Children—*Allen*, bapt. Aug. 23, 1795; *Elsey*, bapt. Aug. 23, 1795.

BURR, TIMOTHY, m. Mary. Children—*Mary*, b. Sept. 8, 1754; *Timothy*,
b. Sept. 1, 1757; *Elizabeth*, b. July 9, 1759; *Eleanor*, b. March 8, 1761;
Esther, b. April 9, 1763; *Nancy*, b. May 7, 1765.

CARRIER, ISAIAH, m. Hannah. Children—*Dau.*, b. Sept. 30, 1771;
Seth Kneeland, b. Jan. 16, 1773, d. Jan. 21, 1779; *Samuel*, b. Jan. 11, 1775,
d. Feb. 2, 1775; *Benjamin*, b. April 28, 1776, d. April 29, 1776; *Samuel*, b.
March 6, 1778; *Seth Kneeland*, b. Sept. 5, 1780; *Hannah*, b. April 13, 1783;
Sarah, b. Sept. 18, 1785; *Nathaniel Montague*, b. Nov. 23, 1787.
"Old Mr. Carrier" d. July 3, 1780.

1. CATLIN, SAMUEL, m. May 30, 1735, Mary Crow. Children—*Samuel
Crow; Mary; Elizabeth*, m. —— Moody; *Irene*, d. Sept. 26, 1753.

2. SAMUEL CROW, s. of Samuel, (1) a saddler, rem. abt. 1770 to S. H.,
and thence to the West. M. Dorcas. Children—*Samuel*, b. Oct. 1, 1766,
d. young; *Irene*, b. May 17, 1769, d. unm. 1825, ae. 56; *Lucretia*, b. Oct. 4,
1771, m.—— Woodworth; *Dorcas*, b. July 27, 1776; *Elizabeth*, b. Nov. 23,
1778, m. Eleazar Goodman, Jr.; *Roxa*, b. April 25, 1781, m. Chester Moody;
Samuel, b. July 23, 1783.

CHAMBERLAIN, JOSEPH, came to Had. as a soldier, in 1676, and rem.
before 1700 to Hat., and before 1709 to Colchester, Ct. where he d. Aug. 7,
1752, ae. 87. M. Mary or Mercy, dau. of John Dickinson. She d. June 30,
1735. Children—*Sarah*, b. Nov. 2, 1690; *Sarah*, b. March 10, 1693; *John*,
b. in March.

1. CHAUNCY, REV. ISAAC, b. in Stratford, Ct., Oct. 5, 1670, s. of Rev.
Israel, grad. H. C. 1693, ord. over Had. chh. Sept. 9, 1696, and d. May 2,
1745, ae. 74. M. (1) Sarah, who d. June 29, 1720, ae. 38; m. (2) Abiel,
wid. of Rev. Joseph Metcalf of Falmouth, and dau. of Rev. William Adams
of Dedham. Children—*Mary*, b. May 10, 1698, d. Aug. 1701; *Israel*, b.
March 15, 1700, grad. H. C. 1724, a preacher, became deranged, and was
burnt to death the latter part of Nov. 1736, in "a small out house," of his
father's; *Abigail*, b. Nov. 13, 1701, m. Sept. 14, 1726, Rev. John Graham of
Southbury, Ct.; *Richard*, b. Oct. 23, 1703; *Catharine*, b. Jan. or June 5, 1705,
m. Rev. Daniel Russell of Rocky Hill, Ct.; *Sarah*, b. Dec. 13, 1707;
Dorothy, b. June 24, 1710, m. May 19, 1738, Rev. Grindal Rawson, of S.
H.; *Charles*, b. June 28, 1712; *Jerusha*, b. Sept. 7, 1714, m. abt. 1747, Rev.
Hobart Estabrook of East Haddam, Ct.; *Josiah*, b. Nov. 14, 1716.

2. RICHARD, s. of Rev. Isaac, (1) res. in Amh. and Whately, and d. Dec. 31,
1790, ae. 87; m. Nov. 6, 1729, Elizabeth, dau. of Jonathan Smith of Hat.
She was b. May 8, 1708, and d. in Wh. May 22, 1790, ae. 82. Children—
Oliver, b. July 9, 1730, m. Dec. 1751, Huldah Moody; *Elizabeth*, b. July 25,

1732; *Eunice*, b. April 2, 1735; *Jerusha*, b. Feb. 8, 1741, d. Sept. 1746; *Medad*, b. July 14, 1744, d. Sept. 1746; *Abigail*, bapt. Sept. 18, 1748.

3. CHARLES, s. of Rev. Isaac, (1) res. in Amh., Sund., &c. M. (1) Jan. 29, 1740, Sarah Ingram; m. (2) Sept. 18, 1746, Mary Gaylord. Children— *Catharine*, bapt. Jan. 4, 1741, m. April 24, 1759, Benjamin Harwood; *Dorothy*, bapt. April 1, 1744; *Isaac*, bapt. Aug. 22, 1745; *Eunice*, bapt. June 5, 1748; *David*, bapt. April 18, 1750.

4. JOSIAH, s. of Rev. Isaac, (1) res. in Had. and Amh. He was a Justice of the Peace, Selectman, Representative to General Court, rem. abt. 1781 to western part of Albany Co., now Schenectady Co., N.Y., where both himself and wife Mary are believed to have died within a year from the time of their removal. Children—*Elizabeth Billing*, b. April 16, 1747; *Mary*, b. Jan. 20, 1749, d. unm., abt. 1796; *Sarah*, b. March 2, 1751; *Josiah*, b. July 5, 1753, d. June 27, 1766; *Isaac*, b. Oct. 16, 1755; *Moses*, b. July 14, 1757, d. 1761; *Moses*, b. April 12, 1761, m. 1792, Sarah Calkin, and d. April 11, 1814; *Samuel*, b. June 3, 1763, d. June 11, 1763; *Samuel*, b. July 28, 1764, d. unm.; *Josiah*, b. July 19, 1767, d. 1813.

CHAUNCY, REV. NATHANIEL, s. of Rev. Charles Chauncy, Pres. of Harv. Col., was b. about 1639, in Plymouth, grad. H. C. 1661, and d. in Hat., Nov. 4, 1685. M. Nov. 12, 1673, Abigail, dau. of John Strong of Nh. She m. (2) Sept. 8, 1686, Medad Pomeroy of Nh. and d. April 15, 1704. Children— *Isaac*, b. Sept. 6, 1674, d. unm. in Durham, Ct., July 23, 1748, ae. 68; *Katharine*, b. Jan. 12, 1676, m. Aug. 23, 1689, Rev. Daniel Brewer of Springfield, and d. May 15, 1754, ae. 78; *Abigail*, b. Oct. 14, 1677, m. (1) Dr. Hudson; (2) or (3) Edward Burroughs; *Charles*, b. Sept. 3, 1679, d. Oct. 31, 1679; *Nathaniel*, b. Sept. 21, 1682, Y. C. 1702, ordained over church in Durham, Ct., Feb. 17, 1711, and there d. Feb. 8, 1756, ae. 74; *Sarah*, b. Sept. 15, 1683, m. July 1, 1712, Rev. Samuel Whittlesey of Wallingford, Ct., and d. Oct. 20 or 23, 1767, ae. 84.

1. CHURCH, RICHARD, Hartford, 1637, rem. in 1659 to Had., and d. Dec. 16, 1667. M. Anne, who d. in Hat., March 10, 1684, in 84th yr. Children—*Edward*, b. abt. 1628; *John*, b. abt. 1636, m. Oct. 27, 1657, Sarah Beckley, res. in Hartford, and was buried Oct. 16, 1691; *Samuel; Mary*, m. Isaac Graves.

2. EDWARD, s. of Richard, (1) deacon, Norwalk, 1654, rem. to Hat., and d. Sept. 19, 1704, ae. 76. M. Mary, who d. Sept. 30, 1690, acc. to Town Rec., but Sept. 17, 1691, ae. 54, acc. to grave-stone. Children—*Rebecca*, per. m. Feb. 11, 1677, Joseph Selden; *Mary*, b. 1656, prob. m. Dec. 25, 1679, Philip Russell; *John*, slain in Falls' fight, May 19, 1676; *Samuel*, b. April 4, 1662, d. May 6, 1662; *Samuel*, b. Aug. 4, 1663; *Naomi*, b. May 12, 1666, m. May 11, 1687, Joseph Bodman; *Sarah*, b. May 18, 1670, per. m. Dec. 3, 1697, William Porter; *Hannah*, per. m. abt. 1691, Ebenezer Billings; *Richard*, b. Jan. 18, 1675.

3. SAMUEL, s. of Richard, (1) freeman of Conn., 1657, d. April 13, 1684. M. Mary, prob. dau. of Josiah Churchill. Children—*Mary*, b. Jan. 23, 1665, m. 1684, Samuel Smith, and d. June 18, 1700; *Samuel*, b. Aug. 19, 1667; *Richard*, b. Dec. 9, 1669, m. Jan. 24, 1696, Sarah Bartlett, and was slain by

Indians Oct. 15, 1696, ae. 26; *Mehitable*, b. Jan. 11, 1672, m. Nehemiah Dickinson; *Josiah*, b. April 10, 1673; *Joseph*, b. May 26, 1678, d. unm., 1721; *Benjamin*, b. Sept. 1, 1680; *John*, b. Dec. 24, 1682.

4. RICHARD, s. of Edward, (2) Hat., d. April 4, 1763. M. Mary, who d. Dec. 22, 1776, in 85th yr. Children—*Mary*, b. Feb. 7, 1713, m. —— Smith; *Hannah*, b. May 1716, m. Richard Church; *John*, b. March 27, 1719, d. young; *Samuel*, b. July 16, 1721, d. Oct. 1, 1725, ae. 4; *Sarah*, d. Jan. 14, 1722; *Sarah*, m. Ebenezer Train; *Edward*, b. Dec. 5, 1726, d. at Cape Breton; *John*, b. July 26, 1729, d. unm., April 25, 1779, ae. 49; *Samuel*, b. Aug. 11, 1731, m. Lydia Billings, and d. May 9, 1786, ae. 55.

5. SAMUEL, s. of Samuel, (3) d. abt. 1737. M. (1) July 7, 1692, Abigail Harrison, who d. Sept. 7, 1717; m. (2) Aug. 12, 1720, Abigail Strong. She m. (2) Oct. 12, 1738, Ebenezer Chapin. Children—*Samuel*, d. April 28, 1703; *Martha*, b. Sept. 23, 1694, m. Jan. 5, 1715, John White; *Abigail*, b. Dec. 25, 1696, m. May 7, 1723, Samuel Warner; *child*, b. and d. June 16, 1699; *Richard*, b. Sept. 20, 1700; *Nathaniel*, b. Feb. 7, 1704; *Samuel*, b. Aug. 21, 1706; *Experience*, b. Feb. 2, 1710, m. June 14, 1733, Joseph Wright; *Joseph*, b. Jan. 28, 1728.

6. JOSIAH, s. of Samuel, (3) m. Nov. 24, 1699, Thankful Brooks. Children—*Mary*, b. Jan. 15, 1701; *Jonathan*, b. Dec. 13, 1702; *John*, b. Oct. 2, 1704; *Elizabeth*, b. April 10, 1707; *Josiah*, b. Nov. 27, 1709; *Mehitable*, b. Sept. 3, 1711; *Joseph*, b. Jan. 12, 1714; *Samuel*, b. April 30, 1716; *Ann*, b. Aug. 31, 1718; *Martha*, b. Oct. 4, 1720.

7. BENJAMIN, s. of Samuel, (3) d. Jan. 15, 1755. M. (1) Jan. 13, 1709, Miriam Hovey; m. (2) Sept. 23, 1714, Hannah Dickinson; m. (3) May 29, 1724, Sarah, wid. of Elisha Perkins. Children—*Benjamin*, b. Dec. 26, 1709; *Meriam*, b. May 12, 1712, m. May 24, 1739, Joseph Smith, and d. 1773; *Nehemiah*, b. July 22, 1715; *John*, b. Sept. 23, 1716, m. March 24, 1741, Jemima Montague; *Esther*, b. Feb. 13, 1718, m. Nov. 1, 1749, Joseph Barnard; *Mary*, b. Aug. 13, 1719, m. Feb. 11, 1746, Phinehas Smith; and prob. others.

8. RICHARD, s. of Samuel, (5) m. Jan. 12, 1727, Mehitable Dickinson. Children—*Moses*, b. Feb. 23, 1728, d. Sept. 9, 1748; *Elisha*, b. May 29, 1730, d. abt. 1766; *Son*, b. Sept. 1732, d. Nov. 5, 1732; *Richard*, b. Nov. 9, 1733, d. Dec. 8, 1733; *Waitstill*, b. Feb. 7, 1735, d. Sept. 12, 1748; *Dau.*, b. Feb. 27, 1737, d. Feb. 1737; *Mary*, b. April 3, 1738, d. abt. 1778; *Martha*, b. March 1, 1740; *Rebecca*, per.

9. NATHANIEL, s. of Samuel, (5) m. 1727, Rachel McCranney of Spr. Children—*Nathaniel*, b. Dec. 5, 1728; *William Harrison*, b. March 3, 1730; *Rachel*, b. April 10, 1731, m. 1750, Joseph Burt of Spr.; *Malachi*, b. June 24, 1732, m. April 30, 1756, Elizabeth Miller; *Jesse*, b. July 14, 1733; *Eber*, b. Dec. 14, 1734; *Timothy*, b. May 12, 1736, m. June 9, 1757, Abigail Church; *Samuel*, b. Dec. 7, 1737; *Ruth*, b. June 24, 1739; *Experience*, b. June 24, 1739; *Mary*, b. Aug. 4, 1741; *David*, b. Dec. 30, 1744; *Jonathan*, b. April 17, 1747; *Benjamin*, b. May 20, 1751.

10. SAMUEL, s. of Samuel, (5) rem. abt. 1743, to Amh. M. Margaret, dau. of Samuel Smith. She d. 1791. Children—*Margaret*, b. Jan. 12, 1735; m. Gideon Smith; *Sarah*, b. Aug. 17, 1736, m. Ebenezer White, and d. abt.

1802; *Abigail*, b. 1738, m. Elisha Smith; *Thankful*, b. 1741, d. in Conway, 1788; *Daniel*, b. 1743, m. Feb. 2, 1775, Hannah Smith; *Eunice*, bapt. Nov. 1747, d. unm.; *Giles*, b. Aug. 20, 1754, m. Lois Billings, and d. in Amh. Feb. 14, 1807, ae. 52.

11. JOSEPH, s. of Samuel, (5) Amh., d. Sept. 7, 1819, ae. 91. M. Jan. 2, 1755, Abigail, dau. of Jonathan Smith. She d. March 22, 1815. Children— *Samuel*, a physician in Sund., m. (1) Sabra Farnum, and d. June 7, 1826, ae. 71; *Abigail*, m. Gideon Henderson, and rem. to Claremont, N. H.; *Joseph*, b. abt. 1760, m. (1) Lydia Wait; m. (2) Elizabeth Kellogg, and d. in Amh., Sept. 20, 1840; *child*, bapt. 1764; *Sylvanus*, b. Nov. 13, 1768, m. Betsey Stevens, and d. in Amh., Sept. 6, 1854, ae. 85.

12. BENJAMIN, s. of Benjamin, (7) S. H., m. Ruth Kellogg. Children— *Joel*, b. Sept. 16, 1740, res. in S. H., m. Hannah; *Benjamin*, b. April 16, 1742, m. Miriam, and d. in Gr., Dec. 15, 1775; *Josiah*, b. July 9, 1744; *David*, b. March 31, 1746; *John*, b. Jan. 13, 1747, d. unm., in S. H., 1831; *Waitstill*, b. Feb. 9, 1752; *Nathan*, b. July 27, 1754, grad. D. C. 1784, settled as a minister in Bridgton, Me., in 1789, and d. Nov. 14, 1836, ae. 82; *Ruth*, b. Nov. 15, 1757; *Dorcas*, b. Aug. 7, 1763.

13. NEHEMIAH, s. of Benjamin, (7) Amh. and Montague, d. 1773. M. Esther Smith. Children—*Medad*, b. Dec. 22, 1747; *Hannah*, b. Oct. 25, 1749; *Samuel*, (?) b. Feb. 21, 1752; *Ebenezer*, bapt. Oct. 15, 1754; *Esther*, bapt. Sept. 4, 1757.

14. WILLIAM HARRISON, s. of Nathaniel, (9) m. Nov. 15, 1750, Jane Wood. Children—*child*, d. March, 1752; *Diadema*, b. March 7, 1755; *child*, b. Dec. 7, 1756, d. Dec. 7; *Jesse*, b. Dec. 7, 1756.

15. EBER, s. of Nathaniel, (9) rem. to Brattleboro', Vt.; m. May 25, 1758, Mary Farrand. Children—*Eber*, b. April 11, 1759, d. May 16, 1759; *Josiah*, b. July 21, 1761; *Eber*, b. July 19, 1763.

CLAPP, PRESERVED, s. of Preserved of Nh., b. 1705, res. in Amh., and d. Oct. 18, 1758, ae. 53. M. Aug. 20, 1730, Sarah, dau. of Christopher West, of Guilford, Ct. She was b. Nov. 9, 1706, and d. 1795. Children—*Preserved*, b. May 6, 1731, m. Eunice Atherton of Bolton; *Sarah*, b. Oct. 4, 1733, m. (1) Jan. 13, 1751, Ebenezer Kellogg of Amh.; m. (2) April 23, 1778, John Nash, of Amh.; *Lucy*, b. Nov. 10, 1737, m. (1) Jan. 4, 1760, Martin Smith of Amh.; m. (2) —— Shattuck, of Hinsdale, N. H.; *Irene*, b. Nov. 12, 1740, m. 1759, Noadiah Lewis, of Amh., and d. Oct. 10, 1830, ae. 89; *Miriam*, b. June 25, 1743, d. young; *Oliver*, b. 1744, m. Elizabeth Mattoon, and d. in Amh. Oct. 25, 1832, ae. 88; *Mary*, bapt. Jan. 25, 1747, m. Timothy Hubbard, and d. April 22, 1835, ae. 88; *Timothy*, bapt. May 21, 1749, m. Sarah Field, and d. in Amh. May 20, 1824, ae. 75; *William*, bapt. Aug. 1752, m. Martha Dickinson, and d. Aug. 28, 1809.

CLARK, ISRAEL, Gr., d. June 17, 1796, in 62d yr. M. Dec. 3, 1756, Mehitable, dau. of Luke Montague. She d. Oct. 23, 1815, in 77th yr. Children—*Sybil*, b. Nov. 9, 1757; *Israel*, b. Nov. 10, 1759; *Luke*, b. Feb. 11, 1762; *Jotham*, b. Nov. 19, 1764; *Joseph*, b. Aug. 7, 1767; *Asa; Joel; Titus.*

1. CLARK, JOHN, b. abt. 1704, in Ireland, m. Mary. Children—*John*, b. abt. 1739; *Moses*, b. Aug. 7, 1749.

2. JOHN, s. of John, (1) m. 1764, Margaret Farrand. Children—*Sarah*, b. July 19, 1766; *Enoch*, b. May 19, 1768; *Peggy*, b. Jan. 19, 1770; *Phyllira*, b. Sept. 14, 1772; *Achsah*, bapt. Sept. 25, 1774, d. Jan. 14, 1776; *Achsah*, b. Aug. 12, 1777.

3. MOSES, s. of John, (1) m. Sarah. Children—*James*, b. Aug. 28, 1773; *Moses*, b. March 9, 1775; *William*, b. Dec. 2, 1776; *David*, b. Nov. 5, 1778; *Phene*, (dau.) b. July 28, 1780: *Jonathan*, b. Sept. 9, 1782.

CLARK, NOAH, b. 1719, came from Nh. to Gr., and d. abt. 1790. M. Rachel, dau. of Samuel Phelps, of Nh. She was b. 1724. Children— *Rachel*, b. Dec. 14, 1745; *Gad*, b. Feb. 27, 1746, d. 1749; *Amaziah*, b. Nov. 26, 1748, joined the Shakers; *Rufus*, b. Feb. 22, 1751; *Eunice*, b. April 27, 1753; *Rhoda*, b. Aug. 28, 1755; *Esther*, b. Aug. 28, 1757; *Kezia*, b. May 21, 1759; *Noah*, b. April 27, 1762.

CLARK, SETH, came from Nh. to Gr., m. Mary Edwards. Children— *Enos*, b. 1747; *Mary*, b. 1748, d. young; *Mary*, b. 1749; *Eleanor*, b. Nov. 13, 1750; *Mary*, b. 1751, d. 1751; *Seth*, b. July 15, 1753; *Mary*, b. Nov. 2, 1755; *Adah*, (dau.) b. May 16, 1759; *Naomi*, b. Jan. 1, 1761; *Levi*, b. Aug. 3, 1762, d. Jan. 11, 1764.

CLARK, SIMEON, b. Oct. 20, 1720, s. of Increase of Nh., deacon in Amh.. where he d. Oct. 28, 1801, ae. 81. M. Nov. 2, 1749, Rebecca, dau. of Nathaniel Strong. She d. Jan. 13, 1811, ae. 86. Children—*Eunice*, b. Aug, 11, 1750, m. Timothy Green of Amh., and d. May 6, 1776, ae. 25; *Simeon*, b. June 25, 1752, m. (1) Lucy Hubbard; m. (2) April 23, 1795, Irene Lewis; res. in Amh., and d. May 3, 1831, ae. 78; *Levi*, b. Aug. 27, 1753, m. —— Lincoln, and d. Sept. 1836, ae. 83; *Judah*, b. April 18, 1756, d. Sept. 9, 1757; *Lois*, b. March 9, 1758, d. June 20, 1759; *Judah*, b. Aug. 16, 1759, m. Nov. 26, 1789, Esther Merrick, and d. July 18, 1842, ae. 82; *Asahel*, b. Feb. 6, 1762, m. Nov. 23, 1786, Irene Hubbard; d. in Amh., March 7, 1800, ae. 38; *Lois*, b. Jan. 3, 1764, m. Jan. 29, 1792, Oliver Cowls of Amh., and d. Dec. 4, 1803, ae. 39; *Justus*, b. Nov. 24, 1765, m. Oct. 26, 1794, Dorcas Pomeroy, and d. Dec. 25, 1847, ae. 82; *Mary*, b. Dec. 13, 1767, m. John Stebbins of Gr.; *Jerusha*, b. May 31, 1770, d. Jan. 19, 1771; *Jerusha*, b. May 12, 1772, m. Nov. 19, 1804, John Stebbins of Gr., and d. March 26, 1815, ae. 42.

CLARKE, MR. HENRY, Windsor 1640, representative 1641–1650, Assist-ant 1650–1661, a first settler of Had., a wealthy and distinguished man. He was one of the Commissioners for holding the courts at Spr. and Nh. (or Associates, as they were called after 1666) from 1663 to 1676. He d. s. p. Dec. 23, 1675. M. Jane, who d. Feb. 25, 1672.

1. CLARY, JOHN, came from Watertown, and d. Feb. 10, 1691. M. Feb. 5, 1644, Sarah Caddett, but Cady, accd. to Savage, and Cassell, accd. to Bond. She d. Dec. 23, 1681. Children—*John; Sarah*, b. Oct. 4, 1647, m. Dec. 13, 1667, John Perry of Watertown; *Gershom*, b. Sept. 7, 1650.

2. JOHN, s. of John, (1) res. in Hat. and North., and d. Aug. 15, 1688. M. Jan. or June 16, 1670, Ann Dickinson, who m. (2) Enos Kingsley. Children—*John*, b. April 3, 1671, slain in Brookfield, 1709, leaving John and Rachel; *Sarah*, b. March 19, 1673, d. young; *Joseph*, b. Nov. 30, 1677; *Mary*, m. —— Hutchinson.

3. JOSEPH, s. of John, (2) Hat. and Sund., d. 1748. M. Nov. 19, 1702, Hannah, dau. of Samuel Belding of Hat. Children—*Joseph*, b. Sept. 3, 1705, m. Sarah Gunn, and d. in Leverett; *Samuel*, b. 1707; *Martha*, b. 1712; *Sarah*, d. 1715; *Sarah*, b. 1717; *Hannah*, b. 1719.

COATS, REUBEN. Child—*Son*, b. Feb. 26, 1777.

1. COLEMAN, THOMAS, doubtless came from Evesham, Eng., Wethersfield 1639, rep. 1652 and 1656, rem. to Had., where he was a first settler, freeman 1661, and buried Oct. 1, 1674. M. Wid. Frances Wells, who d. March, 1678. Children—*John*, b. abt. 1635; *Noah; Esther*,(?) m. Philip Davis; *Sarah*, m. abt. 1661, Richard Treat, Jr.; *Deborah*, m. Daniel Gunn, of Milford, Ct., and d. 1703.

2. JOHN, s. of Thomas, (1) freeman of Conn., 1658, and of Mass., 1672, res. in Hat., where he d. Jan. 21, 1711, ae. 76. M. (1) May 29, 1663, Hannah Porter of Windsor, who was slain Sept. 19, 1677; (2) March 11, 1679, Mehitable Root, who d. Aug. 4, 1689; (3) Mary, wid. of Thomas Stebbins of Spr. She d. Oct. 17, 1725, ae. 84. Children—*Thomas*, b. March 3, 1664, d. unm.; *Hannah*, b. Feb. 14, 1667, m. Thomas Nash; *John*, b. April 11, 1669, res. in Wethersfield; *Noah*, b. Dec. 20, 1671; *Sarah*, b. Feb. 15, 1673, m. John Field; *Bethia*, b. Oct. 14, 1676, slain Sept. 21, 1677; *Ebenezer*, b. Aug. 29, 1680, d. in Colchester, 1741; *Nathaniel*, b. Oct. 18, 1684.

3. NOAH, s. of Thomas, (1) freeman 1671, d. July 20, 1676. M. Dec. 27, 1666, Mary, dau. of John Crow. She m. (2) Sept. 16, 1680, Peter Montague. Children—*Mary*, b. Aug. 31, 1667, d. Sept. 20, 1668; *Thomas*, b. Dec. 23, 1668, d. young; *Twins*, b. and d. 1670; *Mary*, b. Sept. 15, 1671, d. Sept. 25, 1671; *Sarah*, b. Oct. 25, 1672, m. 1692, Westwood Cook; *Mary*, b. Dec. 27, 1675, d. young.

4. NOAH, s. of John, (2) rem. abt. 1705, from Hat. to Colchester, Ct., and d. 1711. M. Hannah. Children—*Hannah*, b. Feb. 16, 1701; *Noah*, b. July 2, 1703; *Joseph*, b. June 28, 1706.

5. NATHANIEL, s. of John, (2) Hat., d. April 7, 1755, ae. 70. M. 1705, Mary Ely. Children—*John*, b. Jan. 16, 1707, d. 1725, ae. 18, in East Windsor, Ct.; *Nathaniel*, b. Sept. 21, 1709; *Mary*, b. July 14, 1712, m. John Dickinson; *Elijah*, b. Nov. 17, 1714; *Noah*, b. March 27, 1718, res. in Hat.; *Samuel*, b. Sept. 22, 1720, d. May 17, 1728; *Amos*, per. res. in Middletown; *John*, b. May 14, 1728, d. abt. 1770, in Hartford.

6. NATHANIEL, s. of Nathaniel, (5) rem. to Amh. in 1742, and d. March 8, 1792, ae. 82. M. March 24, 1739, Mercy Smith, who d. May 16, 1798, ae. 83. Children—*Seth*, b. March 17, 1740; *Thankful*, b. Nov. 13, 1741; *Azubah*, b. April 18, 1749, m. March 27, 1783, Jonathan Dickinson of Amh.; *Enos*, b. Jan. 26, 1751, d. of croup.

7. ELIJAH, s. of Nathaniel, (5) Hat., m. Mary. Children—*Elijah*, b. March 10, 1745, m. Tabitha, and d. Jan. 19, 1818, ae. 73; *Mary*, b. July 31, 1747; *Submit*, b. Dec. 5, 1751.

8. SETH, s. of Nathaniel, (6) grad. Y. C., 1765, studied medicine with Dr. L. Hubbard of New Haven, Ct., and established himself in the practice of the same in Amh., where he d. Sept. 9, 1816, ae. 74. M. (1) Oct. 20,

1765, Sarah Beecher, who d. March 3, 1783, ae. 42; (2) Jan. 27, 1785, Eunice, wid. of Oliver Warner of Had., and dau. of Dea. Jonathan Church, of Spr. She d. Aug. 8, 1822, ae. 81. Children—*William*, b. Sept. 7, 1766, a physician in Pittsfield; *Thankful*, b. May 10, 1768, m. Nov. 8, 1798, Dr. Linus Stevens, of Charlemont, N. H.; *Sarah*, b. Feb. 13, 1770, d. Feb. 14, 1776, ae. 6; *Fanny*, b. March 6, 1772, d. Feb. 9, 1776, ae. 3; *Seth*, b. April 4, 1774, m. Elizabeth Doane; *Sarah*, b. Aug. 2, 1777, d. April 11, 1782, ae. 4; *Eliphalet Beecher*, b. Aug. 30, 1779, grad. W. C. 1800, clergyman, d. in Olivet, Mich., 1856, ae. 76; *Fanny*, b. Aug. 3, 1781, m. Hon. Nathaniel W. Howell, of Canandaigua, N. Y.

COLT, Lt. BENJAMIN, came from Lyme, Ct., and d. Aug. 30, 1781. M. 1761, Lucretia Ely of Lyme. She m. (2) John Walker, and d. March 3, 1826, ae. 83. Children—*Benjamin*, b. Sept. 30, 1762; *Lucretia*, b. Dec. 16, 1763, d. Sept. 12, 1767, ae. 3; *Daniel*, b. July 7, 1767, grad. H. C. 1786, d. 1816 in La.; *Lucretia*, b. June 28, 1769, d. Jan. 7, 1771; *Ethalinda*, b. July 23, 1771, m. Oct. 8, 1790, Joseph Dudley Selden; *Ame*, b. Feb. 7, 1773, m. Aug. 30, 1791, Moses Porter; *Betsey*, b. Sept. 1, 1774; *Lucretia*, b. Nov. 25, 1776; m. 1803, Ebenezer Foot, Esq., of Troy, N. Y.; *Elisha*, b. June 12, 1778, m. Aug. 17, 1800, Rebecca Cook; *Christopher*, b. Aug. 31, 1780, a merchant in Hartford, Ct.

1. COOK, or COOKE, Capt. AARON, bapt. Feb. 21, 1640, s. of Aaron, of Nh., was representative, 1689, 1691, 1693 and 1697, and d. Sept. 16, 1716, in 76th yr. M. May 30, 1661, Sarah, dau. of William Westwood. She d. March 24, 1730, in 86th yr. Children—*Sarah*, b. Jan. 31, 1662, m. Thomas Hovey; *Aaron*, res. in Hartford; *Joannah*, b. July 10, 1665, m. Feb. 22, 1683, Samuel Porter, Jr., and d. Nov. 13, 1713, ae. 49; *Westwood*, b. March 29, 1670 or 1671; *Samuel*, b. Nov. 16, 1672; *Moses*, b. May 5, 1675; *Elizabeth*, b. Jan. 9, 1677, m. July 19, 1698, Ichabod Smith; *Bridget*, b. March 31, 1683, m. (1) June 13, 1701, John Barnard; (2) Dea. Samuel Dickinson.

2. WESTWOOD, s. of Aaron, (1) d. June 3, 1744, ae. 73. M. 1692, Sarah Coleman, who d. after Feb. 1756. Children—*Mary*, b. March 21, 1693, d. June, 1693; *Noah*, b. April 5, 1694; *William*, b. June 20, 1696, grad. H. C. 1716, ord. as pastor of chh. in East Sudbury, March 20, 1723, m. Jane, dau. of Maj. Stephen Sewall of Salem, and d. June 17, 1760, ae. 66; *Aaron*, b. Jan. 14, 1699; *Bridget*, b. Jan. 26, 1701, m. Rev. William Rand; *Westwood*, b. June 20, 1703; *Mary*, b. April 6, 1711, d. Aug. 23, 1730, ae. 19; *Rebecca*, b. April 14, 1717, prob. m. —— Wyman.

3. SAMUEL, Lieut., s. of Aaron, (1) d. Sept. 16, 1746, ae. 73. M. June 21, 1698, Ann, dau. of Jonathan Marsh. She d. March 30, 1758. Children—*Ann*, b. June 6, 1700, m. Feb. 26, 1725, Aaron Cook, and d. Dec. 27, 1776, ae. 76; *Sarah*, b. June 7, 1703, m. Dec. 7, 1726, Timothy Eastman, Jr.; *Hannah*, b. April 22, 1706, m. March 20, 1730, William Dickinson, Jr.; *Samuel*, b. Jan. 10, 1709, grad. H. C. 1735, ord. Sept. 12, 1739, over Second chh. in Cambridge, and d. June 4, 1783, ae. 74. M. (1) 1740, Sarah Porter; (2) Anna, dau. of Rev. John Cotton of Newton; (3) ——, dau. of Rev. Nicholas Bowes, of Bedford; *Mehitable*, b. Nov. 10, 1711, m. Jan. 31, 1734, Jonathan Smith; *Jonathan*, b. March 28, 1714, d. April 12, 1714; *Joanna*,

b. May 10, 1715, d. June 13, 1715; *Miriam*, b. Oct. 14, 1716, m. Nov. 17, 1743, Josiah Pierce; *Jonathan*, b. Jan. 17, 1722.

4. MOSES, Capt., s. of Aaron, (1) d. March, 1758. M. July 4, 1698, Mary Barnard, who d. 1753. Children—*Mary*, b. March 20, 1700, m. (1) June 18, 1734, Stephen Kellogg; (2) Oct. 30, 1744, Moses Nash of West Hartford, and d. Sept. 21, 1775, ae. 75; *Moses*, b. Aug. 1, 1702, d. April 19, 1725, ae. 22; *Joannah*, b. Oct. 13, 1704, m. March 7, 1723, Westwood Cook; *Aaron*, b. Feb. 21, 1707; *Margaret*, b. March 18, 1711, m. (1) Cotton Partridge; (2) Samuel Gaylord; *Elisha*, b. Feb. 22, 1715; *Martha*, b. May 26, 1717, m. April 15, 1741, John Dickinson; *Hannah*, b. Oct. 16, 1719, m. 1739, Moses Marsh.

5. NOAH, s. of Westwood, (2) d. June 17, 1760. M. (1) 1716, Sarah Marsh, who d. Sept. 4 or 5, 1746; (2) 1747, Esther Chapin. Children— *Sarah*, b. Nov. 8, 1717, m. Sept. 8, 1743, Elisha Cook; *Noah*, b. Feb. 24, 1720, d. May 17, 1725, ae. 5; *Coleman*, b. June 12, 1722, d. Aug. 20, 1746, ae. 24; *Joseph*, b. Nov. 24, 1724; *Dorcas*, b. March 28, 1727, m. Aaron Goodrich; *Noah*, b. Feb. 12, 1730.

6. AARON, s. of Westwood, (2) d. May 3 or 30, 1739, ae. 80. M. Feb. 26, 1725, Ann, dau. of Samuel Cook. She d. Dec. 27, 1776, ae. 76. Children— *John*, b. April 11, 1726; *Aaron*, b. Feb. 21, 1728; *Phinehas*, b. July 16, 1730, d. young; *Phinehas*, b. June 25, 1732, d. young; *Jabez*, b. Oct. 29, 1734, d. unm., Aug. 28, 1803, ae. 68; *Phinehas*, b. Aug. 23, 1741, d. June 25, 1759, ae. 17.

7. WESTWOOD, s. of Westwood, (2) rem. to Amh., and d. abt. 1748. M. March 7, 1723, Joanna, dau. of Moses Cook. She d. abt. 1749. Children— *Jane*, b. Oct. 11, 1724, m. 1749, Joseph Wright of Ware; *Moses*, b. May 26, 1726; *Mary*, b. Dec. 16, 1730, d. young; *Joannah*, b. Oct. 23, 1734, d. abt. 1734; *Mary*, b. June 4, 1743, m. Dec. 5, 1764, John Smith.

8. JONATHAN, s. of Samuel, (3) m. Aug. 2, 1744, Ruth Goodman. Children—*Seth*, b. Oct. 4, 1744; *Samuel*, b. Dec. 22, 1746, d. Sept. 12, 1748; *Mary*, b. Aug. 9, 1749, m. June 13, 1771, Dan West; *Hannah*, b. Jan. 24, 1751, m. Jan. 5, 1774, Thomas W. Foster; *Ruth*, b. Jan. 3, 1753, m. Dec. 8, 1774, Maj. John Smith; *Samuel*, b. March 18, 1755, rem. to Worthington, a Judge in Vt.; *Jonathan*, b. 1757, d. Aug. 22, 1758, ae. 1 yr. and 7 mos.; *Jonathan*, b. Oct. 17, 1759, called Doctor, rem. from Had.; *Ann*, b. Nov. 19, 1761, m. April 17, 1788, William Westwood Cook; *Lucretia*, b. June 2, 1764, m. Jan. 15, 1792, Elihu Smith; *David*, b. June 2, 1764, d. June 7, 1764; *Clarissa*, b. Dec. 19, 1768, m. 1792, Eliphalet Baker of Sandisfield.

9. AARON, s. of Moses, (4) d. March 29, 1795, ae. 88. M. May, 1740, Abigail, dau. of Doct. John Barnard. She d. June 18, 1782, ae. 72. Children—*Samuel*, b. June 7, 1741, rem. to N. H.; m. 1761, Mary Fairfield of Belchertown; *William*, b. June 7, 1743; *Moses*, was in Rev. war, d. unm.; *Thankful*, m. Sept. 2, 1773, Walter Fairfield of Lyme; *Mary*, b. Aug. 29, 1756; *Samuel*, b. Jan. 16, 1763; *Elijah*, b. Nov. 20, 1764.

10. ELISHA, Ens., s. of Moses, (4) d. March 7, 1794, ae. 79. M. Sept. 8, 1743, Sarah, dau. of Noah Cook. Children—*Rebecca*, b. June 10, 1744, d. May 23, 1751, ae. 6; *Sarah*, b. Dec. 27, 1745, d. Aug. 23, 1746, ae. 8 mos.;

Coleman, b. Aug. 3, 1747; *Elisha*, b. Sept. 3, 1749; *Waitstill*, b. Feb. 25, 1752, *Perez*, b. Feb. 18, 1754, res. in Gr., and d. July 21, 1844, ae. 90; *Oliver*, b. March 12, 1756, rem. to Vt.; *Gad*, b. Sept. 20, 1758, m. Joanna, dau. of Oliver Smith; *William Westwood*, b. March 3, 1762.

11. JOSEPH, s. of Noah, (5) d. June 14, 1805, ae. 79. M. Abigail, dau. of Luke Smith, Jr., to whom he was pub. March 9, 1751. Children—*Giles*, b. Aug. 23, 1751, d. in Greenfield, April 4, 1834, ae. 82; *David*, b. Nov. 29, 1752; *Joseph*, b. 1754, d. Oct. 2, 1779; *Enos*, b. Dec. 28, 1755, grad. Y. C. 1785, lawyer in Deerfield, whence he rem. to N. Y.; *Sarah*, b. Nov. 18, 1757, d. Oct. 22, 1784; *Irene*, b. May 15, 1759, d. 1759; *Irene*, b. Jan. 21, 1761, d. Jan. 1836; *Caleb*, b. Dec. 10, 1762, d. July 10, 1777; *Lucretia*, b. Sept. 23, 1765, d. 1834; *Louisa*, b. Sept. 23, 1765, d. Jan. 24, 1785.

12. NOAH, Lt., s. of Noah, (5) d. April 8, 1796, ae. 66. M. Oct. 23, 1748, Kezia Parsons of Nh. She d. 1809. Children—*Noah*, b. Oct. 8, 1749, grad. H. C. 1769, minister in Keene, N. H.; *Amasa*, b. April 7, 1751, grad. Bro. Univ., 1776, settled over chh. in Bernardston, Dec. 1783, dis. May 1805, d. 1816, ae. 65; *Elihu*, b. Jan. 16, 1753; *Eleazar*, b. Feb. 11, 1755, rem. to St. Albans, Vt., and d. 1800; *Timothy*, b. Feb. 6, 1757, rem. to Stamford, Vt.; *Josiah*, b. March 29, 1759, d. Jan. 5, 1778, ae. 18; *Parsons*, b. March 8, 1762, d. Dec. 15, 1777, ae. 15; *Solomon*, b. Feb. 11, 1764; *Andrew*, b. Feb. 1, 1766, d. Dec. 21, 1814, ae. 48; *Stephen*, b. Sept. 19, 1768, d. Jan. 1, 1827; *Keziah*, b. Jan. 22, 1773, m. —— Shattuck of Brookfield.

13. JOHN, s. of Aaron, (6) d. Feb. 29, 1805, ae. 74. M. (1) Jan. 24, 1760, Rebecca Smith, who d. May 30, 1762, in 26th yr.; m. (2) Jan. 4, 1770, Elizabeth, wid. of Josiah Smith, and dau. of David Smith. She d. June 20, 1819, ae. 79. Children—*Phinehas*, b. Nov. 15, 1760, d. June 14, 1761; *Silas*, b. Nov. 7, 1770, d. Nov. 1, 1772; *Rebecca*, b. July 31, 1772, m. Feb. 7, 1797, Noah Smith of Winchester, N. H.; *Elizabeth*, b. July 5, 1774, d. Jan. 13, 1776; *John*, b. April 6, 1776, d. April 6, 1856, ae. 80; *Silas*, b. Jan. 9, 1779, d. April 27, 1814, ae. 35; *Phinehas*, b. Oct. 9, 1781, grad. W. C. 1803, clergyman, d. in Amh., April 28, 1853, ae. 71.

14. AARON, s. of Aaron, (6) d. Jan. 24, 1800, ae. 77. M. 1755, Anne Sheldon of Nh., who d. Dec. 29, 1796. Children—*Anne*, b. Aug. 23, 1756, m. April 3, 1794, Samuel Pierce; *Phebe*, b. Dec. 15, 1758, m. Oct. 30, 1798, John Sikes of Ludlow; *Lucy*, b. Nov. 26, 1760, m. March 17, 1782, Daniel Smith; *Persis*, b. Oct. 26, 1762, m. (1) Nov. 7, 1787, William, s. of John Smith; m. (2) —— Bates, and d. Aug. 13, 1848; *Jerusha*, b. Oct. 3, 1764, m. Dec. 15, 1785, Willard Smith, and d. Nov. 28, 1848; *Susannah*, b. Dec. 2, 1766, m. 1798, Nathaniel Bridges; *Dan*, b. July 5, 1770; *Caleb*, b. Jan. 16, 1773, d. Jan. 23, 1838.

15. MOSES, s. of Westwood, (7) Amh., m. July 7, 1748, Hannah Smith Children—*Moses*, bapt. 1751, m. Susanna Henderson and rem. to Vt.' *Preserved*, bapt. Jan. 19, 1755, d. unm., in Ashfield; *Joanna*, bapt. Jan. 29; 1758, m. Nov. 16, 1774, Clark Lawton; *Martin*, bapt. March 14, 1764, m., Jan. 28, 1785, Hannah, dau. of Noah Smith; *Levi*, m. (1) April 27, 1786, Achsah, dau. of Dea. Eleazar Smith, of Amh., and rem. to Ashfield.

16. SETH, s. of Jonathan, (8) d. Nov. 26, 1817. M. March 23, 1775, Elizabeth Stevens, who d. May 4, 1818. Children—*Son*, b. and d. Jan. 1776;

Stephen, b. Feb. 25, 1777; *Betsey*, b. Nov. 5, 1778; *Charlotte*, b. Dec. 15, 1780, d. unm., May. 24, 1854; *Son*, per. Almon, bapt. June 29, 1783, rem. to N. Y.; *Child*, bapt. June 29, 1783; *Winthrop*, b. April 26, 1785; *Child*, b. and d. June, 1787; *Child*, b. and d. July, 1788.

17. WILLIAM, s. of Aaron, (9) d. Oct. 20, 1817. M. April 26, 1770, Martha White, who d. Oct. 14, 1816, ae. 74. Children—*Experience*, b. Nov. 20, 1771, m. 1795, Stephen Cook; *Mary*, b. Nov. 11, 1774, d. unm., Aug. 5, 1806, ae. 31; *Martha*, b. Sept. 18, 1777; *David White*, b. July 26, 1779, m. Nov. 23, 1799, Salome Cady, and d. in Belchertown, Jan. 29, 1854, ae. 74; *William*, b. Aug. 23, 1781, m. —— —— and d. in Hat.

18. COLEMAN, s. of Elisha, (10) m. Jan. 31, 1771, Hannah Smith. She d. Feb. 22, 1824, ae. 80. Children—*David Smith*, b. Nov. 1771; *Sarah*, b. Feb. 14, 1774, m. —— Tyler; *Eliezer*, b. May 4, 1775; *James*, b. Sept. 1777; *Hannah*, b. April 20, 1780, m. —— Rhodes; *Lucinda*, b. April 26, 1783, m. April 19, 1801, Joel Fox; *Coleman*, b. Jan. 25, 1785, rem. to Vt.

19. ELISHA, s. of Elisha, (10) m. Dec. 23, 1774, Martha, wid. of Perez Jones, and dau. of John Dickinson. Children—*Submit*, bapt. May 14, 1775, m. (1) Sept. 12, 1799, Timothy Stockwell; (2) —— Wallis; *Job*, b. Oct. 13, 1775; *Elisha*, b. abt. 1779; *Robert*, bapt. May 20, 1781; *Rebecca*, b. June 21, 1783, m. Aug. 17, 1800, Elisha Colt; *Martha*, b. Dec. 26, 1785, d. unm.; *Margaret*, bapt. May 6, 1787, d. unm.; *Roswell*, b. Jan. 1790, d. in youth.

20. WAITSTILL, s. of Elisha, (10) d. March 7, 1823, ae. 71. M. July 23, 1779, Ruth Ballard, who d. in Nh. Children—*Ruth*, m. —— Edwards of Nh.: *Sylvia; Waitstill; Linda*, b. 1785; *Catharine*, b. Nov. 20, 1786; *Son*, b. Nov. 1788, d. June 22, 1789; *Calvin*, b. April 11, 1790; *Lucius Althea*, b. March, 1792; *Ashbel; Frederick*, d. Feb. 21, 1817.

21. WILLIAM WESTWOOD, s. of Elisha, (10) d. Oct. 28, 1821, [1822?] M. April 17, 1788, Anne, dau. of Jonathan Cook. Children—*Daniel*, b. April 17, 1788; *Sophia*, b. 1793, m. 1814, Allen Clark of Nh.; *Harriet*, m. Feb. 14, 1817, Sylvanus Dickinson; *Louisa*, bapt. June 17, 1798, m. Jacob Edson.

22. ELIHU, s. of Lt. Noah, (12) d. April 5, 1801. M. Cynthia Frink of Spr., to whom he was pub. Dec. 2, 1779. She was b. in Stonington, Ct., July 11, 1758, and d. June 7, 1853, ae. 94. Children—*Dau.* per. *Cynthia*, b. Jan. 17, 1781, m. Jan. 15, 1799, Isaac Daniels of Keene, N. H., and d. Jan. 1849; *Achsah*, b. Oct. 2, 1782, m. (1) Jabez Fairbanks; (2) Caleb Stockbridge, and d. Feb. 1837; *Josiah*, b. Jan. 1, 1785, d. Sept. 10, 1828; *Artemas*, b. April 5, 1787; *Elihu*, b. Jan. 13, 1790; *Eunice*, b. July 26, 1792; *Sophia*, b. July 11, 1795; d. Oct. 19, 1802; *Miriam*, bapt. June 3, 1798; m. James Congdon, and d. July 4, 1850.

23. SOLOMON, s. of Lt. Noah, (12) d. June 21, 1831, ae. 67. M. Jan. 3, 1790, Tryphena Newton, who d. June 10, 1805. Children—*Solomon*, b. Nov. 19, 1790; *Elizabeth*, b. May 4, 1792; *Tryphena*, b. May 1, 1794, d. Dec. 20, 1807, ae. 13; *Sylvester*, b. Feb. 16, 1796; *Noah*, b. May 28, 1798; *Parsons*, b. Feb. 18, 1800, grad. W. C. 1822, pastor of Cong. chh. in Lynn; *Amanda*, b. Feb. 12, 1803.

24. JOHN, s. of John, (13) d. April 6, 1856, ae. 80. M. Jan. 22, 1799, Sarah, dau. of Daniel White. She was b. Jan. 26, 1779. Children—*Maria*,

b. Oct. 19, 1799, m. John Judd Graves; *Zenas*, b. Sept. 1, 1801, m. Lucy Russell; *Ephraim*, b. Sept. 30, 1803, d. Sept. 19, 1804; *Ephraim*, b. June 14, 1805, m. Phebe English; *Roswell Wells*, b. June 7, 1807, m. May 19, 1835, Harriet A. Nash of Greenfield; *Elizabeth Smith*, b. April 28, 1810, m. Norman Hamilton; *Horace*, b. March 8, 1812, d. Oct. 29, 1820; *Sarah Porter*, b. June 17, 1814, d. Sept. 16, 1838, ae. 24; *Silas Wright*, b. Dec. 8, 1816, m. Mary Cook; *John Dudley*, b. Feb. 28, 1821; *Emily White*, b. March 28, 1824, d. Aug. 22, 1831.

25. DAN, s. of Aaron, (14) m. Eunice Smith of Winchester, N. H., pub. July 5, 1795. Children—*Loomis*, b. Dec. 3, 1797, d. Dec. 27, 1802; *Judith*, b. June 26, 1799, d. Aug. 30, 1800; *Aaron*, b. April 21, 1800, d. Oct. 16, 1805, *Julia*; b. Dec. 16, 1802; *Loomis*, b. Sept. 3, 1805; *Charles*, b. March 29, 1807. ·

26. STEPHEN, s. of Seth, (16) rem. to N. Y., m. Jan. 19, 1799, Polly Dewey, who d. Jan. 8, 1827. Children—*Charles*, b. Dec. 16, 1799; *Jonathan*, b. April 26, 1801; *Mary Ann*, b. Feb. 15, 1805; *Adelia*, b. June 9, 1807; *Clarissa*, b. Sept. 2, 1810; *Betsey*, b. Sept. 2, 1812; *Giles*, b. Sept. 16, 1815; *Eveline*, b. Dec. 4, 1818.

27. ALMON, s. of Seth, (16) d. Sept. 1825. M. Lorinda, dau. of Clement Smith. She d. May 10, 1815. Child—*Lewis*, b. Aug. 25, 1809, d. Sept. 17, 1820.

28. WINTHROP, s. of Seth, (16) d. June 11, 1854, ae. 69. M. (1) ——, dau. of Joel Smith of Amh.; (2) Feb. 3, 1814, Sophia, dau. of Erastus Smith. She d. Sept. 1, 1846. Children—*Chester*, b. Nov. 27, 1814, m. April 24, 1856, Laura Briggs; *Charlotte Smith*, b. Oct. 5. 1816, m. April 21, 1847, Elijah H. Bartlett; *Horace*, b. Oct. 21, 1818, d. March 18, 1819; *Elizabeth S.*, b. Jan. 31, 1820, m. May 26, 1841, Charles E. Lamson; *Sophia L.*, b. March 3, 1822, m. Oct. 1, 1845, Josiah S. Smith; *Horace*, b. April 24, 1824, Representative 1861, m. Dec. 19, 1855, Cornelia Asenath, dau. of Theodore Pasco, and had— Herbert Stanley, b. June 27, 1857, d. Dec. 25, 1860; *Charles*, b. Oct. 30, 1826, d. Nov. 15, 1829; *Mary D.*, b. Feb. 12, 1829; *Charles*, b. Feb. 9, 1831, m. Nov. 20, 1856, Harriet M. Flagg, and has Francis Luther, b. March 18, 1859, and Frederick, b. Oct. 14, 1860.

29. DAVID SMITH, s. of Coleman, (18) m. Aug. 3, 1772, Ruth Rood. Children—*Horace*, b. Oct. 11, 1792; *Pamela*, b. April 3, 1795, d. Oct. 13, 1796, ae. 1.

30. JAMES, s. of Coleman, (18) d. 1861. M. (1) Nov. 26, 1797, Polly, dau. of Simeon Rood. She d. April 5, 1800; (2) June 1, 1801, Ruhamah Deane, b. July 1, 1776. She d. 1861. Children—*Erastus*, b. April 14, 1798, m. and res. in Vt.; *Dau.*, b. March 20, 1800; *Elbridge*, b. May 3, 1802, d. Nov. 20, 1820, ae. 18; *Austin*, b. Sept. 20, 1804, d. Oct. 29, 1820; *James*, b. June 12, 1806, d. Sept. 18, 1807; *James*, b. Dec. 5, 1807; *Maria A.*, b. July 30, 1809, m. Charles Austin Kellogg; *Polly Rood*, b. Aug. 14, 1811, m. William E. Mather of Nh.; *Martha H.*, b. June 21, 1813, m. 1853, Rev. Solomon Knapp of Lockport, Ill.; *Rufus*, b. Jan. 1, 1815; *Enos Foster*, b. Oct. 29, 1816; *Elizabeth Ann*, b. March 10, 1819, d. Nov. 30, 1820; *Elizabeth Ann*, b. Sept. 5, 1821, m. May 27, 1846, Sylvester Keith.

31. ELISHA, s. of Elisha, (19) d. Jan. 7, 1846, ae. 67. M. Anne, dau. of Timothy Eastman. She d. Feb. 23, 1841, ae. 59. Children—*Abigail; Mary; Jane; Roswell Dickinson*, b. 1820, d. June 9, 1842, ae. 22, while a member of the Class of 1843, in A. C.; *Henry Martin*, b. abt. 1825, d. April 7, 1842, ae.17.

32. ROBERT, s. of Elisha, (19) d. Oct. 10, 1813. M. Lucy, dau. of Noadiah Warner. Child—*Albert Hunt*, b. April 28, 1810.

33. DANIEL, s. of William Westwood, (21) d. March 25, 1823. M. Sept. 12, 1811, Permelia, dau. of William Smith of Williamstown. She was b. March, 1792, and m. (2) Feb. 11, ——, Lucius Crane. Children—*Nancy Elvira*, b. Sept. 1, 1812, d. Sept. 21, 1828; *William Smith*, b. April 18, 1813; *Martin Franklin*, b. Nov. 18, 1815; *Sarah Ann*, b. May 26, ——; *Sydenham*, b. April 4, 1818; *Daniel*, b. May 23, 1821; *Eliza*, b. Feb. 18, ——.

34. ELIHU, s. of Elihu, (22) m. Nov. 4, 1812, Elizabeth Sparhawk, dau. of —— Hull of Walpole, N. H. She was b. March 27, 1793. Children— *Evander*, b. Oct. 21, 1813, d. Dec. 1, 1813; *Abigail Frank*, b. April 10, 1815; *Charlotte Sparhawk*, b. April 28, 1817; *Enos Evander*, b. Nov. 7, 1819; *Sophia*, b. Nov. 20, 1820; *Adaline*, b. Oct. 20, 1822; *Josiah*, b. Nov. 13, 1824; *John Black*, b. June 6, 1827, d. Sept. 25, 1828; *John Elihu*, b. Aug. 25, 1829; *Jane Elizabeth*, b. Jan. 17, 1831; *Eleazar*, b. May 24, 1826.

35. JAMES, s. of James, (30) m. Sept. 26, 1831, Angeline, dau. of Benjamin Kellogg. Children—*Mary Jane*, b. Oct. 10, 1832, d. Oct. 7, 1833; *George Elbridge*, b. Dec. 1, 1834; *Mary Jane*, b. Jan. 5, 1837, d. June 8, 1837; *James Francis*, b. Nov. 5, 1844, d. March 29, 1848; *Juliette Montague*, b. Oct. 15, 1847; *Maria*, b. July, 1852; *Francis James*, b. Jan. 15, 1855.

36. RUFUS, s. of James, (30) m. May 10, 1848, Sophia, dau. of Rufus Lyman of Norwich. Children—*Austin Eliot*, b. Oct. 8, 1849; *Rufus Lyman*, b. Dec. 9, 1852.

37. ENOS FOSTER, s. of James, (30) Amherst, m. April 22, 1840, Sarah Jane, dau. of Daniel White. Children—*Henry A.*, b. Dec. 8, 1840; *Child*, b. Feb. 9 and d. Feb. 19, 1844; *Wm. E.*, b. April 18, 1845, d. Aug. 31, 1848; *Child*, b. March 16 and d. March 18, 1847; *Martha Jane*, b. Jan. 16, 1850, d. Dec. 29, 1856; *Mary A.*, b. June 20, 1853, d. Sept. 27, 1853; *William Foster*, b. July 1, 1855; *Frederick Louis*, b. Feb. 18, 1858; *Mary Maria*, b. Feb. 1, 1861.

38. ALFRED HUNT, s. of Robert, (32) m. Nov. 20, 1834, Prudence, dau. of Jonathan Lyon. She was b. in Holland, Mass., Dec. 21, 1809, and d. Nov. 26, 1850. Children—*Martha Hunt*, b. Sept. 7, 1835; *Alfred Lyon*, b. Dec. 1, 1836; *Lucy Warner*, b. Sept. 10, 1838; *Ellen Elizabeth*, b. May 7, 1840; *Elmira Fay*, b. Nov. 9, 1841; *Henry Robert*, b. Sept. 10, 1843; *Herbert Jonathan*, b. May 18, 1845; *Lucius Lyon*, b. Nov. 16, 1846, d. Jan. 10, 1849; *Emory Lucius*, b. June 12, 1848.

39. WILLIAM SMITH, s. of Daniel, (33) m. (1) Nov. 28, 1837, Mary E. Phelps of Nh. She d. Feb. 23, 1848; (2) Nov. 30, 1848, Caroline, dau. of Zaccheus Crocker Ingram of Amh. She was b. May 12, 1811, and d. April 27, 1850, ae. 28; (3) Feb. 5, 1851, Catharine, dau. of Asahel Burr of Springfield, Vt. She was b. Jan. 4, 1820. Children—*Horace D.*, b. Dec. 8, 1838, d. Jan. 22, 1839; *Helen N.*, b. Feb. 25, 1840, d. Aug. 28, 1840; *Elizabeth W.*, b. May 15, 1842; *George P.*, b. Nov. 15, 1845; *Nancy D.*, b. Dec. 12, 1847; *Caroline*, b. April 27, 1850, d.

40. MARTIN FRANKLIN, s. of Daniel, (33) d. June 3, 1856, ae. 39. M. (1) March 31, 1840, Elizabeth E., dau. of Levi Wright. She d. July 17, 1853, ae. 37; (2) Aug. 28, 1855, Sabra, dau. of Stephen Montague. Children—*Abbe Greenwood*, b. Feb. 19, 1846; *Harriet Amelia*, b. Oct. 24, 1847.

41. SYDENHAM, s. of Daniel, (33) m. May 7, 1845, Elizabeth, dau. of John Shipman. Children—*Alice Georgianna*, b. March 9, 1846, d. Aug. 9, 1846; *Charles Herbert*, b. May 27, 1847, d. July 23, 1848; *Charles Herbert*, b. Feb. 9, 1852; *Emma Louisa*, b. Jan. 18, 1852, d. March 9, 1854; *Edwin Shipman*, b. May 19, 1860.

42. DANIEL, s. of Daniel, (33) m. Sept 5, 1844, Aurelia, dau. of Josiah Smith. Children—*Francis Edward*, b. Oct. 17, 1845; *Daniel Westwood*, b. July 12, 1846; *Sarah Ann*, b. Sept. 20, 1850, d. May 28, 1859; *Lucius Crane*, b. Oct. 25, 1852, d. April 3, 1859; *Helen Permelia*, b. Aug. 4, 1855, d. April 6, 1859; *Maria Louisa*, b. May 7, 1857, d. Nov. 7, 1857; *Arthur Lyman*, b. Sept. 1, 1858, d. March 28, 1859.

COOK, SAMUEL, b. Aug. 7, 1779, d. April 14, 1854. M. Hannah Gates. She was b. July 3, 1779, and d. Oct. 20, 1809. Children—*Miriam*, b. May 16, 1801, m. May 9, 1825, David, s. of Josiah Pierce; *Samuel Pierce*, b. Oct. 7, 1804; *Eliza*, b. April 7, 1807, d. Jan. 31, 1840.

COOLEY, SAMUEL. Children—*Samuel* and *Tamesin*, bapt. July 28, 1799; *Loi Clark*, (son) bapt. July 20, 1800.

CORKINS, WILLIAM, m. Oct. 30, 1792, Huldah Peck.

1. COWLES, COWLS, and COLE, JOHN, Farmington, 1652, rem. abt. 1664, to Hat., freeman 1666, d. Sept. 1675. M. Hannah, who made her Will at Hartford, 1680. Children—*John*, b. abt. 1641; *Hannah*, b. abt. 1644, m. Caleb Stanley, and d. 1689; *Sarah*, b. abt. 1647, m. Nathaniel Goodwin, and d. 1676, ae. 29; *Mary*, m. [Nehemiah?] Dickinson; *Elizabeth*, m. Richard Lyman; *Samuel*, m. 1661, Abigail, dau. of Timothy Stanley, res. in Farmington, and d. Apr. 17, 1691; *Esther*, prob., m. 1669, Thomas Bull of Farmington.

2. JOHN, s. of John, (1) Hat., freeman 1690, d. May 12, 1711, ae. 70. M. Nov. 22, 1668, Deborah, dau. of Robert Bartlett of Hartford. Children—*Hannah*, b. Nov. 14, 1668, d. unm. Dec. 25, 1711, ae. 41; *Jonathan*, b. Jan. 26, 1671; *Samuel*, b. May 27, 1673; *John*, b. June 15, 1676, d. June 18, 1690; *Abigail*, b. Feb. 1, 1679, d. Dec. 8, 1690; *Sarah*, b. June 5, 1681, m. Joseph Burt; *Mary*, b. Nov. 3, 1683, d. unm. 1742; *Esther*, b. April 14, 1686, m. May 25, 1713, Nathaniel Dickinson.

3. JONATHAN, s. of John, (2) Hat., d. Nov. 13, 1756. M. Jan. 21, 1697, Prudence Frary, who d. July 1, 1756. Children—*Abigail*, b. May 24, 1698; *John*, b. Dec. 27, 1700; *Jonathan*, b. June 30, 1703; *Timothy*, b. April 9, 1706; *Keziah*, b. Sept. 6, 1708, m. Ebenezer Cowles; *Nathaniel*, b. March 21, 1711, m. Anna, dau. of Peter Montague, of S. H., and d. abt. 1761, in Belchertown; *Eleazar*, b. Sept. 18, 1713, m. Dec. 6, 1739, Martha Graves, res. in Hat., d. s. p.; *Elisha*, b. April 19, 1716; *Eunice*, b. Aug. 18, 1719; *Abia*, b. Oct. 27, 1722, d. May 10, 1727.

4.   SAMUEL, s. of John, (2) Hat., d. Aug. 16, 1750, from injuries received by a fall from a cart three days before. M. 1698, Sarah Hubbard. Children—
Mary, b. March 16, 1698, m. March 23, 1720, John Amsden; Sarah, b. abt. Oct. 12, 1703, m. Timothy Cowles; Samuel, b. March 12, 1706, m. Abigail, res. in Coventry, Burlington, Harwinton, Simsbury, and Norfolk, Ct., dying in the latter place, 1762; Elizabeth, b. June 28, 1708, m. Charles Hoar; Ebenezer, b. Dec. 18, 1710, m. Kezia, d. of Jonathan Cowles, and d. in Hat., Oct. 28, 1800; Son, b. Jan. 21, 1713, d. ae. 1 week; Daughter, b. Jan. 21, 1713, d. ae. 1 day.

5.   JOHN, s. of Jonathan, (3) Amh., d. between June and Nov., 1735. M. Mary, who d. in Belchertown, 1795, in 89th yr. Children—Israel, b. Sept. 28, 1726, m. Lydia Bardwell, rem. to Belchertown, and d. 1797; Abia, b. Dec. 22, 1729, m. March 3, 1752, Gideon Hannum of Belchertown; John, b. July 28, 1731, m. Sept. 24, 1757, Hannah Bardwell, and d. in Belchertown; Martha, b. Nov. 14, 1734, m. Dec. 12, 1754, Stephen Crowfoot of Belchertown; Mary, bapt. Oct. 3, 1742.

6.   JONATHAN, s. of Jonathan, (3) Amh., d. May 14, 1776, ae. 73. M. June 13, 1732, Sarah Gaylord, who d. Feb. 2, 1790, ae. 81. Children—Sarah, b. Dec. 29, 1732, m. Abraham Kellogg, and d. Oct. 26, 1819, ae. 87; Oliver, b. July 15, 1735; Jerusha, b. May 5, 1737, m. Oliver Barrett of Leverett; Jonathan, b. Aug. 2, 1739, d. unm., in Amh., March 14, 1772, ae. 32; David b. Aug. 11, 1741; Josiah, b. March 20, 1744, m. (1) Christian ——, (2) Wid. Mary Marsh, and res. in Leverett; Eleazar, b. Oct. 18, 1746; Reuben, b. July 22, 1749; Enos, b. May 5, 1752, m. Jan. 28, 1779, Dorcas Goodrich, and d. s. p., in Amh., Jan. 21, 1825, ae. 72; Simeon, b. Oct. 24, 1755.

7.   TIMOTHY, s. of Jonathan, (3) Hat., d. abt. 1788. M. Sarah, dau. of Samuel Cowles. Children—Sarah, b. Sept. 7, 1740, m. Peter Train; Timothy, b. Dec. 25, 1741.

8.   ELISHA, s. of Jonathan, (3) Hat., d. abt. 1770. Children—Abner, b. May 26, 1749; Justin; Lucy, b. June 4, 1753; Elijah; Prudence.

9.   OLIVER, s. of Jonathan, (6) Amh., d. Jan. 23, 1799, ae. 63. M. Irene, dau. of Nathan Dickinson, of Amh. She d. March 28, 1834, ae. 90. Children—Levi, b. April 24, 1764, m. (1) Dec. 25, 1805, Rebecca Hastings; (2) Submit, wid. of Enoch Bangs, and dau. of John Eastman, res. in Amh., and d. Aug. 22, 1829, ae. 65; Oliver, b. Oct. 27, 1765, m. (1) Jan. 29, 1792, Lois, dau. of Simeon Clark; (2) Jan. 16, 1806, Ruth Lindsay; (3) 1832, Submit, wid. of his brother Levi. He d. in Amh., April 1, 1850, ae. 85; Rufus, b. Dec. 16, 1767, m. (1) Mary Putnam; (2) Sarah, wid. of Solomon Boltwood of Amh., and dau. of Robert Benney. He grad. D. C. 1792, and was a physician in New Salem and Amh., and d. in Amh. Nov. 22, 1837, ae.70; Chester, b. Aug. 14, 1770, a physician, m. (1) March 3, 1796, Abigail, dau. of Levi Dickinson of Granby; (2) April 25, 1811, Sally Wade of Chicopee. He d. in Amh., Feb. 25, 1842, ae. 71; Jonathan, b. Oct. 24, 1755, d. Sept. 19, 1777.

10.   DAVID, s. of Jonathan, (6) Amh., d. Nov. 18, 1817, ae. 76. M. Sarah, dau. of Joseph Eastman of Amh. She d. Aug. 14, 1815, ae. 71. Children—David, b. Dec. 20, 1773, m. Sally Wheelock of Leverett, and d. s. p. May 23, 1814, ae. 40; Sally, b. July 23, 1775, m. Dec. 6, 1778, Rev. Ichabod Draper of Amh., and d. in Mich., Aug. 3, 1848, ae. 73; Joseph, b. May 29,

1777, m. Sept. 1801, Beulah Walkup, and d. in Amh.; *Silas*, b. Nov. 4, 1779, m. Dec. 22, 1805, Zilpha Shumway, and d. in Hadley; *Jonathan*, b. Dec. 2, 1781, m. April 16, 1807, Esther, dau. of Elias Graves of Sunderland, and res. in Amh.

11. ELEAZAR, s. of Jonathan, (6) Amh., d. July 19, 1795, ae. 48. M. Dec. 5, 1771, Hannah, dau. of Azariah Dickinson. She d. Oct. 5, 1821, ae. 70. Children—*Hannah*, b. Nov. 10, 1772, m. Jan. 5, 1797, Israel Scott of Whately, and d. in Hadley, April 20, 1827. ae. 55; *Eunice*, b. Oct. 1, 1775, d. Sept. 5, 1777; *Irene*, b. May 8, 1777, m. Jan. 8, 1801, Israel Thayer, and d.; *John*, b. Dec. 20, 1779, m. Nov. 24, 1799, Deborah Warner, and d. in New Haven; *Eunice*, b. April 22, 1782, m. —— Day; *Eleazar*, b. July 25, 1784, m. Sept. 5, 1810, Sybil Montague, and d. in Amh. 1849; *Stoughton*, b. Jan. 3, 1788, m. —— Osborn, and res. in Parishville, N. Y.

12. REUBEN, (6) Amh., d. March 13, 1824, ae. 74. M. Nov. 26, 1778, Betsey Rice. Children—*Elizabeth*, bapt. Jan. 7, 1780, m. Samuel Church; *Reuben*, bapt. Jan. 6, 1782, d. young; *Lavina*, bapt. June 6, 1784, m. Nov. 23, 1812, Zebina Cowls; *William*, bapt. Oct. 14, 1787; *Jerua*, bapt. Feb. 26, 1792, m. John Randolph; *Reuben*, bapt. July 27, 1794; *Sylvester*, bapt. April 23, 1797, m. Sophronia Mason of Cummington; *Solomon*, bapt. Sept. 15, 1799; *Wealthy*, bapt. Sept. 12, 1802, m. —— Trumbull.

13. SIMEON, s. of Jonathan, (6) Amh., d. July 8, 1831, ae. 75. M. Feb. 12, 1778, Sarah, dau. of Reuben Dickinson of Amh. She d. April 21, 1814, ae. 57. Children—*Simeon*, b. Jan. 11, 1779, m. Nov. 10, 1805, Charlotte, dau. of Gideon Stetson, and d. in Goshen; *Child*, b. Oct. 26, 1780, d. in infancy; *Jerusha*, b. March 4, 1782, m. Noah Smith; *Orinda*, b. Jan. 21, 1784, m. Chester Marshall; *Azubah*, b. April 12, 1786, m. Timothy Baker, and d. in Springfield, May 28, 1828, ae. 42; *Zebina*, b. April 10, 1789, m. Nov. 23, 1812, Lavina Cowls, and rem. to New Haven, Vt., and Lincoln, Vt.; *Moses*, b. July 10, 1791, m. Nov. 10, 1814, Chloe, dau. of Ebenezer Dickinson of Amh. and res. in Amh.; *Aaron*, b. Oct. 23, 1793, m. Ruth Saunders, and res. in Springfield; *Sally*, b. Oct. 14, 1796, m. Nov. 26, 1829, Joseph Spear of Sunderland; *Eli*, b. Jan. 1, 1800, m. Melinda Ball of Holden, and d. Jan. 1844, ae. 44.

COLE, STEPHEN, Amherst, m. Persis. Children—*Persis*, b. Nov. 5, 1772; *Elizabeth*, b. Aug. 28, 1774; *Polly*, b. Aug. 19, 1778; *Stephen*, b. Sept. 9, 1780; *Ebenezer*, b. July 8. 1782; *Persis*, b. June 23, 1784; *Sally*, b. June 23, 1786.

1. CRAFT, THOMAS, Had. 1678, d. Feb. 27, 1692. M. Dec. 6, 1683, Abigail Dickinson. She m. (2) Nov. 30, 1704, Samuel Crowfoot, and d. 1714. Children—*John*, b. Nov. 22, 1685; *Mary*, b. Feb. 3, 1687, m. Thomas Hovey, Jr.; *Abigail*, b. Sept. 29, 1688, m. Feb. 3, 1709, Joseph White; *Thomas*, b. Feb. 27, 1690, d. April 12, 1714; *Elizabeth*, b. April 17, 1691, m. May 2, 1734, Benjamin Smith; *Benoni*, b. Oct. 22, 1692, d. May 20, 1722.

2. JOHN, s. of Thomas, (1) Hat., d. May 2, 1730, ae. 44. M. Martha Graves. Children—*Thomas*, b. Aug. 16, 1717, m. Sarah Graves, and d. in Whately, 1803; *Moses*, b. Oct. 23, 1719; *Rebecca*, b. Oct. 12, 1721; *Benoni*, b. Nov. 17, 1725; *Gaius*, b. Dec. 22, 1727.

CRAFTS, JOSEPH, m. May 20, 1779, Roxelany White. Child—*Mary Parsons*, b. April, 1780.

1.   CROW, JOHN, came to New England in 1635, was an early settler of Hartford, and one of the first settlers of Hadley, freeman 1666. He returned as early as 1676 to Hartford, where he d. Jan. 16, 1686. M. Elizabeth, only child of William Goodwin. Children—*John*, a merchant in Fairfield, d. at sea, s. p., 1667; *Samuel; Nathaniel*, who prob. resided in Hartford, and was buried July 2, 1695. He m. Anna —— who after his death m. Andrew Warner of Windham, and d. 1697; *Daniel*, b. about 1656, prob. res. in Hartford, and was buried Aug. 13, 1693, ae. 37; *Esther*, m. Giles Hamlin, Esq., of Middletown; *Sarah*, b. March 1, 1647, m. Nov. 1, 1661, Daniel White, of Hat., and d. June 29, 1719, ae. 72; *Hannah*, b. July 13, 1649, m. March 7, 1668, Thomas Dickinson; *Elizabeth*, b. 1650, m. William Warren; *Mehitable*, b. abt. 1652, m. Sept. 24, 1668, Samuel Partridge, Esq., and d. Dec. 8, 1730, ae. 78; *Mary*, m. (1) Dec. 27, 1666, Noah Coleman of Hat., (2) Sept. 16, 1680, Peter Montague, and d. Oct. 12, 1720; *Ruth*, m. (1) Dec. 21, 1671, William Gaylord, m. (2) John Haley.

2.   SAMUEL, s. of John, (1) was slain at Falls fight, May 18, 1676. He m. May 17, 1671, Hannah, dau. of Capt. William Lewis of Farmington. She m. (2) 1676, Daniel Marsh. Children—*Mary*, b. Feb. 5, 1672, m. April 9, 1690, Luke Smith, and d. June 19, 1761, ae. 89; *Hannah*, b. Dec. 6, 1673; *Samuel*, b. Feb. 11, 1675.

3.   SAMUEL, s. of Samuel, (2) d. Feb. 13, 1761, ae. 86. M. Jan. 11, 1710, Rebecca Smith, who d. Feb. 26, 1715. Children—*Rebecca*, b. May 22, 1712, m. June 4, 1761, Daniel Noble of Westfield, and d. 1802; *Mary*, b. Feb. 12, 1715, m. May 30, 1735, Samuel Catlin.

CROWFOOT, DANIEL, b. abt. 1721, S. H., came from Middletown, Ct. M. Margaret Hillyer. Children—*Margaret*, b. Oct. 4, 1750; *Abial*, b. Oct. 4, 1750; *Abigail*, b. Feb. 3, 1753; *Joseph*, b. March 26, 1755; *Charles*, b. May 15, 1758.

CROWFOOT, SAMUEL, perhaps s. of Joseph of Springfield, d. Feb. 10, 1733, ae. 71. M. Mary, prob. dau. of Isaac Warner. She d. April 9, 1702; (2) Nov. 30, 1704, Abigail, wid. of John Croft, and dau. of John Dickinson. She d. 1714. Children—*Samuel*, b. Jan. 21, 1694; *Stephen*, b. April 13, 1695; *Mary*, b. April 6, 1697, m. 1719, Peter Domo; *Joseph*, b. July 3, 1699; *Daniel*, b. June 5, 1700; *Ebenezer*, b. April 3, 1702; *Sarah*, b. May 25, 1706.

CUTLER, ROBERT, s. of Rev. Robert, was b. in Epping, N. H., Oct. 2, 1748. He was a physician in Pelham and Amherst, and d. March 10, 1835, ae. 84. M. Dec. 22, 1773, Esther, wid. of Isaac Guernsey of Northampton, and dau. of Elisha Pomeroy. She d. Dec. 11, 1822, ae. 77. Children—*Esther*, b. June 11, 1775, m. Jan. 28, 1806, Wright Warner, and d. in Steubenville, Jan. 22, 1818, ae. 42; *Susan*, b. April 9, 1777, m. May 4, 1808, Jason Mixter of Hardwick, and d. 1861, ae. 84; *Robert*, b. Dec. 1778, d. Nov. 4, 1781; *Elihu Pomeroy*, b. Oct. 18, 1780, grad. W. C. 1798, m. July, 1811, Betsey Delano, was a promising lawyer in Hardwick and North Yarmouth, Me., and d. Aug. 29, 1813, ae. 32; *Isaac Guernsey*, b. Nov. 18, 1782, grad. W. C. 1801, m. Dec. 24, 1807, Nancy Hastings, was a physician in Amherst, where he d. Nov. 29, 1834, ae. 52; *Robert*, b. Sept. 14, 1784, was a physician in Sheldon, Vt., and St. Albans, Miss., and d. Nov. 22, 1817, ae. 33.

DALE, MRS. MEHITABLE. Children—*Samuel; Jeremiah; Green.*

DANA, AMARIAH, s. of Samuel of Pomfret, Ct., was b. May 20, 1738, and rem. abt. 1773 to Amherst, where he d. Oct. 29, 1830, ae. 92. M. (1) June 30, 1763, Dorothy May, who d. Dec. 9, 1779; (2) Oct. 5, 1780, Ruth Williams, who d. April 16, 1822. Children—*Ezra*, b. May 1, 1764, d. Jan. 7, 1776; *Lucinda*, b. Nov. 3, 1765, m. Nathan Sprout; *Eleazer*, b. Aug. 6, 1767, rem. to Weybridge, Vt.; *Dorothy*, b. Sept. 22, 1769; m. —— Marsh; *Lucretia*, b. Nov. 3, 1771, killed by being run over by the wagon while her parents were removing from Conn., March 9, 1773, ae. 1; *Lucretia*, b. Oct. 9, 1773, m. Nathaniel Goddard of Boston; *Mary*, b. April 17, 1775, m. —— Cowan; *Freedom*, b. May 2, 1777; *Son*, b. June 14, 1783; *Ruth*, b. June 8, 1784, m. —— Terry, of Hardwick; *Hannah*, b. Oct. 27, 1786, m. David Dickinson, of Amh.; *Amariah*, b. Nov. 14, 1787, settled in Minerva, N. Y.; *Samuel*, b. March 26, 1790, m. Julia Moody; *Sarah*, b. Dec. 14, 1791, m. Elijah Church of Amherst; *Sylvia*, b. June 1, 1793, d. unm., in Amherst; *Joseph*, b. March 15, 1795.

DAVIS, HERMON, m. June 19, 1781, Mehitable Dean. Child, bapt. Oct. 1782.

DAVIS, SARAH, d. Aug. 31, 1789.

DEAN, FAXON, m. Mehitable. Children — *Samuel; Mehitable; Sarah; Olive*, b. Jan. 6, 1766; *Orange*, b. Sept. 19, 1767.

1. DICKINSON, JONATHAN, from Wethersfield, d. May 28, 1791, ae. 63.

2. LEVI, s. of Jonathan, (1) rem. to Had., abt. 1786, d. Jan. 28, 1843, ae. 88. M. Bethiah Fuller, who d. Feb. 6, 1845, ae 84. Children—*Harvey*, b. 1785; *Levi*, b. Dec. 11, 1786; *Jonathan*, b. Feb. 1789; *Bethiah*, b. May, 1790, m. John Shipman; *Luther*, b. Nov. 7, 1792; *Son*, b. Sept. 1794; *Simeon*, b. Sept. 4, 1796; *Samuel*, b. abt. 1797, d. March 6, 1813, ae. 16; *Fuller*.

3. SIMEON, Deacon, s. of Levi, (2) m. Aug. 17, 1818, Martha, dau. of Enos Nash. Children—*Henry Kirk White*, b. June 8, 1819, res. in West Spr.; *Edwin*, b. July 13, 1826, m. Aug. 14, 1849, Paulina, dau. of Rev. Joseph Bent, of Amh., res. in West Spr.; *Sidney*, b. Feb. 6, 1835; *Simeon*, b. Dec. 10, 1837; *Martha Elizabeth*, b. Dec. 19, 1842.

1. DICKINSON, NATHANIEL, Wethersfield, 1637, town clerk, 1645, representative 1646-56, rem. to Had. 1659, freeman 1661, deacon, and first Recorder, resided for a few years in Hat., but died in Had., June 16, 1676. M. Anne. Children—*Samuel*, b. July, 1638; *Obadiah*, b. April 15, 1641; *Nathaniel*, b. Aug. 1643; *Nehemiah*, b. abt. 1644; *Hezekiah*, b. Feb. 1645; *Azariah*, b. Oct. 4, 1648, slain in Swamp fight, Aug. 25, 1675, m. Dorcas, who m. (2) 1676, Jonathan Marsh; *Thomas; Joseph; John; Anna*, or *Hannah*, m. (1) Jan. or June 16, 1670, John Clary; (2) Enos Kingsley of Nh.

2. SAMUEL, s. of Nathaniel, (1) Hat., freeman 1690, d. Nov. 30, 1711, ae. 73. M. Jan. 4, 1668, Martha, dau. of James Bridgman of Spr. and Nh. She was b. Nov. 20, 1649, and d. July 16, 1711, ae. 61.   Children—*Samuel*, b. Aug. 17, 1669; *Child*, b. Dec. 12, 1671; *Nathaniel*, b. Feb. 10, 1672; *Sarah*, b. Nov. 5, 1675, d. unm., abt. 1750; *Azariah*, b. Dec. 4, 1678; *Ebenezer*, b. Feb. 2, 1681; *Ann*, b. Dec. 17, 1683; *Joseph*, b. Aug. 3, 1686, d. in Sund., Sept. 2, 1755, ae. 69, leaving neither wife or child; *Hannah*, b. April 4, 1689, m. Thomas Hovey of Sund.

3. OBADIAH, s. of Nathaniel, (1.) His house was burnt, and he and child carried in 1677 to Canada. He returned the next year, and rem. from Hat. to Wethersfield, where he d. June 10, 1698, ae. 57. M. (1) Jan. 8, 1669, Sarah Beardsley; (2) Mehitable, prob. dau. of Samuel Hinsdale. Children—*Sarah*, b. Aug. 20, 1669; *Obadiah*, b. Jan. 29, 1672; *Daniel*, b. April 26, 1674; *Eliphalet; Sarah; Noadiah*, b. 1694; *Mehitable*, b. 1696.

4. NATHANIEL, s. of Nathaniel, (1) Hat., freeman 1690, d. Oct. 11, 1710. M. (1) Hannah, who d. Feb. 23, 1679; (2) 1680, Wid. Elizabeth Gillett; (3) 1684, Elizabeth, wid. of Samuel Wright, of Nh. Children—*Nathaniel*, b. May 1, 1663; *Hannah*, b. Jan. 18, 1666, m. Samuel Kellogg of Colchester, Ct., and prob. d. Aug. 3, 1745, ae. 79; *John*, b. Nov. 1, 1667; *Mary*, b. Feb. 2, 1673, m. Nathaniel Smith; *Daniel*, b. March 3, 1675; *Rebecca*, b. March, 1677, m. 1713, Thomas Allen.

5. NEHEMIAH, s. of Nathaniel, (1) freeman 1690, d. Sept. 9, 1723, in 79th yr. M. Mary, prob. Cowles, dau. of John. Children—*Nehemiah*, b. June 5, 1672; *William*, b. May 18, 1675; *John*, b. Feb. 14, 1676, d. Feb. 16, 1676; *Mary*, b. Jan. 4, 1678, m. Aug. 6, 1702, Samuel Gaylord; *John*, (twin,) b. Jan. 4, 1678; *Sarah*, b. April 19, 1680, m. July 4, 1709, Samuel Mighill; *Samuel*, b. Aug. 16, 1682; *Hannah*, b. Sept. 6, 1684, m. Sept. 23, 1714, Benjamin Church; *Esther*, b. March 3, 1687; *Nathaniel*, b. Aug. 23, 1689; *Israel*, b. March 16, 1691; *Abigail*, b. Jan. 14, 1693; *Ebenezer*, b. Sept. 17, 1696; *Rebecca*, b. April 2, 1699, m. Dec. 16, 1725, Jonathan Smith.

6. HEZEKIAH, s. of Nathaniel, (1) a merchant, res. in Hat., Had., and Spr., where he d. June 14, 1707. M. Dec. 4, 1679, Abigail, dau. of Samuel Blackman of Stratford. She m. (2) Jan. 1708, Thomas Ingersol, of West-field and Spr., and d. 1717. Children—*Joanna*, b. Feb. 2, 1684; *Jonathan*, b. April 22, 1688, grad. Y. C., 1706, pastor of 1st Pres. chh. in Newark, N. J., and first President of New Jersey College. He d. Oct. 7, 1747, ae. 59; *Abigail*, b. Dec. 8, 1690; *Elizabeth*, b. March 9, 1693; *Moses*, b. Dec. 12, 1695, grad. Y. C., 1717, settled as clergyman in Maidenhead, N. J., and installed in 1727 over church in Norwalk, Ct. He d. May 1, 1778, ae. 82; *Adam*, b. Feb. 5, 1702.

7. THOMAS, s. of Nathaniel, (1) freeman of Conn., 1657, and of Mass. 1661, a first settler of Had. Having sold out at the latter place in 1679, he removed to Wethersfield, and there d. 1716. M. March 7, 1667, Hannah, dau. of John Crow. Children—*Elizabeth*, b. Dec. 6, 1668, m. —— Adams; *Hannah*, b. May 20, 1670, m. —— Leffingwell; *Thomas*, b. Feb. 15, 1672; *Esther*, b. Jan. 22, 1674, m. (1) Nathaniel Smith of Hartford; (2) Hezekiah Porter, of Hartford; *Mehitable*, b. Oct. 20, 1675; *Nathaniel*, b. Nov. 15, 1677, was buried Jan. 26, 1678; *Elihu; Ebenezer*.

8. JOSEPH, s. of Nathaniel, (1) freeman of Conn., 1657, res. in Nh., from 1664 to 1674, and then rem. to Northfield. He was slain with Capt. Beers, Sept. 4, 1675. M. Phebe Bracy, dau. of Mrs. Martin. Children—*Samuel*, b. May 24, 1666, d. in Hat., in 1690 or 1691; *Joseph*, b. April 27, 1668; *Nathaniel*, b. May 20, 1670; *John*, b. May 2, 1672; *Azariah*, b. May 15, 1674, prob. m. (1) Mary, and (2) Elizabeth, and settled abt. 1704, in Haddam, Ct.

9. JOHN, s. of Nathaniel, (1) Had., 1659, d. 1676. M. Frances, dau. of Nathaniel Foote of Wethersfield. She m. (2) Francis Barnard. Children— *Hannah*, b. Dec. 6, 1648, m. (1) Sept. 23, 1668, Samuel Gillet. (2) May 15, 1677, Stephen Jennings; *Mary*, m. Samuel Northam, of Hat., Deerfield, and Colchester, Ct.; *John*, m. Susanna, dau. of Joseph Smith of Hartford, Ct. and rem. to Ct.; *Jonathan*, d. before March, 1678; *Sarah*, m. (1) Dec. 11, 1677, Samuel Lane; (2) Feb. 27, 1691, Martin Kellogg; *Rebecca*, b. abt. 1658, m. Feb. 11, 1681, Joseph Smith, and d. Feb. 16, 1731, ae. 73; *Elizabeth*, d. before March, 1678; *Abigail*, m. (1) Dec. 6, 1683, Thomas Croft, (2) Nov. 30, 1704, Samuel Crofoot; *Mercy*, b. abt. 1668, m. June 8, 1688, Joseph Chamberlain, of Hat., and Colchester, Ct., and d. June 30, 1735, ae. 67; *Mehitable*, m. June 26, 1689, John Ingram.

10. SAMUEL, s. of Samuel, (2) Hat. M. (1) Sarah, dau. of Samuel Billings, (2) 1706, Rebecca, wid. of Abner Wright. Children—*John*, b. Sept. 1, 1699; *Samuel*, perhaps; *Elisha*, b. Dec. 15, 1708; *Moses*, b. Sept. 28, 1711; *Benoni; Martha*.

11. NATHANIEL, s. of Samuel, (2) Hat., d. Nov. 29, 1741. M. May 25, 1713, Esther Cole, who d. 1750. Children—*Eunice*, b. July 17, 1714, m. Thomas Baker; *Gideon*, b. April 27, 1716; *Joseph*, b. Aug. 30, 1719, m. Submit, and d. 1747; *Meriam*, m. Simeon Morton.

12. AZARIAH, s. of Samuel, (2) Hat., m. Jan. 23, 1707, Sarah Gunn. Child—*Azariah*, b. June 5, 1709, grad. Y. C. 1730, and d. March, 1737, in Branford, Ct.

13. EBENEZER, s. of Samuel, (2) Hat., d. March 16, 1730. M. June 27, 1706, Hannah Frary. Children—*Editha*, b. Aug. 23, 1707, m. John Field; *Elizabeth*, b. Aug. 2, 1709, m. —— Gunn; *Nathan*, b. May 30, 1712; *Hannah*, b. Feb. 17, 1715, m. Remembrance Bardwell; *Reuben*, b. Aug. 2, 1717; *Samuel*, b. Oct. 14, 1718; *Mary*, b. Oct. 14, 1718, d. unm., 1754; *Abner*, b. Jan. 5, 1724, m. Sarah, res. in Wh., and d. Sept. 28, 1799, ae. 75.

14. NATHANIEL, s. of Nathaniel, (4) Hat. made his Will 1743, which was approved 1757. M. (1) Hepzibah Gibbs, who d. 1713, (2) Lydia, wid. of Samuel Wright, of Nh. Children—*Nathaniel*, b. Feb. 25, 1685, slain 1698; *Samuel*, b. Dec. 30, 1687, res. in Deer., and d. abt. 1761; *Ebenezer*, b. Oct. 7, 1690, res. in Hat.; *Daniel*, b. Nov. 13, 1693; *Hepzibah*, b. Aug. 7, 1696, m. 1720, Jonathan Belding; *Nathaniel*, b. Nov. 27, 1698, res. in Northfield, and d. before 1758; *Benjamin*, b. Sept. 11, 1702; *Thankful*, b. Sept. 11, 1702, m. 1726, Japhet Chapin of Spr.; *Catharine*, b. Jan. 8, 1706, m. 1726, Caleb Chapin of Spr.

15. JOHN, s. of Nathaniel, (4) Hat., d. Dec. 21, 1761, ae. 94. M. (1) 1688, Sarah, who d. 1707, (2) Hepzibah, prob. dau. of Lt. Thomas Wells of Deer. Children—*Sarah*, b. April 15, 1689, m. Feb. 15, 1709, John Leonard

of Spr.; *Jerusha*, b. March 20, 1693, m. Daniel Russell; *Lydia*, m. Jan. 12, 1714, Joseph Churchill of Wethersfield; *Eunice*, b. 1697, m. Noah Clark of Nh.; *Hannah*, m. Feb. 20, 1723, William Murray; *Ruth*, m. abt. 1727, Samuel Wells; *John*, b. April 2, 1707; *Thomas*, b. April 6, 1718; *David*, b. Oct. 5, 1720, d. 1726; *Mary*, b. June 20, 1722, d. Dec. 10, 1726; *Salmon; Abigail*, m. Jonathan Wells of Belchertown; *Dorothy*, prob.

16. NEHEMIAH, s. of Nehemiah, (5) d. Oct. 1, 1715, ae. 43. M. Mehitable Church, who d. in S. H., Sept. 25, 1748, in 81st yr. Children—*Mary*, b. June 12, 1701; *Nehemiah*, b. Nov. 6, 1702; *Mehitable*, b. July, 1704, m. Jan. 12, 1727, Richard Church; *Hannah*, b. June 30, 1706, m. Luke Montague; *Sarah*, b. April 13, 1708, m. June 24, 1733, John Moody; *Daniel*, b. Sept. 8, 1710, m. Rachel Goodman, and d. s. p. in Amh., abt. 1793; *John*, b. May 14, 1713.

17. WILLIAM, s. of Nehemiah, (5) d. June 24, 1742, ae. 67. M. Mary, dau. of Jonathan Marsh. Children—*Mary*, b. Feb. 23, 1704; m. April 6, 1727, John Smith, s. of Ebenezer; *William*, b. April 26, 1706; *Dorcas*, b. March 21, 1709, m. May 10, 1728, Hezekiah Smith; *John*, b. Nov. 27, 1715; *Josiah*, b. Aug. 8, 1724; *Elisha*, b. May 18, 1729.

18. SAMUEL, s. of Nehemiah, (5) deacon, removed to Shutesbury, where he d. abt. 1747. M. (1) Oct. 17, 1711, Hannah Marsh, who d. June 10, 1729, ae. 39. (2) 1730, Wid. Bridget Barnard, who d. Aug. 31, 1762. Children—*Samuel*, b. Oct. 16, 1712; *Jonathan*, b. Jan. 16, 1715; *Azariah*, b. July 10, 1717; *Nathaniel*, b. Sept. 3, 1721; *Hannah*, b. March 6, 1723; *Nehemiah*, b. June 15, 1726.

19. NATHANIEL, s. of Nehemiah, (5) rem. to Sund., and d. 1719. M. Dec. 3, 1713, Hannah, dau. of Luke Smith. Children—*Esther*, b. 1716, m. Nov. 12, 1741, John Dickinson of Amh., and d. Jan. 11, 1803, in 88th yr.; *Moses*, b. 1718.

20. ISRAEL, s. of Nehemiah, (5) d. April, 1733. M. (1) Jan. 28, 1719, Mary, dau. of Dea. Nathaniel White. (2) Feb. 13, 1724, Ruth, dau. of Luke Smith. Children—*Ruth*, b. Dec. 5, 1724; *David*, b. March 18, 1726, m. 1753, Hannah Smith; *Ruth*, b. Sept. 27, 1728, d. March 19, 1745; *Rebecca*, b. Dec. 1732, m. June 16, 1762, Moses Clark of Sund., being his fourth wife.

21. EBENEZER, s. of Nehemiah, (5) deacon, rem. abt. 1731 to Amh., where he d. abt. 1780. M. (1) May 26, 1720, Sarah, dau. of Nathaniel Kellogg, who d. March 22, 1743, ae. 42; (2) Wid. —— Hamilton of Brookfield. Children—*Gideon*, b. Dec. 1, 1720; *Ebenezer; Reuben; Joseph*, b. abt. 1731; *Abigail*, m. Oct. 21, 1740, Samuel Ingram of Amh.; *Sarah*, m. Jan. 18, 1753, Asa Adams; *Mary*, b. abt. 1737, m. April 27, 1757, Noah Dickinson of Amh.; *Jerusha*, m. (1) Jan. or Feb. 1763, David Blodgett of Amh.; (2) March 19, 1804, Nathan Dickinson of Amh., and d. Oct. 27, 1818; *Experience*, bapt. June 28, 1741, d. unm. in Had., March 7, 1770, in 29th yr.

22. NATHANIEL, s. of Joseph, (8) deacon, Hat., d. 1745. M. Hannah, dau. of Daniel White, of Hat. Children—*Jonathan*, b. Nov. 7, 1699; *Martha*, b. Dec. 25, 1701, m. March 2, 1727, Elnathan Graves; *Obadiah*, b. July 28, 1704; *Nathan*, b. April, 1707, d. May 10, 1707; *Joshua*, b. Feb. 7, 1709; *Elijah*, b. Feb. 24, 1712, d. June 8, 1714; *Elijah*, b. Sept. 20, 1714, d. May 28, 1715; *Joel*, b. March 23, 1716; *Lucy*, b. Sept. 9, 1718, d. Dec. 24, 1718.

23. MOSES, s. of Samuel, (10) Hat., d. abt. 1787. M. Oct. 24, 1737, Anna, dau. of Joseph Smith. Children—*Samuel*, res. in Wh.; *Rebecca; Martha*, m. William Mather; *Miriam*, m. Silas Billings; *Anna*, m. John Bullard.

24. BENONI, s. of Samuel, (10) Hat., d. abt. 1723. M. Ruth. Children— *Ruth*, m. Elisha Belding; *Ann*, m. Nathaniel Coleman; *Mehitable; Martha*.

25. GIDEON, s. of Nathaniel, (11) Hat., d. abt. 1781. M. Rebecca. Children—*Lois*, b. June 7, 1743, m. Daniel Dickinson, and d. in Hat., Aug. 31, 1834, ae. 91; *Gideon*, b. Dec. 29, 1744; *Joseph*, b. May 9, 1747; *Beulah*, b. May 25, 1754, m. Elijah Stebbins, and removed to Vt.

26. NATHAN, s. of Ebenezer, (13) rem. in 1742, from Hat. to Amh., where he d. Aug. 7, 1796, ae. 84. M. (1) Thankful Warner; (2) Joanna Leonard of Spr.; (3) Judith Hosmer. Children by first wife—*Nathan*, b. Oct. 19, 1735; *Ebenezer*, b. Jan. 3, 1741; *Irene*, b. July 13, 1743, m. Oct. 27, 1762, Oliver Cowls of Amh., and d. March 28, 1834, ae. 90; *Enos*, b. March 28, 1746. Children by second wife—*Azariah*, b. March 6, 1752, m. and res. in Boston, where he d. abt. 1826; *Elihu*, b. Oct. 14, 1753; *Shelah*, b. Sept. 20, 1755, served in Rev. war, and d. April 30, 1777, ae. 21; *Thankful*, b. March 15, 1758, m. Oct. 7, 1802, Eli Smith of S. H.; *Lois*, bapt. Aug. 5, 1759; *Asa*, bapt. May 10, 1761; *Levi; Joanna*, bapt. April 6, 1766, m. July 15, 1817, John Conkey, of Pelham, and d. Nov. 17, 1825, ae. 60. Children by third wife—*Stephen*, bapt. July 6, 1770; *Judith*, m. Daniel Heath.

27. DANIEL, s. of Nathaniel, (14) Hat., d. Oct. 16, 1768. M. (1) Lydia, dau. of Ichabod Allis. She d. Oct. 16, 1737, ae. 35, (2) 1744, Ruth Bagg, who d. Dec. 19, 1791, in 83d yr. Children—*Daniel*, b. June 3, 1745; *Lydia*, b. Nov. 21, 1746, m. Gideon Dickinson; *Aaron*, b. Oct. 9, 1749, rem. to West Brookfield; *Roger*, b. Feb. 23, 1752.

28. BENJAMIN, s. of Nathaniel, (14) was a teacher and occasionally preached. He d. May 18, 1778. M. Sarah Scott. Children—*Azariah*, b. Sept. 18, 1735; *John; Benjamin*, was a physician in Sund. and Wh., but d. in Hudson, N. Y.; *Asenath; William*, b. Feb, 4, 1746, d. 1749.

29. JOHN, s. of John, (15) Hat., a colonel. He d. Feb. 21, 1799, in 92d yr. M. abt. 1734, Mary Coleman. Children — *John; Lemuel; Mary*, m. —— Graves; *Sarah*, m. —— Belding.

30. THOMAS, s. of John, (15) rem. abt. 1753, from Hat. to Deerfield. M. Prudence Smith. Children—*David*, b. Feb. 3, 1745, d. Aug. 22, 1746; *David*, b. Aug. 31, 1747; *Eliphalet*, b. Aug. 22, 1749; *Thomas Wells*, b. June 14, 1751; *Hepzibah*, b. 1753; *Honor*, b. 1755; *Prudence*, b. 1758; *Consider*, b. 1761.

31. SALMON, s. of John, (15) Hat., d. abt. 1782. Children—*Salmon; John; Mary*, m. Feb. 8, 1774, Samuel Dickinson, Jr.; *Hannah*, m. Aug. 31, 1773, Seth Bardwell; *Olive*.

32. NEHEMIAH, s. of Nehemiah, (16) Gr., d. March 20, 1776, ae. 73. M. June 4, 1730, Mary Moody, who d. Nov. 15, 1787. Children—*Nehemiah*, b. Aug. 10, 1731, d. Oct. 25, 1799; *Mary*, b. Oct. 19, 1732, d. 1752; *Joseph*, b. Sept. 13, 1734, d. March 28, 1736; *Azubah*, b. Sept. 7, 1736, m. 1757, Josiah Snow, Jr.; *Joseph*, b. Dec. 15, 1738, m. Susanna, dau. of Samuel

38   DICKINSON.

Church, and d. Nov. 2, 1817, ae. 78; *Editha*, b. Feb. 21, 1742; *Mehitable*, b. Jan. 13, 1745, d. Aug. 25, 1748; *Mehitable*, b. Oct. 28, 1749.

33. JOHN, s. of Nehemiah, (16) Amh., d. abt. 1791. M. Nov. 12, 1741, Esther, dau. of Nathaniel Dickinson of Sund. She d. in Gr., Jan. 11, 1803, in 88th yr. Children—*Nathaniel*, b. Aug. 13, 1742; m. Theoda, dau. of Dea. David Smith, and d. abt. 1795; *Israel*, b. May 15, 1746; *Waitstill*, b. April 17, 1750.

34. WILLIAM, s. of William, (17) S. H., d. Dec. 30, 1740, ae. 35. M. March 30, 1730, Hannah Cook. She d. Oct. 29, 1745, ae. 39. Children—*Hannah*, b. Feb. 5, 1731, d. April 11, 1731; *Son*, b. and d. Dec. 10, 1732; *Silence*, b. Feb. 25, 1734, d. March 26, 1734; *Son*, b. Feb. 25, 1734, d. Feb. 26, 1734; *Waitstill*, b. Feb. 14, 1736; *William*, b. Jan. 9, 1741.

35. JOHN, s. of William, (17) d. Sept. 25, 1753, ae. 37. M. April 15, 1741, Martha, dau. of Moses Cook. She m. (2) June 25, 1761, David Bagg of Blandford, and d. June 29, [30?] 1762. Children—*Mary*, b. Jan. 12, 1742, d. May 12, 1743; *William*, b. Oct. 4, 1743, d. Aug. 30, 1746; *Martha*, b. Sept. 7, 1745, m. (1) Perez Jones; (2) Dec. 23, 1744, Elisha Cook, Jr.; *Marah*, b. Oct. 15, 1747, d. Oct. 17, 1747; *John*, b. Oct. 30, 1748; *Mary*, b. Jan. 20, 1751, m. Nov. 15, 1770, Enos Smith, and d. Feb. 7, 1815, ae. 64; *William*, d. Nov. 24, 1757, ae. 4.

36. JOSIAH, s. of William, (17) d. Oct. 29, 1772, ae. 48. M. Nov. 24, 1748, Sibil Partridge, who d. Oct. 19, 1819, ae. 87. Children—*Josiah*, m. Wealthy Shepard of Hartford, Ct., and d. in Nh., Jan. 17, 1812, ae. 62; *Elisha*, b. July 27, 1752; *Cotton*, b. Nov. 1754; *Elihu*, rem. to Charlestown, N. H.; *Sibil*, m. Dec. 9, 1779, Daniel Dickinson; *Maria*, m. May 10, 1787, Maj. John Smith, and d. May 21, [29?] 1808, ae. 46; *William*, b. June, 1765, m. Nov. 15, 1795.

37. SAMUEL, s. of Samuel, (18) Gr., d. Feb. 10, 1750, ae. 38. M. Esther, dau. of Nathaniel White. Children—*Hannah*, b. Dec. 3, 1743, m. Waitstill Dickinson; *Christian*, b. Oct. 5, 1745, m. —— Barton; *Samuel*, b. May 15, 1747, m. Naomi; *Eli*, b. Nov. 10, 1749.

38. JONATHAN, s. of Samuel, (18) res. in Shutesbury and Amh. M. Sept. 26, 1745, Dorothy, dau. of John Stoughton, of Windsor, Ct. She was b. March 18, 1715. Children—*Lucy*, b. Nov. 9, 1746, m. Zaccheus Crocker of Sunderland; *Dorothy*, b. March 14, 1748, m. April 10, 1788, Joseph Dickinson of Amh., and d. Feb. 27, 1808, ae. 60; *Jonathan*, b. Sept. 5, 1749; *Joel*, b. May 29, 1751, m. Eunice; *Samuel*, b. May 5, 1753, rem. to Brattleboro', Vt.; *Stoughton*, b. Feb. 17, 1755; *Daniel*, b. Oct. 10, 1756.

39. AZARIAH, s. of Samuel, (18) Shutesbury and Amh., d. Nov. 12, 1799, ae. 82. M. Sept. 16, 1747, Eunice, dau. of John Stoughton of Windsor, Ct. She was b. Feb. 19, 1717. Children—*Eunice*, b. April 10, 1749, m. Feb. 6, 1771, Joseph Eastman, of Amh., and d. Aug. 16, 1838, ae. 89; *Hannah*, b. Dec. 24, 1750, m. Dec. 5, 1771, Eleazar Cowles of Amh., and d. Oct 5, 1821, ae. 70; *Azariah*, b. April 13, 1753; *Oliver*, b. March 27, 1757, m. (1) Hannah Strickland, (2) Nov. 20, 1831, Dorothy Whiting, and d. in Amh., s. p., May 12, 1843, ae. 86.

40. NATHANIEL, s. of Samuel, (18) Shutesbury and Amh., d. July 10, 1806, ae. 84. M. (1) Thankful ——, who d. March 9, 1783, ae. 60; (2)

Jan. 18, 1787, Wid. Jemima Wales. Children—*Mary*, b. Dec. 29, 1746, m. Nov. 12, 1772, Ebenezer Eastman, of Amh., and d. March 16, 1825, ae. 78; *Nathaniel*, b. Sept. 1, 1750; *Josiah*, b. Oct. 15, 1753, d. May, 1762; *Elijah*, b. Dec. 26, 1756, d. March, 1762; *Rachel*, b. Oct. 19, 1759; *Elijah*, b. April 1, 1762, d. Nov. 30, 1765; *Rebecca*, b. May 24, 1764, d. young; *Salome*, b. April 1, 1766, d. young; *Salome*, b. Nov. 13, 1768, d. young.

40½. NEHEMIAH, s. of Samuel, (18) Shutesbury and Amh., d. Jan. 23, 1779, ae. 52. M. Nov. 14, 1749, Amy, dau. of John Stoughton of Windsor, Ct. She d. Jan. 27, 1784, ae. 64. Children—*Nehemiah*, b. April 23, 1756, insane, d. unm. May 7, 1794; *John*, b. Oct. 27, 1757; *Simeon*, b. Oct. 9, 1759, m. Sally McClare, rem. to Weybridge, Vt., and d. Jan. 20, 1800, ae. 40.

41. MOSES, s. of Nathaniel, (19) Amh., d. April 9, 1803, ae. 85. M. Thankful, dau. of Chileab Smith. She d. Oct. 18, 1802, ae. 80. Children— *Moses*, bapt. April 27, 1746, d. Jan. 30, 1748; *Hannah*, b. Oct. 7, 1747, m. (1) Aaron Warner, Jr., of Amh., (2) Aaron Moody; *Moses*, b. Sept. 8, 1749; *Lois*, b. May 14, 1751, m. Feb. 20, 1772, Enos Dickinson, of Amh., and d. Sept. 21, 1820; *Aaron*, b. June 24, 1753; *Medad*, b. June 9, 1755; *Mercy*, b. Nov. 21, 1757, d. March 6, 1777, ae. 19; *Elijah*, b. April 20, 1760; *Eli*, b. Oct. 1, 1762, d. Sept. 28, 1767, ae. 5; *Judah*, b. Feb. 12, 1765.

42. GIDEON, s. of Ebenezer, (21) Amh. M. Aug. 19, 1745, Hannah, dau. of Nathaniel Edwards, of Amh. Children—*Gideon*, bapt. Dec. 1, 1745; *Elisha*, bapt. March 22, 1747; *Hannah*, bapt. Jan. 22, 1749, m. Jonathan Smith of Whately; *Abigail*, bapt. Jan. 20, 1751, d. unm., prob. in April, 1822; *Sarah*, bapt. Oct. 28, 1753, m. Simeon Dickinson, Jr.; *Martha*, bapt. Jan. 23, 1757, m. William Clapp of Amh.; *Naomi*, b. abt. 1761, m. May, 1782, Seth Dickinson of Amh.; *Samuel*, bapt. May 13, 1764, d. ae. abt. 21.

43. EBENEZER, s. of Ebenezer, (21) Amh., d. Sept. 12, 1798. M. Chloe Holton, b. abt. 1734, who d. Feb. 18, 1826, ae. 92. Children—*Ebenezer*, b. Feb. 6, 1761; *Chloe*, bapt. March 20, 1763, m. Simeon Dickinson, Jr.; *Experience*, bapt. May 20, 1770, prob. d. young; *Roswell*, b. abt. 1772; *Luther*, bapt. Dec. 4, 1774; *Zimri; Joseph*.

44. REUBEN, s. of Ebenezer, (21) commanded a company from Amh. and vicinity in the Revolutionary war, and after the close of the war rem. to Thetford, Vt. He d. in Amh., Nov. 12, 1803, at the house of his sister Mrs. Jerusha Blodgett, while there on a visit. Children—*Reuben*, bapt. 1755, m. — Kellogg; *Sarah*, bapt. Feb. 12, 1757, m. Feb. 12, 1778, Simeon Cowls, and d. April 20, 1814; *Esther*, bapt. Feb. 11, 1759, m. Amos Ayres of Amh., and d. May 17, 1831; *Ruth*, b. abt. 1763, m. Perez Dickinson of Amh., and d. March 25, 1798, ae. 35; *Josiah*, bapt. Oct. 2, 1768; *Solomon; Elijah; Josiah; Rachel*.

45. JOSEPH, s. of Ebenezer, (21) Amh., d. July 25, 1804, ae. 73. M. (1) Martha, dau. of Jonathan Dickinson, son of Samuel; (2) April 10, 1788, Martha, dau. of Jonathan Dickinson, s. of Nathaniel. Children—*Joseph*, b. Sept. 18, 1768; *Martha*, b. Aug. 2, 1769, m. Luke Blodgett; *Ira*, b. Aug. 14, 1789, m. Dec. 12, 1810, Dolly W. Fairbanks.

46. JONATHAN, s. of Nathaniel, (22) rem. from Hat. to School Meadows in Had. and thence abt. 1748 to Amh., where he d. Dec. 31, 1787, ae. 88. M. April 2, 1724, Mary, dau. of Nathaniel Smith of Hat. She d. April 10, 1763. Children—*Simeon*, b. abt. 1726; *Noah*, b. abt. 1729; *Jonathan; Mary*,

m. April 16, 1752, Hezekiah Belding of Amh.; *Martha*, m. Joseph Dickinson
of Amh., and d. Aug. 12, 1779.

47. OBADIAH, s. of Nathaniel, (22) Hat., d. June 24, 1788, ae. 84. M.
(1) May 26, 1726, Mary, dau. of John Belding of Hat.; (2) Martha ——.
Children—*Elijah*, b. July 31, 1727, prob. d. young; *Elihu*, b. Oct. 11, 1729,
per. d. young; *Lucy*, b. Nov. 20, 1731, m. —— Allis; *Israel*, m. Nov. 20,
1764, Mercy, dau. of Oliver Partridge; *Hannah*, m. Nov. 14, 1755, Julius
Allis; *Submit*, m. 1766, Samuel Gaylord of Hat.; *Lois*, m. 1770, John C.
Williams, and d. Sept. 7, 1787, in 42d yr.; *Elijah*, b. abt. 1733, d. in Hat.,
Jan. 26, 1813, ae. 80; *Elihu; Obadiah; Mary*, m. Jan. 27, 1774, Elisha
Allis, Jr.; *Martha*.

48. JOSHUA, s. of Nathaniel, (22) d. in Belchertown, March 2, 1793, ae.
89. Child—*Violet*, b. Nov. 15, 1738, m. Rev. Justus Forward of Belchertown,
and d. March 27, 1834, ae. 95.

49. NATHAN, s. of Nathan, (26) Amh., d. Aug. 3, 1825, ae. 90. M. (1)
Jan. 15, 1761, Esther Fowler, who d. March 15, 1803, ae. 63; (2) March 19,
1804, Wid. Jerusha Blodgett, who d. Oct. 27, 1818. Children—*Timothy*, b.
June 25, 1761; *Perez*, b. March 26, 1763; *Ezekiel*, b. May 25, 1765, m.
Jan. 19, 1797, Perly Gunn of Montague; *Esther*, b. March 3, 1767, m. Maj.
Medad Dickinson; *Esther*, b. Dec. 14, 1768, m. (1) Judah Dickinson; (2)
March 28, 1805, Daniel Moody; *Irene*, b. Dec. 30, 1770, m. Nov. 15, 1798,
Luke Montague of Amh., and d. 1849; *Samuel Fowler*, b. Oct. 9, 1775; *Anna*,
b. April 15, 1780, m. Oliver Smith of Had.

50. EBENEZER, s. of Nathan, (26) Amh. M. Oct. 30, 1765, Ruth Eastman, who d. Jan. 3, 1833. Children—*William*, b. Feb. 6, 1767, m. Sept. 28,
1789, Tirzah Warner, and d. Nov. 4, 1824; *Lucinda*, b. Nov. 17, 1769, m.
May 11, 1800, David Watson of Amh., and d. Jan. 16, 1842; *Editha*, b.
Dec. 16, 1773, d. Feb. 15, 1774; *Sylvanus*, b. Dec. 2, 1776, m. Deborah Parker,
and rem. to Reedsboro', Vt.; *Ebenezer*, b. April 7, 1779, m. Abigail Barrows,
and rem. to Cincinnati, O.; *Abijah*, b. Dec. 7, 1781, m. Oct. 26, 1806, Mary
Stetson, and d. in Amh., April 11, 1824.

51. ENOS, s. of Nathan, (26) Amh., d. Dec. 31, 1821, ae. 72. M. Lois,
dau. of Moses Dickinson of Amh. She d. Sept. 21, 1820. Children—*Azubah*,
b. July 6, 1773, m. Jan. 22, 1795, Enoch Bangs of Amh., and d. Feb. 23,
1799; *Eli*, b. Aug. 11, 1775, m. Nov. 12, 1798, Lovisa Mattoon; *David*, b.
April 27, 1778, m. March 6, 1800, Mary, dau. of Moses Warner of Amh., and
rem. to Petersham; *Lois*, b. Oct. 7, 1783, m. April 27, 1809, Lt. Enos Dickinson of Amh.; *Philomela*, b. Feb. 16, 1786, m. Jan. 21, 1808, Ebenezer
Williams of Amh.; *Enos*, b. March 27, 1788, m. (1) Jan. 27, 1814, Joanna
Nash; (2) Jan. 7, 1819, Thankful, dau. of Oliver Cowls, of Amh.; *Lucius*,
b. Jan. 23, 1790, m. July 1, 1813, Betsey Shumway; *Mary*, b. Oct. 20, 1792,
d. Jan. 15, 1812; *Horace*, b. Jan. 25, 1797, m. Sept. 11, 1822, Sophia Stetson
of Amh., and res. in Palmer.

52. ELIHU, s. of Nathan, (26) Amh., d. June 5, 1811. M. Sept. 28, 1791,
Susanna, dau. of Noadiah Lewis of Amh. Children—*Joel L.*, bapt. March 9,
1794, d. 1794; *Rufus Leonard*, b. April 19, 1795, m. Electa Perry, and d. abt.
1837, in New Ashford; *Fidelia*, b. May 17, 1796, m. June 2, 1817, James
Kellogg of Amh.; *Austin Lyman*, bapt. May 26, 1799, m. (1) March 26, 1820,

Sarah E., dau. of Rev. Ichabod Draper, of Amh., and d. abt. 1835; *Fanny*, bapt. May 10, 1801, m. March 5, 1821, Learned Scott, of Lanesboro', and d. in L., abt. 1840.

53. ASA, s. of Nathan, (26) Amh., d. Feb. 1, 1824. M. June 9, 1805, Salome, dau. of Thomas Hastings, of Amh. Children—*Friend*, b. April 6, 1806, m. (1) May 28, 1827, Betsey Packard, (2) Betsey Hayes, and d. in Higganum, Ct., Nov. 1851; *Noble*, b. Dec. 14, 1807, res. in Amh.; *Asa*, b. Feb. 24, 1809, m. Jan. 20, 1841, Louisa Sprout.

54. LEVI, s. of Nathan, (26) Amh., m. Margaret Peebles. She m. (2) Andrew Hyde, and (3) —— ——, at the West. Children—*Sarah*, b. May 15, 1783; *Irene*, b. April 21, 1785, m. s. of Simeon Pomeroy; *Elizabeth*, b. June 3, 1787; *Patrick Peebles*, b. Oct. 29, 1789.

55. STEPHEN, s. of Nathan, (26) Amh., d. July 25, 1827, ae. 57. M. (1) Dec. 1, 1793, Mary Eastman. (2) Wid. —— Currier. Children—*Adolphus*, b. Oct. 11, 1794, m. Oct. 16, 1817, Lydia, dau. of Andrew Hyde; *Judith*, m. April 11, 1816, Samuel Thayer of Belchertown; *Asa*, m. May 12, 1812, Sophia Hastings; *Joseph E.*; *Polly*, m. April 15, 1824, Erastus Smith, Jr., of Had.; *Osman*, d. young; *Orin R.*, bapt. Dec. 21, 1806, m. Jan. 19, 1830, Mary Hyde; *Salome*, bapt. May 6, 1810, m. Oct. 21, 1831, Elisha Clark, Jr.; *Elihu E.*, bapt. Oct. 18, 1812, m. April 2, 1835, Susan D. Pettengill; *George*, bapt. Nov. 10, 1816, d. Jan. 11, 1824; *Maria*, bapt. Nov. 15, 1818; *Hosmer*, m. Roxanna Goodale. She m. (2) Wright D. Kellogg, of Amh.

56. AZARIAH, s. of Benjamin, (28) m. Sarah. Children—*Sarah*, bapt. Nov. 8, 1767; *William*, bapt. Nov. 8, 1767; *John*, bapt. May 27, 1770; *John*, bapt. June 14, 1772; *Samuel Steward*, b. Sept. 1, 1774, d. March 13, 1776; *Son*, b. Oct. 28, 1777, d. Nov. 1777; *child*, b. and d. Nov. 1778; *Lucretia* (or *Asenath*) *Scott*, b. April 29, 1782.

57. ISRAEL, s. of John, (33) Amh. M. (1) Sarah, dau. of William Boltwood, of Amh.; (2) Nov. 16, 1786, Abigail Lyon. Children—*Israel*, d. July 25, 1801; *Mary*, m. William Champney, of Pownal, Vt.; *Esther*, bapt. April 8, 1781, m. Jan. 25, 1810, Chester Billings of Amh.

58. WAITSTILL, s. of John, (33) Amh., d. abt. 1792. M. (1) Lucretia Montague of Gr. She m. (2) Benjamin Wilson, and had *Lucretia*, b. Aug. 12, 1801, and d. Oct. 6, 1837, ae. 79. Children—*Chester*, b. July 12, 1780, non compos; *David*, b. Aug. 14, 1785, m. Nov. 29, 1810, Hannah Dana, and d. in Amh., Nov. 19, 1833, ae. 48; *Oliver*, b. June 27, 1789, m. (1) Nov. 17, 1811, Elizabeth, dau. of Moses Billings of Amh.; (2) Clarissa, dau. of Moses Billings; (3) March 9, 1847, Lucy Montague, and d. Sept. 2, 1860, ae. 71.

59. WAITSTILL, s. of William, (34) Gr. M. Phebe. Children—*Hannah*, b. Nov. 1, 1760; *Irene*, b. Sept. 28, 1762; *Waitstill*, b. 1765; *Phebe*, b. Oct. 18, 1766.

60. WILLIAM, s. of William, (34) Gr. M. Esther, prob. dau. of Hezekiah Smith. Children—*Dorcas*, b. Sept. 9, 1764; *William*, b. Nov. 23, 1766.

61. JOHN, s. of John, (35) d. Dec. 2, 1830, ae. 82. M. 1773, Abigail Alexander. She d. Dec. 30, 1832, ae. 84. Children—*Betsey*, b. Oct. 1, 1774, m. Oct. 2, 1798, Lemuel Brown; (2) Sept. 21, 1808, Maj. John Smith, and d. June 22, 1832, ae. 57; *Abigail*, b. Oct. 2, 1776, m. July 21, 1794, Francis Newton; *Martha*, b. Dec. 1778, m. Thomas Reynolds; *John*, b. Dec. 14,

1781; *Elijah*, b. Oct. 10, 1783; *William*, b. 1785; *Polly*, b. Nov. 19, 1787, m. 1813, Thomas Reynolds; *Theodocia*, b. Jan. 1790, d. Feb. 18, 1791, ae. 1.

62. ELISHA, s. of Josiah, (36) d. Sept. 25, 1811, ae. 59. M. Hannah Billings of Conway. She was b. Feb. 24, 1754, and d. April 6, 1829, ae. 75. Children—*Polly*, b. June 4, 1783, m. Enos Smith, Jr.; *Hannah*, b. March 4, 1786, m. Elisha Ely of Rochester, N. Y.; *Elisha*, b. April 15, 1788, m. Azubah Hammond of Winchester, N. H.; *Ruth*, b. Oct. 30, 1790, m. Henry Smith; *Charles*, b. June 25, 1793, m. and res. at the West.

63. COTTON, s. of Josiah, (36) res. in Claremont, N. H., Had., and Nh., and d. in Nh., Jan. 21, 1826, ae. 72. M. Olive, dau. of Seth Field of Northfield. She d. Sept. 10, 1844, ae. 89. Children—*Fanny*, b. Sept. 27, 1780; *Olive*, b. July 23, 1782; *Josiah*, b. Sept. 9, 1784; *Cotton*, b. July 11, 1786; *Susannah*, b. Nov. 11, 1789; *Lucy*, b. Sept. 11, 1791; *Melinda*, b. May 22, 1794.

64. WILLIAM, s. of Josiah, (36) deacon, d. March 15, 1849, ae. 83. M. Nov. 15, 1795, Dorothy, dau. of William Warner. Children—*Maria Partridge*, b. Oct. 15, 1797, m. Rev. Lewis Sabin, D. D. of Templeton; *William*, b. Dec. 17, 1799, d. Dec. 10, 1817; *Roswell*, b. March 11, 1802, d. June 13, 1803; *Dorothy*, b. July 13, 1804, d. Sept. 27, 1810; *Roswell*, b. Dec. 29, 1806, d. Sept. 18, 1807; *Elizabeth*, b. Aug. 20, 1808, m. Horace Goodrich of Ware; *Caroline*, b. March 19, 1811; *Dorothy*, b. March 6, 1813, m. Leonard B. Shearer of Boston; *George*, b. Aug. 24, 1815; *Harriet Newell*, b. March 5. 1818, m. Rev. Ebenezer W. Bullard; *William Phelps*, b. Oct. 17, 1820, m. Feb. 2, 1848, Emeline, dau. of Rev. John Woodbridge, D. D., and res. in Chicago, Ill.

65. JONATHAN, s. of Jonathan, (38) Amh., d. June 2, 1836, ae. 86. M. March 27, 1783, Azubah, dau. of Nathaniel Coleman of Amh. Children— *Nathaniel Coleman*, b. Feb. 4, 1784, m. (1) Jan. 27, 1807, Submit Smith; (2) June 2, 1841, Sybil Strickland; *Enos*, b. Oct. 23, 1785, m. April 27, 1809, Lois Dickinson; *Achsah*, b. Dec. 25, 1786, m. Jan. 20, 1807, Jonathan C. Warner; *Ansel*, b. Oct. 23, 1788, d. 1807; *Jeremy*, b. Aug. 22, 1791, d. Nov. 12, 1809, ae. 18; *Anna*, b. Jan. 25, 1801.

66. STOUGHTON, s. of Jonathan, (38) Amh. M. Dec. 16, 1784, Abigail, dau. of Jonathan Nash, of Amh. Children—*Gardner; Luther; Clarissa; Polly; Joshua*, d. Aug. 1796, ae. 4; *Horace*, d. Aug. 1796, ae. 2; *Joshua; Horace.*

67. DANIEL, s. of Jonathan, (38.) M. Dec. 9, 1779, Sybil, dau. of Josiah Dickinson. Children—*Sophia*, b. Sept. 4, 1780, m. Doct. Josiah Goodhue; *Henry*, b. Feb. 3, 1783, d. unm., 1804; *Charlotte*, b. Feb. 15, 1785, m. (1) John Dickinson, (2) Thomas Cutler, of Bernardston; *Samuel*, b. July 30, 1787, m. Abigail Stockbridge; *Sylvanus*, b. Dec. 6, 1789; *Elihu*, b. April 12, 1791, unm.; *Lucy*, bapt. April 30, 1797, d. ae. 10; *Daniel*, b. 1799, m. Mary Ann Williston, was master of a vessel, and d. in 1832, in St. Jago; *Edward*, bapt. Feb. 1801, m. Catharine Jones, physician in Peoria, Ill.

68. AZARIAH, s. of Azariah, (39) Amh., d. Aug. 31, 1813. M. Dec. 22, 1785, Mary, dau. of Joseph Eastman of Amh. Children—*Sarah I.*, b, June 17, 1787, d. Sept. 1, 1788; *Ransom*, b. May 8, 1789, m. Nov. 17, 1808, Betsey, dau. of Aaron Dickinson, and res. in Sunderland; *Austin*, b. Feb. 15,

1791, grad. D. C. 1813, was a clergyman, m. 1836, Laura W. Camp, and d. Aug. 15, 1849; *Daniel*, b. June 18, 1793, m. (1) Feb. 17, 1819, Louisa Adams; (2) June 25, 1829, Tamer Eastman, and res. in Amh.; *Baxter*, b. April 14, 1795, grad. Y. C. 1817, a clergyman, m. June 4, 1823, Martha, dau. of Col. Jotham Bush and Mary Taylor of Boylston, d. Dec. 7, 1875. She (mother) was b. Feb. 10, 1798, d. Aug. 15, 1892; *Hannah*, b. June 3, 1797, m. Austin Loomis of Amh.

69. NATHANIEL, Esq., s. of Nathaniel, (39) grad. H. C. 1771, Amh., d. Nov. 10, 1802, ae. 51. M. Dec. 9, 1779, Sarah, dau. of Ebenezer Marsh of Had. She d. Dec. 9, 1801, ae. 47. Children—*Susanna*, b. Sept. 6, 1781, m. May 29, 1803, Chester, s. of John Dickinson, and d. Oct. 8, 1836, ae. 55; *Walter*, b. May 2, 1784, m. Nov. 7, 1806, Lydia, dau. of John Dickinson, and d. in Amh., April 9, 1851, ae. 66.

70. JOHN, s. of Nehemiah, (39) Amh., d. Jan. 4, 1850, ae. 92. M. (1) June 8, 1778, Lydia, dau. of Joseph Eastman of Amh.; (2) Nov. 6, 1836, Wid. Susanna Wilder. Children—*Zebina*, b. Sept. 30, 1778, m. 1808, Mary Watson, and d. in Amh., June 2, 1837; *Chester*, b. April 26, 1780, m. May 29, 1803, Susanna, dau. of Nathaniel Dickinson, and d. in Amh., May 10, 1850; *John*, b. Feb. 25, 1782, grad. W. C. 1800, lawyer and Judge of Probate at Machias, Me., returned abt. 1837 to Amh. He m. (1) Oct. 12, 1807, Rebecca Ellis; (2) Jan. 5, 1848, Olive S., wid. of Rev. Samuel Shepard, D. D., of Lenox; *Nehemiah*, b. Feb. 16, 1784, m. Jan. 18, 1826, Wid. Wealthy Cowles, and d. in Amh., March 15, 1837; *Bissel*, b. Sept. 1, 1787, d. Dec. 19, 1789; *Bela*, b. July 6, 1789, d. May 2, 1790; *Lydia*, b. July 9, 1791, m. Nov. 6, 1806, Walter Dickinson, and d. in Amh., March 21, 1827, ae. 35; *Ame Stoughton*, b. April 6, 1796, m. (1) Sept. 19, 1816, Jonathan Dickinson; (2) May 6, 1847, John Kellogg, Esq., of Benson, Vt., and d. 1860, ae. 64.

71. MOSES, s. of Moses, (41) Amh., d. Sept. 18, 1775. M. Mary, dau. of Solomon Boltwood of Amh. She m. (2) Oct. 5, 1780, Daniel Cooley, Esq., of Amh., and d. Jan. 10, 1795. Child—*Mary*, m. Nov. 30, 1797, Joseph Blair, Jr., of Amh.

72. AARON, s. of Moses, (41) Amh., d. April 24, 1802. M. June 8, 1780, Eleanor Morton. Children—*Charles*, b. Sept. 8, 1782, d. unm., at the West; *Aaron*, bapt. April 25, 1784, d. young; *Lucy*, b. June 15, 1785, m. Aaron M. Chandler of Amh.; *Lucinda*, b. Aug. 5, 1786, m. (1) Luke Tuttle; (2) Thomas B. Strong of Pittsfield; *Salmon Morton*, b. Aug. 2, 1788, m. May 10, 1820, Lucretia Smith of Had., and res. in Amh.; *Elizabeth*, b. June 11, 1790, m. Nov. 17, 1808, Ransom, s. of Azariah Dickinson, and d. May 29, 1849, ae. 58.

73. MEDAD, s. of Moses, (41) m. (1) Sally Smith; (2) Eleanor Morton; (3) Esther, dau. of Nathan Dickinson. Children—*Sally Smith*, b. Oct. 7, 1786; *Hannah*, b. March 10, 1788, m. Lorenzo Smith of Had.; *Thankful*, b. June 25, 1789; *Olive*, b. Oct. 9, 1793; *Moses Billings*, b. Sept. 6, 1795, m. Ruth Osburn; *Pliny*, b. March 5, 1797, m. Aurelia Burt, rem. to Syracuse, N. Y.; *Olive*, b. Sept. 25, 1798, m. Doct. Geo. Hill of Ann Arbor, Mich.; *Esther*, b. Aug. 15, 1800; *Aaron*, b. July 5, 1802, res. in Heath; *Eleanor M.*, b. Aug. 3, 1804, m. Obadiah Dickinson; *Medad*, b. May 25, 1806; *Julia*, b. May 3, 1809.

74. ELIJAH, s. of Moses, (41) a Colonel, Amh., d. Feb. 1, 1820. M. June 13, 1780, Jerusha, dau. of Jonathan Smith. She d. April 6, 1853, ae. 89. Children—*Moses*, b. June 15, 1781, grad. W. C. 1800, and d. unm. in Amh.,

Aug. 4, 1841, ae. 60; *Silas*, b. Sept. 24, 1783, d. May 30, 1804; *Lucretia*, b. Jan. 19, 1791, d. Feb. 6, 1792; *J. Smith*, b. Oct. 8, 1793; *Fanny*, b. Aug. 5, 1798, d. June 7, 1802; *Jonathan Smith*, b. Aug. 6, 1803, m. Minerva Bartlett of Leverett, and d. in Amh., June 2, 1836, ae. 32; *Fanny*, b. April 26, 1805, m. (1) Artemas Thompson; (2) Caleb Benjamin; (3) Calvin Merrill.

75. JUDAH, s. of Moses, (41) Amh., d. Aug. 4, 1800, ae. 35. M. (1) Olive ——; (2) Nov. 10, 1791, Thankful Dickinson. Children—*Judah*, b. Aug. 20, 1797, d. July 30, 1803, ae. 5; *Henry*, b. May 11, 1799, d. Aug. 5, 1803, ae. 4; *Thankful*, b. Jan. 9, 1801, m. Doct. John Hubbard.

76. GIDEON, s. of Gideon, (42) rem. after 1787 from Amh. to Washington, Vt. M. (1) Abigail, dau. of John Field; (2) Lydia, dau. of Simeon Dickinson. Children—*Jerusha*, bapt. June 2, 1771; *Rosalinda*, b. March 19, 1775; *Abigail*, b. July 25, 1779; *Gideon*, bapt. Sept. 16, 1781; *Abi*, bapt. Nov. 23, 1783; *Joshua*, bapt. May 29, 1785; *Irene*, bapt. Aug. 12, 1787.

77. ELISHA, s. of Gideon, (42) Amh., d. May 12, 1819, ae. 72. M. Martha, dau. of Simeon Dickinson. She d. March 17, 1848, ae. 92. Children —*Elisha*, b. Aug. 2, 177–, d. ae. 18 mos.; *Martha*, b. Jan. 16, 1778, m. March 19, 1797, Zebina Hawley of Amh., and d. 1852, ae. 74; *Elisha*, b. Jan. 30, 1781, m. (1) Feb. 1807, Lois Marsh; *Roxana*, b. April 3, 1783, m. Philip Hawley; *Susan*, b. Aug. 12, 1785, m. Aug. 1, 1833, Benoni Rust; *Wealthy*, b. Dec. 5, 1787, m. (1) Josiah Cowls; (2) Jan. 18, 1826, Nehemiah Dickinson; *Samuel*, b. Oct. 28, 1789, m. Jan. 1, 1816, Wealthy Cushman; *Elijah*, b. March 9, 1792, m. Oct. 23, 1823, Sarah Belding; *Harrison*, b. April 21, 1794, d. March 4, 1804, ae. 9; *Jerusha*, b. July 29, 1796, d. unm., Sept. 8, 1840, ae. 44.

78. EBENEZER, s. of Ebenezer, (43) Amh., d. Aug. 15, 1818. M. Nov. 17, 1782, Abigail Belding, dau. of Hezekiah. She d. in a fit, June 25, 1839, ae. 76. Children—*Electa*, b. Feb. 8, 1783, d. Jan. 21, 1785; *Rufus*, b. Feb. 20, 1786, m. Aug. 1811, Almira Church, and res. in South Deerfield; *Luther*, b. Aug. 26, 1788, d. Aug. 20, 1789; *Hezekiah*, b. Sept. 26, 1790, d. Dec. 27, 1791; *Chloe*, b. Jan. 26, 1793, m. Nov. 10, 1814, Moses Cowls; *Electa*, b. Feb. 10, 1795, m. May 25, 1825, Lyman, s. of Jonathan Smith, and d. in Amh., April 25, 1859; *Abigail*, b. April 13, 1797, d. unm., Dec. 29, 1851; *Martha*, b. Dec. 26, 1799, d. Feb. 3, 1802; *Hezekiah*, b. March 14, 1802, m. Nov. 22, 1832, Electa Marshall; *Orra*, b. April 14, 1804, m. June 25, 1833, John Milton Smith of Goshen; *Speedy*, b. July 19, 1807, d. Feb. 19, 1808.

79. ROSWELL, s. of Ebenezer, (43) Amh., d. March 4, 1848, ae. 76. M. Rachel, dau. of John Hunt of Belchertown. Children—*Nancy*, b. Sept. 14, 1800, m. Nathaniel Adams Wilder of Chesterfield; *Charlotte*, b. Jan. 14, 1801, unm.; *Rebecca*, b. July 5, 1803, m. Samuel, s. of Eli Parker; *Lovina*, b. April 26, 1805; *Caleb Dexter*, b. May 23, 1807, m. (1) Tryphena Russell; (2) Louisa Billings, res. in North Hadley; *Maria*, b. May, 1808, m. Rev. Eli W. Harrington of Lunenburgh, and d. Aug. 29, 1838, ae. 30; *Charles Holton*, b. Jan. 1810, m. Maria Brainard.

80. ZIMRI, s. of Ebenezer, (43) Amh., d. May 31, 1802. M. Lucy. Children—*Salina; Hiram; daughter*.

81. JOSEPH, s. of Joseph, (45) Amh., d. March 3, 1841, ae. 72. M. Jan. 29, 1795, Sarah, dau. of John Hunt of Belchertown. She was b. in Braintree, May 22, 1776. Children—*Martha*, b. June 9, 1796, d. Dec. 3, 1796;

Harriet, b. Nov. 2, 1798; *Mary Ann*, b. Feb. 2, 1801, m. June 8, 1837, Parker Hastings of Amh.; *Martha*, b. Nov. 26, 1802, m. Oct. 3, 1850, Lucius Church; *Dorothy*, b. May 30, 1807, m. Nov. 9, 1837, Marcus Lyon Goodale of Belchertown; *Sarah Hunt*, b. Jan. 13, 1809, m. Nov. 29, 1832, David Blodgett; *Joseph*, b. Oct. 20, 1810, m. (1) May 8, 1839, Jane Elizabeth Pease of Gr.; (2) June 2, 1841, Fidelia Alvord of Wilmington, Vt.; *Daniel Baxter*, b. May 18, 1813, d. Sept. 10, 1813; *Emily*, b. Jan. 4, 1817, m. Wm. Morton Graves of South Hadley.

82. SIMEON, s. of Jonathan, (46) Amh., d. May 23, 1806, in 81st yr. M. Sept. 15, 1750, Martha, dau. of Aaron Graves of Hat. Children—*Lucy*, b. Sept. 28, 1751, d. unm., Aug. 20, 1823; *Lydia*, b. May 25, 1753, m. March 18, 1810, Gideon Dickinson, Jr. of Washington, Vt., and d. 1854; *Martha*, b. July 17, 1755, m. Elisha Dickinson and d. March 17, 1848, ae. 92; *Simeon*, b. Aug. 28, 1757; *Seth*, b. Oct. 6, 1759; *Gad*, b. Nov. 29, 1761, m. July 11, 1793, Mary Franklin, and d. s. p. in Amh., Dec. 26, 1848, ae. 87; *Eunice*, b. Feb. 6, 1764, m. March 13, 1800, Nathaniel Edwards of Amh., and d. Mch. 2, 1862, ae. 98; *Martin*, b. Oct. 29, 1765, d. unm., May 4, 1818, ae. 52; *Jemima*, b. Nov. 28, 1767, d. unm., June 20, 1820, ae. 52; *Jerusha*, b. March 24, 1770, m. Nov. 29, 1797, Nathan Franklin of Amh., and d. Feb. 21, 1849, ae. 79; *Obed*, b. April 11, 1772, d. Oct. 15, 1775; *William*, b. Jan. 26, 1775, d. unm., Nov. 1824, ae. 49.

83. NOAH, s. of Jonathan, (46) Amh., d. March 28, 1815, ae. 86. M. (1) April 27, 1757, Mary, dau. of Dea. Ebenezer Dickinson, she d. June 1, 1791, ae. 54; (2) March 22, 1792, Susan Ward. Children—*Mary*, b. abt. 1758, m. July 7, 1779, Hon. Ebenezer Mattoon of Amh., and d. July 30, 1835, ae. 77; *Jonathan*, bapt. June 7, 1795, m. Sept. 19, 1816, Ame S., dau. of John Dickinson, and d. Oct. 2, 1840.

84. JONATHAN, s. of Jonathan, (46) Amh., d. in Pittsfield, Sept. 7, 1798. M. (1) Dec. 27, 1759, Mary Hamilton, who d. Dec. 6, 1770, ae. 27; (2) Mary Matthews of New Braintree; (3) Mary Warner. Children—*Salome*, bapt. Aug. 16, 1762, m. March, 1782, Eli Parker, and d. June 16, 1801; *Mary*, bapt. Aug. 10, 1766, d. young; *Silas*, bapt. Nov. 19, 1769, m. Oct. 22, 1789, Eunice, dau. of Jonathan Moody; *Lois*, m. April 5, 1787, John Blodgett, and rem. to Claremont, N. H.; *Polly*, bapt. 1772; *Nancy*, bapt. June 24, 1787, d. unm., in Oct. or Nov. 1833; *Lucy*, bapt. March 14, 1790, m. Jude Hamilton, and rem. to Vt.

85. REV. TIMOTHY, s. of Nathan, (49) grad. D. C. 1785, ord. as pastor of (Cong.) church in Holliston, Feb. 18, 1789, where he d. July 6, 181̖, ae. 52. M. Nov. 26, 1789, Margaret, dau. of Rev. Joshua Prentiss of Holliston. She d. Feb. 16, 1839, ae. 79. Children—*Nancy*, b. Oct. 14, 1790, d. Feb. 2, 1806, ae. 15; *Joshua Prentiss*, b. Aug. 2, 1792, grad. Brown Univ. 1811, was a physician in Bangor, Me., where he d. Nov. 17, 1856, ae. 64; *Thomas*, b. June 24, 1794, m. (1) Nov. 27, 1817, Rhoda Adams; (2) March, 1835, Miranda Pond; (3) Sept. 20, 1836, Susan Grout, and d. in Hol., Nov. 2, 1844, ae. 50; *Edwards*, b. April 22, 1796, grad. H. C. 1818, practiced medicine in Waterford, N. Y., m. April 2, 1824, Susan Henry, and d. in Hol., Feb. 28, 1831, ae. 34; *Irene*, b. Dec. 28, 1797, m. Sept. 10, 1840, Harding P. Woods of Barre; *John*, b. Feb. 11, 1801, d. March, 1801, ae. 4 weeks; *Esther*, b. Oct. 2, 1803, res. in Barre.

46   DICKINSON—DOMO, OR DOMER.

86. PEREZ, s. of Nathan, (49) Amh., d. Aug. 20, 1815, ae. 50. M. (1) June 28, 1787, Ruth, dau. of Reuben Dickinson. She d. March 25, 1798, ae. 35; (2) Lucinda Foster, who d. in Knoxville, Tenn. Children—*Betsey; Electa,* m. Oct. 31, 1815, Horace Gates of Belchertown; *Fanny,* m. Seneca Holland of Belchertown and Amh.; *Ruth,* d. unm., Jan. 9, 1843, ae. 49; *Nancy,* bapt. May 11, 1806; *Appleton,* bapt. March 27, 1808, grad. A. C. 1825; *Lucinda,* bapt. June 2, 1811; *Perez,* bapt. April 25, 1813.

87. HON. SAMUEL FOWLER, (49) Amh., grad. D. C. 1795, was an eminent lawyer in Amh., Representative and Senator in General Court of Mass., rem. 1833 to Cincinnati, O., and thence to Hudson in the same State, where he d. April 22, 1838, ae. 62. M. March 31, 1802, Lucretia Gunn of Montague, who d. in Enfield, May 11, 1840, ae. 64. Children—*Edward,* b. Jan. 1, 1803, grad. Y. C. 1823, a lawyer in Amh., Representative, Senator, Counsellor, and Representative in Congress, m. May 6, 1828, Emily, dau. of Joel Norcross of Monson; *William,* b. Oct. 7, 1804, m. (1) Eliza Hawley; (2) Mary L. Whittier, both of Andover, and res. in Worcester; *Lucretia,* b. Dec. 16, 1806, m. Rev. Asa Bullard of Cambridge; *Mary,* b. Feb. 10, 1809, m. Mark H. Newman, and d. March 31, 1852; *Samuel Fowler,* b. Aug. 16, 1811, res. in Macon, Ga.; *Catharine,* b. Feb. 17, 1814, m. Joseph A. Sweetser of New York; *Timothy,* b. March 11, 1816, m. Jan. 10, 1838, Hannah, dau. of Ezekiel Dickinson, and d.; *Frederick,* b. Aug. 3, 1819, grad. A. C. 1837, m. Feb. 17, 1846, Mary Richardson of Billerica, and res. in B.; *Elizabeth,* b. May 29, 1823.

88. JOHN, s. of John, (61) d. Sept. 29, 1787. M. Jan. 6, 1808, Charlotte, dau. of Daniel Dickinson. She m. —— Cutter of Bernardston, and d. Jan. 12, 1861, ae. 76. Children—*Lucy; Charlotte.*

89. ELIJAH, s. of John, (61) d. March 22, 1848. M. April 4, 1815, Clarine, dau. of Samuel White of So. Hadley. She was b. April 3, 1789. Children—*Elijah Walden,* b. Feb. 29, 1816, m. Nov. 12, 1839, Mary A. Crossett; *Jerusha,* b. Feb. 15, 1819, m. Nov. 25, 1847, Warren S. Judd; *Alphonzo,* b. Nov. 3, 1821, m. Jan. 20, 1853; *Samuel Collins,* b. Dec. 11, 1824, m. May 16, 1846, Rachel S. Parsons; *Emeline,* b. Nov. 5, 1826, d. Sept. 1, 1847; *Luther White,* b. Nov. 30, 1830.

90. GEORGE, s. of Dea. William, (64) m. Aug. 19, 1844, Maria, dau. of Cotton Dickinson of St. Johnsbury, Vt. Children—*William C.,* b. Oct. 18, 1846; *Lewis S.,* b. Jan. 27, 1849; *George,* b. May 2, 1851; *Albert,* b. Sept. 23, 1853; *Arthur E.,* b. Jan. 20, 1859.

91. SYLVANUS, s. of Daniel, (67) m. Feb. 14, 1817, Harriet, dau. of William Westwood Cook. Children — *James P.,* b. Jan. 10, 1818; *Horace Stoughton,* b. Dec. 11, 1819, d. Sept. 18, 1838; *William Westwood,* b. Jan. 21, 1822; *Harriet Sophia,* b. Jan. 1, 1824; *Daniel Henry,* b. Dec. 16, 1825; *Frances Cordelia,* b. Jan. 23, 1828, d. June 27, 1855; *Elisha B.,* b. Dec. 1, 1832; *Horace Stoughton,* b. March 29, 1839.

DOMO, or DOMER, PETER, d. in S. H., Jan. 1, 1763, ae. 78. M. Feb. 20, 1719, Mary Crowfoot, who d. Dec. 17, 1759, ae. 62. Children—*Mary,* b. Nov. 13, 1719; *Martha,* b. May 28, 1721; *Sarah,* b. Oct. 23, 1723, m. Henry Gilbert of Ware; *Martin,* b. July 20, 1730; *Comfort,* (dau.) d. unm., in Gr., March 17, 1798.

1. EASTMAN, ROGER, b. abt. 1611, sailed from Southampton, Eng., for New England, April, 1638, in the ship Confidence of London, John Jobson, master, settled in Salisbury, where he d. Dec. 16, 1694, ae. 83. M. Sarah, who d. March 11, 1698. Children—*John*, b. April 9, 1640, m. Nov. 5, 1670; *Nathaniel*, b. May 18, 1643; *Philip*, b. Dec. 20, 1644; *Thomas*, b. Nov. 11, 1646; *Timothy*, b. Nov. 29, 1648; *Joseph*, b. Jan. 8, 1651; *Benjamin*, b. Feb. 12, 1653, m. April, 1678, Anna Joy; *Sarah*, b. Sept. 25, 1655, m. (1) June 13, 1678, Joseph French, Jr., of Salisbury; (2) Aug. 4, 1684, Solomon Shepard of S. and d. Dec. 1, 1748, ae. 93; *Samuel*, b. Nov. 20, 1657, m. (1) 1686, Elizabeth Severance, (2) Shuah, and d. Feb. 27, 1725, ae. 67; *Ruth*, b. April 22, 1662.

2. TIMOTHY, s. of Roger, (1) rem. to Suffield, and thence abt. 1690, to Had., where he d. April 1, 1733, ae. 85. M. May 16, 1682, Lydia, dau. of William Markham. Children—*William*, b. April 9, 1684, d. April 22, 1705, ae. 21; *Lydia*, b. May 2, 1691, d. unm., Oct. 5, 1746, ae. 55; *Sarah*, b. Oct. 11, 1694, m. Jan. 24, 1716, William Montague, and d. Sept. 29, 1747, ae. 52; *Timothy*, b. Jan. 10, 1697.

3. JOSEPH, s. of Roger, (1) rem. as early as 1682, from Salisbury to Had., where he d. April 4, (14?) 1692. M. Mary, dau. of Hon. Peter Tilton of Had. She m. (2) Feb. 17, 1693, James Guernsey. Children—*Joseph*, b. Aug. 2, 1683; *Mary*, b. Dec. 11, 1684, d. April 10, 1685; *Peter*, b. Jan. 20, 1686, prob. m. Nov. 28, 1708, Mehitable Root, and rem. to Whipanung, N. J.

4. TIMOTHY, s. of Timothy, (2) d. March 25, 1733, ae. 36. M. Dec. 7, 1726, Sarah Cook. She d. March 10, 1793. Children—*Sarah*, b. June 16, 1728, m. Dec. 4, 1746, Ebenezer Marsh; *Joanna*, b. Jan. 2, 1731, m. April 5, 1750, Phinehas Lyman; *Elizabeth*, b. Jan. 31, 1733, m. June 2, 1757, Olivei Smith, and d. Aug. 13, 1811, ae. 78.

5. JOSEPH, s. of Joseph, (3) deacon, was in 1704 taken captive at Deerfield, by French and Indians, and after his return settled in Had., on the place of his grandfather, Hon. Peter Tilton, where he d. Sept. 29, 1769, ae. 86. M. Nov. 22, 1711, Mercy Smith, who d. Jan. 10, 1784, in 90th yr. Children—*Mary*, b. Oct. 11, 1712, m. Nov. 27, 1735, Fellows Billings of Conway; *Joseph*, b. Feb. 1, 1715; *William*, b. Aug. 25, 1718; *John*, b. March 20, 1721; *Mercy*, b. Sept. 5, 1723, m. Experience Smith of Gr.; *Rachel*, b. Jan. 2, 1725, m. Nov. 23, 1749, John Clary of Sunderland; *Benjamin*, b. Jan. 2, 1725; *Abigail*, b. May 28, 1728, m. Dec. 26, 1751, Josiah Smith of Granby; *Ruth*, b. Nov. 13, 1731, d. March 13, 1740; *Kezia*, b. Nov. 5, 1733, m. Dec. 28, 1763, Jonathan Belding of Northfield; *Timothy*, b. Sept. 9, 1739.

6. JOSEPH, s. of Joseph, (5) Amh., d. Oct. 29, 1790, ae. 75. M. May 17, 1746, Sarah Ingram. She d. Aug. 30, 1811, ae. 86. Children—*Sarah*, b. Jan. 28, 1744, m. David Cowles of Amh., and d. Aug. 14, 1815, ae. 71; *Ruth*, b. Aug. 10, 1745, m. Oct. 30, 1765, Ebenezer Dickinson of Amh., and d. Jan. 3, 1833, ae. 87; *Joseph*, b. March 21, 1747, m. Feb. 6, 1771, Eunice, dau. of Azariah Dickinson of Amh., and d. s. p. in Amh., March 26, 1826, ae. 79; *Ebenezer*, b. May 31, 1749; *John*, b. May 7, 1751; *Mercy*, b. Oct. 14, 1754, m. Dec. 15, 1778, Daniel Kellogg of Amh., and d. Jan. 12, 1823, ae. 68; *Lydia*, b. Jan. 13, 1757, m. June 8, 1778, John Dickinson of Amh., and d.

May 10, 1834, ae. 77; *Mary*, b. Aug. 2, 1761, m. Dec. 22, 1785, Azariah Dickinson of Amh., and d. Nov. 20, 1836, ae. 75; *Hannah*, b. Feb. 21, 1766, m. April 3, 1786, David Billings, and d. June 18, 1786, ae. 20; *Tilton*, b. April 28, 1769, d. Aug. 17, 1773, ae. 4.

7.   WILLIAM, s. of Joseph, (5) Gr., deacon, d. July 20, 1793, ae. 74.   M. (1) Dec. 11, 1744, Mary, dau. of Dea. Joseph White of S. H.   She was b. June 25, 1727, and d. Nov. 19, 1752, ae. 25; (2) Elizabeth Moseley of Glastenbury, Ct.   Children—*Mary*, b. Sept. 12, 1745, m. Joel Lyman; *Mercy*, b. Dec. 31, 1746, d. Jan. 22, 1747; *Mercy*, b. Feb. 17, 1748, d. Dec. 31, 1752; *William*, b. Nov. 10, 1749, d. 1759; *Joseph*, b. July 14, 1751, d. Feb. 26, 1752; *Joseph*, b. Nov. 13, 1754; *Elizabeth*, b. Dec. 1, 1756; *Rachel*, b. Dec. 15, 1759, m. —— Dickinson; *Lois*, b. July 8, 1761, m. —— Kellogg; *William*, b. Nov. 20, 1763; *Abigail*, d. Jan. 26, 1767; *Abigail; Ruth*.

8.   JOHN, s. of Joseph, (5) d. March 28, 1790, ae. 69.   M. Dec. 3, 1763, Submit, wid. of David Keyes of Western (Warren) and dau. of Jonathan Belding of Northfield.   She d. in East Hartford, Ct., May 23, 1816, ae. 84. Children—*Lois*, b. Sept. 27, 1764, m. Dec. 9, 1788, William Porter, and d. Dec. 12, 1792, ae. 28; *Anne*, b. April 22, 1766, d. Aug. 22, 1767, ae. 1; *John*, b. May 18, 1768, d. Aug. 29, 1769, grad. Y. C. 1788, a physician in Flushing, L. I., where he d. unm.; *Joseph*, b. Feb. 22, 1772, d. Aug. 21, 1775, ae. 3; *David*, b. Aug. 31, 1774, left home at the age of 21 for the West, and has never since been heard from; *Submit*, b. Aug. 24, 1776, d. Aug. 24, 1778.

9.   BENJAMIN, s. of Joseph, (5) Gr., d. Nov. 28, 1792, ae. 67.   M. 1758, Eunice Day of Spr.   Children—*Benjamin*, b. May 23, 1760; *John*, b. April 24, 1762, d. 1762; *Eunice*, b. Nov. 8, 1763, m. Samuel White of Gr.; *John*, b. Dec. 23, 1765, grad. Y. C. 1795, a clergyman, d. 1834; *Mercy*, b. April 14, 1768, m. James Smith of Gr.; *Kezia*, m. Oct. 21, 1792, Asa Nash of Gr., and d. July 29, 1806.

10.   TIMOTHY, s. of Joseph, (5) d. Aug. 19, 1818, ae. 78.   M. (1) Nov. 15, 1770, Anna, dau. of Jonathan Smith.   She d. Dec. 7, 1777; (2) 1780, Ruth, dau. of Timothy Sheldon of Suffield, Ct.   She d. Feb. 7, 1830, ae. 76. Children—*Anna*, bapt. April 25, 1773; *Timothy*, b. Sept. 1, 1775, d. Sept. 15, 1775; *Anna*, b. May 22, 1781, m. Dec. 30, 1807, Elisha Cook, and d. Feb. 23, 1841, ae. 59; *Lucinda*, b. July 12, 1783; *Samuel*, b. Sept. 27, 1785; *Joseph*, b. April 8, 1788; *Ruth*, b. March 21, 1791, m. Jan. 1, 1834, Eleazar Wright of Nh., and d. Jan. 1, 1834, ae. 32; *Grace*, b. Nov. 5, 1793, m. Nov. 7, 1815, Dea. Aaron Breck of Nh.; *Timothy*, b. Sept. 15, 1796.

11.   EBENEZER, s. of Joseph, (6) Amh., d. Nov. 7, 1820, ae. 71.   M. Nov. 12, 1772, Mary, dau. of Nathaniel Dickinson, of Amh.   She d. March 16, 1825, ae. 78.   Children—*Tilton*, b. Aug. 15, 1773, grad. D. C. 1796, Cong. clergyman in Randolph, Vt., where he d. July 8, 1842.   M. Speedy Smith; *Polly*, b. Nov. 8, 1775, m. Dec. 11, 1794, Stephen Dickinson of Amh., and d. May 25, 1822; *Elijah*, b. March 13, 1777, m. Oct. 24, 1802, Rebecca Hall, and d. March 26, 1820; *Zebina*, b. Sept. 28, 1778, d. unm. in Carlisle, Nov. 6, 1855, ae. 77; *Salome*, b. Oct. 25, 1780, m. (1) April, 1803, Silas Adams of Shutesbury; (2) David Putnam; *Samuel*, b. March 18, 1783, grad. D. C. 1802, res. in Amh., m. Sally Pynchon; *Clarissa*, b. Nov. 9, 1784. m. Nov. 27, 1801, Asa Adams of Shutesbury; *Achsah*, b. Oct. 19, 1786, m.

April 15, 1805, Josiah Warner, Jr.; *Theodore*, b. Dec. 17, 1788, m. Jan. 3, 1811, Susanna Scott, and d. May 27, 1816; *Ebenezer*, b. Nov. 22, 1790, enlisted in U. S. Army, in war of 1812, and died.

12. JOHN, s. of Joseph, (6) Amh., d. Aug. 6, 1829, ae. 78. M. Dec. 22, 1779, Hepzibah, dau. of John Keyes. She d. 1837. Children—*Submit*, b. Oct. 20, 1780, m. (1) Nov. 19, 1801, Enoch Bangs of Amh.; (2) Levi Cowls of Amh.; (3) 1832, Oliver Cowls of Amh.; *Emelia*, b. March 7, 1782, m. Jan. 25, 1814, John Hawks of Deerfield; *Joseph*, b. Nov. 4, 1783; *Beulah*, b. and d. June 1, 1785; *Hannah*, b. June 22, 1786, d. unm., Sept. 14, 1818; *Solomon Keyes*, b. July 12, 1788, m. Nov. 10, 1819, Almira Richardson, res. in Amh.; *Jonathan*, b. March 21, 1790, grad. Y. C. 1811, a lawyer, d. unm. in New York City, Sept. 7, 1830, ae. 40; *Ornan*, b. March 30, 1793, d. Dec. 28, 1793; *Lois*, b. Aug. 17, 1794, m. Aug. 26, 1824, Lewis Whittemore; *Ornan*, b. March 26, 1796; grad. Y. C. 1821, a Secretary of the American Tract Society in New York City, m. Nov. 1832, Mary Reed; *Anna*, b. Sept. 14, 1797, m. Oct. 31, 1821, Archimedes Ferry, and res. in Amh.; *John*, b. May 3, 1799, d. Nov. 1799; *Hepzibah*, b. Jan. 8, 1802, m. (1) Aug. 31, 1826, Henry Clary; (2) Nov. 25, 1835, Matthew O. Halsted of Orange, N. J.; *John*, b. July 19, 1803, m. (1) Prudence Dale; (2) Prudence Hathaway; *David*, b. June 16, 1806, grad. A. C. 1835, minister in Leverett, m. (1) Sarah Smith, (2) Emily Pomeroy.

13. SAMUEL, s. of Timothy, (10) d. May, 1837. M. Nov. 21, 1815, Abigail Smith of Chester. She d. Oct. 1837. Children—*Samuel Sheldon*, b. Nov. 2, 1816, res. in Greenfield, and is editor of the Gazette & Courier; *Charles Baxter*, b. March 12, 1819, res. in Chicopee; *William Smith*, b. Feb. 7, 1821, d. April 28, 1821; *Child*, b. May 20, 1822, d. May 23, 1822; *Harriet Sophia*, b. May 4, 1824, d. Jan. 25, 1853; *William Merrick*, b. July 10, 1827, res. in Macon, Ga.; *Lucy Ann Smith*, b. July 27, 1831, res. in Springfield; *Sarah Maria*, b. Nov. 1, 1834, res. in Springfield.

14. JOSEPH, s. of Timothy, (10) d. Jan. 13, 1860, ae. 71. M. Nov. 1819, Susan, dau. of Oliver Sheldon of Suffield, Ct. She was b. 1786, and d. Jan. 13, 1853, ae. 67. Children—*Timothy Phelps*, b. Nov. 27, 1820, m. April 24, 1860, Susan Phelps, dau. of Milton Woodville of Chicopee; *Henry B.*, b. Aug. 2, 1823, d. June 29, 1850, ae. 27.

15. JOSEPH, s. of John, (12) rem. in 1814 to State of New York, and now (1861) res. in Bleeker, N. Y. M. (1) July 24, 1806, Lois Root of Montague. She was b. Sept. 19, 1786, and d. Feb. 14, 1810; (2) Dec. 30, 1810, Eunice Parker of Whately. She was b. April 11, 1785. Children—*Rilus*, b. Nov. 23, 1807; *Lucius Root*, b. Sept. 15, 1809; *Martin*, b. Jan. 20, 1812.

16. RILUS, s. of Joseph, (15) res. in Bleeker, N. Y. M. May 5, 1831, Catharine Maria Jipson, b. Oct. 12, 1812. Children—*Lois Root*, b. Feb. 27, 1832; *Ornan*, b. Sept. 20, 1833, d. July 19, 1857, ae. 23; *Catherine Lucinda*, b. May 17, 1835; *Elizabeth Jane*, b. May 25, 1837; *Rilus*, b. Oct. 24, 1839; *Joseph*, b. Jan. 29, 1842; *David*, b. May 24, 1844; *Sarah Ann*, b. Sept. 27, 1846; *Aloney*, b. May 23, 1849; *Lucius Root*, b. Dec. 8, 1851; *Lena Harriet*, b. Feb. 28, 1857.

17. LUCIUS ROOT, s. of Joseph, (15) grad. A. C. 1833, Andover Theo.
Sem. 1836, has been pastor of Cong. church in Sharon, but now (1862)
resides in Amherst. M. Dec. 20, 1837, Sarah Ann, dau. of Aaron Belden of
Amh. She was b. July 20, 1817. Children—*Lucius Root*, b. Jan. 25, 1839,
grad. A. C. 1857, and Andover Theo. Sem. 1861; *Mary Louisa*, b. March 27,
1841; *Sarah Hibbard*, b. Nov. 5, 1850.

EDWARDS, JONATHAN, Amh., s. of Nathaniel, was b. in Northampton,
Dec. 1722. M. Sept. 6, 1748, Rebecca, dau. of Samuel Smith of Sunderland.
Children—*Jonathan*, bapt. Aug. 20, 1749, d. young; *Jonathan*, bapt. Sept. 8,
1751, d. Dec. 6, 1831, ae. 80; *Rebecca*, bapt. March 17, 1754, m. Zechariah
Hawley of Amh., and d. Jan. 17, 1832, ae. 78; *Nathaniel*, b. April 25, 1756,
m. (1) Jan. 16, 1794, Mary, dau. of Simeon Pomeroy; (2) Eunice, dau. of
Simeon Dickinson, and d. July 22, 1830; *Lydia*, bapt. March 26, 1758, m.
April, 1780, Reuben Nash of Amh., and d. May 20, 1823; *Philip*, bapt. Feb.
10, 1760, m. Jan. 23, 1783, Jerusha Pomeroy; *Sarah; Mary*, bapt. Feb. 23,
1766, m. May 1, 1791, Gideon Ingram; *Hannah; Martha*, bapt. April 17,
1768, m. March 5, 1793, Samuel Marsh of Montague.

EVENS, JOHN, Hatfield, rem. abt. 1685 to Deerfield. M. (1) Mary;
(2) July, 1677, Mercy or Mary, wid. of Ephraim Hinsdale, and dau. of ——
Hawks. Children—*Peter*, b. in Roxbury, June 21, 1674; *Elenor*, b. Jan. 8,
1678; *Jonathan*, b. March 10, 1679.

FELLOWS, RICHARD, Hartford, 1643, rem. 1659, to Springfield, thence
to Nh., and in 1661 to Hat., where he d. 1663. M. Ursula, who d. Sept. 21,
1690. Children—*Richard*, slain Aug. 25, 1675, at Swamp fight above Hatfield; *Samuel*, d. unm.; *Sarah*, m. (1) abt. 1661, Samuel Billings of Hat.;
(2) Oct. 9, 1678, Samuel Belding, Jr., of Hat., and d. Feb. 5, 1713; *John*,
bapt. Nov. 1, 1646; *Mary*, bapt. Feb. 9, 1650, m. March 24, 1671, Joseph
Leonard of Spr.

1. FERRY, NOAH, s. of Charles, Jr. of Springfield, d. in Gr., Nov. 4,
1798, ae. 86. M. 1736, Experience Allis of Hat. She d. Nov. 4, 1794.
Children—*Noah*, m. Hannah, and res. in Gr.; *Charles*, b. Jan. 7, 1739;
Daniel, b. Feb. 15, 1743; *Rebecca*, b. April 9, 1745.

2. CHARLES, s. of Noah, (1) Gr., d. Oct. 19, 1804, ae. 65. M. Mary, who
d. Nov. 22, 1789. Children—*Charles*, b. 1763; *Mary*, b. 1766; *Experience*,
b. 1769; *Luther*, b. 1773; *Rhoda*, b. 1776, d. 1777; *Asa*, b. 1779; *Chester*,
b. 1782.

1. FIELD, ZACHARIAH, Hartford, 1639, rem. abt. 1659, to Nh., and as
early as 1663, to Hat., where he was buried June 30, 1666. M. Mary.
Children—*Mary*, m. Oct. 2, 1663, Joshua Porter of Nh.; *Zechariah*, m. Dec. 17,
1668, Sarah, dau. of John Webb, res. in Nh. and Deerfield, and d. 1674;
John; Samuel; Joseph.

2. JOHN, s. of Zechariah, (1) Hat., freeman, 1690, d. June 26, 1717.
M. Dec. 17, 1670, Mary, dau. of Alexander Edwards of Nh. Children—*John*,
b. May 11, 1672; *Mary*, b. Feb. 2, 1674; *Zechariah*, b. Aug. 1676; *Benjamin*,
b. Feb. 14, 1679; *Mary*, b. Feb. 20, 1681, m. March 6, 1701, Dr. Thomas
Hastings of Hat.; *Bethia*, b. abt. 1684, m. John Allis; *Sarah*, b. Feb. 2,

1687, m. 1709, Nathaniel Peck of Swanzey, N. H.; *Abilene*, d. May 6, 1689; *Ebenezer*, b. July 2, 1690, prob. slain by Indians, in Deerfield, Oct. 26, 1708, *Abilene*, b. July 2, 1690, m. —— Nash.

3. SAMUEL, s. of Zechariah, (1) Hat., slain by Indians June 24, 1697. M. Aug. 9, 1676, Sarah, dau. of Thomas Gilbert of Springfield. Children— *Samuel*, b. Sept. 27, 1678; *Thomas*, b. June 30, 1680; *Sarah*, b. June 30, 1683, m. Nov. 18, 1702, Samuel Warner of Springfield; *Zechariah*, b. Aug. 29, 1685; *Ebenezer*, b. March 17, 1688; *Mary*, b. July 23, 1690, m. June 26, 1712, Jonathan Hoyt; *Josiah*, b. Nov. 5, 1692, rem. to Somers, Ct.; *Joshua*, b. April 9, 1695, rem. to Springfield and Bolton.

4. JOSEPH, s. of Zechariah, (1) res. until about 1714 in Hat., when he rem. to Sunderland, where he d. Feb. 15, 1736, in 78th yr. M. (1) June 28, 1683, Joanna, dau. of John Wyatt of Hartford. She d. March 23, 1722; (2) Jan. 2, 1723, Wid. Mary Belding. Children—*Mary*, b. July 18, 1684; *Joanna*, b. Dec. 9, 1686, d. Aug. 30, 1689; *Joseph*, b. June 9, 1689; *Daughter*, b. March 15, 1691, d. April 19, 1691; *Joannah*, b. Jan. 9, 1693, m. June 11, 1713, Thomas French; *Lydia*, b. June 26, 1695, m. 1724, John Bliss of Springfield; *Jonathan*, b. Oct. 13, 1697, and d. 1781. He m. (1) March 30, 1721, Mary Billings; (2) July 25, 1739, Esther Smith; *Martha*, b. Oct. 19, 1699; *Abigail*, b. Sept. 4, 1702, d. in Sunderland, Jan. 10, 1721; *Israel*, b. June 29, 1705, d. July 16, 1705; *Thankful*, b. Sept. 19, 1707, d. Oct. 11, 1707.

5. JOHN, s. of John, (2) Hat., d. May 28, 1747, ae. 75. M. Sarah, dau. of John Coleman of Hat. Children — *John*, b. Sept. 14, 1700; *Sarah*, m. Joshua Belding; *Hannah*, b. July 8, 1704, m. Dec. 24, 1729, Samuel Dickinson of Deerfield; *Amos*, b. June 24, 1708; *Eliakim*, b. Nov. 27, 1711; *Mary*, b. June 18, 1715.

6. ZECHARIAH, s. of John, (2) an early settler of Amh., where he d. abt. Jan. 1738. M. May 25, 1705, Sarah, dau. of Dea. John Clark of Nh. Children—*Ebenezer*, b. Aug. 8, 1709, prob. imbecile; *Rebecca*, b. abt. 1711, m. Jan. 13, 1737, Joseph Hawley of Amh.; *Sarah*, b. March 18, 1714, m. abt. 1736, Samuel Hawley of Amh.; *Mary*, b. Jan. 21, 1716, m. May 18, 1738, Moses Warner of Amh.; *John*, b. Jan. 12, 1718.

7. SAMUEL, s. of Samuel, (3) rem. as early as 1720 from Hat. to Deerfield, and d. 1762. M. 1706, Mary Hoyt, who d. 1747. Children—*Elizabeth*, b. April 16, 1707; *Samuel*, b. Feb. 20, 1709, d. 1726; *Eunice*, b. May 29, 1714, m. Joseph Smead; *David*, b. Jan. 4, 1712, d. in Deerfield, 1792; *Ebenezer*, b. 1723.

8. THOMAS, s. of Samuel, (3) rem. after 1728 to Longmeadow. M. 1713, Abigail, dau. of Hezekiah Dickinson. Children—*Abigail*, b. Oct. 5, 1714, m. Abial Abbot of Windsor, Ct.; *Samuel*, b. May 10, 1718, d. Aug. 10, 1721; *Moses*, b. Feb. 16, 1722; *Simeon*, a physician in Enfield; *Samuel*, b. Oct. 10, 1725, physician in Saybrook, Ct.; *Sarah*, b. Nov. 28, 1728.

9. ZECHARIAH, s. of Samuel, (3) rem. first to Deerfield, and thence to Northfield, and d. 1746. M. Sarah Mattoon. Children — *Seth*, b. 1712; *Catharine*, b. 1715, m. —— Willard of Winchester, N. H.; *Gaius*, b. 1716; *Ebenezer*, b. 1717; *Samuel*, b. 1719; *Paul*, b. 1721.

10. EBENEZER, s. of Samuel, (3) Northfield, d. Sept. 12, 1723. M. Elizabeth, who m. (2) Azariah Wright. Children — *Ebenezer*, b. 1715;

Joanna, b. 1717, m. Phinehas Wright; *Moses*, b. 1719; *Aaron*, b. 1722; *Elizabeth*, b. 1723.

11. JOSEPH, s. of Joseph, (4) deacon, Sunderland, d. 1754. M. Sept. 13, 1716, Mary Smith. Children—*Elisha*, b. 1717; *Mary*, b. 1719, m. Daniel Clark; *Abigail*, b. 1721, m. 1745, Samuel Field; *Joseph*, b. 1723, d. 1798; *Thankful*, b. 1726; *Martha*, b. 1729; *Experience*, b. 1732, m. Elijah Clark; *Sarah*, b. 1735, m. Simeon Lyman; *Jonathan*, b. 1737; *Israel*, b. 1741.

12. JOHN, s. of John, (5) Hat., d. May 26, 1762, ae. 61. M. (1) Editha Dickinson, who d. 1740; (2) Ann Bagg. Children—*Medad*, b. Aug. 8, 1734; *Editha*, b. June 15, 1737, m. —— Fitch of Ct.; *Hannah*, b. Oct. 5, 1740, m. Silas Graves.

13. AMOS, s. of John, (5) Hat., perhaps d. Oct. 10, 1759. M. Aug. 30, 1739, Mehitable, dau. of Thomas Day of Hartford. Child — *Zechariah*, b. Jan. 6, 1744.

14. ELIAKIM, s. of John, (5) Hat., d. Feb. 8, 1786, ae. 75. M. 1752, Esther Graves of Whately. Children—*Zenas*, b. Aug. 10, 1753; *Sarah*, b. April 22, 1755, m. D. Scott; *Zilpah*, b. Nov. 13, 1756, m. Abner Loomis; *Rhoda*, b. Oct. 26, 1758, m. Elisha Wait; *John*, b. Aug. 25, 1760, rem. to Conway; *Abigail*, b. July 21, 1762, m. Roger Dickinson; *David*, b. April 11, 1764, rem. to Conway; *Esther*, b. April 4, 1767, an invalid, d. unm.; *Hannah*, b. June 21, 1769, m. (1) —— Grimes; (2) —— Cooley.

15. JOHN, s. of Zechariah, (6) Lt., Amh. M. July 10, 1739, Hannah, dau. of Samuel Boltwood of Amh. Children—*John*, bapt. May 18, 1740, m. (1) Jan. 15, 1767, Elizabeth Henderson; (2) Wid. —— Wells; *Abigail*, bapt. July 11, 1742; *Martha Boltwood*, bapt. Oct. 2, 1743, m. (1) Col. Nathan Allen; (2) Thomas Bascom; *Mary*, bapt. July 27, 1746, m. Joel Billings of Amh., and d. Aug. 18, 1813; *Abigail*, bapt. June 5, 1748, m. Gideon Dickinson, Jr. of Amh.; *Sarah*, bapt. May 27, 1750, m. Timothy Clapp of Amh., and d. abt. Feb. 1799; *Ebenezer*, bapt. March 22, 1752, m. Oct. 1, 1782, Sarah Gould; *Samuel*, bapt. Jan. 20, 1754, m. June 15, 1779, Miriam Nash; *Jemima*, bapt. May 25, 1755, m. Jan. 15, 1778, Oliver Bridgman; *Jonathan*, bapt Dec. 9, 1759, m. (1) Jan. 2, 1780, Sally Smith; (2) —— Johnson; *Zechariah*.

FOOTE, NATHANIEL, b. Jan. 10, 1648, s. of Nathaniel of Wethersfield, Ct., rem. abt. 1674 from Hat. to Springfield and thence abt. 1681 to Wethersfield. He d. Jan. 12, 1703, ae. 55. M. May 2, 1672, Margaret, dau. of Nathaniel Bliss of Springfield. She d. in Colchester, Ct., April 3, 1745, ae. 95. Children—*Sarah*, b. Feb. 25, 1673, m. Nov. 1691, Thomas Olcott of Hartford, Ct., and d. July 24, 1756, ae. 84; *Margaret*, b. Dec. 1, 1674; *Elizabeth*, b. June 23, 1677, m. June, 1701, Robert Turner of Coventry, Ct.; *Mary*, b. Nov. 24, 1679, m. May 14, 1706, Daniel Rose, Jr. of Coventry, Ct.; *Nathaniel*, b. Sept. 9, 1682, m. (1) July 4, 1711, Ann Clark; (2) Sept. 13, 1727, Wid. Hannah Coleman, resided in Colchester, and d. Aug. 20, 1774, ae. 91; *Ephraim*, b. Feb. 13, 1685, m. June, 1708, Sarah Chamberlain, and d. in Colchester, June 10, 1765, ae. 79; *Josiah*, b. Sept. 27, 1688, m. Sarah Welles, res. in Colchester, and d. Dec. 1778, ae. 90; *Joseph*, b. Dec. 28, 1690, m. (1) Dec. 12, 1719, Ann Clothier; (2) Sept. 2, 1740, Wid. Hannah Northam, and d. in Colchester, April 21, 1756, ae. 55; *Eunice*, b. May 10, 1694, m. Dec. 3, 1712, Michael Taintor, Jr., of Colchester.

1. FOOTE, SAMUEL, b. May 1, 1649, s. of Nathaniel of Wethersfield, settled in Hat., and d. Sept. 7, 1689, ae. 40. M. 1671, Mary, dau. of Thomas Merrick of Springfield. She d. Oct. 3, 1690. Children—*Nathaniel; Mary*, b. July 9, 1674, slain in Canada; *Samuel*, slain by Indians at Deerfield, Feb. 29, 1704; *Mary*, b. Feb. 28, 1680, m. Feb. 13, 1707, Samuel Sykes of Springfield, and d. Feb. 18, 1752, in 72d yr.; *Sarah*, b. Feb. 26, 1682, m. June 21, 1706, William Scott of Springfield and Kingston, (Palmer;) *Eliezer*, b. Sept. 5, 1684; *Thomas*, b. 1687; *Daniel*, b. 1688.

2. NATHANIEL, s. of Samuel, (1) Hat., m. Nov. 5, 1707, Mary Ward. Children—*Dinah*, b. Oct. 5, 1708; *Ezra*, b. June 28, 1713; *Benoni*, b. June 28, 1713, d. July 2, 1713.

3. ELIEZER, s. of Samuel, (1) res. in Springfield, until abt. 1730, when he rem. to Brimfield, where he d. Nov. 17, 1758, ae. 73. M. (1) May 24, 1717, Lydia Bidwell, who d. Feb. 9, 1719; (2) Sarah, who d. Dec. 17, 1773. Children—*Eliezer*, b. Feb. 8, 1719, d. in infancy; *Lydia*, b. Feb. 8, 1719.

4. THOMAS, s. of Samuel, (1) res. in Springfield, Brimfield and Monson, and d. in M. abt. 1766. Children—*Samuel*, b. Nov. 12, 1728, res. in Norfolk, Ct., Spencertown, N. Y., and New Haven, Vt., dying in the latter place, Dec. 16, 1790, ae. 62; *Joseph*, res. in Monson, and Spencertown, N. Y., and d. 1795, ae. 65. M. (1) Roselle, dau. of David Chapin of Enfield, Ct.; (2) Thankful Parcy; (3) Wid. Sawyer.

5. DANIEL, s. of Samuel, (1) res. in Hartford and Simsbury, Ct., and d. in S., July 15, 1740, ae. 51, from injuries received by being run over by a cart. M. Nov. 19, 1718, Mary, dau. of Joseph Collier of Hartford, Ct. She d. June, 1769, ae. 71. Children—*Samuel*, b. Oct. 4, 1719, res. in Simsbury, Ct., and d. Sept. 18, 1775, ae. 55. M. Nov. 24, 1743, Lois Loomis; *Mary*, b. Nov. 20, 1721, m. (1) 1737, Joel Gillett of Wintonbury Society, (Windsor,) Ct., and Nine Partners, N. Y.; (2) —— Fillemore; *Daniel*, b. April 27, 1724, res. in Simsbury, Ct., Washington and Dalton, Mass., Middlebury, Vt., and Canton, N. Y., and d. in C., May 10, 1801, ae. 77. M. Jan. 14, 1748. Martha, dau. of Dea. John Stillman of Wethersfield, Ct.; *Joseph*, b. Feb. 17, 1727, res. in Simsbury, Ct., and d. Sept. 16, 1779, ae. 52. M. Dec. 8, 1757, Azubah, dau. of Nathaniel Griswold of Windsor, Ct.; *John*, b. 1729, res. in Simsbury, Ct., and d. Sept. 15, 1813, ae. 82. M. (1) 1753, Rosanna, dau. of Jonathan Humphrey of Simsbury, Ct.; (2) Mary Fowler of Salem, Ct.; *Rachel*, b. 1731, d. Jan. 21, 1737; *Sarah*, b. 1732, m. June 9, 1762, Daniel Boardman of Wethersfield, Ct.; *Rachel*, b. March, 1736, m. June 5, 1760, Timothy Phelps of Simsbury, Ct.

1. FOX, ABRAHAM. Children—*Abraham; Joseph Kneeland*, b. June 25, 1782; *Son*, b. and d. June, 1785; *Patience*, b. Sept. 22, 1786.

2. ABRAHAM, s. of Abraham, (1.) Child—*Jesse Anson*, b. March 30, 1803.

FOX, JOEL. Children—*Cynthia*, b. Nov. 14, 1801; *Eliza*, b. July 19, 1804. See page 165.

FOX, NATHANIEL, m. Martha. Children—*Mary*, b. July 7, 1740; *Nathaniel*, b. June 7, 1742; *Martha*, b. Sept. 20, 1744; *Ebenezer*, b. Sept. 1, 1746; *Eunice*, b. March 20, 1748; *Moses*, b. March 1, 1752, d. April 15, 1752; *Catharine*, b. March 14, 1753.

FRANKLIN, Henry Johnson, came in 1766 from Pomfret, Ct., to Amh., where he d. Aug. 3, 1800, ae. 59. M. Mary Williams of Pomfret. Children—*Mary*, b. Nov. 13, 1765, m. July 11, 1793, Gad Dickinson of Amh., and d. Sept. 23, 1851, ae. 85; *Nathan*, b. July 27, 1767, m. Jerusha, dau. of Simeon Dickinson, res. in Amh., and d. March 11, 1832, ae. 64; *Persis*, b. Dec. 25, 1768, m. Edward Stanley, and d. March 26, 1803, ae. 34; *Francis*, b. Sept. 26, 1772, m. John Thayer of Belchertown, and d. Feb. 25, 1843, ae. 70; *Elizabeth*, b. Dec. 16, 1775, m. Dea. Eliab Thomas, and d. Sept. 23, 1837, ae. 61; *Sophia*, b. Nov. 30, 1778, d. Nov. 2, 1802, ae. 23.

1. FRARY, Eliezer, prob. son of John of Dedham and Medfield, freeman 1680, Hat., d. Dec. 19, 1709. M. Jan. 28, 1666, Mary, dau. of Isaac Graves. Children—*Eliezer*, b. July 7, 1669, d. Aug. 5, 1669; *Samuel*, b. April 15, 1674; *Prudence*, b. May 7, 1677, m. Jonathan Cowls of Hat.; *Eliezer*, b. May 12, 1680, res. in 1750 in Hat.; *Hannah*, b. March 23, 1683, m. Ebenezer Dickinson; *Isaac*, b. March 2, 1686; *Jonathan*, b. Nov. 13, 1689.

2. Samuel, s. of Eliezer, (1) rem. to Middletown, Ct. M. Sarah. Children—*Joseph*, b. 1696; *Sarah*, b. 1698.

3. Isaac, s. of Eliezer, (1) Hat., d. abt. 1760. M. Dec. 8, 1715, Lydia, dau. of Jonathan Parsons of Nh. Children—*Eleazar*, b. Dec. 19, 1716; *Phineas*, b. April 29, 1718; *Moses; Lydia*, m. Thomas Hastings; *Hannah; Martha; Elisha*, b. Aug. 18, 1729; *Mary*, m. Jonathan Morton.

4. Jonathan, s. of Eliezer, (1) Hat., d. May 18, 1728. M. July 23, 1719, Mary, dau. of John Graves, 2d. She m. (2) Oct. 30, 1729, Eliakim King of Nh. Children—*Jonathan*, b. Oct. 27, 1721; *John*, b. Dec. 7, 1726.

5. Eleazar, s. of Isaac, (3) Hat., d. 1801. M. (1) 1745, Deborah Chapin of Springfield; (2) Margaret. Children—*Nathaniel*, b. abt. 1754, d. 1832, ae. 78; *Eleazar; Seth*, b. 1758, d. Feb. 24, 1847, ae. 88; *Mary*, m. John Wait; *Esther*, m. David Scott of Whately; *Sarah*, m. Jacob Cooper.

6. Moses, s. of Isaac, (3) rem. from Hat. to Whately, and thence as early as 1773, to Ashfield. M. Abigail Fairfield. Children—*Submit*, b. Nov. 21, 1744; *David*, b. Sept. 12, 1747; *Moses*, b. Feb. 8, 1750; *Jerusha*, b. Aug. 13, 1752; *Julius*, b. July 27, 1755; *Abigail*, b. July 3, 1759; *Mercy*, b. July 7, 1762; *Moses*, b. 1764.

7. Jonathan, s. of Jonathan, (4) Hat., m. Eunice Cowles. Children—*Prudence*, b. Oct. 28, 1743; *Asa*, b. Sept. 17, 1745; *Eunice*, b. March 11, 1752.

1. FRARY, Sampson, prob. s. of John of Dedham and Medfield, settled in Hat., whence he rem. in 1673 to Deerfield, where he was slain by French and Indians, Feb. 29, 1704. M. Mary, who was slain 1704. Children—*Mary*, m. 1681, Jacob Root of Nh.; *Mehitable*, m. 1682, Hezekiah Root of Nh.; *Susanna*, b. March 4, 1668, d. March 28, 1668; *John*, b. Sept. 17, 1669; *Nathaniel*, b. Nov. 29, 1675.

2. Nathaniel, s. of Sampson, (1) res. in Deerfield, where he d. April 30, 1727. M. Mehitable. Children—*Obadiah; Nathan; Eunice; Amos*, d. before 1729.

GARDNER, Jacob, Hat. M. Hannah. Child—*Jacob*, b. 1676.

GARDNER, Joseph, Hat. M. Mary. Child—*Mehitable*, b. May 20, 1679.

GARDNER, Samuel, Hartford or Wethersfield, 1641, rem. 1663 to Had. where he d. Nov. 22, 1696, ae. abt. 81. M. Elizabeth, who d. June 21, 1676. She may have been his second wife, for at settlement of Samuel Gardner, Jr.'s estate in 1677, Joanna and Sarah are called his only sisters. Children— *Samuel*, d. without family, Jan. 12, 1677; *John*, m. 1681, Wid. Mehitable Hinsdale, and d. leaving no children, Nov. 26, 1684; *Joannah*, m. Feb. 3, 1681, Nathaniel Warner; *Sarah*, m. March 25, 1678, John Preston; *Hannah*, m. 1675, Nathaniel Bancroft; *Elizabeth*, m. Nov. 21, 1664, John Ingram; *Abigail*, m. 1673, Isaac Morgan; *Mary*, d. June 6, 1662; *Martha*, b. Jan. 8, 1664, d. Feb. 15, 1664; *Nathaniel*, d. Dec. 8, 1676.

1. GAYLORD, William, b. in Windsor, Ct., Feb. 25, 1651, settled in Had., and d. 1680. He was s. of William and Ann (Porter) Gaylord, and grandson of Dea. William Gaylord of W., who prob. came over from old England in 1630, in the Mary and John, and was one of the first deacons of the Dorchester Church. M. Dec. 21, 1671, Ruth, dau. of John Crow. She m. (2) John Haley. Children—*Ruth*, b. April 1, 1673; *Child*, b. Oct. 23, 1674; *Samuel*, b. Oct. 19, 1676; *William*, b. Oct. 1, 1678.

2. Samuel, s. of William, (1) d. 1734. M. 1702, Mary Dickinson, who was living in 1751. Children—*Ruth*, b. April 6, 1703, d. June 20, 1703; *William*, b. Oct. 4, 1704; *Mary*, b. Jan. 27, 1707, prob. m. Sept. 18, 1746, Charles Chauncey; *Sarah*, b. Feb. 1, 1709, m. Jan. 13, 1732, Jonathan Cowles of Amh., and d. Feb. 2, 1790, ae. 81; *Samuel*, b. May 5, 1711; *John*, b. Sept. 27, 1713; *Nehemiah*, b. Nov. 30, 1715; *Nathaniel*, b. Sept. 8, 1718; *Ruth*, b. Feb. 16, 1721, m. Sept. 10, 1751, John Strickland.

3. William, s. of William, (1) Deacon, rem. to West Hartford, Ct., where he d. Dec. 19, 1770, ae. 92. M. 1702, Hope, dau. of Thomas Butler of Hartford. She d. June 16, 1763, in 83d yr. Children—*William*, b. Jan. 13, 1703, d. Oct. 21, 1703; *Ruth*, b. Oct. 18, 1704; *Twins*, b. and d. Aug. 1706; *William*, b. Nov. 24, 170[9?]; *Samuel*, b. Dec. 10, 1711; *Sarah*, b. May, 1714.

4. William, s. of Samuel, (2) rem. from Had. to S. H., and d. Aug. 20, 1798. M. 1733, Elizabeth Scovill. Children—*Elizabeth*, b. Aug. 31, 1734; *Mary*, b. Jan. 7, 1735; *Catharine*, b. Nov. 8, 1737, m. Dec. 22, 1762, Ezekiel Day of West Springfield, and d. Sept. 28, 1824, ae. 86; *William; Oliver*, b. Dec. 7, 1740; *Nathaniel*, b. Sept. 8, 1742; *Eliphalet*, b. Oct. 28, 1744; *Meribah*, b. July 3, 1746, m.—— Ashley; *Ebenezer*, b. Sept. 12, 1749.

5. Samuel, s. of Samuel, (2) bought the homestead of Josiah Chauncy, Esq., Nov. 23, 1749, his former house at the upper end of the street having been washed away by the river. He d. Sept. 3, 1785, ae. 74. M. (1) 1736, Margaret, wid. of Cotton Partridge. She d. March 15, 1756; (2) 1758, Elizabeth Worthington of Springfield. Children—*Cotton*, b. Oct. 2, 1737, d. in a fit; *Margaret*, b. April 11, 1740, m. Dec. 17, 1761, Edmund Hubbard, Jr.; *Samuel*, b. Oct. 20, 1742; *Martha*, b. July 3, 1747, m. Nov. 27, 1771, Enos Nash, and d. Sept. 25, 1788, ae. 41; *Child*, b. March 10, 1756, d. March 11, 1756.

6. John, s. of Samuel, (2) res. in S. H., d. abt. 1799. He m. (1) 1746, Abigail Miller of Springfield, who d. 1775, in 53d yr.; (2) abt. 1775, Dolly Taylor. Children by second wife—*Abigail; John; Moses; Josiah*.

7. NEHEMIAH, s. of Samuel, (2) d. June 21, 1796, ae. 80. M. ——,
who d. Oct. 20, 1783, ae. 61. Child—*Nehemiah.*

8. OLIVER, s. of William, (4) S. H. M. Betty. Children—*Lois,* b. May
13, 1773, m. Martin Wait; *William,* b. March 1, 1775; *Benjamin Evens,*
b. Sept. 10, 1777; *Keturah,* b. Aug. 6, 1779, m. (1) Ferry Parsons of Easthampton; (2) Seth Phelps of Chester.

9. SAMUEL, s. of Samuel, (5) d. June 10, 1816, ae. 73. M. (1) 1766,
Submit, dau. of Obadiah Dickinson of Hat. She d. Oct. 25, 1766, in 24th yr.;
(2) Nov. 15, 1770, Penelope Williams. She d. April 10, 1815, ae. 70.
Children—*Samuel,* b. Oct. 25, 1771, and d. Feb. 7, 1797, ae. 25. He m. Dec.
31, 1795, Lucretia, dau. of Chileab Smith. She m. (2) Jan. 6, 1799, Samuel
Dexter Ward; *Submit Dickinson,* b. Aug. 24, 1773, d. Dec. 7, 1775; *Submit
Dickinson,* b. Jan. 8, 1776, m. 1793, Eliakim Smith; *Chester Williams,* b.
Dec. 25, 1777, d. Sept. 10, 1779; *Penelope,* b. Oct. 15, 1780, m. June 4, 1804,
Erastus Nash, and d. 1861, ae. 80; *Chester,* b. Sept. 3, 1782; *Elizabeth,* b.
July 3, 1784, d. unm.; *Israel,* b. Aug. 4, 1788.

10. NEHEMIAH, s. of Nehemiah, (7) m. Sept. 4, 1766, Rebecca, dau. of
Dea. Enos Nash. She d. Aug. 15, 1794. Children—*Joanna,* d. unm.;
Lucinda, bapt. 1774, m. Richard Osborn; *Moses,* b. June 6, 1776, m. (1)
Polly Baker; (2) Clarissa Stockwell; *Rebecca,* b. Jan. 6, 1780, m. Isaac
Baker of Amh.; *Nehemiah,* bapt. March 24, 1782, d. April, 1782; *Child,*
b. Dec. 1783; *Jerusha,* bapt. Jan. 25, 1784, m. Francis Strickland of Amh.

GILLETT, JOSEPH, b. Nov. 2, 1664, s. of Joseph, of Simsbury, settled in
Hat., whence he rem. to West Hartford. M. (1) Nov. 3, 1687, Esther Gull;
(2) Mercy Griswold at Hartford. Child—*Elizabeth,* b. 1689.

1. GILLETT, SAMUEL, b. in Windsor, Ct., Jan. 22, 1643, s. of Jonathan,
settled in Hat., and was slain in the Falls' fight, May 9, 1676. M. Sept. 23,
1668, Hannah Dickinson. She m. (2) May 15, 1677, Stephen Jennings.
Children—*Hannah,* b. Sept. 20, 1669, was burned to death, Feb. 1671; *Mary,*
b. Dec. 20, 1671; *Samuel,* b. May 14, 1672; *Hannah,* b. Sept. 5, 1674.

2. SAMUEL, s. of Samuel, (1) Hat., d. abt. 1769. M. Hannah, dau. of
Dr. Thomas Hastings of Hat. Children — *Hannah,* b. Jan. 9, 1698, m.
—— Benton of Guilford, Ct.; *Margaret,* b. May 1, 1699, m. Joseph Belding; *Samuel,* b. Dec. 26, 1703; *Elizabeth,* b. Dec. 29, 1705, m. —— Bardwell; *Mary,* b. July 31, 1711, m. —— Evetts of Killingsworth, Ct.

3. SAMUEL, s. of Samuel, Jr. (2) Hat., d. abt. 1745. M. April 8, 1730.
Sarah Billings. Children—*Sarah,* d. unm.; *Martha,* m. May 16, 1754, Perez
Graves; *Hannah,* m. Nov. 10, 1757, Oliver Morton.

GOLDING, MR. PETER, b. abt. 1635, rem. abt. 1690, from Boston to Had.,
and thence to Sudbury, where he d. Oct. 11, 1703. M. (1) Jane; (2) Sarah.
Children—*Mary,* b. Jan. 21, 1666; *Frances,* b. Feb. 22, 1668; *Elizabeth,*
b. Oct. 6, 1673; *Windsor,* b. March 3, 1675; *Thomas,* b. Jan. 23, 1678;
Sarah, b. Aug. 19, 1679, m. (1) April 13, 1704, Daniel Warner; (2) Jan. 6,
1714, Thomas Horton; *Jane,* b. Jan. 1, 1684; *Mercy,* Sept. 8, 1686, m.
Dec. 19, 1710, Chileab Smith, and d. Aug. 6 or 7, 1756, ae. 69.

GOODELL, ISAAC, b. abt. 1730, d. in Amherst, Jan. 14, 1808, in 77th yr.
M. (1) 1753, Huldah, dau. of Thomas Burt of Nh. She was b. Feb. 9, 1733;

(2) Oct. 24, 1805, Wid. Prudence Billings. Children — *Isaac*, bapt. 1755, m. Jemima, dau. of Daniel Warner of Nh., and rem. to Broome Co., N. Y.; *Mercy*, bapt. July 24, 1757, m. Aug. 6, 1778, Elijah Elmer; *Thomas*, bapt. Oct. 29, 1758, m. Hannah Parker; *David*, bapt. April 20, 1760, m. 1784, *Mercy*, dau. of Gideon Clark of Nh. She was b. Jan. 6, 1760; *Eleanor*, bapt. Feb. 21, 1762, m. Sept. 26, 1780, Silas Wright of Amh.

1. GOODMAN, RICHARD, Deacon, Cambridge, 1632, Hartford, 1639, was one of the first settlers of Had. Having been slain by the Indians, he was buried April 3, 1676, ae. abt. 67. M. Dec. 8, 1659, Mary, dau. of Stephen Terry of Windsor. She was b. Dec. 31, 1635, and d. in Deerfield, 1692. Children—*John*, b. Oct. 13, 1661; *Richard*, b. March 23, 1663, res. in Hartford, Ct., and d. May 4, 1730, ae. 67; *Stephen*, b. Feb. 6, 1664; *Mary*, b. Nov. 5, 1665, m. 1684, John Noble of Westfield and New Milford, Ct.; *Thomas*, b. March 20, 1668, d. Aug. 24, 1670, ae. 2; *Elizabeth*, b. Feb. 5, 1671, m. Jacob Warner; *Thomas*, b. Sept. 16, 1673; *Samuel*, b. May 5, 1675.

2. JOHN, s. of Richard, (1) freeman 1690, d. Jan. 17, 1725. M. abt. 1685, Hannah, dau. of Thomas Noble of Westfield. She m. (2) Oct. 12, 1728, Nathaniel Edwards of Nh. She was b. Feb. 24, 1664, and d. abt. 1741, ae. 77. Children—*John*, b. Sept. 29, 1686; *Hannah*, b. May 29, 1689, d. March, 1690; *Hannah*, b. Jan. 15, 1696, d. Feb. 4, 1718, ae. 21; *Stephen*, b. Aug. 17, 1699, d. Feb. 4, 1718, ae. 18; *James*, b. Feb. 7, 1707.

3. THOMAS, s. of Richard; (1) d. Oct. 5, 1748, ae. 75. He m. Grace, dau. of Samuel Marsh of Hat. She d. May 28 or 29, 1756. Children—*Mary*, b. Nov. 15, 1699, d. unm., Jan. 3, 1769, ae. 69; *Thomas*, b. Dec. 15, 1701; *Samuel*, b. March 10, 1704, taken captive at Fort Massachusetts, in 1746, and d. in Canada. Perhaps m. Rebecca ——; *Rachel*, b. Oct. 1, 1706, per. m. June 14, 1750, Daniel Dickinson; *Abigail*, b. July 3, 1709, d. unm., Jan. 24, 1795, ae. 84; *Eleazar*, b. Sept. 4, 1711; *Nathan*, b. Dec. 29, 1713.

4. JAMES, s. of John, (2) d. Sept. 8, 1746, ae. 39. He m. (1) 1736, Anna Phelps of Springfield; (2) Sept. 22, 1743, Sarah Sikes of Springfield. Children—*Hannah*, b. April 28, 1740, m. Aug. 8, 1771, Timothy Stockwell; *Stephen*, b. Dec. 26, 1742; *Oliver*, drowned in Springfield, March 26, 1747.

5. THOMAS, s. of Thomas, (3) d. Nov. 4, 1761, ae. 59. He m. (1) 1724, Mary Scovill, who d. March, 1736, ae. 33; (2) Rebecca Shepard of Hartford. Children—*Ruth*, b. Jan. 12, 1726; *Mary*, b. 1728, d. 1731; *Miriam*, b. 1731, d. 1732; *Noah*, b. Feb. 9, 1734; *Asa*, b. Aug. 6, 1738, res. in West Hartford, Ct.; *Simeon*, b. Dec. 14, 1739; *Rebecca*, b. July 21, 1743, m. Joel Moody of Amh.; *Susannah*, b. Feb. 2, 1745; *Thomas*, b. July 19, 1746; *Thankful*, b. Dec. 3, 1748, m. Ephraim Smith; *Enos*, b. March 4, 1751, rem. to Masonville, N. Y.; *Elihu*, b. April 5, 1753, rem. to Greenfield; *Ruth*, m. Jonathan Cook.

6. ELEAZAR, s. of Thomas, (3) res. in S. H., and d. July 27, 1849, ae. 37. He m. Dec. 25, 1746, Hannah Rugg. Children—*Samuel; Eleazar*.

7. STEPHEN, s. of James, (4) d. June 28, 1802, ae. 59. He m. (1) 1761, Mercy Dewey of Westfield, who d. Dec. 28, 1764; (2) Feb. 28, 1765, Joanna Kellogg, who d. Aug. 31, 1831, ae. 89. Children—*Joanna*, b. Dec. 1, 1765, d. Dec. 3, 1765; *James*, b. May 13, 1767, d. in Mobile, Ala.; *Joanna*, b. Feb. 20, 1769. m. Perez Jones, and rem. to Windsor, Vt.; *Stephen*, b. Nov. 19,

1770, d. at the West; *Mercy*, b. Nov. 17, 1773, d. Sept. 12, 1776; *John Kellogg*, b. June 18, 1776, rem. in 1802, to Jersey City, and d. Oct. 29, 1853, ae. 77; *Sylvester*, b. Nov. 19, 1778; *Spencer*, b. June 5, 1781; *Mercy*, b. Aug. 18, 1783, m. Cotton Smith.

8. NOAH, s. of Thomas, (5) res. in S. H. He m. Oct. 25, 1756, Abial Smith. Children—*Ithamar*, b. Feb. 1, 1757; *Titus*, b. Oct. 23, 1763; *Simeon; Abial*, m. Dec. 25, 1798, Ebenezer Bartlett of Williamsburgh; *Mary*, m. Bezaleel Alvord; *Clarissa*, d. ae. abt. 14.

9. ENOS, s. of Thomas, (5) rem. to Masonville, N. Y. He m. Esther, dau. of Jonathan White of S. H. Children—*Cynthia*, b. Aug. 25, 1775; *Erastus*, b. Aug. 15, 1777; *Phineas*, b. May 12, 1780; *Enos*, b. July 16, 1782; *Cleopas*, b. Dec. 8, 1784; *Esther*, b. July 23, 1787; *Thomas*, b. Aug. 22, 1789; *Tryphosa*, b. April 15, 1792; *Sophia*, b. Dec. 17, 1794.

10. SAMUEL, s. of Eleazar, (6) res. in S. H. He m. (1) Joanna Smith; (2) Huldah Montague. Children by second wife—*Calvin*, b. May 12, 1778; *Luther*, b. Jan. 6, 1780.

11. ELEAZAR, s. of Eleazar, (6) rem. from S. H. to Lake George. He m. Rebecca, dau. of Joseph White. Children—*Justin*, b. Feb. 7, 1771; *Eleazar; Eldad; Nathan; Samuel; Oren*.

GOODRICH, AARON, d. Jan. 27 or 28, 1769, ae. 48. He m. Dorcas Cook. Children—*Sarah*, b. Oct. 16, 1747, m. Oct. 21, 1773, Nathaniel Montague; *Aaron*, b. Sept. 30, 1749, d. April 14, 1776, ae. 26; *Dorcas*, b. Dec. 16, 1751, m. Jan. 28, 1779, Enos Cowls of Amh., and d. Aug. 11, 1824, ae. 72; *Joanna*, b. Aug. 9, 1754, m. 1775, Jonathan Russell of Chesterfield; *Mary*, b. Oct. 13, 1756, d. Oct. 17; *Rebecca*, b. Aug. 8, 1759.

GOODWIN, MR. WILLIAM, sailed from London, in ship Lyon, June 22, 1632, and arrived in New England, Sept. 16, 1632. He was made freeman in Mass. Nov. 6, 1732, and was in May 1634, Deputy from Cambridge to the General Court. He was an early settler of Hartford, Ct., where he was a man of great influence, both in Church and State. Having resided in Hadley about ten years from its first settlement, abt. 1620 he returned to Ct., and d. in Farmington, March 11, 1673. He m. Susanna, who d. in F., May 17, 1676. Child—*Elizabeth*, m. John Crow of Had. and Hartford.

GOULD, SOLOMON, Amherst. Children—*David*, bapt. April 6, 1760; *Samuel*, bapt. May 8, 1763; *Noah*, bapt. May 8, 1763, m. Jan. 30, 1794, Mary Williams; *Child*, bapt. March 17, 1765; *Miriam*, bapt. Feb. 9, 1766; *Reuben*, bapt. July, 1767; *Bashmotte*, bapt. July 4, 1771.

GRANGER, HOLCOMB, m. Electa, who d. Sept. 6, 1793. Children—*Electa; Achsah; Lydia; Thaddeus.*

GRANIS, EDWARD, a shoemaker, came from Hartford to Had., and rem. abt. 1677, to New Haven, Ct. He m. (1) May 3, 1654, Elizabeth Andrews of Hartford; (2) 1662, Hannah, dau. of John Wakefield of New Haven. Children—*Joseph*, b. March 31, 1656, d. young; *Hannah*, m. Jan. 31, 1681, John Hill; *Mabel*, m. March 2, 1684, John Johnson; *Abigail*, m. 1689, John Allen, Jr.; *Sarah*, b. Oct. 20, 1671, m. 1690, Nathaniel Bishop; *John*, b. Dec. 5, 1674; *Joseph*, b. March 12, 1677; *Ann*.

1. GRAVES, THOMAS, Hartford, 1645, rem. to Hat., and d. Nov. 1662. He m. Sarah, who d. Dec. 17, 1666. Children—*Isaac; John; Samuel;* perhaps a *Daughter,* whose name is unknown.

2. ISAAC, s. of Thomas, (1) Hat., was slain by Indians, Sept. 19, 1677. He m. Mary, dau. of Richard Church. She d. 1694 or 1695. Children— *Mary,* b. July 5, 1647, m. Jan. 28, 1665, Eleazar Frary; *Isaac,* b. Aug. 21, 1650, prob. d. young; *Rebecca,* b. July 3, 1652; *Samuel,* b. Oct. 1, 1655; *Sarah,* m. April 27, 1677, Benjamin Barrett; *Elizabeth,* b. March 6, 1662, m. Benjamin Hastings of Hat.; *John,* b. 1664; *Hannah,* b. Jan. 24, 1666, m. William Sacket of Westfield; *Jonathan; Mehitable,* b. Oct. 1, 1671, m. (1) Jan. 29, 1690, Richard Morton; (2) William Worthington.

3. JOHN, s. of Thomas, (1) Hat., slain by Indians, Sept. 19, 1677. He m. (1) Mary, dau. of Lt. Samuel Smith. She prob. d. Dec. 16, 1668; (2) Mary, widow of John Wyatt of Haddam, Ct. Children—*John; Mary,* m. (1) Jan. 15, 1671, Samuel Ball of Springfield, (2) April, 1679, Edward Stebbins; *Isaac; Samuel; Sarah,* m. Edward Stebbins; *Elizabeth,* b. Dec. 9, 1662, m. Thomas Jones; *Daniel,* b. Dec. 7, 1664; *Ebenezer,* b. Nov. 20, 1666; *Bethiah,* b. June 17, 1668, d. Jan. 21, 1669; *Nathaniel,* b. June 10, 1671.

4. SAMUEL, s. of Isaac, (1) Hat., d. Feb. 8, 1692. He m. (1) Oct. 1, 1678, Sarah Colton. She d. July 11, 1689; (2) Jan. 1, 1690, Deliverance ——. She m. (2) Isaac, s. of John Graves. Children—*Rebecca,* b. 1681; *Samuel,* b. March 2, 1685; *Joseph;* perhaps *Sarah,* b. Jan. 1, 1688; *Elizabeth,* b. Oct. 8, 1689; *Thomas,* b. Oct. 21, 1690.

5. JOHN, s. of Isaac, (2) Hat. He m. Sarah. Children—*Isaac,* b. July 10, 1687; *Benjamin,* b. Aug. 12, 1689; *Jemima,* b. April 30, 1693, m. (1) May 5, 1715, John Graves, (2) Eleazar Allis; *Mary,* b. Nov. 9, 1695, m. (1) Jonathan Frary, (2) —— King; *Elnathan,* b. Aug. 20, 1699; *Hannah,* b. June 4, 1701, m. Eleazar King; *Eunice,* b. Sept. 29, 1705; *Aaron,* b. Feb. 2, 1707; *Sarah,* perhaps, b. 1691.

6. JONATHAN, s. of Isaac, (2) tanner, Hat., d. Oct. 12, 1737, ae. 71. He m. (1) Sarah, dau. of John Parsons. She d. March 15, 1711; (2) Mary, wid. of Benjamin King of Nh., and dau. of Abel Janes of Nh. Children—*Moses,* b. Feb. 1, 1700; *Jonathan,* b. March 6, 1702; *Joseph,* b. June 4, 1704; *Perez,* b. Nov. 26, 1707, d. in Belchertown, April 12, 1728, ae. 22; *Mary,* b. Aug. 20, 1722, m. Noah Loomis of Harwinton, Ct.; *Elijah,* b. Dec. 20, 1723, d. 1739; *Sarah,* b. Feb. 9, 1726.

7. JOHN, s. of John, (3) Hat., d. Dec. 2, 1750. He m. Feb. 12, 1678, Sarah, dau. of John White, Jr. Children—*Sarah,* b. Feb. 15, 1679, m. Oct. 27, 1702, Nathaniel Clark of Middletown, Ct.; *John,* b. March 23, 1682; *Mary,* b. Feb. 24, 1683, m. Jeremiah Wait; *Thomas,* b. July 4, 1685, d. Oct. 1689; *Abigail,* b. Oct. 29, 1687, m. —— Wilcox; *Martha,* b. Nov. 4, 1689, m. May 17, 1716, John Crafts; *Daniel,* b. Oct. 13, 1690, d. young; *Thomas,* b. June 5, 1693; *Daniel,* b. Jan. 20, 1698; *Rebecca,* b. May 4, 1700, m. Moses Nash, and d. in West Hartford, Ct., Oct. 6, 1743.

8. ISAAC, s. of John, (3) Hat., d. abt. 1740. He m. (1) April 1, 1679, Sarah Wyatt, who d. June 9, 1695; (2) 1697, Abigail ——, who d. July 13, 1697; (3) Deliverance, wid. of Samuel Graves. Children—*Mary,* b. Oct. 31, 1682, d. Dec. 26, 1684; *Sarah,* b. Oct. 23, 1684, m. Nov. 22, 1705, Daniel Kelsey; *Elizabeth,* b. Oct. 23, 1686, m. —— Hull; *Isaac,* b. Nov. 3, 1688;

Mary, b. Sept. 23, 1690, m. —— Smith; *Lydia*, b. March 11, 1693, m. Jan. 1, 1719, Thomas Graves, and d. in Belchertown, 1777, ae. 85; *Abigail*, b. Aug. 16, 1696, m. March 14, 1717, Stephen Crowfoot.

9. SAMUEL, s. of John, (3) rem. prior to 1718, from Hat. to Sunderland, and d. March 11, 1731. He m. Sarah, who d. Oct. 15, 1734. Children— perhaps *Sarah*, b. Jan. 1, 1688; *Jonathan*, b. Oct. 27, 1689; *Abraham*, b. Dec. 12, 1691, m. May 23, 1717, Thankful Bardwell, and was of Deerfield in 1749; *David*, b. Dec. 9, 1693; *Noah*, b. Dec. 19, 1695; *Mehitable*, b. Dec. 19, 1695, prob. m. John Bardwell; *Samuel*, b. Jan. 30, 1698.

10. NATHANIEL, s. of John, (3) Hat., d. abt. 1757. He m. April 30, 1702, Rebecca Allis. Children—*Rebecca*, b. Oct. 25, 1703; *Mary*, b. Feb. 22, 1706, m. Isaac Graves; *Nathaniel*, b. Nov. 16, 1707; *Ruth*, b. Aug. 16, 1709; *Eleazar*, b. Dec. 12, 1711; *Israel*, b. abt. 1716, rem. to Whately; *Martha*, b. Oct. 29, 1718, m. Eleazar Cowls; *Oliver*, b. abt. 1725, rem. to Whately.

11. JOSEPH, s. of Samuel, (4) Hat., d. April 22, 1728. He m. Bridget, dau. of Edward Scott. She d. 1756. Children—*Sarah*, b. Nov. 13, 1717, m. Thomas Crafts; *Miriam; Elizabeth*, b. May 14, 1721.

12. THOMAS, s. of Samuel, (4) rem. from Hat. to Belchertown, and d. 1784, ae. 92. He m. Jan. 1, 1719, Lydia, dau. of Isaac Graves. She d. in Belchertown, 1777. Children—*John*, b. Oct. 16, 1719; *Lydia*, b. June 20, 1726, d. unm., 1779, ae. 53.

12½. BENJAMIN, prob. s. of John, (5) Sunderland, d. Oct. 1, 1756, ae. 67. He m. 1720, Mary Warner. She d. in S. H., April 10, 1779, in 86th yr. Children—*Mary*, b. Dec. 23, 1720, m. June 20, 1745, Jonathan Warner; *Elizabeth*, b. Aug. 17, 1723, m. 1749, Orange Warner of Had.; *Sarah*, b. Sept. 16, 1726, m. Sept. 22, 1748, Moses Montague; *Daniel*, b. Nov. 5, 1728, d. in Sund., Feb. 5, 1793, ae. 64; *Benjamin*, b. Feb. 29, 1734; *Moses*, b. Oct. 10, 1736; *Aaron*, b. Oct. 10, 1736; *Eunice*, b. Jan. 25, 1741, m. Seth Lyman.

13. ELNATHAN, s. of John, (5) Hat., d. Feb. 17, 1785, ae. 85. He m. (1) March 2, 1727, Martha, dau. of Dea. Nathaniel Dickinson of Hat. She d. Jan. 9, 1756, ae. 55; (2) Wid. Dorothy Belding, dau. of —— Morton. She d. May 9, 1800, ae. 80. Children—*Seth*, b. Dec. 27, 1727; *Perez*, b. April 26, 1730; *Silas*, b. Feb. 8, 1732; *Lucy*, b. May 8, 1734, m. Benjamin Wells; *Martha*, b. Feb. 26, 1739, m. John Nash of Williamsburgh.

14. AARON, s. of John, (5) rem. from Hat. to Williamsburgh, and d. 1788, ae. 81. Children—*Jemima*, b. April 11, 1730; *Martha*, b. March 9, 1732, m. July 12, 1752, Simeon Dickinson of Amh., and d. Dec. 3, 1822, ae. 90; *Mary*, b. Oct. 19, 1733, m. May 22, 1754, John Nash, Jr., of Amh.; *Eunice*, m. March 1, 1759, Jonathan Moody, Jr. of Amh., and d. Dec. 15, 1813; *Beulah*, m. Aug. 20, 1761, Asahel Moody of Amh., and prob. d. Dec. 30, 1826; *Lucius; Aaron*, b. abt. 1749, d. in S. H., Nov. 18, 1834, ae. 85.

15. MOSES, s. of Jonathan, (6) Hat. He m. Feb. 24, 1743, Martha Marsh of Had. She d. Feb. 3, 1755, ae. 35; (2) Catharine. Children— *Judith*, b. Dec. 4, 1743, killed by lightning, June 19, 1754; *Elijah*, b. Nov. 14, 1745; *Moses*, b. Feb. 3, 1748; *John*, b. Jan. 13, 1750, d. Aug. 6, 1751; *John*, b. March 13, 1752; *Martha*, b. April 6, 1754; *Jonathan*, b. June 26, 1762; *Judith*, b. Feb. 16, 1764.

16. JONATHAN, s. of Jonathan, (6) rem. to Belchertown, and d. 1787, ae. 84. Children—*Perez*, who in May, 1758, being about to go into the army made his will, which was proved in Oct. following; *Joseph*, bapt. Oct. 5, 1735, d. in Belchertown, 1796; *Penelope*, b. May 8, 1753, m. (1) 1757, Elihu Dwight; (2) —— Hollister.

17. JOHN, s. of John, (7) Hat., d. Aug. 1716. He m. May 5, 1715, Jemima Graves. Child—*Nathan*, b. March 20, 1716, res. in Whately, where he was deacon in the Church.

18. DANIEL, s. of John, (7) rem. from Hat. to Greenfield, was taken captive by the Indians, Aug. 12, 1756, and slain shortly after. He m. 1724, Thankful, dau. of Ebenezer Smead. Children—*Ebenezer*, b. March 15, 1726; *Jerusha*, b. March 29, 1728, m. Ebenezer Allen; *Thankful*, b. June 8, 1730; *Daniel*, b. July 2, 1732, d. 1755; *Esther*, b. 1734; *Joel*, b. April 27, 1737, d. 1760; *John*, m. Sarah Judd of Nh.

19. ISAAC, s. of Isaac, (8) rem. to Sunderland. He m. 1713, Mary, dau. of Jonathan Parsons of Nh. She was b. July 8, 1688. Children—*Sarah*, b. Dec. 22, 1713; *Jerusha*, b. June 13, 1717; *Simeon*, b. Jan. 20, 1720, d. Dec. 20, 1747; *Phinehas*, b. April 30, 1726; *Submit*, b. Jan. 7, 1731.

20. JONATHAN, s. of Samuel, (9) Sunderland. He m. June 2, 1715, Mrs. Elizabeth Combs. Children—*Jonathan*, who prob. d. young; *Ebenezer*, b. Sept. 10, 1717.

21. DAVID, s. of Samuel, (9) d. in Whately, 1781. He m. June 6, 1720, Abigail, dau. of Robert Bardwell. She d. 1786. Children—*Elijah*, b. July 18, 1720; *Simeon*, b. April 13, 1722; *Martha*, b. March 7, 1731; *David*, b. 1733; *Matthew; Martin; Abigail; Esther; Anna; Hannah*.

21½. NOAH, s. of Samuel, (9) Sunderland, prob. d. March 17, 1773. He m. Rebecca ——, who d. Feb. 8, 1744. Children—*Noah*, b. Jan. 25, ——; *Reuben*, b. Nov. 23, 1724; *Noah*, b. Oct. 21, 1726; *Silas*, b. Sept. 3, 1728, d. Sept. 15, 1728; *Rebecca*, b. Feb. 14, 1731; *Rhoda*, b. Feb. 9, 1734; *Benoni*, b. Feb. 16, 1736; *Martha*, b. Aug. 1, 1739; *Martin*, b. Dec. 5, 1741, d. Dec. 17, 1743.

22. SAMUEL, s. of Samuel, (9) settled in Sunderland, whence he rem. to South Deerfield, where he d. May 6, 1774. He m. Grace. Children—*Azubah*, b. Jan. 1, 1730; *Child*, b. Sept. 1, 1731; *Elizabeth*, b. Feb. 1, 1734; *Bethula*, b. Oct. 8, 1736; *Sarah*, b. May 2, 1739; *Zebadiah*, b. June 15, 1741; *Eunice*, b. March 30, 1745.

23. NATHANIEL, s. of Nathaniel, (10) Sunderland. He m. Hannah. Children—*Mehitable*, b. Oct. 21, 1732; *Hannah*, b. Aug. 27, 1735; *Lydia*, b. Sept. 5, 1738; *Martha*, b. July 8, 1744.

24. ELEAZAR, s. of Nathaniel, (10) Hat. He m. Oct. 1, 1736, Sarah Belding. Children—*Samuel*, b. Oct. 12, 1737; *Mary*, b. Oct. 14, 1739; *Sarah*, b. Feb. 20, 1742; *Lucy*, b. April 10, 1744.

25. BENJAMIN, s. of Benjamin, (12½) Sunderland. He m. Sept. 15, 1757, Thankful Field. Children—*Rufus*, b. Sept. 27, 1758, grad. D. C. 1791; *Benjamin*, b. Oct. 4, 1760, d. in S., March 22, 1832, ae. 71; *Thankful*, b. Oct. 18, 1764; *Timothy*, b. Oct. 18, 1764; *Electa*, b. Feb. 5, 1767.

26. MOSES, s. of Benjamin, (12½) Leverett. He m. (1) Sarah. She was b. March 20, 1740, and d. Oct. 23, 1767; (2) Jan. 12, 1768, or Jan. 11, 1769, Experience Oakes. She was b. March 17, 1742. Children—*Enos*, b. May 20, 1763; *Mary*, b. Dec. 20, 1764; *Sarah*, b. March 27, 1767; *Naomi*, b. Nov. 4, 1769; *Achsah*, b. May 4, 1772; *Lucy*, b. Jan. 4, 1774; *Experience*, b. April 9, 1776; *Martha*, b. April 9, 1776; *Moses*, b. April 11, 1778; *Elihu*, b. Oct. 20, 1780.

27. PEREZ, s. of Elnathan, (13) Hat. He m. (1) May 16, 1754, Martha, dau. of Samuel Gillett; (2) Feb. 19, 1795, Zeruiah, wid. of Elihu White of Hat., and dau. of Ebenezer Cole of Hat. She was b. Nov. 30, 1741, and d. Dec. 13, 1820, ae. 79. Children—*Samuel*, b. May 4, 1755; *Elisha*, b. Sept. 2, 1757; *Martha*, b. April 28, 1759, m. M. Montague; *Perez*, b. Jan. 2, 1761, d. 1848; *Elnathan*, b. Feb. 2, 1763; *William*, b. Feb. 11, 1766; *Solomon*, b. March 2, 1768; *Levi*, b. Jan. 12, 1771; *Timothy*.

28. JOSEPH, s. of Jonathan, (16) Belchertown, d. 1796, ae. 62. He m. Eunice, dau. of Nathaniel Dwight of Belchertown. She d. 1807, ae. 66. Children—*Perez*, b. 1762; *Margaret*, m. 1785, Benjamin Howe; *Susanna*, m. 1787, Nathan Parsons, Jr., and rem. to Bangor, Me.; *Electa*, m. 1788, Dea. Aaron Lyman; *Josiah Dwight*, b. 1772, rem. in 1828, to Manchester, N. Y.; *Jonathan*, b. 1774; *Elijah*, b. 1779, d. 1799; *Joseph*, b. 1783, rem. in 1828, to Manchester, N. Y.

29. REUBEN, s. of Noah, (21½) Sunderland, d. March 11, 1778, ae. 53. He m. Sept. 18, 1748, Hannah Fuller. Children—*Patience*, b. June 20, 1749; *Noah*, b. June 7, 1751; *Gideon*, b. June 4, 1753; *Asa*, b. Nov. 4, 1755; *Selah*, b. March 19, 1758; *Randall*, b. May 31, 1760; *Submit*, b. May 1, 1763; *Martin*, b. Feb. 23, 1766; *Hannah*, b. Aug. 21, 1769.

30. ENOS, s. of Moses, (26) Leverett. He m. Oct. 6, 1785, Sybil, dau. of Abraham Kellogg. She was b. Sept. 24, 1761. Children—*Walter*, b. June 13, 1786; *Sally*, b. June 28, 1788; *Fanny*, b. March 6, 1791, d. Aug. 6, 1808; *Kellogg*, b. Aug. 20, 1793; *Nancy*, b. June 3, 1796; *Moses*, b. July 21, 1798; *Enos*, b. Nov. 5, 1800; *Sybil*, b. Aug. 8, 1803.

GREEN, ELIPHALET, Gr., d. Feb. 16, 1777. He m. 1754, Mercy, dau. of Jonathan Selden. Children—*Elizabeth*, b. Feb. 10, 1755; *Eliphalet*, b. Jan. 14, 1757; *Jared*, b. July 5, 1759; *Hepzibah*, b. Oct. 7, 1761; *David*, b. April 14, 1766; *Rhoda*, b. June 28, 1768; *Phebe*, b. Sept. 26, 1771.

GREEN, TIMOTHY, b. Jan. 4, 1748, Amherst, d. Sept. 7, 1821, ae. 73. He m. (1) Eunice, dau. of Simeon Clark of Amherst. She d. May 6, 1776, ae. 25; (2) Sybil Peck. Children—*Timothy*, b. March 27, 1771, m. Dec. 25, 1800, Huldah Harris; *Zera*, b. June 18, 1773, m. Eleanor Morton, and d. in Amh., March 28, 1813, ae. 40; *Clark*, b. April 11, 1776, m. April 26, 1798, d. in Amh., Nov. 27, 1848, ae. 72; *Eunice*, b. Nov. 16, 1781, m. (1) Oct. 22, 1807, Josiah Ayres of Amh.; (2) Chester Hawley, and d. Feb. 1862, ae. 80; *Sybil*, b. Aug. 19, 1783, m. Nov. 28, 1805, Elijah Clark, and res. (1862) in Rockford, Ill.; *Joel*, b. Oct. 4, 1785, d. March 19, 1788; *Lucretia*, b. May 21, 1787, d. Nov. 6, 1803; *Joel*, b. Dec. 10, 1788, m. Oct. 30, 1809, Philomela, dau. of Simeon Clark of Amh.; *Rufus*, b. Sept. 8, 1790, m. Jan. 17, 1813, Mary Sheldon, dau. of Wm. Boltwood of Amh., and res. in Frewsburg, Chautauque Co., N. Y.; *Lucina*, b. July 16, 1792, m. Jan. 19, 1817, Chester Rice; *Polly*, b. June 28, 1794, d. Jan. 27, 1813, ae. 18; *Judith*, b. Nov. 19, 1796.

GREY, JAMES, perhaps rem. abt. 1760, to Stockbridge. He m. July 28, 1732, Sarah Marsh, prob. wid. of John Marsh, and dau. of —— Williams. She d. June 1, 1759. Children—*James*, b. Sept. 24, 1752; *John*.

GROVER, HOSEA, m. 1797, pub. Feb. 1, Diadema Grover of Glastenbury, Ct. Children—*Josiah*, b. Nov. 8, 1798; *Phineas*, b. July 23, 1800; *Leonard*, b. Sept. 29, 1803; *Leonard*, perhaps same with the last, bapt. Jan. 5, 1806; *Ruth Marilla*, bapt. Aug. 21, 1808.

GULL, WILLIAM, rem. from Wethersfield, Ct. to Hat., freeman 1673, made will April 12, 1701, which was proved Dec. 18, 1701. He m. Elizabeth, wid. of Nathaniel Foote, Jr., and dau. of Lt. Samuel Smith. Children— *Mary*, m. Nov. 29, 1676, Robert Bardall; *Anna*, m. Jonathan Root; *Esther*, b. Nov. 21, 1665, m. Joseph Gillett; *Mercy*, b. June 27, 1668, m. Jeremiah Alvord.

GUNN, MOSES, m. Jan. 18, 1739, Sarah Mighill. Child — *Rufus*, b. 1752.

GUNN, SAMUEL, s. of Nathaniel of Hartford, settled in Hat., but rem. in 1714 to Sunderland, where he was a deacon in the Church, and d. Aug. 1, 1755, in 93d yr. He m. Jan. 22, 1685, Elizabeth, dau. of John Wyatt. She d. Oct. 2, 1737. Children—*Sarah*, b. April 3, 1686, m. Jan. 23, 1707, Azariah Dickinson; *Elizabeth*, b. Nov. 8, 1689, m. May 4, 1709, Simon Cooley; *Nathaniel*, b. July 30, 1693, res. in Sunderland, m. 1724, Esther Belding; *Samuel*, b. March 22, 1696; *Mary*, b. Aug. 9, 1698, m. Daniel Hubbard; *Abel*, b. July 17, 1700; *Christian*, b. Sept. 5, 1702, m. Isaac Hubbard of Sunderland; *Editha*, b. April 26, 1705, m. Ebenezer Billings, Jr.; *John*, b. Dec. 3, 1707; *Sarah*, b. Oct. 27, 1711, m. 1729, Joseph Clary.

HALE, THOMAS, rem. to Enfield, Ct., and d. abt. 1725. He m. Priscilla, dau. of William Markham. Children — *Martha*, b. Oct. 10, 1676; *Thomas*, b. Oct. 8, 1678; *John*, b. Nov. 26, 1680; *Samuel*, b. July 2, 1683, d. Aug. 6, 1689; *Priscilla*, b. Sept. 9, 1685; *William*, b. Feb. 18, 1687; *Son*, b. and d. Jan. 10, 1689; *Joseph*, b. March, 1691; *Samuel*.

HALEY, JOHN, d. abt. 1688. He m. (1) Mrs. Ruth Gaylord, dau. of John Crow; (2) Hannah, dau. of Samuel Bliss. She m. (2) May 1, 1689, Simon Smith.

HAMMOND, TIMOTHY, m. Nov. 16, 1769, Hannah Clark. Children— *Martha*, bapt. Sept. 27, 1772; *Nathaniel*, bapt. Oct. 11, 1772; *Molly*, bapt. April 11, 1775; *Timothy*, b. Sept. 1777; *Hannah*, bapt. Jan. 30, 1780; *Dau.*, bapt. Feb., 1786; *Child*, b. Nov. 13, 1779; *Child*, b. and d. 1782.

HARRISON, ISAAC, was slain after the Falls fight, May 19, 1676. He m. Dec. 1, 1671, Martha, dau. of Richard Montague. She m. (2) Henry White. Children—*Abigail*, b. Sept. 11, 1673, m. July 7, 1692, Samuel Church; *Sarah*, m. March 24, 1698, John Selden.

HARWOOD, BENJAMIN, m. Bridget. Child—*Abigail*, b. Nov. 13, 1753.

HASTINGS, BENJAMIN, b. in Watertown, Aug. 9, 1659, s. of Thomas, res. in Hat., Nh., Deerfield and Hat., and d. Dec. 18, 1711, ae. 60. He m. (1)

Elizabeth, dau. of Isaac Graves of Hat. She d. abt. 1695; (2) abt. 1697, Mary, prob. wid. of Jonathan Parsons of Nh. Children—*Samuel*, b. March 15, 1684, taken captive by Indians at Deerfield, Feb. 29, 1704, and carried to Canada, whence he never returned; *Elizabeth*, b. March 8, 1693; *Hannah*, d. Feb. 8, 1697; *Benjamin*, b. May, 1699, res. in Greenfield; *Zeruiah*, b. Aug. 30, 1701; *Joseph*, b. Dec. 27, 1703; *Dau.*, b. June 30, 1706, d. July 9, 1706; *Submit*, b. July 16, 1707, m. Sept. 19, 1723, John Wait.

1. HASTINGS, THOMAS, b. in Watertown, July 1, 1652, s. of Thomas, physician, settled in Hat., where he d. July 23, 1712, ae. 60. He m. (1) Oct. 10, 1672, Anna, dau. of John Hawkes. She d. Oct. 25, 1705; (2) Feb. 14, 1706, Mary, dau. of David Burt of Nh. She m. (2) May 17, 1703, Samuel Belding, and d. Feb. 14, 1706. Children—*Margaret*, b. July 7, 1674, m. May 7, 1707, Nathaniel Evetts of Guilford, Ct.; *Hannah*, b. Jan. 19, 1677, m. Samuel Gillett; *Thomas*, b. Sept. 24, 1679; *Hepzibah*, b. April 16, 1682, m. April 5, 1705, Jonathan Curtis of Wethersfield; *Mehitable*, b. Jan. 23, 1685, m. Nov. 25, 1714, John Burk; *John*, b. Sept. 17, 1689; *Silence*, b. Feb. 26, 1707, m. Josiah Hadlock of Williamsburgh; *Thankful*, b. May 5, 1711, d. July 15, 1711; *Sylvanus*, b. Sept. 10, 1712, d. Feb. 27, 1713.

2. THOMAS, s. of Thomas, (1) a physician in Hat., d. April 14, 1728, ae. 48. He m. March 6, 1701, Mary, dau. of John Field of Hat. Children— *Mary*, b. Dec. 24, 1701, d. Jan. 10, 1702; *Thomas*, b. Nov. 6, 1702, d. Nov. 4, 1703; *Mary*, b. July 26, 1704, m. Nov. 13, 1729, Benjamin Billings; *Anna*, b. Oct. 13, 1706, m. —— White; *Dorothy*, b. July 27, 1709, d. July 29, 1711; *Thomas*, d. Dec. 12, 1713, ae. 9 mos., according to grave stone, but 1½ yrs., accd. to Town Rec.; *Waitstill*, b. Jan. 3, 1714; *Tabitha*, b. Oct. 6, 1715, m. Jan. 4, 1739, John Strickland; *Hopestill*, b. April 13, 1718; *Dorothy*, b. March 20, 1720, d. April 6, 1720; *Thomas*, b. Jan. 28, 1721; *Lucy*, b. Feb. 1, 1723, m. Jonathan Taylor.

3. JOHN, s. of Thomas, (1) res. for some years in Hat., whence he rem. up the Conn. river, and was at Fort Dummer, in 1735. He m. (1) Lydia ——, who d. June 21, 1716; (2) July 4, 1720, Hannah, dau. of Dea. John White of Hat. She was b. March 26, 1695. Children—*Lydia*, b. 1714, d. Dec. 24, 1714; *Lydia*, b. June 8, 1716, d. July 5, 1716; *Sylvanus*, b. March 22, 1721, res. in Charlestown, N. H.; *John*, b. Nov. 14, 1722, res. in Charlestown, N. H.; *Oliver*, b. Nov. 22, 1724; *Lemuel*, b. Feb. 5, 1727, res. in Charlestown, N. H., *Hannah*, b. July 28, 1729; *Lydia*, b. Aug. 19, 1732; *Mehitable*, b. 1735.

4. WAITSTILL, s. of Dr. Thomas, (2) was a physician in Hat., where he d. April 22, 1748. He m. Oct. 1, 1736, Abigail, dau. of John Marsh of Had. She m. (2) Col. Buckley of Colchester, Ct.; (3) Rev. —— Little of Colchester, and d. as early as 1758. Children—*John*, b. Jan. 10, 1738; *Abigail*, b. Feb. 28, 1739, m. Solomon Woolcott of Williamstown; *Hannah Barnard*, b. March 16, 1742, m. Nathaniel Kellogg of Dalton; *Mary*, b. Jan. 10, 1744; *Samuel*, b. March 14, 1747, d. Feb. 28, 1748.

5. HOPESTILL, s. of Dr. Thomas, (2) Hat., d. Dec. 24, 1766. He m. Lydia Frary. She m. (2) Windsor Smith. Children—*Abner*, b. July 7, 1742, d. July 10, 1742; *Lydia*, b. July 5, 1743, d. Oct. 5, 1746; *Seth*, b. Dec. 6, 1745; *Lydia*, b. Nov. 21, 1747, d. Oct. 4, 1751; *Tabitha*, b. Oct. 1, 1749, d.

unm., in Amh., in 1795; *Elihu*, b. Aug. 17, 1751, d. unm. in Hat., Feb. 25, 1837, ae. 75; *Elijah*, b. June 6, 1753; *Perez*, b. Dec. 23, 1754; *Hopestill*, b. Oct. 30, 1756, d. Oct. 31, 1756; *Oliver*, b. Aug. 25, 1757, d. in Hammondsport, N. Y.

6. THOMAS, s. of Dr. Thomas, (2) rem. abt. 1753, from Hat. to Amh., where he d. Jan. 22, 1787, ae. 66. He m. Mary, dau. of Joseph Belden of Hat. She d. July 31, 1801, ae. 78. Children—*Esther*, b. Feb. 1, 1743, m. Ephraim Kellogg of Amh.; *Sarah*, b. July 13, 1744, m. Jan. 17, 1771, Nathaniel Alexander Smith of Amh., and d. Oct. 7, 1810; *Thomas*, b. May 20, 1746; *Anna*, b. April 22, 1748, m. Jonathan Nash of Amh.; *Waitstill*, b. May 8, 1750; *Samuel*, b. March 1, 1752; *Sybil*, bapt. Oct. 14, 1753, m. (1) Joseph Peck; (2) Timothy Green, Jr. of Amherst; *Moses*, bapt. Aug. 31, 1755; *Mary*, bapt. April 24, 1757, d. April 24, 1757; *Mary*, bapt. Aug. 12, 1759, m. Dec. 30, 1779, Simeon Pomeroy of Amh.; *Elisha*, bapt. April 12, 1761, accidentally killed by his brother with an axe; *Tabitha*, m. Ethan Smith; *Lucy*, bapt. March 31, 1765, d. unm., Feb. 21, 1814.

7. HON. JOHN, s. of Dr. Waitstill, (4) Hat., was a magistrate 36 yrs. and a Senator or Counsellor of Mass., 28 yrs. He d. Dec. 6, 1811. He m. Content Little, who d. April 9, 1829, in 89th yr. Children—*John*, b. Oct. 1765; *Content*, b. Sept. 14, 1767; *Mary*, b. Jan. 1769, m. Daniel Wait; *Waitstill*, b. May 14, 1771, a physician in Margaretta, O.; *Elizabeth*, b. March 7, 1773, d. unm. in Hat., Nov. 5, 1823; *Abigail*, b. May 7, 1775; *Samuel*, b. April, 1777, rem. to Springfield; *Ephraim*, b. Nov. 17, 1780, rem. to Nashua, N. H.; *Justin*, b. Feb. 14, 1786.

8. SETH, s. of Hopestill, (5) settled as a physician in Washington, Ct., whence in 1797, he rem. to Clinton, Oneida Co., N. Y., and d. April 29, 1830. He m. Nov. 10, 1779, Eunice Parmalee, b. Dec. 30, 1763. She d. May 2, 1821. Children—*Seth*, b. Aug. 23, 1780, a physician in Clinton, N. Y., m. Sept. 12, 1802, Huldah Clark; *Betsey*, b. Aug. 28, 1782, m. April 13, 1802, Elnathan Judd, M. D., of Troy, Mich.; *Thomas*, b. Oct. 15, 1784, a teacher of music in New York City, m. Mary Seymour; *Eunice*, b. Oct. 22, 1786, d. Jan. 10, 1788; *Orlando*, b. March 7, 1789, a lawyer in Rochester, N. Y., m. (1) Nov. 12, 1812, Betsey Clarke; (2) Aug. 31, 1823, his cousin, Mrs. Lydia F. Hamilton, dau. of Elijah Hastings of Amh.; *Eurotas Parmalee*, b. July 20, 1791, a merchant in Detroit, Mich., m. (1) Jan. 26, 1819, Electa Owen; (2) Aug. 23, 1826, Mrs. Philema Moody; (3) Oct. 14, 1835, Theodocia C. Petit; *Charles*, b. Sept. 2, 1793, a tanner in Mich., m. (1) May 21, 1818, Patty Barker; (2) July 8, 1837, Julia Trowbridge; *Polly Sophia*, b. April 14, 1796, d. June 10, 1803; *Truman*, b. Aug. 29, 1798, a lawyer in Genesee, Buffalo and New York, m. (1) Aug. 11, 1828, Elizabeth Vail; (2) April 6, 1837, Mary Williams; *Albert Merwin*, b. July 16, 1804, m. 1827, Frances Barry, and d. Oct. 4, 1828; *Eunice Sophia*, b. Sept. 22, 1809, m. (1) July 24, 1833, Washington Smith, M. D.; (2) Sept. 10, 1840, Levi Trowbridge of Southfield, Mich. She d. Oct. 1, 1849.

9. ELIJAH, s. of Hopestill, (5) a blacksmith in Amh., d. Oct. 4, 1803, ae. 50. He m. (1) April, 1782, Jerusha, dau. of Dea. John Billings of Amh. She d. July 3, 1798, ae. 34; (2) Rebecca ——, who m. (2) April 25, 1805, Levi Cowls of Amh., and d. Nov., 1826, ae. 63. Children—*Lucinda*, m. April 2, 1809, Calvin Hamilton; *Lydia*, m. (1) May 14, 1810, Chauncey Hamilton;

(2) Aug. 31, 1823, her cousin, Orlando Hastings, Esq., of Rochester, N. Y.;
Nancy, m. Dec. 24, 1807, Dr. Isaac Guernsey Cutler of Amh., and d. Jan. 28,
1849; *Elijah*.

10. PEREZ, s. of Hopestill, (5) a blacksmith in Hat., where he d. March
11, 1822. He m. Oct. 31, 1787, Elizabeth, dau. of Dea. Salmon and Mary
(Wait) White of Whately. Children—*Elizabeth*, b. Nov. 15, 1788, m. June,
1814, Horace Hastings of Geneva, N. Y., and d. Aug. 15, 1837; *Eurotas*, b.
May 15, 1790, m. Eroe Arms, was a banker in Buffalo, N. Y., and d. May 22,
1858; *Electa*, b. Jan. 15, 1792, m. July 4, 1816, Dr. David Field of Geneva,
N. Y.; *Perez*, b. May 29, 1794, m. May, 1822, Eunice Hastings, was a merchant in Geneva, N. Y., and d. April 26, 1852.

11. THOMAS, s. of Thomas, (6) Amh., d. Jan. 22, 1827, ae. 81. He m.
Hannah, dau. of Dea. John Billings of Amh. She d. Oct. 5, 1823, ae. 74.
Children—*Salome*, b. July 22, 1770, m. June 9, 1805, Asa Dickinson of Amh.,
and d. Sept. 5, 1846, ae. 76; *Jerusha*, b. Aug. 8, 1772, m. Sept. 6, 1792, Luke
Rich; *Hannah*, b. Nov. 10, 1774, d. Sept. 15, 1777; *Submit*, b. May 13, 1777,
m. April 26, 1798, Clark Green of Amh.; *Hannah*, b. Jan. 15, 1780, m. Oct. 31,
1799, Martin Kellogg of Had.; *Thomas*, b. Feb. 6, 1782, m. Nov. 1, 1803,
Eunice Clark, and d. in Amh., Oct. 11, 1858, ae. 76; *Eli*, b. June 1, 1784, m.
Sarah Paine, and d. in Ohio, March, 1835, ae. 51; *Judith*, b. Oct. 1, 1786, m.
Dec. 21, 1809, George Nutting of Amh.; *Mary*, b. Oct. 27, 1788, m. May
7, 1808, Samuel Smith; *Lucius*, b. Oct. 13, 1791, m. Feb. 8, 1810, Olive, dau.
of Joel Smith, and d. in Amh., Sept. 25, 1823; *David*, b. April 15, 1795, d.
Aug. 17, 1796.

12. SAMUEL, s. of Thomas, (6) Amh., Oct. 1, 1807. He m. Sept. 15,
1774, Lucy, dau. of Simeon Pomeroy of Amh. She m. (2) Martin Kellogg
of Amh., and d. Dec. 23, 1839, ae. 87. Children—*Waitstill*, b. June 15, 1775
d. Jan. 3, 1776; *Waitstill*, b. July 24, 1778, m. (1) Elsy, dau. of David Shaw
of East Windsor, Ct.; *Elisha*, b. July 31, 1780, m. Jan. 31, 1813, Abigail,
dau. of Benjamin Potwine, and d. July 18, 1856; *Samuel*, b. Nov. 14, 1785,
m. Sarah Spear, and rem. to Reedsborough, Vt.; *Daughter*, b. and d. July 19,
1788.

13. MOSES, s. of Thomas, (6) Amh., rem after 1820 to Vt., and d. June 6,
1844. He m. Aug. 29, 1776, Elizabeth, dau. of Eli Parker of Amh. Children
—*Twins*, b. Oct. 3, 1776; *Rachel*, b. Nov. 20, 1777, m. Benjamin Cooley of
Whately, rem. to Brownhill, O.; *Elizabeth*, b. Aug. 31, 1779, m. Luther
Lathrop of Wilmington, Vt.; *Polly*, b. Sept. 12, 1781, m. Nov. 23, 1800,
Joseph Cutler of Chicopee; *Otis*, b. July 17, 1783, m. June 13, 1804, Clarissa
Kellogg, and d. Oct. 1846; *Pickering*, b. June 28, 1785, d. unm. in Amh.,
Feb. 15, 1808; *Matilda*, b. June 14, 1787, m. Benoni Rust of Amh., and d.
Nov. 30, 1832; *Sarah*, b. Nov. 15, 1789, m. Oct. 16, 1806, Zaccheus Crocker
Ingram of Amh., and d. Aug. 30, 1832; *Moses*, b. Jan. 13, 1792, m. March 3,
1814, Anna Smith, and d. in Ia., Jan. 12, 1842; *Aaron*, b. Feb. 7, 1794, d.
Sept. 18, 1796; *Parker*, b. July 18, 1796, m. (1) Sept. 21, 1819. Martha
Graves, dau. of Seth Dickinson of Amh.; (2) June 8, 1837, Mary A., dau. of
Joseph Dickinson of Amh., and res. in Amh.; *Aaron*, b. Sept. 7, 1798, m.
Barbara Alvord, and d. Feb. 15, 1846, in Brunswick, N. Y.; *David*, b. Nov. 12,
1800, d. Jan. 8, 1801.

14. JOHN, s. of John, (7) a physician in Hat., d. May 2, 1845. He m. Feb. 1, 1790, Sybil Dickinson. She d. July 29, 1843. Children—*Chester*, b. Dec. 2, 1790, res. in Hat., m. Sept. 20, 1818, Lois Dickinson; *John*, b. Dec. 22, 1791, m. Lucretia Ward of Petersham, rem. to Onondaga Hollow, N. Y.; *Mary* b. 1794, m. Dr. Chester Bardwell of Whately; *Sybil*, b. July 31, 1796, d. young; *Justin*, b. July 23, 1800, m. Dolly Wait of Hat.; *Sophia*, b. Nov. 10, 1802.

1. HAWKES, JOHN, came abt. 1660, from Windsor, Ct., and was buried June 30, 1662. He m. Elizabeth ——. She m. (2) Robert Hinsdale; (3) June 25, 1683, Thomas Dibble of Windsor, Ct. Children—*John*, bapt. Aug. 13, 1643; *Nathaniel*, bapt. Feb. 16, 1645, d. young; *Elizabeth*, bapt. Jan. 10, 1647, m. Nov. 24, 1664, Joseph Gillett; *Anna*, bapt. Oct. 1, 1648, m. (1) Oct. 10, 1672, Thomas Hastings, and d. Oct. 25, 1705; *Isaac*, b. Aug. 11, 1650, drowned in Conn. river, June 22, 1659; *Mary*, b. May 23, 1652, m. (1) Oct. 10, 1672, Experience Hinsdale; (2) July, 1677, John Evans; *Joanna*, b. Feb. 8, 1654, m. William Arms of Deerfield, and d. Nov. 22, 1729; *Eliezer*, b. Dec. 20, 1655; *Sarah*, b. Sept. 29, 1657, m. (1) 1677, Philip Mattoon of Deerfield; (2) Daniel Belden, and d. Dec. 17, 1751; *Gershom*, b. Aug. 12, 1659, d. young.

2. JOHN, s. of John, (1) settled in Hat., whence he rem. to Deerfield, and subsequently to Waterbury, Ct., where he d. He m. (1) Dec. 26, 1667, Martha, (probably Baldwin,) who d. Jan. 7, 1676; (2) Nov. 20, 1696, Alice, wid. of Samuel Allis of Hat. She was slain by French and Indians, Feb. 29, 1704. Children—*John*, b. June 26, 1671, d. young; *John*, m. Thankful ——, and was slain, Feb. 29, 1704; *Hannah*, m. 1694, Jonathan Scott of Waterbury, Ct., and d. April 7, 1744; *Elizabeth*, b. 1697, taken captive in 1704, and was slain on the way to Canada.

3. ELIEZER, s. of John, (1) was deacon in Deerfield, where he d. March 22, 1727. He m. April 30, 1689, Judith, dau. of William Smead of Nh. Children —*Thankful*, b. 1690, m. (1) Thomas Taylor; (2) Daniel Ashley of Westfield; *Eliezer*, b. 1693; *Mary*, b. 1695, m. Jonathan Pattison; *Elizabeth*, b. 1697, m. Hezekiah Stratton; *Nathaniel*, b. 1699; *Sarah*, b. 1701, m. 1726, Thomas Wells; *Hannah*, b. 1703, m. 1727, Samuel Allen; *John*, b. 1707.

1. HAWLEY, SAMUEL, b. Feb. 23, 1686, s. of Joseph of Nh. and grandson of Thomas of Roxbury, settled in Hat., whence he rem. to Amh. He m. Dec. 2, 1708, Mehitable, dau. of Samuel Belding. Children—*Lydia*, b. April 3, 1710, m. Aug. 4, 1730, John Morton of Amh.; *Samuel; Joseph; Moses*, b. April 3, 1718; *John*, probably the man who in 1762 was warned out of Sunderland; *Dorothy*, b. abt. 1723, m. May 1, 1741, Ephraim Kellogg of Amh., and d. July 26, 1812, ae. 89; *Mary*, m. Jonathan Nash of Amh.

2. SAMUEL, s. of Samuel, (1) Amh., d. in the army, Dec. 15, 1750. He m. abt. 1736, Sarah, dau. of Zechariah Field of Amh. Children—*Anne*, perhaps; *Elijah*, d. in the army, Nov. 30, 1756; *Sarah*, m. (1) Benjamin Buckman; (2) —— Hodden; *Zechariah*, bapt. April 10, 1743, d. young; *John*, bapt. Dec. 28, 1746; *Miriam*, bapt. Jan. 1, 1749; *Mehitable*, m. her cousin, David Hawley of Amherst; *Zechariah*, bapt. May 13, 1753, m. Rebecca, dau. of Jonathan Edwards of Amh., was a dea. in Amh., and d. June 1, 1824, ae. 71.

3. JOSEPH, s. of Samuel, (1) Amh., d. abt. 1756. He m. (1) Jan. 13, 1737, Rebecca, dau. of Zechariah Field of Amh.; (2) 1753, (pub. April 12,) Thankful Alexander. She m. (2) Daniel Kellogg of Amh. Children— *Asenath*, bapt. Dec. 1739, m. 1758, (pub. Sept. 1,) Jonathan Scott of Sunderland; *Joseph*, b. July 1, 1744, d. young; *Joseph*, bapt. Oct. 10, 1748; *Abigail*, d. July 15, 1758; *Rebecca*.

4. MOSES, s. of Samuel, (1) Amh., d. July 27, 1802, ae. 84. He m. (1) Jan. 10, 1744, Eunice Houghton; (2) 1750, (pub. April 2,) Rebecca Gould. Children—*Rebecca*, b. abt. 1751, d. unm., Jan. 26, 1846, ae. 88; *Asenath*, b. abt. 1760, d. unm., Dec. 20, 1847, ae. 87; *Eunice*, b. abt. 1763, d. Oct. 20, 1843, ae. 80; *David*, m. his cousin, Mehitable Hawley, and d. in Amh., April 23, 1829; *Noah*, rem. to Natick; *Samuel*, m. Dec. 28, 1803, Fanny Perry.

1. HENDERSON, GIDEON, resided for a few years after marriage in Nh., whence abt. 1745 he rem. to Sunderland, and thence to Amh., where he d. Dec. 6, 1791. He m. Aug. 4, 1740, Sarah Baker. She d. Aug. 25, 1803. Children—*Sarah*, b. July, 1741, d. 1742; *Sarah*, b. Sept. 12, 1743, d. Oct. 13, 1760; *Gideon*, b. Aug. 30, 1745, d. Sept. 4, 1745; *Mehitable*, b. July 23, 1746, d. Nov. 24, 1760; *Elizabeth*, b. Jan. 1, 1748, m. Jan. 15, 1767, John Field, and d. April 6, 1783; *Mary*, b. April 24, 1751, d. Oct. 15, 1760; *Gideon*, b. Oct. 9, 1753, m. Abigail, dau. of Joseph Church of Amh., rem. to Claremont, N. H., and d. July 10, 1825, ae. 61; *Timothy*, b. Jan. 18, 1756; *Susanna*, b. March 15, 1758, m. Moses Cook, and d. 1824.

2. TIMOTHY, s. of Gideon, (1) Amh., d. Oct. 14, 1833, ae. 77. He m. Anna Wales. Children—*Ira*, b. Sept. 10, 1781, d. in Orange, O., 1850; *Timothy*, b. March 30, 1784, m. (1) Aug. 26, 1811, Mary Parker; (2) Tryphena, wid. of Charles Kellogg of Amh., and d. in Had., Oct. 28, 1861; *Zebina*, b. June 18, 1786, d. in Hudson, N. Y., Sept., 1812; *Luther*, b. Aug. 5, 1788; *Gideon*, b. Sept. 28, 1790, rem. to Mt. Morris, N. Y.; *Seth Smith*, b. Sept. 6, 1794, m. (1) Lima Farnum; (2) ———, and d. in Euclid, N. Y., in 1844; *Nancy*, b. Jan. 14, 1797, m. March, 1819, Ashley Hubbard of Sunderland; *Horace*, b. March 1, 1801, m. (1) Oct. 28, 1824, Martha Hubbard; (2) May 23, 1832, Caroline Rowe of Sunderland, and res. in Amherst.

HENRY, JAMES, rem. from Had. to S. H., as early as 1763, and d. April, 1767. He m. Elizabeth. Children — *Josiah; Sarah; Margaret*, b. Feb. 17, 1731; *William*, b. July 8, 1732; *Samuel*, b. May 25, 1734; *Elizabeth*.

1. HIBBARD, GEORGE, came to Had. from Windham, Ct., abt. 1780, and d. July 15, 1823. At the date of his death, he had had 16 children, 109 grandchildren, and 51 great grandchildren. Children — *John; George; Eliphaz*, b. April 1, 1782; *Son*, b. Aug. 6, 1784; *Sally*, b. March 12, 1786; *Dau.*, b. May 18, 1788; *Dau.*, b. March 29, 1790; *Dau.*, April, 1791.

2. JOHN, s. of George, (1) d. Sept. 1, 1855, ae. 87, at which date he had had 14 children, 30 gr. children, and 27 great gr. children. He m. 1792, (pub. Jan. 29,) Irene Belding of Whately. Children—*Child*, d. April 29, 1793; *Elias*, b. Feb. 7, 1794; *John*, bapt. July 12, 1795; *Lucy*, bapt. Feb. 5, 1797; *John*, b. June 10, 1798; *Albert*, bapt. May 4, 1800; *Chester*, b. Oct. 17, 1802; *Eliphaz*, b. Oct. 24, 1803; *Irene*, bapt. Nov. 5, 1809.

3. GEORGE, s. of George, (1) d. Dec. 1849, ae. 69. He m. Nov. 30, 1797, Susanna Washburn. Children—*Clarissa; Truman; Elizabeth; Eliphaz; Isaiah Washburn.*

4. ELIAS, s. of John, (2) d. Jan. 2, 1828. He m. (1) Phila, (2) Lydia C. ——. Children—*Richard M.*, b. Jan. 16, 1823; *Elias Worcester*, b. June 30, 1830; *Phila Elizabeth*, b. Dec. 9, 1832; *Rufus Pomroy; Emily Jane*, b. April 29, 1836; *Henry Harrison*, b. June 6, 1840.

HICKSON, WALTER, Hat., d. April 3, 1696. He m. Feb. 1679, Sarah, wid. of Barnabas Hinsdale, and dau. of John White. She d. Aug. 10, 1702. Children—*John*, b. Nov. 7, 1679, d. July 2, 1691; *Elizabeth*, b. Jan. 26, 1681, prob. d. young; *Jacob*, b. Jan. 26, 1683, captured by Indians and slain in 1704, at Cowas, N. H., while on the way to Canada.

1. HILLIARD or HILLYER, JOHN, b. June 3, 1637, s. of John of Windsor, Ct., rem. to Nh., and thence to Had., where he d. Dec. 29, 1729, ae. 85. He m. Sept. 30, 1664, Anne Baxter, who d. June 5, 1728, ae. 84. Children—*John*, b. Dec. 26, 1669; *Mary*, b. Dec. 28, 1671; *Timothy*, b. Nov. 4, 1686.

2. TIMOTHY, s. of John, (1) rem. to S. H., and d. Dec. 9, 1759, ae. 72. He m. Mehitable. Children—*Margaret*, b. May 6, 1716, m. Daniel Crowfoot; *John*, b. Feb. 5, 1717; *Mehitable*, b. Nov. 22, 1721, m. Oct. 25, 1740, William Thompson; *Mary*, b. May 22, 1725, m. Ephraim Crowfoot; *Timothy*, b. Dec. 15, 1728; *Joseph*, b. Feb. 21, 1735.

3. JOHN, s. of Timothy, (2) S. H. He m. Mary. Children—*John*, b. Sept. 14, 1744; *Patience*, b. Feb. 18, 1746; *Warham*, b. Aug. 1, 1747, d. 1747; *Submit*, b. 1749, d. 1749; *Anne*, b. 1750, d. Jan. 8, 1832, ae. 81; *Uriah*, b. 1752; *Joseph*, b. 1755; *Warham*, b. 1757.

4. TIMOTHY, s. of Timothy, (2) S. H. Child—*Hannah*, b. Oct. 23, 1756, m. —— Fuller.

1. HINSDALE, ROBERT, Dedham, 1638, freeman March 13, 1639, rem. to Medfield, thence as early as 1672 to Had., and later to Deerfield, where together with his sons Barnabas, John and Samuel, he was slain by Indians. He m. (1) Ann; (2) Elizabeth, wid. of John Hawkes. She m. (3) 1683, Thomas Dibble of Windsor, Ct. Children—*Elizabeth*, m. July 7, 1657, James Rising; *Barnabas*, b. Nov. 13, 1639; *Gamaliel*, perhaps mistake for Samuel, b. March 5, 1642; *Mary*, b. Feb. 14, 1644; *Experience*, b. Jan. 23, 1646; *John*, b. Jan. 27, 1648, slain by Indians, Sept. 18, 1675; *Ephraim*, b. Sept. 26, 1650.

2. BARNABAS, s. of Robert, (1) rem. from Hat. to Deerfield, and was slain Sept. 18, 1675, at Bloody brook, being one of Capt. Lathrop's Co. He m. Oct. 15, 1666, Sarah, wid. of Stephen Taylor, and dau. of John White. She m. (3) Feb. 1679, Walter Hickson, and d. Aug. 10, 1702. Children— *Barnabas*, b. Feb. 20, 1668, m. Nov. 9, 1693, Martha Smith, settled in Hartford, Ct., and d. Jan. 25, 1725; *Sarah*, m. Jan. 8, 1691, Samuel Hall of Middletown, Ct.; *Elizabeth*, b. Oct. 29, 1671, d. March 8, 1672; *Isaac*, b. Sept. 15, 1673, m. Jan. 6, 1715, Lydia Loomis, settled in Hartford, Ct., and d. abt. March 1, 1739; *Mary*, b. March 27, 1677.

3. SAMUEL, s. of Robert, (1) rem. from Had. to Deerfield, where he was killed by Indians, Sept. 18, 1675. He m. Oct. 31, 1660, Mehitable Johnson, perhaps dau. of Humphrey of Roxbury. She m. (2) John Root, (3) Dea. John Coleman. Children—*Mehitable*, b. Oct. 18, 1663, prob. m. Obadiah Dickinson; *Ann*, b. Feb. 22, 1666; *Mary*, m. 1685, Thomas Sheldon, and d. Sept. 1738; *Sarah*, m. 1692, Samuel Janes; *Samuel*, m. Abigail ——, and d. in Medfield, Jan. 1730; *Mahuman*, m. Mary, and d. in Deerfield, May 9, 1736.

4. EXPERIENCE, s. of Robert, (1) Deerfield, d. 1676. He m. Oct. 10, 1672, Mary, dau. of John Hawks. She m. (2) July, 1677, John Evens of Hat. and Deerfield. Children—*Elizabeth*, m. John Cornwell of Middletown; and another daughter, whose name is not known.

5. EPHRAIM, s. of Robert, (1) rem. from Hat. to Deerfield, but returned to Hat., and d. Aug. 20, 1681. He m. Mehitable ——, who m. (2) John Gardner. Children—*John*, b. Aug. 7, 1677; *Experience*, b. July, 1679, m. Nathaniel Clark of Medfield; *Mehitable*, b. abt. 1681, m. Nathaniel Wright of Medfield.

HITCHCOCK, CHARLES, deacon, s. of Enos of Brookfield, was b. Jan. 27, 1798. He m. (1) May 12, 1823, Sophia, dau. of Moses Porter; (2) Aug. 21, 1843, Cornelia Hubbard Wells, b. May 29, 1807, dau. of Roswell Hubbard of Northampton.

HITCHCOCK, MRS. THANKFUL, wid. of Enos, d. June 27, 1853, ae. 75.

HODGE, GEORGE, a tailor, resided for a time in Nh., but removed, and finally settled in Had. He m. 1757, Jane Question. She d. March, 1804, ae. 80. Children—*William*, b. Sept. 30, 1758; *John*, b. Oct. 19, 1760, m. March 19, 1789, Sarah Dickinson; *George*, b. March 18, 1763.

2. WILLIAM, s. of George, (1.) He m. (1) Dec. 22, 1785, Amanda Hopkins; (2) Nov. 6, 1808, Esther Edwards. Children—*George*, b. Oct. 14, 1786; *William*, b. April 9, 1788; *Emily*, b. Feb. 7, 1790; *Timothy*, b. Dec. 23, 1791; *Charles*, b. Aug. 23, 1793; *Mary*, b. April 25, 1795; *Henry*, b. April 13, 1797; *Robert Wilson*, b. Dec. 13, 1799; *Giles*, b. April 29, 1801; *Anna*, b. Oct. 20, 1803; *Hannah*, b. March 25, 1807; *Esther*, b. Oct. 10, 1808.

3. HENRY, s. of William, (2.) He m. Nov. 20, 1823, Eliza, dau. of John Nash. Children—*Mary Guilford*, b. Sept. 27, 1824, d. July 26, 1826; *Harriet Merrick*, b. Feb. 6, 1826, m. Oct. 7, 1847, Hon. Thomas F. Plunkett of Pittsfield; *Lester Porter*, b. Feb. 2, 1828, graduated A. C. 1850, and d. in Athens, O., May 28, 1851; *Elizabeth Hervey*, b. July 16, 1831, d. May 2, 1833; *Lephe Nash*, b. Oct. 22, 1833, d. Oct. 25, 1835; *William Henry*, b. July 24, 1841.

HODGE, BENJAMIN, Children—*Charles D.*, b. Nov. 15, 1826; *James W.*, b. July 8, 1828; *Harriet M.*, b. Feb. 22, 1830; *Eliza*, b. May 10, 1832; *Samuel*, b. Sept. 20, 1835; *Sarah G.*, b. March 1, 1837; *Susan A.*, b. Nov. 21, 1839.

HOLT, MOSES PIKE. Children—*Moses Pike*, b. May 15, 1806; *William Henry*, b. May 26, 1808; *Giles*, b. May 22, 1810.

1. HOPKINS, Rev. Samuel, D. D., s. of Rev. Samuel of West Springfield, was b. Oct. 31, 1729, grad. Y. C. 1749. Tutor in Y. C. 1751-4, ord. as pastor of church in Had., Feb. 26, 1755, received the degree of Doctor of Divinity from Y. C. in 1802, and d. March 8, 1811, ae. 81. He m. (1) Feb. 17, 1756, Sarah, wid. of his predecessor, Rev. Chester Williams, and dau. of Eleazar Porter, Esq., of Had. She d. Feb. 5, 1774; (2) Oct. 1776, Margaret, dau. of Rev. Sampson Stoddard of Chelmsford. Children—*Samuel*, b. Oct. 31, 1756, d. in Martinico, July 11, 1782, ae. 25; *Mabel*, b. Aug. 28, 1758, m. Oct. 28, 1779, Moses Hubbard, and d. April 19, 1829, ae. 70; *Hannah*, b. Aug. 10, 1760, m. Nov. 4, 1779, Rev. Samuel Spring, D. D. of Newburyport, and d. June 11, 1819, ae. 58; *Jerusha*, b. July 14, 1762, m. Sept. 14, 1788, Rev. Samuel Austin, D. D., of Worcester, and d. March 26, 1841, ae. 78; *Stephen*, b. June 1, 1764, m. (1) Nancy Turner, was a joiner in Hanover, N. H., Brookfield, Vt., and Peacham, Vt.; *Polly*, b. March 6, 1766, m. Dec. 15, 1785, Benjamin Colt, and d. Sept. 14, 1813, ae. 47; *Lucy*, b. Feb. 6, 1768, m. Sept. 4, 1797, Rev. William Riddel of Bristol, Me.; *John*, b. Jan. 17, 1770; *Elizabeth*, b. June 12, 1772, m. Nov. 1, 1793, Rev. Leonard Worcester of Peacham, Vt.

2. John, s. of Rev. Samuel, (1) a merchant, rem. April, 1814, from Hadley to Boston, and thence in Oct. 1824 to Northampton, where he d. Jan. 9, 1842, ae. 71, leaving a very large estate. He m. 1797, Lydia, dau. of Thomas Thompson of Newburyport. She was b. April 17, 1773, and d. in Newburyport, April 10, 1842, ae. 68. Children—*Sarah Ann Wait*, b. Jan. 20, 1799, m. Sept. 23, 1822, Rev. John Wheeler, then of Windsor, Vt., but afterwards President of University of Vermont at Burlington. She d. in Burlington, Nov. 2, 1847; *Elizabeth*, b. May 18, 1802, d. Aug. 1, 1802; *Thomas Thompson*, b. Dec. 13, 1804, d. June 27, 1805; *Samuel*, b. April 11, 1807, grad. D. C. 1827, was ordained and installed over the 1st church in Montpelier, Vt., Oct. 26, 1831, and dismissed May, 1835, was installed over 1st church in Saco, Me., Feb. 1836, and dismissed 1841, reinstalled over the same church in 1842, and dismissed 1845. He now resides in Nh. and is an author of note. He m. May 29, 1832, Caroline W., dau. of Josiah Dwight of Nh.; *Erastus*, b. April 7, 1810, grad. D. C. 1830, was settled May, 1835, in the ministry at Beech Island, Edgefield District, S. C., and dismissed 1837. He was settled in the fall of 1837 over the 2d Presbyterian church in Troy, N. Y., and dismissed in the fall of 1841. He has since resided in Nh., and has represented that town in the Legislature. As a political speaker, he has in the State few superiors. He m. (1) June 25, 1835, Sarah H. Benedict of Charleston, S. C., who d. May 3, 1838; (2) Nov. 18, 1841, Charlotte Frelinghuysen, dau. of Rev. William Allen, D. D., of Nh.; *George*, b. Sept. 13, 1812, d. at the Santa Cruz, West Indies, March 16, 1830, ae. 17, while a member of Yale College; *Lewis Spring*, b. Sept. 18, 1815, entered in 1831 the University of Vermont, but left before graduation, pursued his medical studies at Northampton, and in Boston, New Haven, Ct., and Philadelphia, Pa., and graduated at Med. Col. at Charleston, S. C. About the year 1840, he commenced the practice of his profession in Northampton, but after two years was compelled by failing health to abandon the same. His residence has since been at Northampton. He m. Oct. 14, 1846, Fanny J. Washburn of Boston.

HOPKINS, Timothy, deacon, b. April 9, 1762, s. of Timothy and nephew of Rev. Samuel, D. D., came from West Springfield, and d. March 17, 1840. He m. Aug. 9, 1792, Rebecca, dau. of Eliakim Smith. She d. Aug. 17, 1848. Children—*Charles*, b. June 13, 1793, grad. Y. C. 1814, and d. Dec. 28, 1816; *Mehitable*, b. April 30, 1795, m. —— Hunt; *Emily*, b. Jan. 19, 1805, m. Sept. 12, 1838, Sherman Peck; *William Smith*, b. Feb. 4, 1807, a farmer in New Salem, m. Sept. 3, 1848, Adeline Fitts.

HOVEY, Joseph, s. of Daniel of Ipswich, settled in Had., but rem. perhaps (says Savage) to Cambridge, d. in Milton, May or June, 1690. He m. May 31, 1677, Hannah Pratt, perhaps dau. of John of Hartford, Ct. Children—*Joseph*, b. Feb. 28, 1678; *Ebenezer*, b. Nov. 5, 1680; *Hannah*, b. Nov. 21, 1682; *John*, b. Aug. 21, 1684; *Caleb*, b. June 4, 1687; *Thomas*, b. June 6, 1681, says record, perhaps a mistake for 1689.

1.   HOVEY, Lt. Thomas, from Ipswich, per. s. of Daniel, freeman 1681, lieut., representative, 1699 and 1703, and d. 1739, ae. 91.   He m. Sarah, dau. of Aaron Cook.   Children—*Thomas*, b. 1678; *Sarah*, b. Dec. 25, 1680, m. Jan. 21, 1704, Jonathan Winchell; *Abigail*, b. Jan. 8, 1682, m. Jan. 27, 1701, Nathaniel Austin, Jr.; *Joanna*, b. abt. 1684, m. —— Wadsworth; *Elizabeth*, b. abt. 1686, m. John Smith, s. of Joseph; *Miriam*, b. Aug. 27, 1689, m. Jan. 30, 1709, Benjamin Church; *Hannah*, b. Nov. 5, 1691, buried March 7, 1694; *Three daughters*, b. and d. Nov. 12, 1693; *Daniel*, b. Dec. 1, 1694, d. Feb. 13, 1716; *Dorcas*, b. Feb. 1, 1698, d. unm., March 3, 1795, ae. 97; *Rachel*, b. Jan. 20, 1700, d. Oct. 12, 1703.

2.   Thomas, s. of Thomas, (1) d. in Sunderland, in 1728.   He m. (1) Mary Crafts, who d. Jan. 6, 1714; (2) Nov. 5, 1719, Hannah, dau. of Samuel Dickinson of Hat.   She became deranged, and d. abt. 1757.   Children—*Mary*, b. Feb. 12, 1710; *Martha*, m. (1) 1746, Nathaniel Barstow; *Thomas*, b. and d. 1720; *Hannah*, b. 1721, d. March 30, 1730; *Sarah*, b. 1723, d. young; *Miriam*, b. 1726, d. young.

1.   HOYT, David, deacon, s. of Nicholas, b. in Windsor, Ct., April 22, 1651, rem. to Hat. and thence to Deerfield.   He, together with his wife and children, Jonathan, Sarah, Ebenezer, and Abigail, was taken captive in the sack of Deerfield, Feb. 29, 1704, and carried away towards Canada, and perished of hunger near the lower Cohoes. He m. (1) April 3, 1673, Sarah, dau. of Thomas Wells, who d. before Sept. 1676; (2) Mary; (3) Abigail, wid. of Joshua Pomeroy, and dau. of Nathaniel Cook of Windsor. She m. (3) Dea. Nathaniel Rice of Wallingford, Ct.   Children—*Samuel*, b. June 12, 1674; *David*; *Mary*, m. April 4, 1707, Judah Wright; *Sarah*, b. May 6, 1686, m. —— Nims; *Jonathan*, b. April 6, 1688; *Benjamin*, b. Sept. 15, 1692, rem. to Wallingford, Ct.; *Ebenezer*, b. Aug. 21, 1695, remained among the Indians; *Abigail*, b. May 1, 1702, killed on the way to Canada, March, 1704.

2.   David, s. of David, (1) Deerfield, slain by Indians, Feb. 29, 1704. He m. April 14, 1699, Hannah, dau. of Joseph Edwards of Nh.   She was b. Sept. 1675, and m. (2) 1706, Samuel Field.   Children—*Sarah*, b. Jan. 16, 1700, d. April 12, 1700; *Mary*, b. April 20, 1703, m. July 4, 1723, Jonathan Wells, and d. Nov. 22, 1750.

3. JONATHAN, s. of David, (1) Deerfield, d. May 23, 1779. He m. Mary
Field, who d. June 26, 1780. Children—*Mary*, b. Oct. 5, 1714, m. Oct. 24,
1740, Ebenezer Sheldon; *Abigail*, b. Sept. 10, 1716, m. (1) Oct. 18, 1743,
Matthew Clesson; (2) John Nims; *Sarah*, b. July 9, 1719, m. Dec. 6, 1740,
John Burk; *David*, b. Oct. 26, 1722, m. (1) 1743, Mercy Sheldon; (2) April
25, 1754, Silence King, and d. in Deerfield, Sept. 6, 1814; *Hannah*, b. April
8, 1726, d. Dec. 22, 1728; *Jonathan*, b. Feb. 20, 1728, m. July 11, 1751,
Experience Childs, and d. May 7, 1813.

HUBBARD, HEZEKIAH, came from Lebanon, Ct., and d. May 1, 1775,
ae. 38. He m. Jan. 31, 1760, Mabel, dau. of Edmund Hubbard. She d.
May 3, 1816, ae. 81. Children—*Lucinda*, b. Feb. 13, 1761, d. July 11, 1761,
ae. 4 mos.; *Lucinda*, b. Nov. 25, 1761, m. (1) Sept. 7, 1780, William Jones;
(2) —— Haskell; *Mabel*, b. Aug. 19, 1768, d. unm. May 20, 1842; *Hezekiah*,
b. Oct. 6, 1770, rem. to the West; *Hannah*, b. Aug. 19, 1772, d. unm. 1860;
John Hancock, b. 1774.

1. HUBBARD, JOHN, s. of George of Wethersfield, Milford and Guilford,
Ct., came abt. 1660 from Wethersfield, Ct., and d. abt. 1705. He m. Mary
(perhaps Merriam of Concord) who survived him. Children—*Mary*, b. Jan.
27, 1651, d. young; *John*, b. April 12, 1655; *Hannah*, b. Dec. 5, 1656, d.
1662; *Jonathan*, b. Jan. 3, 1659, m. —— Merriam, and d. in Concord, 1728,
ae. 70; *Daniel*, b. March 9, 1661; *Mercy*, b. Feb. 23, 1664, m. Oct. 12,
1685, Jonathan Boreman of Wethersfield, Ct.; *Isaac*, b. Jan. 16, 1667;
Mary, b. April 10, 1669, m. 1688, Daniel Warner; *Sarah*, b. Nov. 12, 1672,
m. Samuel Cowles of Hat.

2. JOHN, s. of John, (1) settled in Glastenbury, Ct. Children—*John;
David; Ephraim; Isaac; Sarah.*

3. DANIEL, s. of John, (1) d. Feb. 12, 1744, ae. 82. He m. Nov. 1,
1683, Esther Rice, or Rise. She d. Feb. 11, 1737, ae. 67. Children—*Esther*,
b. Jan. 17, 1685, m. Nov. 13, 1707, Leonard Hoar; *Anna*, b. July 13, 1687,
d. May 13 or 25, 1688; *Daniel*, b. May 7, 1689, per. moved to Brimfield;
Anna, b. July 10, 1691; *Mary*, b. Jan. 11, 1694, m. Dec. 15, 1715, Peter
Montague, Jr.; *Elizabeth*, b. April 5, 1695; *Samuel*, *b.* April 9, 1697, m.
Hannah Bliss of Springfield, and rem. to Brimfield; *Rachel*, b. Oct. 16, 1698,
m. Sept. 13, 1729, Gabriel Williams; *Edmund*, b. July 18, 1700; *Joseph*, b.
June 5, 1702, d. Nov. 26, 1706; *Joshua*, b. July 23, 1705, d. Aug. 7, 1705;
Rebecca, b. Sept. 19, 1706, m. May 13, 1727, Jacob Williams of Hartford, Ct.

4. ISAAC, s. of John, (1) settled in Hat., whence in 1714, he rem. to
Sunderland, where he was a deacon, and d. Aug. 7 or 9, 1750, ae. 83. He
m. Ann, dau. of Daniel Warner. She d. June 26, 1750. Children—*John*, b.
April 20, 1693; *Isaac*, b. Jan. 14, 1695; *Mary*, b. Feb. 25, 1697; *Daniel*,
b. April 30, 1699; *Hannah*, b. Sept. 7, 1701, m. 1727, Nathaniel Mattoon;
Jonathan, b. Dec. 29, 1703, grad. Y. C. 1724, settled as first pastor of church
in Sheffield, Oct. 22, 1735, dismissed in 1764, and d. July 6, 1765, ae. 61;
Joseph, b. April 8, 1708; *David*, b. March 9, 1712.

5. EDMUND, s. of Daniel, (3) d. April 27, 1766. He m. Ruth, who d.
Nov. 25, 1775. Children—*Anna*, b. July 4, 1729, d. unm. Feb. 1, 1764;
Ruth, b. Aug. 1, 1732, m. May 4, 1758, James Meacham; *Edmund*, b. Feb. 11,
1734; *Mabel*, b. March 17, 1737, m. Jan. 31, 1760, Hezekiah Hubbard, and d.
May 3, 1816; *Esther*, b. March 22, 1738, m. Oct. 14, 1773, Peter Strong of

Chesterfield; *Moses*, b. May 30, 1740, d. Jan. 17, 1743; *Moses*, prob. grad. Y. C. 1765, teacher, m. Oct. 28, 1779, Mabel, dau. of Rev. Samuel Hopkins, D. D., d. in Brookfield, Vt.

6. JOHN, s. of Isaac, (4) Hat., a deacon, d. Aug. 25, 1778, ae. 85. He m. Hannah Cowles of East Hartford, Ct., who d. Feb. 19, 1777, in 85th yr. Children—*Mary*, b. July 28, 1719, m. Joseph Warner, and rem. to Cummington; *Elisha*, b. Sept. 4, 1721; *Hannah*, b. March 28, 1724, d. March 20, 1727, ae. 3; *John*, b. Nov. 6, 1726, grad. Y. C. 1747, settled May 30, 1750, over the church in Northfield, where he d. Nov. 28, 1794, ae. 68.

7. ISAAC, s. of Isaac, (4) Sunderland, d. abt. 1763. He m. (1) July 4, 1723, Christian, dau. of Dea. Samuel Gunn of Hat. and Sunderland; (2) Abigail, wid. of Jonathan Atherton of Amh. and dau. of John Kellogg. Children—*Israel*, b. Jan. 18, 1725, m. 1747, Abigail Smith, and d. in Sunderland, April 21, 1817, ae. 92; *Hannah*, b. July 11, 1727, m. (1) 1745, Simeon Graves; (2) Absalom Scott; *Isaac*, b. Jan. 6, 1730; *Elijah*, b. Dec. 16, 1731; *Christian*, b. Dec. 17, 1733, m. Paul Field of Northfield; *Anna*, b. March 8, 1739; *Giles*, b. Sept. 7, 1742, d. in Sunderland, Aug. 21, 1824, ae. 81.

8. DANIEL, s. of Isaac, (4) Sunderland, d. May 30, 1779, ae. 80. He m. 1732, Mary, dau. of Samuel Gunn of Hat. and Sunderland. Children— *Mary*, b. 1734; *Daniel*, b. 1736; *Martha*, b. 1739, d. young; *Martha*, b. 1741, m. Timothy Parsons.

9. JOSEPH, s. of Isaac, (4) rem. from Had. to Leverett, and d. abt. 1783. He m. Nov. 4, 1737, Joanna, dau. of Samuel Porter. She d. Dec. 12, 1766. Children—*Susanna*, b. July 6, 1738, m. Jan. 29, 1760, Wilder Willard of Fort Dummer; *William*, b. Aug. 22, 1742, d. Aug. 16, 1752; *Anna*, m. Israel Hubbard; *Joanna*, m. Nahum Ward.

10. DAVID, s. of Isaac, (4) Sunderland, and m. 1743, Miriam Cooley, doubtless dau. of Simon of Sunderland. Children—*Moses*, b. 1743; *David*, b. 1748; *Gideon*, b. 1751; *William*, b. 1754.

11. EDMUND, s. of Edmund, (5) d. May 5, 1791. He m. Dec. 17, 1761, Margaret, dau. of Samuel Gaylord. She d. Dec. 9, 1825, ae. 85. Children— *Lucy*, b. Feb. 24, 1764, m. Oct. 26, 1786, Samuel Porter, and d. Jan. 23, 1848; *Daniel*, b. Feb. 19, 1766, d. Nov. 12, 1775; *Elisha*, b. June 6, 1768; *Samuel*, b. Aug. 18, 1770, d. Nov. 12, 1775; *Susanna*, b. Sept. 17, 1772; *Elizabeth*, b. Sept. 1, 1774, m. Elihu Smith; *Daniel*, b. Sept. 24, 1776, rem. to the vicinity of Troy, N. Y.; *Edmund*, b. March 8, 1779, rem. to Chester; *William*, b. March 6, 1781, d. Dec. 30, 1846, in Cummington; *David*, b. Dec. 25, 1788, d. ae. abt. 14.

12. ELISHA, s. of John, (6) Hat., d. April 11, 1768, ae. 46. He m. June 7, 1748, Lucy, dau. of Thomas Stearns of Worcester. She was b. Oct. 6, 1727. Children—*Hannah*, b. Feb. 2, 1750, m. Aug. 2, 1770, Simeon White, Jr., of Williamsburgh, and d. Feb. 17, 1786, ae. 36; *Elisha*, b. Nov. 12, 1751; *Lucy*, b. Sept. 26, 1753, m. Gershom Clark Lyman of New Marlboro', Vt.; *Anna*, b. Dec. 26, 1755, m. Nov. 27, 1799, Josiah Allis of Whately, and d. June 21, 1839, ae. 83; *Elisha*, b. Sept. 13, 1758; *Lucretia*, b. Sept. 23, 1760, m. Epaphroditus Champion of Haddam, Ct.; *Sarah*; *John*.

13. ISAAC, s. of Isaac, (7) rem. from Sund. after 1756 to Amh., and thence in his old age to Wilmington, Vt., where he d. abt. 1810. He m. Oct. 29, 1752, Submit, dau. of Isaac Graves of Sunderland. Children—*Elihu*, b. March 24, 1754, m. March 3, 1779, —— Smith of Leverett, and d. in Goshen; *Stephen*, b. July 27, 1756, m. Feb. 10, 1780, Lucy, dau. of William Boltwood of Amh., and d. in Manchester, Ct., Dec., 1828, ae. 72; *Lucy*, b. abt. 1758, m. Simeon Clark of Amh., and d. March 19, 1793, ae. 35; *Irene*, bapt. May 29, 1763, m. (1) Nov. 23, 1786, Asahel Clark of Amh.; (2) Feb. 18, 1808, William Boltwood of Amh., and d. Aug. 6, 1831, ae. 68; *Elijah*, prob. bapt. Sept. 20, 1767, m. Feb. 15, 1795, Abi, dau. of Noadiah Lewis of Amh., and d. in Amh., March 24, 1814, ae. 47; *Chester*, bapt. March 14, 1770, m. Dorothy, dau. of Martin Kellogg of Amh., and rem. to Wilmington, Vt.

14. ELISHA, s. of Edmund, (11) settled in Chesterfield, but returned to Had., and d. Feb. 24, 1827. He m. Feb. 9, 1797, Lucinda, dau. of Stephen Noble of Westfield. She was b. Jan. 27, 1774, and d. Oct. 29, 1857, ae. 83. Children—*Maria*, b. Feb. 7, 1798; *Harriet*, b. June 7, 1799; *Lucinda*, b. April 4, 1801, m. Aug. 15, 1826, Lyman Selby; *Margaret Gaylord*, b. June 13, 1804, m. July 6, 1836, Seth Barlow; *Elizabeth*, b. Nov. 24, 1807, m. Nov. 1834, Erastus Hall; *Eunice Noble*, b. Oct. 30, 1809, m. April 13, 1831, Theodore Bartlett of Nh.; *Susan*, b. Dec. 19, 1812, m. April 9, 1843, Erastus Nash, Jr.

15. ELISHA, s. of Elisha, (12) Williamsburgh, where he kept a public house and was town clerk. He d. May 17, 1843, ae. 84. He m. June 22, 1780, Hannah, dau. of Daniel White of Hat. She d. March 27, 1824, ae. 64. Children—*Lucinda*, b. Aug. 27, 1780; *Sally*, b. Oct. 10, 1782, d. Oct. 11, 1782; *Jeremiah*, b. Oct. 10, 1783, d. Nov. 25, 1786; *Jeremiah*, b. Nov. 24, 1786, m. Feb. 25, 1813, Huldah Nash, and d. May 18, 1850, ae. 63; *Elisha*, b. Sept. 29, 1789, grad. W. C. 1811, a lawyer in Williamsburgh, d. unm., Aug. 30, 1853, ae. 64; *Erastus*, b. Feb. 27, 1792, m. 1818, Wealthy Amanda Mayhew, and d. Sept. 14, 1850, ae. 58; *Hannah*, b. July 4, 1794, d. ae. 7 yrs.; *Lucretia*, b. Dec. 25, 1796, m. Jan. 5, 1815, Walter Price of Williamsburgh; *Sally*, b. Sept. 7, 1799, m. 1818, Moses Putney, resided in Munroe Co., N. Y., and d. 1838, ae. 39; *Hannah*, b. Oct. 1800.

1. HUNT, JOHN, d. Dec. 20, 1840. He m. Jan. 4, 1816, Mehitable Hopkins. Children—*Charles*, b. Feb. 18, 1818, d. March 17, 1825; *Harriet Mills*, b. May 17, 1819, m. Nov. 3, 1836, Otis S. Baker, and d. Dec. 24, 1840, ae. 21; *Timothy Edwards*, b. Dec. 3, 1820; *Emily Hopkins*, b. Sept. 15, 1822, m. May 26, 1842, Henry A. Ferry; *John*, b. Dec. 10, 1824; *Charles*, b. Aug. 10, 1826, d. Aug. 31, 1826; *Mary Ann*, b. Dec. 15, 1827.

2. JOHN, s. of John, (1) m. Jan. 2, 1851, Sarah Angeline, dau. of David Gould of Heath. Children—*John Gould*, b. Aug. 8, 1853; *Charles Hopkins*, b. Dec. 7, 1854; *Harriet Baker*, b. March 12, 1857; *Lewis Frederick*, b. Jan. 2, 1859; *Helen Emily*, b. Dec. 29, 1859, d. Feb. 24, 1860.

HUNTER, STEPHEN, m. Hannah. Child—*Mary Elizabeth*, b. Nov. 13, 1836.

1. INGRAM, JOHN, b. abt. 1642, freeman 1683, d. June 22, 1722, ae. 80. He m. 1660, Elizabeth, dau. of Samuel Gardner. She d. Nov. 29, 1684. Children—*John*, b. June 29, 1661; *Jadiah*, b. Aug. 16, 1668; *Samuel*, b.

Oct. 8, 1670; *Ebenezer*, b. Feb. 3, 1673, d. April 11, 1690; *Nathaniel*, b. Oct. 8.
1674; *Jonathan*, b. 1676, slain at Deerfield, Feb. 28, 1704; *Elizabeth*, b.
May 1, 1679, d. Jan. 3, 1702; *Abigail*, b. Jan. 12, 1683.

2. JOHN, s. of John, (1) rem., when advanced in years, to Amh., where
he was living Oct. 1742. He m. June 26, 1689, Mehitable, dau. of John
Dickinson. Children—*Elizabeth*, b. March 15, 1691, m. (1) March 27, 1712,
Philip Panthorn; (2) Dec. 13, 1716, Ebenezer Kellogg; *John*, b. Jan. 9,
1693; *Ebenezer*, b. Dec. 10, 1694, d. Nov. 21, 1695; *Hannah*, b. Oct. 17, 1697,
m. Nov. 1716, Dea. John Nash of Had. and Amh.; *Mehitable*, b. Sept. 13,
1698, m. Nov. 6, 1724, Aaron Smith; *Mary*, b. July 10, 1702; *Ebenezer*, b.
Nov. 10, 1701, d. Jan. 6, 1702; *Rebecca*, b. Nov. 5, 1704, m. Nov. 11, 1726,
Nathaniel Smith; *Jonathan*, b. Dec. 15, 1708, d. Jan. 26, 1709; *Experience*,
b. April 17, 1714, d. Aug. 21, 1714; *Elisha*, b. Sept. 7, 1717.

3. SAMUEL, s. of John, (1) prob. resided in Had. until after 1703, and
then removed. He is named March 19, 1722, in his father's will. He m.
Oct. 14, 1696, Hannah, dau. of Daniel Warner of Hat. She d. June 28, 1699.

4. NATHANIEL, s. of John, (1) is said to have lived to an advanced age.
He m. 1696, Esther Smith. Children—*Esther*, b. July 23, 1697, m. Oct. 14,
1725, Isaac Selden; *Elizabeth*, b. April 6, 1699, m. Sept. 26, 1726, Samuel
Belding of Deerfield; *Abigail*, b. Aug. 24, 1700; *Mercy*, b. April 15, 1702,
m. Oct. 6, 1732, Jonathan Selden; *Ebenezer*, b. Nov. 18, 1703, d. in Amh.,
March 26, 1735. Perhaps he m. Jane, who in 1737 or 1738 m. Robert Rogers;
Nathaniel, b. May 18, 1708; *Hannah*, b. April 14, 1711, m. May 18, 1743,
Dea. Nathaniel Montague; *Jonathan*, b. June 5, 1713; *Sarah*, b. Oct. 2, 1717,
m. Jan. 27, 1740, Charles Chauncey.

5. JOHN, s. of John, (2) Amh., d. Nov. 11, 1737, ae. 45. He m. June 29,
1719, Lydia, dau. of Samuel Boltwood. She d. abt. 1779. Children—*Samuel*,
b. Dec. 18, 1720; *Sarah*, b. Sept. 25, 1725, m. Dec. 9, 1743, Joseph Eastman
of Amh., and d. Aug. 30, 1811, ae. 86; *Philip*, b. Aug. 27, 1727; *John*, b.
Nov. 19, 1730; *Reuben*, b. Nov. 18, 1732; *Ebenezer*, b. May 21, 1737, d.
May 25, 1738.

6. ELISHA, s. of John, (2) Amh., d. May 23, 1783. He m. Aug. 14,
1743, Elizabeth, wid. of Noadiah Lewis of Farmington, Ct., and dau. of
Dea. Ichabod Smith. She prob. d. Oct. 1789. Children—*Anna*, b. June 10,
1744, m. Martin Wait of S. H.; *Elizabeth*, b. Sept. 16, 1746, m. Barnabas
Sabin; *Eunice*, b. Sept. 23, 1748, m. Lieut. —— Williams of Leverett;
Lucy, b. July 22, 1750, m. Perez Moody; *Azubah*, b. April 15, 1752, m. Paul
Newton; *Elenor*, b. Jan. 2, 1754, m. Doct. Moses Gunn of Montague; *Jerusha*,
b. May 7, 1756, m. Dec. 16, 1781, Joseph Kellogg of Amh., and d. Dec. 5,
1824, ae. 69; *Susannah*, b. June 10, 1758, d. Sept. 26, 1760.

7. NATHANIEL, s. of Nathaniel, (4) S. H., m. Nov. 11, 1742, Martha,
dau. of Joseph Kellogg of S. H. Children—*Nathaniel*, b. Aug. 23, 1743;
Sarah, b. Sept. 18, 1745; *Martha*, b. Nov. 23, 1747.

8. JONATHAN, s. of Nathaniel, (4) d. Nov. 12 or 14, 1748, ae. 35. He
m. May 18, 1743, Mary, dau. of John Montague, Jr. Children—*Jonathan*,
b. Jan. 5, 1745; *John*, b. Aug. 9, 1746; *Mary*, b. Nov. 21, 1748.

9. SAMUEL, s. of John, (5) Amh., d. abt. 1769. He m. (1) Oct. 21, 1740,
Abigail, dau. of Dea. Ebenezer Dickinson of Amh.; (2) July 11, 1751, Mary,

dau. of Solomon Boltwood of Amh. She d. abt. 1780. Children—*Lydia*, bapt. Aug. 29, 1744, m. John Morton of Amh., and d. June 21, 1834, ae. 90; *Sarah*, bapt. Aug. 16, 1747, m. Oliver Cooley of Sunderland; *Ebenezer*, bapt. June 19, 1752, d. Oct. 6, 1752; *Abigail*, bapt. Sept. 9, 1753, m. April 3, 1783, Abraham Parker of Whately; *John*, bapt. April 13, 1755, m. Susannah Crocker; *Samuel*, bapt. Jan. 2, 1757, m. June 17, 1783, Jerusha Blodgett; *Mary*, bapt. Feb. 24, 1760, m. Elisha Ellis of Whately; *Elisha*, bapt. June 24, 1764, d. ae. 19; *Hannah*, b. Dec. 18, 1767, m. June 22, 1786, Ebenezer Morton of Hat., and d. Aug. 28, 1848; *Lucretia*, bapt. May 20, 1770, d. unm., ae. abt. 20.

10. PHILIP, s. of John, (5) Amh., m. March 10, 1757, Experience Peirce, prob. wid. of Jonathan, and dau. of Peter Montague of S. H. Children—*Lodeona*, bapt. Oct. 1, 1758; *Philip*, b. April 27, 1760; *Experience*, bapt. Nov. 1, 1761, m. Sept. 29, 1785, Gideon Shattuck, and d. in Ticonderoga, N. Y., Sept. 12, 1837, ae. 76; *William*, bapt. May 15, 1763; *Jonathan Peirce*, bapt. Oct. 12, 1766; *Lucretia* and *Lucinda*, (twins,) bapt. May 22, 1768; *Asa*, bapt. Jan. 27, 1771; *Phebe*, bapt. Aug. 9, 1772; *Roswell*, bapt. July 30, 1775.

11. JOHN, s. of John, (5) Amh., d. Aug. 30, 1809. He m. Feb. 9, 1758, Thankful Rose. Children—*Ebenezer*, m. 1789, Esther Rood; *Gideon*, m. (1) May 1, 1791, Mary, dau. of Dea. Jonathan Edwards of Amh.; (2) Mary King, and d. in Amh., July 1, 1798, ae. 35; *Naomi*, m. Eliab Alvord of Westhampton; *Gershom*, m. Martha Belden; *Oshee; Robert*, m. 1790, Sarah Bolles; *Ezekiel*, rem. to Vt.; *Joab; Peter*, d. young.

12. REUBEN, s. of John, (5) Amh., d. June 16, 1791, ae. 57. He m. 1755, (pub. June 6,) Phebe, dau. of Capt. Daniel Shattuck of Hinsdale, N. H. She was b. Dec. 27, 1729, and d. Aug. 4, 1806. Children—*Joanna*, bapt. May 23, 1756, d. April 9, 1783, ae. 27; *Phebe*, d. Oct. 25, 1767, ae. 8; *David*, bapt. March 6, 1763, d. Jan. 23, 1827; *Jonathan*, bapt. April 21, 1765, d. Oct. 22, 1767, ae. 2; *Nathaniel*, bapt. April 21, 1765, d. March 20, 1776, ae. 11; *Nathan*, bapt. July 30, 1769, d. Feb. 24, 1818, ae. 49; *Phebe; Nathaniel; Sarah.*

13. NATHANIEL, s. of Nathaniel, (7) S. H., d. Aug. 19, 1815. He m. Hannah, who d. July 8, 1838. Children—*Hannah*, b. Feb. 16, 1772, d. March 15, 1797; *Ebenezer*, b. Nov. 3, 1775; *Martha*, b. Feb. 2, 1777; *Nathaniel*, b. March 26, 1779; *Esther*, b. April 19, 1781; *Abigail*, b. July 2, 1784; *Artemas*, b. March 11, 1787, d. 1830; *Alpheus*, b. Oct. 31, 1789; *Warren*, b. Oct. 31, 1793.

14. JONATHAN, s. of Jonathan, (8.) Children—*Jonathan*, b. April, 1779; *Samuel*, b. March, 1781; *Son*, b. April 20, 1783; *Joanna*, bapt. April 17, 1785; *Ira*, bapt. Dec. 31, 1786; *Elisha*, bapt. April 17, 1789.

INGRAM, WILLIAM, m. Jan. 1, 1789, Esther White. Children—*Oliver*, bapt. Sept. 30, 1792; *Experience*, (dau.) bapt. Sept. 30, 1792; *Quartus*, bapt. Nov. 24, 1793; *Charles*, bapt. Jan. 29, 1797; *Child*, b. Nov. 1791; *Child*, b. 1793.

JENNINGS, STEPHEN, freeman 1690, came perhaps from Brookfield to Hat., and returned thither. He m. probably, (2) May 15, 1677, Hannah, wid. of Samuel Gillett, and dau. of John Dickinson of Had. She with two of her Gillett children was in 1667 carried to Canada. Children—*Captivity*,

b. March 14, 1678, m. Abijah Bartlett; *Stephen*, b. June 16, 1680. He or his father was slain by the Indians, July 20, 1710; *Joseph*, b. Aug. 23, 1682; *Sarah*, b. Aug. 29, 1684; *Benjamin*, slain by the Indians, July 20, 1710; *John: Jonathan*, b. Nov. 24, 1692.

JUDD, ASAHEL, b. in Nh., s. of Thomas of Nh., who was s. of Samuel of Nh., who was s. of Dea. Thomas of Cambridge, Hartford, and Windsor, settled in S. H. He was an Ensign in a colonial company in Nova Scotia, in the French war, and d. near Minas, N. S., in 1756. He m. (1) Rachel Wait of Nh., who d. April 26, 1751, in 24th yr.; (2) 1754, (pub. Feb. 3,) Mary Ely of Springfield. She m. (2) —— Sikes. Children—*Simeon*, d. unm., in Nh., Nov. 2, 1826, ae. 77; *Martha*, m. Aaron Bush of Westfield.

1.　JUDD, REUBEN, b. in Nh., 1733, (s. of Thomas of Nh., who was s. of Samuel of Nh., who was s. of Dea. Thomas of Cambridge, 1632, Hartford, 1636, and Farmington, 1644,) settled in S. H., where he d. March 7, 1815, ae. 81. He m. (1) Elizabeth, dau. of Moses White of S. H. She d. May 9, 1765, ae. 24; (2) Elizabeth, dau. of John Smith. She d. March 31, 1781, ae. 31; (3) Dec. 12, 1784, Submit, dau. of Moses Graves of Hat. She d. in Had., Dec. 24, 1830. Children—*Achsah*, b. Oct. 8, 1759, m. abt. 1778, Thomas Wells of Leyden, and d. Jan. 1847, ae. 87; *Reuben*, b. Jan. 10, 1761, m. Nov. 27, 1791, Rachel Smead, and d. in Streetsborough, Portage Co., O.; *Lydia*, b. June 10, 1762, m. Eli Day of Nh., and d. May 8, 1812; *Elizabeth*, b. Jan. 10, 1764; *Salathiel*, b. Aug. 31, 1769; *Elizabeth*, b. Jan. 9, 1771, m. (1) Nov. 29, 1792, Dr. Asahel Merrill of Shelburne; (2) Dec. 22, 1809, Levi Clapp of Easthampton; (3) Asahel Judd of Charlemont; *Lucy*, b. Oct. 28, 1772, d. unm.; *Supplina*, b. Nov. 4, 1774, m. Jan. 26, 1797, Jemima Pooler, rem. to Alleghany Co., N. Y.; *Mahlah*, b. March 26, 1777, m. Luther Stebbins of Caldwell, N. Y.; *Samuel*, b. April 24, 1779; *Tirzah*, b. Feb. 26, 1781, m. —— Beckwith; *Lucinda*, b. Sept. 1785, d. unm. in Had., Oct. 3, 1838, ae. 53; *Mary*, b. Nov. 1787, d. in Chester, ae. abt. 15; *Horace*, b. Oct. 1789.

2.　SALATHIEL, s. of Reuben, (1) rem. to Chester, and d. 1821. He m. Irene, dau. of Abraham Day. She d. in S. H. Children—*Harvey*, b. abt. 1793, d. unm., 1820, ae. 27; *Salathiel*, b. May 3, 1795; *Alfred*, b. April 3, 1798; *Alvin*, b. March, 1800, rem. to Ill., m. Jan. 3, 1822, Eliza White; *Quartus*, m. Jan. 13, 1842, Mrs. Julia M. Crawford, and res. in S. H.; *Theodosia*, m. Daniel Blair of Warren, and rem. to Ill.; *Lucy*, m. James Hamilton of Chester; *Irene*, m. Ira Bacon; *James Madison*, rem. to Ill., m. (1) Aurelia White; *Elizabeth*, m. Andrew Hayward of Hartford, rem. to Ill., and d.

3.　SAMUEL, s. of Reuben, (1) S. H., d. March 2, 1825. He m. Nov. 23, 1800, Fidelia, dau. of Justus Wright. She d. June 17, 1843, ae. 62. Children—*Fidelia*, b. Dec. 13, 1801, d. Sept. 26, 1802; *Samuel*, b. Jan. 25, 1803, d. Dec. 17, 1805; *Fidelia*, b. May 15, 1804, m. Alanson Dickinson of Had., and d. in Michigan, April 15, 1846; *Samuel*, b. May 29, 1806; *twin daughters*, b. and d. Jan. 12, 1808; *Melissa*, b. Jan. 8, 1809, m. Nov. 1827, Asa Clark; *Dorcas*, b. April 5, 1811, m. Josiah W. Goodman; *Andrew Wright*, b. Oct. 29, 1812, drowned July 9, 1823; *Edwin Smith*, b. Sept. 27, 1814, d. at sea, Oct. 29, 1836; *Daniel Austin*, b. April 16, 1816, res. in Springfield; *Albert*, b. June 22, 1818, has changed his name to Albert Judd Wright, is a painter in Boston; *George*, b. April 28, 1820, d. April 15, 1822.

4. HORACE, s. of Reuben, (1) d. in Had., Jan. 4, 1831, ae. 41. He m. abt. 1820, Joanna, dau. of Eli Smith of Had. She m. (2) 1845, Asa Brown of Had. Children—*Henry M.*, d. Sept. 19, 1827, ae. 7; *Martha Smith*, d. Sept. 17, 1827, ae. 5; *Eliza Ann*, b. April, 1825, d. Sept. 1830; *Charles Porter*, b. Sept. 2, 1826, m. Algenette Moody of S. H., and res. in S. H.; *Martha Smith*, b. April 11, 1829; *Lucinda*, b. Dec. 20, 1830, d. Dec. 19, 1844.

5. SALATHIEL, s. of Salathiel, (2) S. H., d. March 28, 1842, ae. 46. He m. Laura Taylor of Chester. Children—*Ellen*, b. Nov. 14, 1819, m. Feb. 14, 1849, Jonathan Burnet, Jr.; *Harvey*, b. Oct. 7, 1822, m. Catharine Kellogg of S. H., and res. in S. H.; *Mary Miller*, b. Jan. 9, 1825, m. Henry M. Goodman; *Lewis Strong*, b. Aug. 19, 1827, m. Nancy Jane Trip of Fair Haven, and res. in S. H.; *Edward Hooker*, b. Dec. 27, 1829, m. Mary Ann Brainard of S. H., and res. in S. H.; *Alfred Salathiel*, b. Sept. 19, 1833, d. Sept. 27, 1848.

6. ALFRED, s. of Salathiel, (2) S. H., m. Oct. 13, 1822, Polly, dau. of Selah Smith of S. H. Child—*Irene Sophia*, b. Jan. 5, 1824, m. 1848, Joseph Strong Preston.

7. SAMUEL, s. of Samuel, (3) rem. abt. 1852, from S. H. to Grand Rapids, Mich. Children—*Emily Sophia*, b. Jan. 27, 1833, d. Aug. 31, 1833; *Samuel Adolphus*, b. May 21, 1834, m. Clarissa Smith of S. H.; *George Edwin*, b. March 23, 1838; *Elliot Eugene* and *Ellen Eugenia*, (twins,) b. Sept. 13, 1841.

1. JUDD, THOMAS, b. in Nh. 1723, s. of Thomas of Nh., who was s. of Samuel of Nh., who was s. of Dea. Thomas of Cambridge, 1632, Hartford, 1636, and Farmington, 1644, res. in S. H., and d. Dec. 21, 1802, in 80th yr. He m. (1) 1749, (pub. Oct. 26,) Esther Jones of Springfield. She d. Jan. 8, 1760, in 35th yr.; (2) Esther, dau. of Daniel Graves of Greenfield. She d. May 30, 1772, in 38th yr.; (3) Thankful, dau. of John Allen of Greenfield. She d. Feb. 9, 1775, in 39th yr.; (4) Ruth Taylor of West Springfield. She d. Nov. 16, 1793, in 57th yr. Children—*Thomas*, b. Nov. 11, 1750; *Levi*, b. Jan. 15, 1753, d. young; *Esther*, b. Jan. 4, 1755, m. Joseph Bascom of Greenfield; *Asahel*, b. Sept. 4, 1757, d. young; *Silva*, b. March 10, 1764, m. Luther Smith of S. H.; *Levi*, b. Oct. 27, 1765; *Asahel*, b. Sept. 28, 1767, d. abt. 1852, in Charlemont. He m. (1) Dec. 18, 1790, Azubah, dau. of Josiah Snow; (2) Sept. 21, 1795, Margaret, dau. of Capt. Thomas Lothrop of Martha's Vineyard; (3) his cousin Elizabeth, wid. of Levi Clapp of Easthampton, and dau. of Reuben Judd of S. H.; *Elijah*, b. June 29, 1769; *Allen*, b. Jan. 25, 1775.

2. THOMAS, s. of Thomas, (1) S. H., d. March, 1813. He m. Hannah Stanley of S. H. She d. Dec. 5, 1841. Children—*Sarah*, b. Oct. 22, 1784, m. May 18, 1826, Seth Smith of Gr.; *Simeon*, b. March 9, 1786; *Hannah*, b. July 27, 1788, d. unm., Feb. 1848; *Lydia*, b. May 2, 1790, d. July 6, 1791; *Lydia*, b. Feb. 3, 1792, d. unm., Jan. 1848; *Sophia*, b. June 26, 1794, d. unm., in Gr., Feb. 11 or 16, 1841; *Tirzah*.

3. LEVI, s. of Thomas, (1) deacon in S. H., whence in April, 1827, he rem. to Geneva, N. Y., and d. Sept. 1829. He m. 1786, Lucy, dau. of Josiah Snow of S. H. She m. Dea. Wilder of Geneva, N. Y., and d. there, June, 1846. Children—*Zebina*, b. Sept. 24, 1787; *Ruth*, b. July 7, 1789; *Lucy*,

b. Aug. 21, 1791, m. Halsey Brainard of S. H.; *Azubah*, b. Nov. 1, 1793, m.
Oct. 2, 1821, Smith Kentfield, and res. in Ohio; *Levi*, b. Feb. 18, 1796, m.
Jan. 25, 1820, Elvira Taylor, and rem. to Waterloo, N. Y., but d. in Geneva,
N. Y.; *Hervey*, b. April 7, 1798; *Nabby*, b. Oct. 26, 1800, m. Moses C. Wright;
Milton, b. Nov. 17, 1802, m. Theodocia Thompson, and settled in Geneva,
N. Y.; *Thomas*, b. April 4, 1805, m. Mary Ann Brewster, and moved to
Fredonia, N. Y.; *Lorenzo*, b. April, 1807, d. July, 1807.

4. ELIJAH, s. of Thomas, (1) res. in S. H., Charlemont and Gr., and d.
March 7, 1837. He m. (1) May 3, 1795, Elizabeth, dau. of Josiah Snow of
S. H.; (2) Wid. Lucy Tufts, dau. of Benjamin Smith. Children—*Quartus*,
b. Nov. 21, 1795, d. in S. H., of consumption; *Betsey*, b. Sept. 14, 1797, d. in
Gr., of consumption; *Esther*, b. May 24, 1799, d. in Gr. of consumption;
Jemima, b. March 12, 1801, d. in Gr. of consumption; *Cordelia*, b. March 16,
1803, m. Algernon Sidney Bartlett, and d. of consumption; *Elijah*, b. Feb. 20,
1805, d. in Geneva, N. Y.; *Josiah*, b. Feb. 28, 1807, res. in Wisconsin;
Climene, b. July 22, 1809, m. —— Burt of Springfield; *Sylvester*, b. Aug. 24,
1811, res. in Collinsville, Ct.; *Jonathan Jones*, b. Jan. 25, 1814, res. in Wis.

5. ALLEN, s. of Thomas, (1) S. H., d. Aug. 26, 1828. He m. Jan. 2,
1797, Sarah, dau. of Ebenezer Snow.   Children—*Willard*, b. Dec. 26, 1797;
Otis, b. March 16, 1800, d. Nov. 3, 1826; *Sally*, b. May 20, 1802; *Allen*, b.
March 14, 1804, res. in Chicopee; *William*, b. April 3, 1807, d. young; *Asaph*,
b. Jan. 22, 1810; *Thankful*.

6. SIMEON, s. of Thomas, (2) S. H., m. Lydia, dau. of Eli Day of Nh.
Children—*Alethea Day*, b. Sept. 30, 1823, m. Elam Hitchcock of South-
ampton; *Andrew Thomas*, b. Feb. 9, 1826, m. June 26, 1851, Sarah H. Day;
Lydia, b. July 24, 1828, m. Levi Stockwell of Had.

7. ZEBINA, s. of Levi, (3) S. H., m. Nov. 23, 1812, Laura, dau. of Silas
Smith.   Children—*Zebina*, b. Feb. 23, 1814, m. Eliza Turner, and rem.
to Fredonia, N. Y.; *Warren Smith*, b. March 27, 1816, d. Oct. 23, 1817;
Warren Smith, b. Sept. 6, 1820, m. Jerusha Dickinson of Had.; *Henry Holden*,
b. Oct. 30, 1822, m. Mary Bonney of Had., and res. in S. H.; *Lucy Asenath*,
b. March 30, 1826, m. Oliver Bonney of Had.

8. HERVEY, s. of Levi, (3) S. H., was killed in his cellar, by lightning,
Aug. 8, 1853, ae. 55. He m. Maria Alvord of Nh.   Children—*Harriet Maria*,
b. Jan. 26, 1827; *Edwin Hervey*, b. June 20, 1828, m. Elvira Thorp; *Levi
Harrison*, b. Oct. 29, 1829; *Twins*, b. Aug. 27, 1833, d. Aug. 31, 1833;
Samuel Emerson, b. Oct. 5, 1835, d. May 9, 1836; *Louisa Irene*, b. Nov. 23,
1836; *John Dwight*, b. Nov. 4, 1840, d. young.

9. WILLARD, s. of Allen, (5) S. H., m. Sophia Searl of Norwich. Children — *Otis Allen*, b. Sept. 6, 1829, m. Celia Thorp; *Elizabeth Sophia*,
b. Sept. 12, 1831, m. March 14, 1851, George White of Had.; *Henry W.*, b.
Nov. 20, 1833; *Watson S.*, b. Oct. 20, 1835; *Sarah Ellen*, b. Sept. 15, 1837;
Child, b. and d. Dec. 13, 1840; *John Dwight*, b. May 8, 1843.

10. ASAPH, s. of Allen, (5) S. H., d. June 8, 1856, ae. 46. He m. Lucretia,
dau. of John Bates of Westhampton. She d. May, 1855.   Children—
Frances Jane, b. Jan. 22, 1836; *William Asaph*, b. March 4, 1838; *John
Harrison*, b. April 7, 1840.

1. KELLOGG, JOSEPH, weaver, of Farmington, Ct., in 1651, rem. as early as 1659 to Boston, and thence as early as 1662 to Hadley, where he was a lieutenant and often one of the selectmen. He d. ae. abt. 80, in 1707 or 1708, as appears from the fact, that his will dated 1707, was proved Feb. 4, 1708. He m. (1) Joanna ——, who d. Sept. 14, 1666; (2) May 9, 1667, Abigail, dau. of Stephen Terry of Windsor, Ct. She was living as late as 1714, at which date she gave land to her son Ebenezer. Children—*Elizabeth*, b. March 5, 1651, d. young; *Joseph*, b. Aug. 11, 1653, d. between 1680 and 1684; *Nathaniel*, bapt. Oct. 29, 1654, d. young; *John*, bapt. Dec. 29, 1656; *Martin;* *Edward*, b. Oct. 1, 1660; *Samuel*, b. Sept. 28, 1662; *Joanna*, b. Dec. 8, 1664, m. Nov. 29, 1683, John Smith; *Sarah*, b. Aug. 27, 1666, m. April 27, 1686, Samuel Ashley of Westfield; *Stephen*, b. April 9, 1668; *Nathaniel*, b. Oct. 8, 1669; *Abigail*, b. Oct. 9, 1671, m. Nov. 14, 1688, Jonathan Smith of Hat.; *Elizabeth*, b. Oct. 9, 1673, m. Nov. 27, 1691, John Nash; *Prudence*, b. Oct. 14, 1675, m. April 18, 1699, Dea. Abraham Merrill of West Hartford, Ct., and d. Sept. 21, 1747, ae. 71; *Ebenezer*, b. Nov. 22, 1677, rem. to Colchester, Ct., as early as 1726; *Jonathan*, b. Dec. 25, 1679, rem. to Colchester, Ct., and d. Aug. 8, 1771, ae. 91; *Daniel*, b. March 22, 1682, d. July 5, 1684; *Joseph*, b. April or May 12, 1684, res. in Hat., and d. s. p., Sept. 9, 1724, ae. 40. He m. July 5, 1710, Elizabeth Colton. She m. Joseph Billings; *Daniel*, b. June 10, 1686, d. young; *Ephraim*, b. —— 2, 1687, d. young.

2. JOHN, s. of Joseph, (1) d. between 1723 and 1728. He m. (1) Dec. 23, 1680, Sarah, dau. of Samuel Moody. She d. Sept. 10, 1689; m. (2) Ruth ——, who was alive in 1732. Children—*Sarah*, b. May 2, 1682; *John*, b. March 21, 1684, d. March, 1691; *Joseph*, b. Nov. 6, 1685; *Samuel*, b. April 1, 1687, res. in Westfield; *Son*, b. and d. Sept. 9, 1689; *Ruth*, b. April 5, 1693, d. Nov. 15, 1705; *Joanna*, b. June 12, 1694, m. 1719, Samuel Taylor; *Esther*, b. Feb. 17, 1696; *Abigail*, b. Sept. 20, 1697, m. (1) Feb. 14, 1729, Jonathan Atherton; (2) Jan. 24, 1745, Isaac Hubbard of Sunderland; *John*, b. Oct. 1699, d. June 10, 1727, ae. 28; *James*, b. July 10, 1701.

3. MARTIN, s. of Joseph, (1) Hat., whence he afterwards rem. to Hat., and later to Suffield, Ct. He m. (1) Dec. 10, 1684, Anna, dau. of Samuel Hinsdale. She d. July 19, 1689, ae. 23; (2) Feb. 27, 1691, Sarah, wid. of Samuel Lane, and dau. of John Dickinson. She d. Feb. 11, 1732; (3) Oct. 5, 1732, Sarah, wid. of Ebenezer Smith of Suffield, and dau. of Thomas Huxley of Suffield. Children—*Martin*, b. Oct. 26, 1686, res. in Newington, Ct., and d. Nov. 15, 1753, ae. 67. He m. Jan. 3, 1716, Dorothy, dau. of Stephen Chester of Wethersfield, Ct. She was b. Sept. 5, 1692; *Anna*, b. July 14, 1689, m. 1712, Joseph Severance; *Joseph*, b. Nov. 8, 1691, an Indian interpreter, was for several years at Fort Dummer, was at the Albany treaty in 1754, and d. in 1756 on the Oswego expedition. He was buried in Schenectady, N. Y.; *Joanna*, b. Feb. 8, 1693, was captured in 1704, by French and Indians, and married an Indian chief in Canada; *Rebecca*, b. Dec. 22, 1695, m. Benjamin Ashley of Westfield, and d. 1757, at Onohogwage; *Jonathan*, b. Dec. 17, 1698.

4. EDWARD, s. of Joseph, (1) rem. abt. 1713, to Brookfield. He m. Dorothy. Children—*Joseph*, b. Oct. 29, 1692, d. July 22, 1709; *Joanna*, b. Oct. 5, 1694; *Thomas*, b. Dec. 17, 1696; *Dorothy*, b. March 6, 1700; *Catha-*

rine, b. Feb. 1, 1702; *Mary*, b. March 29, 1703; *Ephraim*, b. April 19, 1707, sold in 1729, to Thomas Kellogg of Lebanon, Ct., all lands in Brookfield; *Elinor*, b. Jan. 20, 1710; *Edward*, b. Aug. 25, 1713, sold in 1729, to Thomas Kellogg of Lebanon, Ct., all lands in Brookfield.

5. SAMUEL, s. of Joseph, (1) a deacon in Hartford, Ct., d. 1717. He m. Sept. 22, 1687, Sarah Merrill, who d. 1719. Children—*Samuel*, b. —— 27, 1688, m. May 11, 1711, Hannah Benton; *Margaret*, b. Jan. 1690; *Abraham*, b. 1692, m. 1718, Miriam Cook, and d. 1718; *John*, b. Dec. 16, 169–; *Isaac*, b. Jan. 169–; *Jacob*, b. April 17; *Benjamin*, b. Jan., m. Nov. 9, 1721, Abigail Sedgwick; *Joseph*, b. April 13; *Daniel*, b. Apr., m. Nov. 27, 1729, Deborah Moor.

6. STEPHEN, s. of Joseph, (1) removed in 1697 from Had. to Westfield, where he d. June 5, 1722. He m. May 8, 1695, Lydia Belding. Children— *Stephen*, b. Feb. 3, 1695; *Lydia*, b. Jan. 24, 1697, perhaps m. Jan. 17, 1734, Benjamin Lewis of Colchester, Ct.; *Moses*, b. Oct. 26, 1700, d. Sept. 15, 1704; *Abigail*, b. Dec. 27, 1702, m. Benjamin Sheldon; *Daniel*, b. Dec. 16, 1704, m. May 13, 1731, Hannah, dau. of Matthew Noble of Westfield, and d. Jan. 11, 1756; *Ephraim*, b. July 2, 1707, prob. m. 1737, Lydia ——, res. in Northfield, Shutesbury, &c., and was slain 1759, in Capt. Smith's Co.; *Mercy*, b. Oct. 30, 1709; *Noah*, b. Feb. 13, 1711; *Silas*, b. April 7, 1714, m. May 10, 1739, Ruth Root, and d. in Sheffield, Jan. 24, 1792, ae. 77; *Amos*, b. Sept. 30, 1716, m. May 27, 1747, Prudence Sedgwick, and d. in Sheffield, Nov. 26, 1770, ae. 54.

7. NATHANIEL, s. of Joseph, (1) rem. abt. 1739 to Amh., and d. Oct. 30, 1750, ae. 80. He m. June 28, 1692, Sarah, dau. of Samuel Boltwood. She was living Jan. 26, 1761. Children—*Nathaniel*, b. Sept. 22, 1693; *Ebenezer*, b. May 31, 1695; *Ezekiel*, b. April 15, 1697; *Samuel*, b. April 4, 1699; *Sarah*, b. March 12, 1701, m. May 26, 1720, Ebenezer Dickinson of Amh., and d. March 22, 1743; *Abigail*, b. March 19, 1703, m. Sept. 7, 1726, Benjamin Sheldon of Westfield; *Mary*, b. March 9, 1706, m. Nov. 14, 1732, Doct. Richard Crouch, and d. Dec. 29, 1788, ae. 82; *Ephraim*, b. Aug. 2, 1709; *Experience*, m. Oct. 15, 1736, Timothy Nash of Shutesbury.

8. JOSEPH, s. of John, (2) rem. to S. H. His son John was appointed his administrator in 1788, several years after his death. He m. March 15, 1711, Abigail, dau. of Ebenezer Smith. Children—*Abigail*, b. Dec. 8, 1711; *Sarah*, b. Jan. 8, 1714, prob. m. Joseph Moody; *Ebenezer*, b. Dec. 26, 1715; *Ruth*, b. Jan. 18, 1717, m. Dec. 21, 1739, Benjamin Church; *Martha*, b. May 21, 1720, m. Nov. 11, 1742, Nathaniel Ingram; *Esther*, b. Sept. 19, 1722; *Joseph*, b. Dec. 24, 1724; *John*, b. Oct. 13, 1727.

9. JAMES, s. of John, (2) d. July 15, 1758, ae. 57. He m. Aug. 11, 1727, Experience, dau. of Dea. John Smith. She d. Aug. 23, 1762. Children— *John*, d. unm., Sept. 7, 1771, in 41st yr.; *Experience*, m. July 21, 1772, Eli Root; *Ruth*, m. 1757, (pub. Dec. 27,) Joshua Ballard, and d. 1776; *Jemima*, m. Feb. 23, 1769, Stephen Nash, Jr., of Stockbridge, and d. Feb. 17, 1790, ae. 53; *Jerusha*, m. Nov. 14, 1771, Eliakim Smith; *Joanna*, m. 1765, (pub. Feb. 28,) Stephen Goodman, and d. 1831, ae. 89; *Mercy*, prob. m. Sept. 18, 1777, Peter Strong of Chesterfield.

10. STEPHEN, s. of Stephen, (6) a trader and innkeeper, d. Dec. 11, 1738. He m. June 18, 1734, Mary, dau. of Moses Cook. She m. (2) Oct. 30, 1744, Moses Nash of West Hartford, Ct., and d. Sept. 21, 1775. Children—*Stephen*, b. July 2, 1736, d. Dec. 1738; *Abigail*, b. Aug. 10, 1738, m. 1757, Ashbel Wells of West Hartford, Ct.

11. NATHANIEL, s. of Nathaniel, (7) was a noted surveyor, and d. Aug. 6, 1770. He m. (1) March 4, 1714, Sarah, dau. of John Preston. She d. Oct. 16, 1756; (2) 1758, (pub. July 1,) Mrs. Martha Hammond of Hardwick, dau. of Ichabod Allis of Hat. She d. Sept. 13, 1764; (3) 1765, (pub. Oct. 5,) Mrs. Elizabeth Smith of Ware. Children—*Daniel*, b. abt. 1717; *Joel*, b. abt. 1724, res. in Whately, and d. 1798, ae. 74. He m. 1748, (pub. Aug. 7,) Joanna, dau. of Samuel Clark of Nh.; *Abraham; Gardner; Moses; Prudence*, b. abt. 1723, m. June 27, 1751, Josiah Parsons, Jr., of Nh., and d. June 27, 1791, ae. 68; *Phebe*, m. Nov. 9, 1749, Eleazar Nash of Gr., and d. abt. 1777; *Sarah*, d. unm.; *Nathaniel*, d. Nov. 8, 1756; *Abigail*, d. Oct. 15, 1756.

12. EBENEZER, s. of Nathaniel, (7) was a captain, res. in Had., Amh., New Salem and Stow, and d. in Had., at the house of his sister, Mrs. Crouch, Aug. 17, 1766. He m. (1) Dec. 13, 1716, Elizabeth, wid. of Philip Panthorn, and dau. of John Ingram; (2) 1756, (pub. Sept. 18,) Mrs. Sarah Stevens of Stow. Children—*Martin*, b. Sept. 24, 1718; *Ebenezer*.

13. EZEKIEL, s. of Nathaniel, (7) was a trader in Had, and New Salem. He m. Elizabeth, dau. of Samuel Partridge. Children—*Elizabeth*, d. 1726, ae. 2; *Dau.*, d. 1725; *Maria*, d. 1726; *Ezekiel*, b. Sept. 22, 1728; *Cotton*, b. Nov. 2, 1732, d. unm., 1756; *Giles Crouch*, b. May 7, 1733, grad. H. C. 1751, a physician in Had., d. Aug. 28, 1793; *William*, b. Feb. 1, 1739; *Samuel*, b. Feb. 1, 1739; *Elizabeth*, b. Dec. 20, 1740, d. unm.

14. SAMUEL, s. of Nathaniel, (7) S. H., d. abt. May, 1741. He m. May 22, 1724, Sarah, dau. of Dea. John Smith. She m. (2) Jan. 1749, William Montague. Children—*Samuel*, b. March 17, 1725, m. June 22, 1751, Mary Nash, and d. in Westfield, Jan. 19, 1777; *Joanna*, d. Dec. 19, 1756; *Gad, Dan; Huldah*, d. Oct. 3, 1756; *Mary; Lucy; Sarah*, d. June 12, 1747.

15. EPHRAIM, s. of Nathaniel, (7) Amh., d. March 16, 1777, ae. 67. He m. May 1, 1741, Dorothy, dau. of Samuel Hawley of Amh. She d. July 26, 1812, ae. 89. Children—*Ephraim*, bapt. Jan. 3, 1742; *Martin*, bapt. Jan. 8, 1744; *Dorothy*, bapt. Feb 23, 1746, m. William Field of Leverett, and d. Aug. 1, 1773, ae. 27; *Abigail*, bapt. Oct. 16, 1748, m. (1) Ezra Rood; (2) Feb. 12, 1801, John Pynchon of Springfield, and d. March 1, 1836, ae. 87; *John*, bapt. April, 1751, d. May 15, 1753; *Sarah*, bapt. Oct. 7, 1753, m. Sept. 6, 1773, Jonathan Field of Leverett; *Joseph*, b. Nov. 28, 1758.

16. EBENEZER, s. of Joseph, (8) S. H., m. Dec. 15, 1748, Sarah Snow. Children—*Amos*, b. Oct. 1, 1749; *Lois*, b. March 4, 1752; *Sarah*, b. Aug. 25, 1754; *Seth*, b. Sept. 5, 1767.

17. JOSEPH, s. of Joseph, (8) S. H., d. Oct. 14, 1810, ae. 83. He m. Dorothy Taylor. She d. Aug. 26, 1803. Children—*Eli*, b. June 2, 1757, res. in S. H.; *Eliakim*, b. Sept. 10, 1759, res. in S. H.; *Elijah*, b. Aug. 17, 1761; *Joseph*, b. May 1, 1773.

18. DANIEL, s. of Nathaniel, (11) Amh., d. Jan. 14, 1799. He m. (1) 1751, (pub. Sept. 21,) Esther, dau. of John Smith of S. H. She d. Dec. 18,

1756; (2) 1758, (pub. April 15,) Thankful, wid. of Joseph Hawley of Amh., and dau. of —— Alexander; (3) Sarah, dau. of Josiah Parsons of Nh. She was b. May 29, 1723, and d. Feb. 26, 1807. Children—*Daniel*, bapt. July 26, 1752; *Aaron*, bapt. Nov. 16, 1755, grad. Y. C. 1778, was deranged, and d. unm., in Amh., Dec. 11, 1830, ae. 76; *David*, bapt. Nov. 16, 1755; *Jonathan*, bapt. Nov. 16, 1755, d. young.

19. ABRAHAM, s. of Nathaniel, (11) Amh., prob. removed before his death to Leverett. He m. Dec. 7, 1758, Sarah, dau. of Jonathan Cowls of Amh. She d. in Leverett, Oct. 26, 1819. Children—*Sybil*, b. Sept. 24, 1761, m. Oct. 6, 1785, Enos Graves of Leverett; *Sarah*, bapt. April 15, 1764; *Samuel*, bapt. May 20, 1770, m. Hannah Marsh, and rem. to Waterbury, Vt; *Abraham*, bapt. Dec. 13, 1772.

20. GARDNER, s. of Nathaniel, (11) d. Oct. 6, 1814. He m. Thankful Chapin of West Springfield. She d. Feb. 24, 1805. Children—*Nathaniel*, C. Oct. 1, 1763; *Gardner*, b. Sept. 22, 1765, grad. Y. C. 1791, was a clergyman in Bradford, N. H., and in Me.; *Josiah*, b. July 15, 1767; *Lucy*, b. Nov. 2, 1769, m. June 27, 1819, Henry Chapin of Springfield, and d. Dec. 10, 1843.

21. MOSES, s. of Nathaniel, (11) d. May 28, 1815, ae. 82. He m. April 3, 1758, Mary Sheldon of Sheffield, who d. Dec. 22, 1812, ae. 75. Children—*Whiting; Moses*, b. Feb. 16, 1761; *Benjamin*, b. Aug. 7, 1763; *Polly*, b. 1766, d. unm., Aug. 1785; *Abigail Sheldon*, bapt. Nov. 4, 1768, m. Feb. 9, 1796, Elisha Belding of Whately; *Experience*, bapt. May 12, 1771, m. Feb. 2, 1797, Aristobulus Smith, and d. 1854; *Electa*, b. Nov. 1773, m. 1822, Elisha Wait; *Samuel*, bapt. Nov. 9, 1777.

22. EBENEZER, s. of Ebenezer, (12) Amh., d. at Fort Independence in the Revolutionary war. He m. Jan. 13, 1751, Sarah, dau. of Preserved Clapp of Amh. She was b. Oct. 4, 1733. She m. (2) April 23, 1778, John Nash of Amh. Children—*Sarah*, bapt. May 13, 1753, m. Joseph Bolles; *Ebenezer*, bapt. July 14, 1754, m. (1) Elizabeth Crocker; *Jonathan*, bapt. Oct. 24, 1760; *Betsey*, m. Reuben Dickinson, Jr. of Amh.

23. EPHRAIM, s. of Ephraim, (15) Amh., d. Jan. 29, 1815. He m. Esther ——, who d. Nov. 30, 1823. Children—*John; Ephraim*, m. April 7, 1791, Martha, dau. of Lt. David Smith of Amh., and removed to Weybridge, Vt., and thence to Malone, N. Y.; *Electa*, m. Jan. 15, 1789, Nathaniel Bangs, and removed to New Salem; *Esther*, m. Dec. 21, 1785, Elijah Prouty; *Elijah*, m. Hannah Herrick, rem. to Weybridge, Vt., and thence to the State of New York; *Elisha*, rem. to Weybridge, Vt.; *David*, m. (1) —— Ashley; (2) Submit, dau. of David Blodgett, Jr., and rem. to Weybridge, Vt., and thence to Malone, N. Y.; *Joel*, b. abt. 1780, m. Elizabeth Alexander of Deerfield, and d. in Amh., June 27, 1827, ae. 47; *Philomela*, m. Feb. 27, 1810, Elisha Smead of Weybridge, Vt.

24. MARTIN, s. of Ephraim, (15) Amh., d. Nov. 7, 1827, ae. 84. He m. (1) Hannah, dau. of Zaccheus Crocker of Shutesbury. She d. Aug. 9, 1812, ae. 69; (2) Lucy, wid. of Samuel Hastings, and dau. of Simeon Pomeroy. She d. Dec. 23, 1839, ae. 87. Children—*Sylvanus*, bapt. Sept. 24, 1769, d. Nov. 30, 1774; *Elizabeth*, b. 1771, d. Dec. 4, 1774, ae. 3 yrs.; *Dorothy*, bapt. March 20, 1774, m. Chester Hubbard, and rem. to Wilmington, Vt.; *Betsey*, bapt. May 26, 1776, d. Feb. 15, 1814; *Martin*, b. Oct. 27, 1778, m.

Oct. 31, 1799, Hannah, dau. of Thomas Hastings, and d. in Had., April 14, 1856; *Bela*, b. Aug. 24, 1780; *Clarissa*, bapt. Feb. 2, 1783, m. June 13, 1804; Otis Hastings, and rem. to Weybridge, Vt.; *Hannah Crocker*, bapt. June 23, 1786, m. Aug. 6, 1807, Otis Cady of Bolton, Ct., and d. Feb. 1839; *Sarah Beals*, bapt. July 23, 1786, m. Samuel Morgan; *Achsah*, bapt. May 30, 1790, m. Dec. 10, 1812, Thomas Barnes.

25. JOSEPH, s. of Ephraim, (15) Amh., d. March 11, 1838, ae. 79. He m. Dec. 16, 1781, Jerusha, dau. of Elisha Ingram of Amh. She d. Dec. 5, 1824, ae. 69. Children—*Dau.*, b. and d. 1782; *William*, b. May 12, 1784, m. Susanna Ingram of Amh.; *Mary*, b. July 25, 1785, m. Luke Wait of Whately, and d. Feb. 19, 1827; *Joseph*, b. July 16, 1786, m. (1) Nov. 28, 1809, Joanna, dau. of John Kellogg of Amh., and res. in Amh.; *Lucy*, b. Oct. 25, 1788, m. Feb. 26, 1810, Rufus Crafts of Whately; *Rufus*, b. July, 1794, m. June 22, 1820, Nancy Stetson, and d. in Amh., April 9, 1845, ae. 48; *Jerusha Ingram*, b. Oct. 13, 1798, d. June 27, 1826, ae. 27.

26. DANIEL, s. of Daniel, (18) Amh., d. March 1, 1826, ae. 73. He m. Dec. 15, 1778, Mercy, dau. of Joseph Eastman of Amh., and d. Jan. 12, 1823, ae. 68. Children—*Sarah*, d. Feb. 25, 1786; *Esther Smith*, bapt. March 6, 1780, m. Feb. 22, 1802, Martin Field, Esq., of Newfane, Vt., in which place she now (June, 1862) resides; *Mercy*, bapt. Sept. 22, 1782, m. Alden Cooley; *Sally*, bapt. Dec. 6, 1787; *Rufus*, bapt. Nov. 23, 1788, d. in Amh., Dec. 2, 1833, ae. 45. He m. (1) Esther Mayo of Orange. She d. April 18, 1813, ae. 28; (2) Oct. 26, 1815, Abigail Chamberlain. She d. May 8, 1824, ae. 33; (3) Mary Smith of Had.; *Daniel*, bapt. Feb. 13, 1791, grad. W. C. 1810, res. in Brattleboro', Vt., and was for many years one of the Judges of the Supreme Court of Vt.; *Charles*, bapt. Dec. 9, 1792, m. Oct. 29, 1812, Tryphena, dau. of Caleb Hubbard of Sunderland, and d. in Amh., June 20, 1834, ae. 42; *Henry*, b. Dec. 10, 1794, grad. Y. C. 1815, is a lawyer in Bennington, Vt., and m. (1) Jan. 27, 1825, Margaret V. D. S. Hubbell; (2) Oct. 16, 1831, Ann Maria Hubbell.

27. DAVID, D. D., s. of Daniel, (18) grad. D. C. 1775, studied divinity with Rev. David Parsons of Amh., was ordained Jan. 10, 1781, as pastor of the Cong. church in Framingham, and remained pastor of the same until abt. 1830. He d. April 13, 1843, ae. 87. He received the degree of Doctor of Divinity from his Alma Mater in 1824. He m. May 27, 1781, Sally Bridge, who d. Feb. 14, 1826, ae. 73. Children—*Mary*, b. Feb. 25, 1782, m. July 19, 1801, Dr. John Ball Kittredge, and d. Aug. 20, 1836; *Sally*, b. Sept. 28, 1783, m. May 9, 1808, Dea. William Brown, Jr., of Boston; *Nancy*, b. July 16, 1785; *Gardner*, b. Aug. 20, 1788, m. Wid. —— Fairbanks, and d. April 29, 1842; *Martha*, bapt. May, 1787; *David*, bapt. April, 1791; *Charles*, bapt. April, 1793.

28. NATHANIEL, s. of Gardner, (20) m. (1) —— Drake of Buckland; (2) Wid. —— Moody of Amh. Children — *Nathaniel; Chloe; Roswell; Molly; Gardner; Charles Austin.*

29. JOSIAH, s. of Gardner, (20) m. Hannah Smith of Ashfield. Children— *Thankful*, b. Sept. 8, 1795, m. Sylvester Cook; *Merub*, b. July 4, 1797, d. Sept. 30, 1788; *Lucy*, b. April 26, 1799, d. ae. abt. 15; *Diathena*, b. Feb. 12, 1801; *Naomi Parsons*, b. Jan. 26, 1803, m. Thaddeus Chapin; *Josiah*, b. Feb.

17, 1805, m. Cynthia Chapin; *John Preston*, bapt. March 22, 1806; *Gardner; Merub*, m. —— Rice; *Priscilla.*

30. WHITING, s. of Moses, (21) res. in Ashfield and Montgomery, but d. in Had., Jan. 16, 1838. He m. Elizabeth Cross of Ashfield. Children— *Spencer*, d. young; *Richard*, m. —— Hatch of West Springfield; *Elizabeth*, m. Daniel Stearns, and rem. to Wisconsin; *Emily*, d. young.

31. BENJAMIN, s. of Moses, (21) d. July 25, 1811, ae. 48. He m. Dec. 11, 1788, Patty, dau. of Wareham Smith. She d. Nov. 20, 1835, ae. 67. Children—*Marma*, b. Sept. 12, 1789, m. Seth M. Warner of Sunderland; *Horace*, b. Sept. 16, 1791, m. Aug. 12, 1813, Almira, dau. of Joel Smith, and d. in Amh., Oct. 4, 1858, ae. 67; *Amelia*, b. Dec. 25, 1795, d. Sept. 8, 1828, ae. 32; *Elizabeth*, b. Oct. 11, 1798, d. unm. April 8, 1861; *Martha*, b. June 7, 1801; *Mary*, b. Jan. 1804, d. Aug. 18, 1805; *Sarah*, b. Aug. 25, 1806, d. April 7, 1807; *Charles Austin*, b. April 29, 1808, m. Maria Cook; *Angeline*, b. Feb. 18, 1811.

32. JONATHAN, s. of Ebenezer, (22) shoemaker in Amh., d. Feb. 28, 1823, ae. 62. He m. June 5, 1783, Mary Holland of Pelham. She d. March 5, 1823. Children—*Ira*, res. in Montague; *Chester*, b. Jan. 21, 1788, a shoemaker in Amh., d. Jan. 7, 1849, ae. 61. He m. (1) June, 1808, Lois, dau. of Silas Dickinson of Amh. She d. Dec. 13, 1809; (2) Aug. 1, 1816, Maria, dau. of Rufus Bixbee of Amh.; *David*, res. in Granby.

33. JOHN, s. of Ephraim, (23) Amh., was a deacon in First church, and d. Dec. 6, 1844, ae. 79. He m. (1) Roxana, dau. of Ebenezer Mattoon. She d. Sept. 2, 1804; (2) Mrs. Martha Ingram. She d. May 10, 1837. Children—*John*, b. May 31, 1786, a lawyer in Benson, Vt., m. (1) Harriet Nash; (2) May 6, 1847, Ame Stoughton, wid. of Jonathan Dickinson, and dau. of John Dickinson, all of Amh.; *Son and dau.*, (twins,) b. and d. Jan. 31, 1788; *Joanna*, b. Jan. 4, 1789, m. Nov. 28, 1809, Joseph Kellogg of Amh., and d. Dec. 19, 1852; *Prudence*, b. Feb. 7, 1791, m. Oct. 27, 1814, Samuel James; *Elizabeth*, b. April 27, 1795, m. Jan. 26, 1820, Hon. Ithamar Conkey of Amh.; *Roxa Mattoon*, b. Dec. 24, 1797, m. Dec. 13, 1818, William Field of Leverett; *Eleazar*, b. March 16, 1800; *Stillman*, b. May 31, 1802, d. April 14, 1832, ae. 29; *Charles*, b. March 31, 1804, d. Oct. 1, 1804; *Henry*, b. March 31, 1804, d. April 16, 1805.

34. BELA, s. of Martin, (24) grad. W. C. 1800, studied theology with Rev. Nathaniel Emmons, D. D. of Franklin, was ordained 1813 over the (Cong.) church in Brookfield, Ct., dismissed 1817, ord. in Avon, Ct., 1819, dis. 1830, on account of ill health, and d. April 30, 1831. He m. June 6, 1805, Lydia, dau. of Samuel Candee. She was b. in New Haven, Ct., Nov. 1, 1778, and d. in Avon, Dec. 3, 1843, ae. 65. Children—*Cordelia*, b. March 17, 1806, m. Dr. Alfred Kellogg, and d. April 30, 1831; *M. A.*, b. April 23, 1808, m. April 30, 1829, Marilla Cooley of Hartford, Ct., and res. in Philadelphia, Pa.; *Bela C.*, b. April 27, 1811, m. Oct. 15, 1839, Mary G., dau. of Rev. John Bartlett of West Avon, Ct., and res. in Avon; *Lucius Storrs*, b. Oct. 6, 1813, d. June 21, 1822; *Cynthia Amelia*, b. Dec. 12, 1815, m. Dec. 12, 1838, Rev. James Kilbourn of Sandwich, De Kalb Co., Ill.; *Mary Elizabeth*, b. Sept. 18, 1821, m. Sept. 1843, E. M. Woodford of West Avon, Ct.; *Martha L.*, b. Dec. 9, 1823.

KELLOGG, GILES CROUCH, b. Aug. 12, 1781, grad. Y. C. 1800, read law with Jonathan E. Porter, Esq., was admitted to the bar in Hampshire County, opened an office in Hadley, and there spent his life. By his townsmen he was honored with many private and public trusts. For many years he was town clerk and treasurer, and for thirteen years Register of Deeds for Hampshire County. He was often representative to the General Court of the State, and was a member of the Constitutional Convention of 1853. In the war of 1812, he served as an adjutant in one of the Massachusetts regiments. For several years he taught successfully in the Hopkins Academy in Hadley. He d. June 19, 1861, ae. 80. He m. 1814, Martha Hunt, dau. of Noadiah Warner. She was b. Oct. 9, 1787. Children—*Ebenezer White*, b. Feb. 6, 1815; *Francis*, b. Jan. 25, 1817; *Giles*, b. March 2, 1819; *Maria Catlin*, b. June 18, 1821; *Martha Hunt*, b. Oct. 25, 1823; *Lucy Warner*, b. March 22, 1826; *Anna Marsh* b. Aug. 11, 1828; *William*, b. Aug. 1830, d. March 20, 1831.

KELLOGG, SAMUEL, Hat., d. July 17, 1711. He m. (1) Nov. 24, 1664, Sarah, wid. of Nathaniel Gunn of Hartford, Ct., and dau. of Robert Day of Hartford. She was slain by Indians, Sept. 19, 1677; (2) March 20, 1679, Sarah Root of Westfield. Children—*Samuel*, b. April 11, 1669; *Nathaniel*, b. June 4, 1671; *Ebenezer*, b. June 2, 1674; *Joseph*, b. Sept. 19, 1676, slain by Indians, Sept. 19, 1677; *John*, b. April 25, 1680, res. in Hat., d. prob. unm., made his Will in 1755; *Thomas*, b. Oct. 1, 1681, non compos, d. unm. in Hat. previous to 1758; *Sarah*, b. April 14, 1684, m. May 8, 1701, Abraham Morton of Hat.

2. SAMUEL, s. of Samuel, (1) rem. after 1701 from Hat. to Colchester, Ct., and d. 1708. He m. Hannah, dau. of Nathaniel Dickinson, Jr. She d. in Colchester, Ct., Aug. 3, 1745. Children—*Samuel*, b. May 18, 1694; *Joseph*, b. June 18, 1696; *Hannah*, b. Sept. 11, 1699; *Eunice*, b. Aug. 3, 1701.

3. NATHANIEL, s. of Samuel, (1) rem. after 1699 from Hat. to Colchester, Ct., and d. Aug. 22, 1757, ae. 86. He m. (1) Margaret, who d. Dec. 15, 1747, in 71st yr.; (2) May 29, 1748, Widow Priscilla Williams of Colchester. Children—*Margaret*, b. Feb. 15, 1698; *Editha*, b. Nov. 13, 1699; *Nathaniel*, b. Aug. 8, 1703; *Sarah*, b. Dec. 27, 1706; *Lydia*, b. May 29, 1710; *Ezra*, b. Sept. 6, 1724.

4. NATHANIEL, s. of Nathaniel, (3) res. in Colchester, Ct., and d. April 1, 1762, ae. 59. He m. July 1, 1725, Elizabeth, dau. of Charles Williams. She was b. in Colchester, Feb. 13, 1703. Children—*Charles*, b. Sept. 17, 1726; *Elizabeth*, b. July 8, 1729; *Sarah*, b. Feb. 22, 1732; *Delight*, b. Oct. 5, 1734; *Margaret*, b. Jan. 17, 1737.

5. EZRA, s. of Nathaniel, (3) Hat., d. in Colchester, Ct., Jan. 5, 1754, ae. 29. He m. Ruth, who m. (2) Nov. 4, 1757, Henry Stiles, and d. 1812, ae. 86. Children—*Sarah; Russell*, b. July 16, 1750; *Oliver*.

KELSEY, MATTHEW, m. Sarah. Child—*Elijah*, b. Feb. 28, 1762.

KING, ELISHA, b. Nov. 11, 1717, s. of Benjamin of Nh., who was s. of John of Nh., res. in Had. 1762-4, but rem. to Hat. where he d. 1785 or 1786. He m. May 20, 1753, Jemima Graves. Children—*Mary*, m. June 4, 1779, Dea. Moses Warner; *Jemima*, non compos.

KING, Thomas, b. July 14, 1662, s. of John of Nh., settled in Hat., but rem. to Hartford, Ct., where he d. Dec. 26, 1711, ae. 49. He m. (1) Nov. 17, 1683, Abigail, dau. of Jedediah Strong of Nh. She d. July 24, 1689, ae. 23; (2) 1691, Mary, dau. of Robert Webster of Hartford. She d. in Hartford, Sept. 27, 1706; (3) —— ——, who d. Jan. 2, 1712. Children—*Thomas,* b. Dec. 3, 1684, d. young; *Abigail,* b. Jan. 31, 1687; *Mary,* b. Oct. 5, 1691, per. m. 1711, Thomas Clapp; *Thomas; Robert.*

KING, William, m. Nov. 12, 1684, Sarah Allison. Children—*Thomas,* b. Jan. 3, 1686; *Elizabeth,* b. March 29, 1690, prob. d. Jan. 11, 1715.

KNEELAND, Edward, Jr., m. Dec. 31, 1788, Betsey Peck. Children—*Hannah; Joseph; Samuel,* bapt. Aug. 31, 1794; *Betsey,* b. Feb. 8, 1795; *Edward,* bapt. Oct. 23, 1796; *Lucinda,* bapt. Oct. 13, 1799; *Elmira; Lydia; Electa.*

KNIGHT, Benjamin, m. Sarah, who d. June 2, 1754. Children—*Catharine,* b. May 11, 1748; *Lucius,* b. May 30, 1750.

1. LANE, John, probably s. of Samuel of Suffield, d. 1745 or 1746. He m. Susanna, dau. of Samuel Strong. Children—*John,* b. Sept. 12, 1717; *Elizabeth,* b. Oct. 26, 1719, m. Jacob Taylor of Granby; *Samuel,* b. Nov. 13, 1721, a soldier of So. Had. 1756.

2. John, s. of John, (1) m. Olive. Children—*John,* b. Nov. 15, 1754; *Samuel,* b. Dec. 7, 1757; *Ruth,* b. Aug. 15, 1760; *Elizabeth,* b. Oct. 6, 1762; *Jonathan,* b. Dec. 18, 1764.

LAWRENCE, John, after the birth of his children removed to Brookfield, and was slain by Indians, 1694. He m. Oct. 16, 1684, Sarah, dau. of Samuel Smith. She m. (2) Aug. 15, 1705, Ebenezer Wells of Hatfield. Children—*John,* b. Oct. 1, 1686, d. Jan. 1687; *daughter,* b. and d. Nov. 15, 1687; *Mary,* b. Nov. 1, 1688, m. Jan. 29, 1708, John Allis, and d. Nov. 8, 1713; *Child,* b. and d. Jan. 16, 1689; *Deliverance,* b. June 20, 1693, m. Dec. 1, 1715, John Belden; *Sarah,* b. Sept. 8, 1694, m. Aug. 19, 1714, Samuel Smith.

LAWRENCE, Stephen, s. of Eleazar, d. Feb. 6, 1851. He m. Nov. 2, 1842, Ethelinda, dau. of Wm. Smith. Children—*Julia Ann,* b. Jan. 11, 1846, d. Aug. 24, 1848; *George Smith,* b. Sept. 23, 1847, d. Sept. 7, 1850; *William Smith,* b. May 29, 1849.

LEVENS, or LEAVENS, Andrew, d. Feb. 19, 1698.

1. LEWIS, William, came over from England in the Lion, arrived at Boston, Sept. 16, 1632, was admitted freeman Nov. 6, 1632, belonged to the Braintree company, which in Aug., 1632, rem. from Braintree to Cambridge. He was in 1636 one of the earliest settlers of Hartford, and subsequently a founder of Hadley, and representative for Hadley, 1662, and for Northampton, 1664. Prior to Nov. 29, 1677, he had removed to Farmington, Ct., where he d. Aug. 2, 1683. He m. Felix, who d. in Had., April 17, 1671. Child—*William.*

2. William, s. of William, (1) was in 1644 a resident of Farmington, and the first recorder of the town on its incorporation in 1645. Though one

of the original "engagers," there is no evidence that he ever removed to Had. He d. in Farmington, Aug. 18, 1690. He m. (1) Mary Hopkins, dau. of the wife of Richard Whitehead of Windsor, Ct. Savage supposes her the dau. of William Hopkins, Esq., of Stratford, Ct. He m. (2) Nov. 22, 1671, Mary Cheever, b. Nov. 29, 1640, dau. of the famous schoolmaster, Ezekiel Cheever of New Haven, &c. After the death of Lewis, she m. Jan. 3, 1692, Dea. Thomas Bull, and d. Jan. 10, 1728, ae. 87. Children—*Mary*, b. May 6, 1645, m. Benjamin Judd of Farmington; *Philip*, bapt. Dec. 13, 1646, res. in Hartford and Fairfield; *Samuel*, b. Aug. 18, 1648, res. in Farmington; *Sarah*, b. abt. 1652, m. Samuel Boltwood; *Hannah*, m. (1) Samuel Crow; (2) Daniel Marsh; *William*, bapt. March 15, 1656, m. Phebe More, resided in Farmington, and d. 1737; *Felix*, bapt. Dec. 12, 1658, m. Thomas Selding; *Ebenezer*, m. Elizabeth, resided in Wallingford, Ct., and d. abt. 1710; *John*, b. May 15, 1665, d. abt. 1694; *James*, b. July 10, 1667, a trader, ran away to Jamaica; *Elizabeth*, b. Oct. 20, 1672, d. 1674; *Ezekiel*, b. Nov. 7, 1674, grad. H. C. 1695, and was a merchant of Boston, where he d. Aug. 14, 1755, ae. 81. He m. (1) March 18, 1702, Mary Breaden; (2) Oct. 11, 1704, Abigail Kilcup; *Nathaniel*, b. Oct. 1, 1676, res. in Farmington, and d. Feb. 24, 1752, ae. 75. He m. (1) Nov. 25, 1699, Abigail Ashley; (2) July 4, 1726, Thankful Lyman; *Abigail*, b. Sept. 19, 1678, m. Dec. 10, 1696, William Wadsworth of Farmington, and d. 1707; *Joseph*, b. March 15, 1679; *Daniel*, b. July 16, 1681.

3. NOADIAH, s. of Noadiah of Farmington and gr.-s. of William, (2) was b. Nov. 24, 1736. He m. 1759, Irene, dau. of Preserved Clapp of Amh. She d. Oct. 10, 1830, ae. 89. Children—*Elisha*, d. April 16, 1760; *Susannah*, b. abt. 1762, m. Elihu Dickinson of Amh., and d. March 12, 1819, ae. 57; *Irene*, b. April 20, 1763, m. April 23, 1795, Simeon Clark of Amh., and d. May 11, 1855, ae. 92; *Abi*, m. Feb. 15, 1795, Elijah Hubbard; *Elisha*, m. Ziba Bryant; *Salome*, m. Aug. 16, 1792, Moses Nash of Amh.; *Elizabeth*, m. Oct. 13, 1799, Benjamin Cooley of Whately; *Mary*, m. March 5, 1797, Daniel Heath; *Rachel*, m. Seth Belding of Whately.

LOOMIS, JOHN, m. Mary. Children—*John*, b. Oct. 19, 1670; *John*, b. July 22, 1676, d. Jan. 20, 1677; *Mary*, b. Dec. 14, 1677. Savage says he was prob. son of Joseph the second of Windsor, and that after 1683 he rem. to Windsor, Ct., and according to Stiles, m. Aug. 30, 1705, Esther Gillett, and had children—*John*, b. Feb. 12, 1707; *Esther*, b. Sept. 13, 1708; *Sarah*, b. Sept. 26, 1710; *Damaris*, b. Dec. 1, 1712; *John*, b. Sept. 21, 1713; *Abel*, b. Aug. 3, 1716.

LOOMIS, THOMAS, Hatfield, d. Aug. 12, 1688. He m. March 31, 1680, Sarah, dau. of Daniel White. She m. (2) Nov. 12, 1689, John Bissell. Children—*John*, b. Jan. 1, 1681; *Thomas*, b. April 20, 1684.

LOTRIDGE, JAMES. Child—*Esther*, b. Nov. 26, 1797.

LOVELAND or LOVEMAN, WILLIAM, m. Nov. 12, 1795, Parthena Gilbert. Child, prob. by former wife—*William*, b. Nov. 28, 1789.

LYMAN, ELIJAH, s. of Gideon of Nh., bapt. Aug. 8, 1736, d. April 7, 1783. He m. Esther Pomeroy. Children—*Elijah*, bapt. Sept. 7, 1777, d. Aug. 24, 1778; *Esther*, m. Elijah Arms, Jr.; *Martha*, m. 1795, Jacob Smith.

LYMAN, GIDEON, s. of Gideon of Nh., b. abt. 1730, m. Eunice, dau. of Noah Clark. Children—*Gideon*, b. Jan. 26, 1758; *Eunice*, b. Nov. 8, 1760, d. Nov. 9, 1760.

LYMAN, ISRAEL, b. Feb. 7, 1746, d. June 8, 1830. He m. Jan. 4, 1770, Rachel Beals, b. in Willington, Ct., June 8, 1747. She d. Dec. 27, 1824. Children—*Sarah*, b. Sept. 12, 1770, m. Stephen Johnson, and d. Sept. 19, 1835; *Rachel*, b. March 10, 1772, m. Elijah Montague, and d. Dec. 27, 1803; *Zadoc*, b. March 26, 1774, d. Dec. 8, 1849; *Israel*, b. Aug. 9, 1775, d. Aug. 10, 1775; *Israel*, b. Oct. 17, 1776, d. Aug. 18, 1830; *Achsah*, b. April 27, 1778, m. Chester Clark, and d. Nov. 21, 1819; *Cynthia*, b. April 8, 1780, m. Aaron Graves Lyman of Northfield, and d. Dec. 2, 1839; *Amaziah*, b. Feb. 13, 1782, d. Aug. 12, 1858; *Hannah*, b. Oct. 9, 1783, m. Perez Smith; *Elijah*, b. Nov. 13, 1785, d. June 30, 1786; *Elijah*, b. May 23, 1787; *Enos*, b. Jan. 2, 1790, d. Feb. 23, 1848; *George*, b. Dec. 13, 1792.

LYMAN, JOHN, b. in Nh., Oct. 2, 1693, s. of John, d. Jan. 3, 1783. He m. (1) 1718, Abigail, dau. of Joseph Mosely of Westfield and Glastenbury, Ct. He m. (2) Feb. 15, 1753, Theoda, wid. of Isaac Sheldon of Hartford. She d. 1763. Children—*Zadoc*, b. 1719; *Mindwell*, b. July 29, 1721, m. Ebenezer Pomeroy, 3d; *John*, b. Oct. 7, 1723, res. in Nh., and d. Nov. 4, 1797, ae. 74, m. Hannah Strong; *Abigail*, b. abt. 1725, burnt to death in the house Dec. 8, 1742; *Dorcas*, b. abt. 1727, m. (1) Noah Clapp; (2) 1753, Josiah Moody of S. H.; *Sarah*, b. abt. 1730, m. Dec. 30, 1756, Supply Clapp; *Hannah*, b. abt. 1733, burnt to death Dec. 8, 1742; *Elinor*, b. Oct. 29, 1735, m. (1) Dec. 19, 1759, Stephen Pomeroy; (2) Sept. 13, 1775, Oliver Morton; *Caleb*, bapt. July 2, 1738, rem. to Cazenovia, N. Y., m. 1763, Mehitable Strong.

1. LYMAN, PHINEHAS, s. of Gideon of Nh., d. April 27, 1792, ae. abt. 67. He m. (1) April 5, 1750, Joanna Eastman, who d. Feb. 5, 1759, in 29th yr.; (2) Elizabeth, wid. of Elisha Hawley. Children—*Phinehas*, b. Jan. 22, 1750, committed suicide by hanging, April 23, 1779; *Timothy*, b. Aug. 15, 1753; *Elihu*, b. Sept. 23, 1756, committed suicide by hanging, prior to 1792.

2. TIMOTHY, s. of Phinehas, (1) studied medicine with Dr. Hunt of Nh., and d. June 12, 1792, ae. 42. He m. June 1, 1780, Elizabeth Pomeroy, who m. after his death Ebenezer Clark of Lunenburgh, Vt. Children— *Joanna*, prob. b. May 4, 1782, m. Abel Brown of Spr., and abt. 1839 rem. to Wisconsin; *Elizabeth*, bapt. March 28, 1784, a cripple; *Naomi*, b. March, 1787, m. Asa Clark of Lunenburgh, Vt.; *Elihu*, b. July, 1789, went to Vt., and thence to Wisconsin; *Phinehas*, b. Feb. 20, 1786.

MARKHAM, WILLIAM, b. abt. 1621, was a kinsman of Nathaniel Ward, and d. abt. 1690. He m. (1) ——, dau. of George Graves; (2) Elizabeth, prob. dau. of Gov. John Webster. She d. abt. 1688. Children, by 1st wife— *Priscilla*, m. abt. 1675, Thomas Hale. By second wife—*William*, slain by the Indians, near Northfield, Sept. 4, 1675; *Lydia*, m. May 16, 1682, Timothy Eastman of Suffield; *John*, b. July 3, 1661, d. Sept. 12, 1664; *Mercy*, b. Sept. 22, 1663.

1. MARSH, JOHN, Hartford, 1639, was one of the first settlers of Hadley, but rem. thence first to Northampton, and then to Hartford, where he died 1688. He m. (1) Anne, dau. of Gov. John Webster. She d.

June 9, 1662; (2) Oct. 7, 1664, Hepzibah, wid. of Richard Lyman of Nh., and dau. of Thomas Ford. She d. April 11, 1683. Children—*John*, m. Nov. 28, 1666, Sarah Lyman, and d. in Hartford, Ct., about 1727; *Samuel*, b. abt. 1645; *Joseph*, bapt. Jan. 24, 1647; *Joseph*, bapt. July 15, 1649; *Jonathan*, b. abt. 1650; *Daniel*, b. abt. 1653; *Hannah*, m. Jan. 28, 1675, Joseph Loomis; *Grace*, m. Jan. 26, 1673, Timothy Baker of Nh., and d. May 31, 1676; *Lydia*, b. Oct. 9, 1667, m. Dec. 8, 1692, David Loomis of Windsor.

2. SAMUEL, s. of John, (1) res. in Hat., where he was freeman 1690, representative 1705 and 1706, and d. Sept. 7, 1728, ae. 83. He m. May 6, 1667, Mary Allison, who d. Oct. 13, 1726, ae. 78. Children—*Mary*, b. Feb. 27, 1668; *Samuel*, b. Feb. 11, 1670; *John*, b. Nov. 6, 1672; *Rachel*, b. Oct. 15, 1674, m. John Wells; *Grace*, b. Jan. 7, 1677, m. Thomas Goodman; *Mary*, b. May 24, 1678, m. Joseph Morton; *Thomas*, b. Jan. 10, 1680; *Hannah*, b. Sept. 18, 1681, m. Richard Billings; *Elizabeth*, b. July 31, 1683, m. 1714, Maynard Day of Hartford, Ct.; *Ruth*, b. June 16, 1685; *Ebenezer*, b. May 1, 1687.

3. JONATHAN, s. of John, (1) was freeman 1690, representative 1701, and d. July 3, 1730, ae. 80 yrs. He m. 1676, Dorcas, wid. of Azariah Dickinson. She d. Aug. 15, 1723, ae. 69. Children—*Dorcas*, b. Dec. 29, 1677, m. July 4, 1700, Ichabod Porter; *Ann*, b. Sept. 13, 1680, m. June 21, 1698, Samuel Cook; *Mary*, b. Feb. 9, 1683, m. William Dickinson; *Jonathan*, b. Aug. 7, 1685, grad. H. C. 1705, was minister of Windsor, Ct., and d. Sept. 8, 1747, ae. 62. He m. July 3, 1710, Mrs. Margaret Whiting; *Sarah*, b. Dec. 4, 1687, m. Nov. 1716, Noah Cook; *Hannah*, b. Feb. 12, 1690, m. Oct. 17, 1711, Samuel Dickinson; *Daughter*, b. July 27, 1692, d. July 29, 1692; *Son*, b. Sept. 14, 1698, d. Sept. 1698.

4. DANIEL, s. of John, (1) freeman 1690, representative 1692, and often after, d. Feb. 24, 1725, ae. 72. He m. Nov. 5, 1676, Hannah, wid. of Samuel Crow, and dau. of William Lewis of Farmington. Children—*Daniel*, b. Oct. 29, 1677, d. unm. Feb. 15, 1770, ae. 92; *John*, b. March 9, 1679; *Joseph*, b. Jan. 16, 1685, grad. H. C. 1705, was minister of Braintree, and d. March 8, 1726, ae. 41. He m. Anne Fiske; *Ebenezer*, b. April 22, 1688; *Job*, b. June 11, 1690; *Hannah*, b. May 17, 1694, m. Dec. 1, 1731, Daniel Kent; *William*, b. Jan. 3, 1697.

5. THOMAS, s. of Samuel, (2) res. in Hat. and Ware, and d. 1759. He m. 1702, Mary Trumbull of Suffield, Ct. Children—*Thomas*, b. May 1, 1703, d. unm. 1728; *Mary*, b. Oct. 27, 1704, m. 1726, Moses Smith; *Samuel*, b. 1706; *Rachel*, b. 1708; *Ruth*, b. Feb. 15, 1710; *Judah*, b. July 25, 1712; *Joseph*, b. April 14, 1714; *Ephraim*, b. Jan. 5, 1717; *Daniel*, b. June 12, 1719, insane; *Martha*, b. April 12, 1721.

6. EBENEZER, s. of Samuel, (2) rem. to Sunderland, and d. 1747. He m. Elizabeth. Children—*Ebenezer; Elizabeth*, b. June 4, 1710; *Ephraim*, b. June 12, 1712, d. Aug. 1, 1714; *Esther*, b. July 15, 1714; *Ephraim*, b. 1718; *Dorothy*, b. 1723, m. —— Gunn; *Mary*, b. 1725; *Thankful*, b. 1728; *Hannah*, b. 1733.

7. JOHN, s. of Daniel, (4) d. Sept. 2, 1725. He m. (1) June 27, 1704, Joanna Porter; (2) Feb. 2, 1715, Hannah Barnard; (3) Sarah Williams,

92   MARSH.

who after his decease prob. m. July 28, 1732, James Grey, and d. June 1, 1759. Children—*John*, b. Aug. 25, 1710; *Abigail*, m. (1) Oct. 1, 1736, Dr. Waitstill Hastings of Hat.; (2) Col. Bulkley of Colchester, Ct.; (3) Rev. —— Little of Colchester, Ct.; *Martha*, m. Feb. 24, 1743, Moses Graves; *Anne*, m. Dec. 20, 1744, Elisha Allis; *John*, d. July 3, 1726, ae. 3; *Judith*, b. 1725, d. Nov. 1, 1725, ae. 8. mos.

8. EBENEZER, s. of Daniel, (4) d. 1772. He m. (1) 1710, Mary Parsons, who d. July 2, 1759; (2) Miriam, who d. July 30, 1765. Children—*Elisha*, b. March 27, 1713, grad. H. C. 1738, minister in Westminster, d. July, 1784, in Lancaster, from the effects of injuries received by falling from his horse in Roxbury; *Ebenezer; Hannah*, m. Samuel Ely of Lyme, Ct.; *Jonathan*, res. in Ct.; *John*.

9. JOB, s. of Daniel, (4) a captain, d. Aug. 29, 1746. He m. (1) Sept. 24, 1713, Mehitable Porter, who d. July 13, 1739; (2) 1742, Rebecca Pratt. Children—*Daughter*, b. and d. Oct. 18, 1714; *Moses*, b. March 20, 1718; *Samuel*, b. April 19, 1721; *Daniel*, b. Jan. 28, 1725; *Perez*, b. Oct. 25, 1729, grad. H. C. 1748, was a physician in Pittsfield; *Joseph*, b. Nov. 6, 1743, d. Sept. 22, 1746.

10. WILLIAM, s. of Daniel, (4) d. Nov. 3, 1727. He m. Feb. 28, 1722, Hannah, dau. of Experience Porter. She m. (2) Maj. Joseph Storrs. Children—*William*, d. 1726; *William*, b. 1727, d. unm., in Mansfield, Ct.

11. EBENEZER, s. of Ebenezer, (6) d. May 29, 1795. He m. Dec. 4, 1746, Sarah Eastman, who d. Jan. 31, 1794. Children—*Timothy*, b. July 6, 1747, d. May 12, 1751; *Daniel*, b. June 26, 1749, d. April 30, 1751; *Timothy*, b. Oct. 5, 1751, m. Mercy Smith, and d. Oct. 19, 1796; *Sarah*, b. July 20, 1754, m. Dec. 9, 1779, Nathaniel Dickinson, Jr., Esq., of Amh., and d. Dec. 9, 1801; *Ebenezer*, b. Sept. 8, 1757, d. Jan. 25, 1761; *Elijah*, b. Dec. 25, 1760, d. Jan. 11, 1761; *Ebenezer*, b. Jan. 5, 1762, d. unm. abt. 1818; *Mary*, b. and d. May 9, 1765; *Susanna*, b. Jan. 26, 1766, d. Feb. 26, 1766.

12. MOSES, s. of Capt. Job, (9) subsequent to the American revolution rem. to Worthington, and d. Oct. 4, 1796. He m. Nov. 2, 1739, Hannah Cook. Children—*Moses*, b. Oct. 22, 1740, d. Aug. 16, 1746; *Hannah*, b. Oct. 2, 1744, d. Aug. 12, 1746; *Moses*, b. June 11, 1747, d. Nov. 16, 1757; *Hannah*, b. Feb. 2, 1749, d. Sept. 15, 1753; *Job*, b. May 4, 1752, d. Jan. 26, 1754; *Mehitable*, m. 1780, Samuel Cook, and prob. d. in Morristown, Vt.; *Hannah*, m. Daniel Marsh, and d. in Belchertown; *Job*, b. abt. 1756; *Joseph*, b. Oct. 26, 1754.

13. SAMUEL, s. of Capt. Job, (9) d. Oct. 2, 1760. He m. Dec. 5, 1745, Phebe Porter, who d. Oct. 1, 1779, ae. 60. Children—*Daughter*, b. and d. Aug. 23, 1746; *Phebe*, m. Benoni Dickinson of Northfield; *Rebecca*, m. Eleazar Cook, who rem. to St. Albans, Vt.; *Samuel*.

14. DANIEL, s. of Capt. Job, (9) d. Jan. 4, 1810, ae. 84. He m. 1751, Hannah, dau. of Timothy Parsons of Durham, Ct. She d. Feb. 9, 1800, ae. 74. Children—*Mehitabel*, b. Dec. 3, 1751, d. Aug. 30, 1752; *William*, b. Oct. 26, 1753, was a soldier at the capture of Cornwallis, and d. unm., in Warren; *Sarah*, m. Joseph Field of Warren; *Eliphalet*, b. Feb. 2, 1761, res. in Coleraine and Belchertown; *Parsons*, b. Sept. 7, 1766, res. in Coleraine and Belchertown.

15. JOB, s. of Moses, (12) grad. Y. C. 1777, established himself as a physician in Worthington, but returned to Had., and d. July 26, 1797. He m. Sept. 10, 1783, Elizabeth, dau. of Oliver Smith. She d. June 7, 1823, ae. 64. Children—*Elizabeth*, b. March 22, 1784, m. Dec. 17, 1805, Wm. Smith, and d. Dec. 18, 1856; *Joseph*, b. Feb. 16, 1786; *Timothy*, d. young; *Moses*, d. young; *Moses*, d. May, 1851; *Ethelinda*, m. Ebenezer Harrington of Worcester, and d. in Had., Aug. 5, 1840.

16. JOSEPH, s. of Moses, (12) rem. to Brookfield, Vt., and was there killed by the falling of a tree, Aug. 1783, ae. 28. He m. Mindwell Pomeroy. She m. 1784, Ebenezer Clark of Lunenburgh, Vt. Children—*Sally*, b. June 10, 1782, m. 1800, Lemuel Holmes of Lunenburgh, Vt.; rem. to Malone, N. Y., where she was living in 1853; *Joannah*, b. Jan. 1784, [Jan. 12, 1785?] m. Daniel Clark of Lunenburgh, Vt., rem. to Huntsburg, Ohio, and there res. in 1853.

17. SAMUEL, s. of Samuel, (13) d. 1798. He m. 1775, Abigail Briggs. Children—*Augustus; Phebe Porter; Samuel; Lucinda.*

18. JOSEPH, s. of Dr. Job, (15) m. (1) Jan. 26, 1814, Roxa, dau. of Stephen Johnson. She d. Nov. 20, 1828; (2) Oct. 13, 1829, Roxana, dau. of Luther Wright of Easthampton. She was b. March 30, 1798, and d. April 29, 1836; (3) Feb. 13, 1839, Catharine, dau. of Nathaniel Cooledge of Worcester and Hadley. She d. Aug. 20, 1842; (4) April 7, 1844, Harriet, wid. of George Newhall of Amh., and dau. of William Boltwood of Amh. Children— *Elvira Minerva*, b. Sept. 5, 1814, m. 1834, Willard M. Kellogg of Amh.; *Mary Lyman*, b. Feb. 18, 1818, m. 1840, William Watson Dickinson of Amh.; *Margaret*, b. July 28, 1820, m. May, 1844, Lucius Nash; *Henry Martyn*, b. Dec. 21, 1827, m. May 10, 1854, Almira Sophronia, dau. of John Alden Morton, *Charles*, b. Nov. 24, 1845.

MATTHEWS, SILAS, Amherst, rem. abt. 1800 to Leverett. Children— *Salome*, b. Sept. 1, 1772; *Elijah*, b. May 27, 1777; *David*, b. Dec. 27, 1779; *Aaron*, b. Oct. 27, 1781; *Huldah*, b. Dec. 7, 1784.

1. MATTOON, ELEAZAR, b. in Deerfield, March 1, 1690, s. of Philip of Springfield and Deerfield, res. for several years in Northfield, whence prior to 1739 he rem. to Amh., where he was deacon in the (Cong.) church, and d. Feb. 1767, ae. 78. Children—*Elizabeth*, b. Nov. 1, 1718, m. Joseph Day of West Springfield, and d. Oct. 13, 1776, ae. 58; *Ebenezer*, b. Dec. 21, 1720, *Sarah*, b. Feb. 21, 1723, m. March 27, 1746, Ephraim Marsh of Montague, and d. April 9, 1797, ae. 74.

2. EBENEZER, s. of Eleazar, (1) Amh., d. April 27, 1806, ae. 87. He m. (1) 1747, Dorothy, dau. of Dr. Nathaniel Smith of Amh. She d. June 3, 1756; (2) 1759, Sarah, dau. of John Alvord of Nh. She was b. March 2, 1726, and d. Feb. 27, 1803, ae. 76. Children—*Dorothy*, bapt. April 16, 1749, m. Stephen Smith of Amh.; *Elizabeth*, bapt. July 21, 1751, m. Oliver Clapp of Amh.; *Ebenezer*, bapt. Aug. 24, 1755; *Sarah*, b. abt. 1761, d. April 11, 1803, ae. 42; *Eleazar*, bapt. Aug. 19, 1764, d. unm.; *Roxana*, b. Aug. 31, 1766, m. 1785, John Kellogg of Amh., and d. Sept. 2, 1804, ae. 37; *Lovisa*, b. abt. 1770, m. Eli Dickinson of Amh., and d. Jan. 31, 1845, ae. 75.

3. HON. EBENEZER, s. of Ebenezer, (2) Amh., grad. D. C. 1776, was Representative and Senator in General Court, Member of Congress, Sheriff of Hampshire County, Adjutant General of Mass. With the exception of his eye sight, he retained all his faculties until the close of his long life. He d. Sept. 11, 1843, ae. 88. He m. July 7, 1779, Mary, dau. of Noah Dickinson of Amh. She d. July 30, 1835, ae. 77. Children—*Mary Dickinson*, b. April 4, 1780, m. Dec. 24, 1807, Daniel Dwight, Esq., of Westmoreland, N. H.; *Ebenezer*, b. Sept. 29, 1781, m. Dec. 30, 1804, Lucina Mayo of Orange; *Noah Dickinson*, b. Sept. 19, 1783, grad. D. C. 1803, lawyer in Amh. and Painsville, O., and is supposed now (1861) to be a resident of Unionville, O. He m. ——— Billings; *Dorothy Smith*, b. June 25, 1785, m. April 20, 1815, Dr. Timothy J. Gridley of Amh., and d. Feb. 16, 1820, ae. 34; *Fanny*, b. Sept. 1787, d. Jan. 28, 1790, ae. 2; *Fanny*, b. June, 1790, d. Sept. 4, 1792, ae. 2.

MEACHAM, JAMES, m. (1) June 23, 1756, Lucy Rugg; (2) May 4, 1758, Ruth Hubbard. Children—*Asa*, b. 1759; *Ruth*, b. 1761; *James*, b. 1761; *Anna*, b. July 6, 1764; *David*, b. June 13, 1766; *Ashbel*, b. 1768, (bapt. April 24;) *Seth*, b. 1771, (bapt. Feb. 10;) *Benjamin*, b. Dec. 30, 1773; *Esther*, b. Feb. 1777.

1. MEEKINS, THOMAS, Hat., d. Dec. 10, 1687. He m. (1) Sarah, who d. Jan. 21, 1651; (2) Elizabeth ———, Feb. 14, 1651, who d. May 12, 1683. Children—*Joseph*, bapt. in Boston, May 3, 1639; *Sarah*, b. in Braintree, April 24, 1641; *Thomas*, b. June 8, 1643; *Hannah*, bapt. in Roxbury, March 13, 1647; *John*, b. Feb. 28, 1649, d. May 10, 1649. He had also, as Savage supposes, dau. *Mary*, who m. (1) Nathaniel Clark of Nh.; (2) Dec. 14, 1669, John Allis of Hat.; (3) abt. 1691, Samuel Belden; and *Hannah*, who m. Joseph Belknap, and d. Dec. 26, 1688. They, together with the heirs of his only son, shared his property.

2. THOMAS, s. of Thomas, (1) Hat., was slain by the Indians, Oct. 19, 1675. He m. Mary, dau. of Thomas Bunce of Hartford. She was b. Sept. 17, 1645, and m. (2) July 20, 1676, John Downing. Children—*Sarah*, b. Feb. 25, 1666, m. Peletiah Jones; *Mary*, b. March 28, 1670, m. James Lewis of Hartford; *John*, b. Jan. 12, 1674 [1672?]; *Thomas*, b. Nov. 8, 1673, m. Wid. Sarah Wells, and in 1711 was a resident of Hartford; *Mehitable*, b. Aug. 1675, m. Thomas Dickinson, Jr.

3. JOHN, s. of Thomas, (2) Hat., prob. d. 1754, as his will executed 1753, was presented for probate Feb. 1754. He m. April 24, 1696, Ruth Belknap. Children—*Hannah*, b. Jan. 18, 1698; *Ruth*, b. Jan. 6, 1700, m. Zechariah Billings; *Joseph*, b. March 20, 1703, d. childless abt. 1756; *Mary*, b. Oct. 17, 1705, m. Thomas Miller; *Martha*, b. Feb. 1, 1708, was unm. in 1756; *Lydia*, d. Dec. 24, 1711; *Thomas*, b. Oct. 1718, m. Feb. 18, 1742, Martha Smith, and d. 1793.

MERRICK, JAMES, b. Dec. 22, 1729, s. of James of Monson, settled in Amherst, and d. Oct. 30, 1813, ae. 85. He m. Oct. 1754, Esther Colton of Longmeadow. She d. Sept. 20, 1803, in 75th yr. Children—*Mary*, b. June 11, 1755, m. Feb. 7, 1782, Nathaniel Sikes of Walpole, N. H.; *Lucy*, b. March 27, 1757, m. Elijah Yale of Amh., Jan. 25, 1788, and d. Nov. 14, 1824, ae. 57; *Sarah*, b. Oct. 29, 1758, m. Feb. 1782, Henry Chandler; *James*, b. Sept. 8, 1760, d. in infancy; *Samuel*, b. Sept. 8, 1760, d. young; *James*, b. May 8, 1762, d. unm. in Amh., July 8, 1825, ae. 63; *Esther*, b. Sept. 11, 1764, m.

Nov. 26, 1789, Judah Clark of Amh., and d. Aug. 30, 1849, ae. 84; *Samuel*, b. May, 1767, d. ae. 8; *Aaron*, b. May, 1770, m. Mary Howe, June 22, 1800, d. in Amh., Dec. 3, 1843, ae. 73.

MIGHILL, SAMUEL, s. of Rev. Thomas, b. in Scituate, 1685, grad. H. C. 1704, taught the Grammar School in Had., and d in So. H., April 11, 1769. He m. 1709, Sarah Dickinson. Child—*Sarah*, b. April 12, 1710, m. Jan. 18, 1739, Moses Gunn.

MIGHILL, SAMUEL, perhaps the same with the above, formerly of Hartford, m. 1714, Sarah Prentice, and in Nov. 1728 deserted his wife and rem. to Had. She in 1733 sued for divorce. They had no children.

1. MONTAGUE, RICHARD, b. abt. 1614, s. of Peter, s. of William, s. of Robert, of Bourney, in Parish of Burnham, England, is said in 1646 to have rem. from Wells, Me. to Boston, and thence in 1651 to Wethersfield, Ct. In 1659 or 1660 he settled in Had. and d. Dec. 14, 1681. He m. Abigail Downing of Norwich, Eng. She d. Nov. 8, 1694. Children—*Mary*, b. abt. 1642, m. Nov. 25, 1668, Joseph Warriner, and d. July 2, 1689, ae. abt. 47; *Sarah*, b. June 15, 1646, d. in Boston, June 19, 1646; *Martha*, b. June 16, 1647, m. (1) Dec. 1, 1671, Isaac Harrison; (2) Henry White; *Peter*, b. July 8, 1651, d. s. p., March 27, 1725, ae. 73. He m. (1) Sept. 1679, Mary, wid. of John Smith, and dau. of William Partridge. She d. May 20, 1680; (2) Sept. 16, 1680, Mary, wid. of Noah Coleman and dau. of John Crow. She d. Oct. 12, 1720; (3) April 22, 1721, Mary, wid. of Preserved Smith, and dau. of Chileab Smith; *Abigail*, m. Dec. 8, 1671, Mark Warner; *John*.

2. JOHN, s. of Richard, (1) d. abt. 1732. He m. March 23, 1681, Hannah, dau. of Chileab Smith. Children—*John*, b. Dec. 31, 1681; *Richard*, b. March 16, 1684, settled in Wethersfield, Ct., and d. Dec. 24, 1751, ae. 67. He m. July 28, 1715, Abigail Camp; *Hannah*, b. Aug. 8, 1687, d. Nov. 1688; *Hannah*, b. March 21, 1689, d. April 19, 1689; *Peter*, b. May, 1690; *William*, b. Dec. 16, 1692; *Samuel*, b. April 2, 1695; *Hannah*, b. May 28, 1697, m. Josiah Willard of Wethersfield; *Luke*, b. Oct. 4, 1699; *Nathaniel*, b. Oct. 6, 1704.

3. JOHN, s. of John, (2) d. Sept. 28, 1722, ae. 40. He m. (1) Jan. 17, 1712, Mindwell Lyman of Nh., prob. dau. of Thomas, and if so, b. April 10, 1681. She d. April 4, 1713; (2) Sept. 29, 1714, Abigail Smith. Children— *Abigail*, b. March 20, 1713, m. March 16, 1735, Nathan Moody; *Mindwell*, b. Sept. 1714, d. Dec. 2, 1715; *John*, b. Jan. 5, 1716; *Jemima*, b. Jan. 28, 1719, m. March 24, 1741, John Church; *Mary*, b. Nov. 8, 1721, m. Oct. 24, 1743, Jonathan Ingram.

4. PETER, s. of John, (2) So. H. His estate was settled 1749, but inventory was not presented until Feb. 1756. He m. Dec. 15, 1715, Mary Hubbard. Children—*Mary*, b. March 4, 1717, m. (1) Daniel Alexander of Nh.; (2) John Brown; (3) J. Clark; *Anna*, b. Oct. 31, 1718, m. Nathaniel Cole of Hat. and Belchertown; *Elizabeth*, b. Nov. 13, 1720, m. (1) —— Montague; (2) James Smith; *Peter*, b. Jan. 2, 1723, per. d. at Louisbourg, 1745; *Moses*, b. Nov. 17, 1724; *Rachel*, m. Nov. 29, 1753, Stephen Warner of Granby; *Experience*, m. (1) 1751, Jonathan Pierce; (2) March 10, 1756, [1757?] Philip Ingram of Amh.; *Adonijah*, d. unm. in Amh. in 1754.

5. WILLIAM, s. of John, (2) d. Dec. 22, 1767, ae. 75. He m. (1) Jan. 24,
1716, Sarah, dau. of Timothy Eastman. She d. Sept. 29, 1747; (2) Jan. 5,
1749, Sarah, wid. of Samuel Kellogg, and dau. of Dea. John Smith.
Children—*Sarah*, b. Oct. 26, 1717, m. John Stanley of Killingworth, Ct.;
William, b. April 9, 1720, d. Oct. 19, 1745, ae. 25; *John*, b. Sept. 14, 1723,
a Canada soldier, d. Oct. 6, 1746, ae. 23; *Joseph*, b. Dec. 31, 1725; *Hannah*,
b. March 16, 1729, d. Nov. 5, 1745, ae. 16; *Timothy*, b. Feb. 23, 1732.

6. SAMUEL, s. of John, (2) Sunderland, deacon, d. Jan. 31, 1779. He
m. (1) June 24, 1716, Elizabeth White. She d. Oct. 15, 1753; m. (2) June
13, 1754, Mary, wid. of Jonathan Billings, and dau. of Joseph Root. Children—*Samuel*, b. June 30, 1720, rem. to Vt.; *John*, b. Jan. 10, 1723, d. unm.
Feb. 15, 1748; *Daniel*, b. Jan. 13, 1725, m. Lydia Smith; *Giles*, b. Jan. 20,
1727, d. 1732; *Richard*, b. May 7, 1729, m. Lucy Cooley; *Caleb*, b. July 27,
1731, res. in Sunderland, was a Captain in Revolutionary war, and d. Nov. 11,
1782, ae. 51. He m. Oct. 30, 1751, Eunice Root; *Giles*, b. Dec. 16, 1733,
d. Sept. 10, 1734; *Elizabeth*, b. Sept. 18, 1735, d. 1743; *Nathaniel*, b. Feb. 13,
1739, slain in battle at Lake George, Aug. 7, 1757; *Ebenezer*, b. Oct. 1, 1741,
d. Sept. 26, 1743.

7. LUKE, s. of John, (2) So. Had., d. Aug. 25, 1775, ae. 75. He m. (1)
Hannah, dau. of Nehemiah Dickinson, Jr. of Had. She d. Sept. 3, 1765;
(2) Deborah. Children—*Luke*, b. March 9, 1729, d. Nov. 18, 1752; *Hannah*,
b. Jan. 5, 1731, d. unm. Aug. 31, 1773, ae. 41; *Abigail*, b. Feb. 18, 1733,
m. March 4, 1756, Josiah Montague, and d. Aug. 28, 1833, ae. 99; *Giles*,
b. June 28, 1736, d. May 3, 1738; *Mehitable*, b. Oct. 3, 1738, m. Dec. 3, [23?]
1756, Israel Clark, and d. Oct. 23, 1817, ae. 77; *Mary*, b. Nov. 1, 1740, m.
Titus Pomeroy; *Huldah*, b. April 20, 1743, m. Samuel Goodman; *Miriam*,
b. Jan. 25, 1745.

8. NATHANIEL, s. of John, (2) deacon in Had. church, d. Nov. 16, 1753,
ae. 49. He m. May 18, 1743, Hannah Ingram. She d. Aug. 28, 1798, ae. 87.
Children—*Hannah*, b. Feb. 29, 1744, m. Nov. 15, 1770, Isaiah Carrier of
Belchertown; *Nathaniel*, b. July 26, 1745; *Esther*, b. March 2, 1747, m. Feb.
21, 1775, Moses Church; *Sarah*, b. Nov. 21, 1748, d. May 3, 1764, ae. 15;
Eunice, b. July 25, 1751, m. Feb. 15, 1780, Joseph Church of New Marlboro';
Elizabeth, b. Feb. 8, 1753, m. Feb. 23, 1773, Abner Phillips.

9. JOHN, s. of John, (3) d. April 18, 1783, ae. 67. He m. (1) 1747,
Thankful Sheldon of Suffield, Ct. She d. April 27, 1758, in 39th yr. He m. (2)
Aug. 28, 1758, Rhoda Selden. Children—*Abigail*, b. Aug. 15, 1748, m. (1)
Jan. 30, 1777, William Chapin of Springfield; (2) John Ely of West Springfield; *John*, b. May 6, 1750; *Lois*, b. June 29, 1752, d. July 21, 1752, ae. 21
days; *Elisha*, b. June 8, 1753, was run over by a cart and killed Nov. 12,
1757, ae. 4; *David*, b. Nov. 11, 1755, d. near West Point Oct. 26, 1781, ae. 26;
Elisha, b. March 6, 1758, d. March 13, 1758; *Seth*, b. April 6, 1762, d. April 8,
1762; *Seth*, b. April 26, 1764, d. Dec. 17, 1764; *Jedediah*, b. July 24, 1766.

10. MOSES, s. of Peter, (4) captain, So. Had., d. Dec. 18, 1792, ae. 68.
He m. 1748, Sarah Graves of Sunderland. She d. Oct. 17, 1810. Children—
Penelope, b. July 16, 1749; *Peter*, b. Nov. 18, 1751; *Sarah*, b. March 4, 1754;
Moses, b. May 7, 1756; *Irene*, b. Aug. 28, 1758; *Selah*, b. Feb. 17, 1761;
Seth, b. July 2, 1763; *Mary*, b. Sept. 14, 1765; *Lucinda*, b. April 25, 1768;
Elijah, b. April 21, 1771.

11. Josiah, s. of Peter, (4) Granby, d. July 11, 1810, ae. 84. He m. March 4, 1756, Abigail, dau. of Luke Montague. She d. Aug. 28, 1833, ae. 99. Children—*Luke*, b. June 20, 1757; *Lucretia*, b. Jan. 9, 1759, m. Waitstill Dickinson of Amh.; *Abigail*, b. April 4, 1761; *Lovisa*, b. March 18, 1763; *Beulah*, b. Jan. 2, 1768; *Hannah*, b. Aug. 8, 1770; *Giles*, b. May 20, 1774.

12. Joseph, s. of William, (5) Granby, d. Aug. 10, 1786. He m. March 21, 1752, [1753?] Sarah Henry. She d. Oct. 16, 1800, ae. 77. Children— *Elizabeth*, b. Feb. 4, 1754, m. Aaron Dickinson of Granby, and d. Nov. 1842; *Hannah*, b. Jan. 3, 1756, m. Noah Ferry of Granby, and d. June 2, 1845, ae. 89; *William*, b. Sept. 23, 1757, grad. D. C. 1784, was an Episcopal clergyman in Boston and Dedham, and d. July 22, 1833, ae. 75. He m. Jane Little; *John*, b. March 6, 1760, m. Melinda Chapin; *Joseph*, b. Oct. 2, 1763, grad. D. C. 1788, d. May 1, 1849, ae. 85. He m. Mrs. Mary Abbott.

13. Timothy, s. of William, (5) So. Had., d. Feb. 1, 1800, ae. 67. He m. Mary Smith of Ashford, Ct. Child—*Timothy*, b. Sept. 27, 1772, m. Mindwell, dau. of Benoni Chapin of Chicopee.

14. Nathaniel, s. of Nathaniel, (8) d. Nov. 4, 1784, ae. 39. He m. Oct. 21, 1773, Sarah Goodrich. She m. (2) Aug. 19, 1792, John Chester Williams, and d. Feb. 5, 1798. Children—*Son*, b. Aug. 7, 1774, d. Aug. 8, 1774; *Sarah*, b. Dec. 15, 1775, d. Sept. 17, 1777; *Mary*, b. Aug. 26, 1777, m. ——— Kingsley; *Stephen*, b. Sept. 24, 1779; *Elijah*, b. June 24, 1781, rem. to Batavia, N. Y.

15. John, s. of John, (9) Lieut., d. June 14, 1808, ae. 53. He m. March 4, 1773, Sibil Hall. Children—*Seth*, b. Oct. 8, 1774, d. in Hartford, Ct.; *Lucinda*, b. June 6, 1777; *Thankful*, b. Dec. 2, 1778, m. (1) June 24, 1795, Stephen Rider; *Sibil*, b. Dec. 4, 1780, m. Eleazar Cowls of Amh.; *David*, b. Nov. 27, 1782, fell and was killed while raising a house in Had., Dec. 1819; *Caroline*, b. March 1, 1785, m. ——— Williams; *Zebina*, b. Nov. 18, 1786, d. Sept. 27, 1787; *Zebina*, b. May 9, 1788, d. in Hartford, Ct., Nov. 18, 1811; *Lois*, b. Oct. 10, 1791, m. Cotton Smith.

16. Jedediah, s. of John, (9) d. Aug. 29, 1824, ae. 58. He m. Dec. 26, 1787, Dorcas, dau. of Josiah Grover, of Ellington, Ct. She was b. Dec. 26, 1769, and d. Aug. 9, 1858, ae. 89. Children—*William*, b. Oct. 7, 1789; *Rhoda*, b. June 25, 1791, d. June 26, 1829; *Heman*, b. March 18, 1793, m. Martha Smith, and d. March 23, 1827; *Sarah*, b. Dec. 27, 1794; *Abigail*, b. April 29, 1797, d. Oct. 7, 1802; *John*, b. June 5, 1799, d. July 1, 1824; *Anna*, b. May 26, 1801, m. Sherman Sabin of Belchertown; *Abigail*, b. Feb. 21, 1803, d. Aug. 21, 1804; *Ephraim*, b. May 6, 1805, a deacon of Cong. church in Belchertown. He m. Jan. 13, 1829, Laura Sabin; *Elizabeth*, b. Feb. 26, 1807; *Harvey*, b. Jan. 30, 1809, res. in Belchertown, m. Jane A. Moody; *Sylvester*, b. Jan. 10, 1812, d. April 23, 1850.

17. Stephen, s. of Nathaniel, (14) d. May 18, 1851. He m. Nov. 20, 1801, Grace Grant, dau. of Daniel White. Children—*Sarah Goodrich*, b. Sept. 9, 1803, d. unm. Dec. 2, 1839, ae. 36; *Sophronia*, b. May 15, 1807, d. April 10, 1827, ae. 19; *Mary*, b. Feb. 2, 1809, d. May 8, 1848, ae. 39; *Daniel Nathaniel*, b. June 9, 1811, m. May, 1840, Mary Pierce; *Henry*, b. July 30, 1813, m. Oct. 19, 1836, Abigail Kingsley; *Susan Grant*, b. Feb. 12, 1817,

m. Jan. 18, 1838, Elijah Ayres of Amh.; *Stephen Stone*, b. Dec. 8, 1818, m. (1) Sept. 24, 1841, Mary C. Kellogg; (2) Oct. 2, 1844, Lucy W. Kellogg; *Harriet Maria*, b. Nov. 30, 1820, m. Nov. 30, 1842, Edmund Bartlett; *Sabra Ward*, b. Dec. 28, 1822, m. Aug. 28, 1855, Martin F. Cook; *Pamela White*, b. March 9, 1825.

18. EPHRAIM, s. of Jedediah, (16) rem. to Belchertown, where he is a deacon in the (Cong.) church. He m. Jan. 13, 1829, Laura Sabin, b. in Wilbraham, March 4, 1809. Children—*William Lewis*, b. April 6, 1831, grad. A. C. 1855, m. Aug. 9, 1858, Rebecca W. Pope, has been Tutor and is now (1862) Instructor in Latin and French in Amh. Col.; *Laura A. M.*, b. July 28, 1835, m. Aug. 5, 1857, Rev. Chester L. Cushman (A. C. 1856) of East Townshend, Vt.; *John L.*, b. July 23, 1838; *James H.*, b. March 8, 1841; *Harlan Page*, b. Jan. 5, 1846; *Alice Louisa*, b. Oct. 28, 1858.

MOODY, SARAH, wid. of Dea. John of Hartford, d. in Hadley, 1671.

1. MOODY, SAMUEL, supposed to have been the only child of Dea. John Moody of Hartford, and grandson of George Moody of Moulton, Suffolk Co., Eng., d. Sept. 22, 1689. He m. Sarah, dau. of John Deming of Wethersfield, Ct. She d. Sept. 29, 1717. Children—*Sarah*, m. Dec. 23, 1680, John Kellogg, and d. Sept. 19, 1689; *John*, b. July 24, 1661, settled in Hartford, Ct., and d. Nov. 5, 1732, ae. 71; *Hannah*, b. March 5, 1663, d. unm. Jan. 6, 1713; *Mary*, m. (1) June 30, 1689, Alexander Panton; (2) June 29, 1689, James Munn; *Samuel*, b. Nov. 28, 1670; *Ebenezer*, b. Oct 23, 1675.

2. SAMUEL, s. of Samuel, (1) d. Nov. 10, 1744, ae. 82. He m. Sept. 5, 1700, Sarah, dau. of Samuel Lane of Suffield, Ct. She was alive in Jan. 1758. Children—*Samuel*, b. Sept. 10, 1702; *John*, b. Sept. 10, 1702; *Nathan*, b. June 27, 1706; *Jonathan*, b. June 2, 1708; *David*, b. Dec. 3, 1711; *Sarah*, b. May 30, 1717, d. May 22, 1719; *Sarah*, b. Sept. 29, 1720.

3. EBENEZER, s. of Samuel, (1) d. Nov. 11, 1757, ae. 82. He m. Editha, who d. Aug. 19, 1757, in 75th yr. Children—*Jonathan*, b. Jan. 13, 1703, d. April 3, 1703; *Mary*, b. Dec. 28, 1705, m. 1730, Nehemiah Dickinson of Granby, and d. Nov. 15, 1787; *Ebenezer*, b. Feb. 22, 1707; *Sarah*, b. Jan. 13, 1709; *Joseph*, b. Jan. 13, 1712; *Daniel*, b. March 12, 1715, d. s. p. in So. H., April 20, 1792. He m. 1744, Mercy Morgan of Springfield. She d. Nov. 6, [7?] 1786, ae. 73; *Josiah*, b. 1721; *Editha*, m. Oct. 23, 1746, Joseph White; *Miriam*, m. Jan. 19, 1748, Reuben Smith.

4. SAMUEL, s. of Samuel, (2) Granby, d. Dec. 11, 1765. He m. Oct. 13, 1729, Mary Hovey. She d. Sept. 15, 1775, in 65th yr. Children—*Samuel*, b. July 2, 1730, d. unm. Dec. 4, 1820, ae. 90; *Gideon*, b. March 24, 1733, d. 1755; *Thomas Hovey*, b. Aug. 31, 1736; *Elisha*, b. Jan. 14, 1738; *Reuben*, b. Jan. 21, 1740, d. unm. Jan. 1831, ae. 91; *Simeon*, b. July 4, 1743, d. 1746; *Simeon*, b. Oct. 30, 1747; *Enos*, b. April 7, 1753.

5. JOHN, s. of Samuel, (2) Granby, d. 1769. He m. June 24, 1733, Sarah Dickinson. Children—*John*, b. July 8, 1734, d. unm. Oct. 4, 1815, ae. 81; *Sarah*, b. Jan. 9, 1736, d. unm. Nov. 21, 1819, ae. 83; *Moses*, b. Aug. 28, 1737, d. unm. 1774; *Aaron*, b. Oct. 1, 1739, d. Oct. 14, 1819, ae. 80. He m. (1) Elizabeth Catlin; (2) Hannah, wid. of Aaron Warner; *Hannah*, b. Sept. 17, 1741, m. Timothy Smith; *Joel*, b. Oct. 27, 1743, d. in Amh. March

22, 1824, ae. 80. He m. Rebecca Goodman; *Rachel*, b. Jan. 13, 1746, m. 1777, David Church of Gr.; *Lois*, b. June 24, 1750, m. Aaron Ayres.

6. NATHAN, s. of Samuel, (2) res. in Amh. and Ludlow, and d. abt. 1791. He m. March 16, 1735, Abigail Montague. Children—*John*, b. Feb. 27, 1736; *Josiah*, b. Feb. 24, 1740, d. 1780; *Abigail*, bapt. 1750, d. 1750; *Abigail*, bapt. 1752.

7. JONATHAN, s. of Samuel, (2) Amh., d. March 9, 1798, ae. 89. He m. Nov. 20, 1730, Bridget Smith. She d. March 12, 1786. Children—*Huldah*, b. May 31, 1731, m. Oct. 26, 1751, Oliver Chauncey; *Jonathan*, b. Jan. 10, 1734, res. in Amh., and d. April 9, 1804. He m. March 1, 1759, Eunice Graves of Hat.; *Asahel*, b. July 7, 1736, res. in Amh., and d. Aug. 9, 1813; *Lemuel*, b. June 27, 1739, res. in Amh., m. ——— Williams, and d. Jan. 22, 1818; *Eldad*, b. Oct. 17, 1746, res. in Amh., m. Nov. 21, 1782, Abigail Pratt, and d. June 16, 1814; *Medad*, b. Oct 17, 1746, res. in Amh., m. Rebecca Lee, and d. Jan. 8, 1813; *Perez*, b. Dec. 25, 1749, m. Lucy Ingram.

8. EBENEZER, s. of Ebenezer, (3) rem. to Belchertown, and d. 1789. He m. (1) Feb. 1, 1739, Joanna Warner of Belchertown. She d. Nov. 14, 1772; (2) Wid. Anna Chapin. Children—*Elijah*, b. Sept. 7, 1739, m. 1762, Elijah Wheeler, and d. 1773; *Joanna*, b. 1742, m. David Warriner, Jr. of Wilbraham; *Ebenezer*, b. 1743, d. young; *Ebenezer*, b. Sept. 10, 1744, m. Lois Smith, and d. in So. H., June 23, 1833, ae. 88; *Jerusha*, b. 1747, d. unm. 1775; *Matthew*, b. 1749, d. unm. 1779.

9. JOSEPH, s. of Ebenezer, (3) So. Had., d. Sept. 15, 1803, in 92d yr. He m. Sarah Kellogg, who d. June, 1782, in 69th yr. Children—*Joseph*, b. Feb. 2, 1738, d. Jan. 5, 1757; *Lois*, b. Oct. 29, 1740, d. Feb. 29, 1741; *Noah*, b. March 29, 1742; *Eunice*, b. Dec. 23, 1746, d. 1746; *Silence*, b. May, 1748, d. 1749; *Seth*, b. Jan. 16, 1750, d. 1752; *Seth*, b. Sept. 28, 1752; *Daniel*, b. Jan. 17, 1755.

10. JOSIAH, s. of Ebenezer, (3) So. Had., m. (1) Jan. 17, 1745, Rebecca White, who d. Sept. 15, 1751, ae. 27; (2) Dorcas, wid. of Noah Clapp of Nh. She d. Nov. 16, 1762, ae. 34; (3) Sarah, wid. of Matthew Clark. She d. March 11, 1810, ae. 82. Children—*Eliphaz*, b. Nov. 23, 1745, d. May 15, 1752; *Josiah*, b. Aug. 7, 1748; *Rebecca*, b. July 21, 1750, d. Sept. 6, 1758; *Dorcas*, b. Aug. 8, 1754; *Mercy*, b. Oct. 18, 1756; *Sarah*, b. July 16, 1764; *Eliphaz*, b. Sept. 20, 1766; *Sylvester*, b. May 20, 1771.

11. THOMAS HOVEY, s. of Samuel, (4) So. Had., d. Sept. 8, 1772. He m. Eunice. Children—*Gideon*, b. March 15, 1765; *Mary*, b. April 28, 1767; *Eunice*, b. April 6, 1769; *Martha*, b. Feb. 14, 1772.

12. ELISHA, s. of Samuel, (4) Gr., d. Jan. 17, 1825, ae. 87. He m. April 15, 1766, Elizabeth, dau. of Martin Nash of Gr. She d. July 3, 1833. Children—*Elisha*, b. March 12, 1767, d. Oct. 16, 1770; *Miriam*, b. Aug. 19, 1768, d. unm. July 2, 1801; *Samuel*, b. April 4, 1770, res. in Gr.; *Elisha*, b. Jan. 14, 1772, d. Jan. 23, 1772; *Azor*, b. Dec. 26, 1772, d. Sept. 25, 1775; *Elizabeth*, b. June 5, 1774, d. March 1, 1795; *Finis*, b. Dec. 13, 1776, m. Jahiel Warner; *Azor*, b. Oct. 17, 1778, grad. D. C. 1808, and settled in Bainbridge, N. Y.; *Sibil*, b. Aug. 9, 1780, m. ——— Johnson, and d. April 10, 1809; *Mary*, b. Aug. 28, 1782, d. unm. Aug. 12, 1801, ae. 18; *Elisha*, b. Feb. 26, 1786, res. in Gr.

13. SIMEON, s. of Samuel, (4) Gr., d. July 16, 1815, ae. 67. He m. Mercy ——— who d. Sept. 14, 1815, ae. 67. Children—*Simeon*, b. 1774; *Lois*, b. 1776; *Thomas*, b. 1778; *Ruth*, b. 1781; *Levi*, b. Feb. 10, 1784; *Mercy*, b. 1786; *Reuben*, b. 1789; *Calvin*, b. 1794.

1. MORTON, RICHARD, a blacksmith, rem. in 1670 from Hartford to Hat., and d. April 3, 1710. He m. Ruth ———, who d. Dec. 31, 1714. Children —*Thomas; Richard*, d. in Hat., Feb. 4, 1692, m. Jan. 29, 1690, Mehitable, dau. of Isaac Graves. She m. (2) William Worthington, and d. in Colchester, Ct., March 22, 1742, ae. abt. 70; *John*, b. Jan. 21, 1670, d. April 26, 1670; *Joseph*, b. April, 1672; *John*, b. April, 1674, d. young; *Abraham*, b. May, 1676; *Elizabeth*, b. March 31, 1680, m. Dec. 27, 1704, John Warner of Wethersfield, Ct., and d. 1741; *Ebenezer*, b. Aug. 11, 1682; *Jonathan*, b. Nov. 2, 1684.

2. JOSEPH, s. of Richard, (1) Hat., d. Sept. 28, 1730. He m. Mary (prob. Marsh.) Children—*Ruth*, b. Dec. 15, 1699, d. Oct. 30, 1730; *Elizabeth*, b. April 4, 1704, m. Samuel Warner of Hat.; *Abigail*, b. July 18, 1707, d. young; *John; Thankful*, b. May 21, 1713, m. Ephraim Allen of Hat.; *Joseph*, b. Oct. 24, 1715, d. prob. abt. 1744, in Amh., leaving no family; *Abigail*, b. Oct. 18, 1720; *Mary*, d. April 10, 1723.

3. ABRAHAM, s. of Richard, (1) Hat., m. May 8, 1701, Sarah Kellogg. Children—*Abraham*, b. May 2, 1703, perhaps settled in Athol; *Richard*, b. Oct. 1, 1704, was of Athol in 1750; *Sarah*, b. April, 1707, m. Samuel Smith; *Samuel*, b. Sept. 8, 1709, m. 1731, Lydia Smith, and was of Athol in 1750; *Abigail*, b. Jan. 6, 1711, d. Feb. 1, 1715; *Moses; Daniel*, b. Dec. 23, 1720; *Abigail*, b. Feb. 1, 1723, d. Dec. 24, 1726; *Noah*, m. Rhoda ———, and settled in Athol.

4. EBENEZER, s. of Richard, (1) Hat., d. abt. 1760, as is inferred from the fact, that his will executed Jan. 1754, was proved April, 1760. He m. Sarah Belding. Children—*Son*, b. 1711, d. ae. 5 weeks; *Dorothy*, b. Dec. 6, 1712, m. (1) ——— Belding; (2) Elnathan Graves, and d. abt. 1801; *Lydia*, b. March 24, 1715, m. 1735, Joseph Bardwell of Belchertown; *Elisha*, b. April 1, 1717; *Eunice*, b. May 14, 1721, m. Elijah Morton; *Simeon; Oliver; Ebenezer*, b. Dec. 8, 1725, m. Azubah, and d. in Hat. abt. 1797; *Seth*, b. Sept. 6, 1729.

5. JONATHAN, s. of Richard, (1) blacksmith in Hat., d. April 23, 1767. He m. 1710, Sarah, dau. of Chileab Smith. She d. Oct. 5, 1760, in 73d yr. Children—*Jonathan*, b. Jan. 25, 1711, d. March 10, 1711; *Martha*, b. Nov. 18, 1713; *Jonathan*, b. July 12, 1716, m. Eleanor, dau. of Joseph Smith, and d. abt. 1788; *Elijah*, b. Nov. 10, 1718, m. Eunice Morton, and d. Oct. 5, 1798; *David*, b. Sept. 12, 1721; *Sarah*, b. Oct. 12, 1725, m. 1750, Ephraim Doolittle; *Mary*, b. Sept. 29, 1727, m. Samuel Smith; *Lucy*, b. Sept, 21, 1732, d. 1766.

6. JOHN, s. of Joseph, (2) Amh., m. Aug. 4, 1730, Lydia, dau. of Samuel Hawley of Amh. She d. abt. 1793. Children—*Ruth*, b. March 2, 1732, m. 1758, [pub. June 17,] John Keet of Amh.; *Rhoda*, b. Aug. 8, 1735, m. April 24, 1755, Peletiah Smith of Amh.; *Thomas*, b. Oct. 18, 1739, m. (1) April 29, 1762, Sarah Barrett; (2) Mrs. Hannah Root; *Lydia*, b. May 19, 1742, m. John Williams of Amh.; *John*, b. May 13, 1745, m. Lydia, dau. of Samuel

Ingram of Amh., and d. May 11, 1834, ae. 89; *Joseph*, b. March 13, 1750, m. ——— Wilson of Sunderland.

7. DANIEL, s. of Abraham, (3) rem. from Hat. to Whately, and d. 1786. He m. (1) 1743, Esther Bardwell, who d. Oct. 27, 1762; (2) Eleanor Wait. Children—*Hannah*, b. Sept. 7, 1744, m. Matthew Graves, and rem. to Norwich, Chenango Co., N. Y.; *Tabitha*, b. Aug. 2, 1747, m. Dr. Charles Doolittle of Hardwick; *Sarah*, b. Dec. 14, 1749, m. Oliver Smith of Northfield; *Mercy*, b. Nov. 25, 1751, m. John Lamson of Cummington; *Joel*, b. Jan. 22, 1754, rem. to Norwich, N. Y.; *Daniel*, b. Feb. 12, 1756, res. in Whately; *Esther*, b. Nov. 3, 1758, m. Dr. Lucius Doolittle of Hardwick; *Justin*, b. Sept. 25, 1760, res. in Whately; *Consider*, b. Oct 12, 1762, res. in Whately; *Tirzah*, m. Wm. Mather, and rem. to Spencertown, N. Y.; *Roxa*, m. Isaac Smith, and rem. to New York.

1. MURRAY, WILLIAM, Amh., d. abt. 1784. He m. Feb. 20, 1723, Hannah, dau. of John Dickinson of Hat. Children—*Elijah*, b. Nov. 28, 1723, d. March, 1742; *William*, b. July 30, 1726; *Dorothy*, b. Aug. 4, 1729, m. May 9, 1754, Abner Adams; *David*, b. Nov. 3, 1735; *Seth*, b. May 21, 1736; *Hannah*, b. abt. 1744, m. Nov. 22, 1764, Timothy Abbot of Bennington, Vt.

2. WILLIAM, s. of William, (1) d. abt. 1762. He m. Mercy Scott of Sunderland. Children—*Elihu*, b. Oct. 13, 1753; *Elijah*, b. June 6, 1756; *Mercy*, b. Sept. 16, 1758; *Martha*, b. July 14, 1761.

3. SETH, s. of William, (1) Hat., d. while on a visit in Canandaigua, N. Y., Sept. 26, 1795, ae. 59. He m. Dec. 22, 1768, Elizabeth, dau. of Daniel White of Hatfield and Bolton, Ct. She d. Feb. 4, 1814, ae. 77. Children—*Lucinda*, b. Dec. 9, 1770, m. Nov. 10, 1790, Isaac Maltby of Hat., (Yale Col. 1786) who d. 1819. She d. abt. 1836.

1. NASH, TIMOTHY, s. of Thomas of New Haven, Ct., by trade a blacksmith, rem. from New Haven to Hartford about 1661, and thence in 1663 to Hadley. He was Representative 1690, 1691 and 1695. He d. March 13, 1699, in 73d yr. He m. abt. 1657, Rebekah, dau. of Rev. Samuel Stone of Hartford. She d. March or April, 1709. Children—*Rebecca*, b. March 12, 1658, d. young; *Samuel*, b. Feb. 3, 1660, was killed 1668, by a fall from a horse; *Thomas*; *Joseph*, b. Jan. 27, 1664, d. unm. in Granby, March 28, 1740, ae. 76; *Timothy*; *John*, b. Aug. 21, 1667; *Samuel*, b. June 17, 1669, d. unm. May 3, 1738, ae. 69; *Hope*, b. Nov. 26, 1670, m. Jan. 24, 1694, Isaac Warner; *Ebenezer*, b. Oct. 25, 1673; *Daniel*, m. June 1, 1710, Experience Clark, and d. March 10, 1760, ae. 84; *Mary*, d. Dec. 19, 1687; *Ephraim*, b. abt. 1682.

2. THOMAS, s. of Timothy, (1) Hat., d. Jan. 19, 1728. He m. Aug. 1685, Hannah Coleman, who d. July 4, 1722. Children—*John*, b. Oct. 28, 1686; *Hannah*, b. Sept. 2, 1689, m. Oct. 27, 1712, John Arms; *Thomas*, b. Feb. 26, 1693; *Rebeccah*, b. April 20, 1699, m. 1720, William Marsh, and d. May 12, 1768, ae. 69; *Sarah*, b. July 9, 1704, d. unm.

3. JOHN, s. of Timothy, (1) blacksmith, representative 1707, 1716, 1719, 1720, 1724, 1728, 1731, d. Oct. 7, 1743, ae. 76. He m. (1) March 29, 1689, Hannah Porter, who d. May 26, 1689; (2) Nov. 27, 1691, Elizabeth Kellogg,

who d. in West Hartford, Ct., July 4, 1750, in 77th yr. Children—*Rebecca*, b. Feb. 27, 1693, d. Nov. 1, 1703, ae. 10; *John*, b. July 2, 1694; *Moses*, b. July 2, 1696, settled in West Hartford, Ct., and d. Jan. 26, 1760, ae. 63. He m. (1) Rebecca Graves; (2) Oct. 30, 1744, Mrs. Mary Kellogg; *Elizabeth*, b. Dec. 15, 1698, d. Dec. 31, 1698; *Timothy*, b. Nov. 13, 1699, settled in Longmeadow, and d. March 15, 1756, ae. 56; *Abigail*, b. April 10, 1702, m. Dec. 1, 1725, Dea. Abraham Merrill of West Hartford, Ct., and d. April 3, 1782, ae. 82; *Stephen*, b. Sept. 20, 1704, settled in Westfield, and d. 1764. He m. May 22, 1728, Elizabeth Smith; *Daniel*, b. Dec. 8, 1706; *Samuel*, b. Jan. 29, 1709, res. in Farmington, Ct. and Goshen, Ct. He m. (1) Jan. 24, 1734, Margaret Merrill; (2) Mrs. —— Dickinson; *Phineas*, b. Jan. 18, 1713, d. March 24, 1713; *Enos*, b. April 21, 1714.

4. EBENEZER, s. of Timothy, (1) removed after the birth of his children, to Suffield, Ct., where he d. 1748. He m. July, 1701, Mary, dau. of John Scott of Springfield. She d. Oct. 19, 1747. Children—*Jonathan*, b. May 30, 1702, d. Nov. 7, 1704, ae. 2; *Mary*, b. Oct. 29, 1704, m. Nov. 18, 1730, John Hovey of Mansfield, Ct., and d. Oct. 3, 1746; *Miriam*, b. Jan. 27, 1710, m. Aug. 24, 1742, Moses Scott of Bernardston.

5. EPHRAIM, s. of Timothy, (1) So. Had., d. Nov. 9, 1759, in 78th yr. He m. Jan. 10, 1705, Joanna, dau. of Dea. John Smith. Children—*Timothy*, b. Jan. 26, 1707; *Ephraim*, b. Jan. 16, 1710, d. Feb. 15, 1710; *Aaron*, b. Feb. 23, 1712; *Joanna*, b. July 4, 1715, d. ae. 4 days; *Joanna*, b. Aug. 28, 1716, d. Oct. 20, 1716; *Martin*, b. Jan. 19, 1718; *Eleazar*, b. Feb. 10, 1720; *Elisha*, b. Oct. 8, 1729.

6. JOHN, s. of Thomas, (2) Hat., d. April 7, 1764, ae. 77. He m. Dec. 29, 1715, Abilene, dau. of John Field of Hat. She d. July 15, [18?] 1764, ae. 75. Children—*Hannah*, b. Sept. 16, 1716, m. Sept. 30, 1736, Ebenezer Belding of Ashfield; *Noah*, b. March 26, 1719, d. March 9, 1795, ae. 75. He m. (1) 1753, Hepzibah Bodman; (2) Abigail Belding; *Mary*, b. abt. 1721, d. Nov. 11, 1725, ae. abt. 4; *Martha*, m. Feb. 11, 1752, Phinehas Warner of New Braintree; *Abigail*, m. Dea. Hezekiah Belding of Amh.; *Daughter*, m. —— Carpenter.

7. THOMAS, s. of Thomas, (2) Hat. and Williamsburgh, d. March 12, 1773, ae. 80. He m. June 8, 1727, Martha, dau. of Joseph Smith of Hat. Children—*Submit*, b. May 18, 1728, d. June 11, 1728; *Rebecca*, b. Feb. 26, 1730, d. unm; *Submit*, b. Feb. 13, 1732, d. unm.; *Elisha*, b. Aug. 2, 1734, d. Dec. 25, 1739; *John*, b. Oct. 20, 1736, settled in Williamsburgh, and d. May 31, 1773, ae. 36. He m. Dec. 27, 1758, Martha Graves; *Moses*, b. Sept. 29, 1739, d. unm.; *Martha*, b. Feb. 21, 1742, d. unm.; *Elisha*, b. Oct. 1, 1744, d. Sept. 15, 1827, ae. 83. He m. (1) Aug. [July 14?] 1767, Elizabeth Smith; (2) Oct. 8, 1783, Naomi Sheldon; (3) Feb. 27, 1812, Mrs. Sarah Clark; (4) May 27, [30?] 1827, Mrs. Mary Johnson.

8. JOHN, s. of John, (3) rem. to Amh., was deacon in the Cong. church, and d. abt. 1778. He m. Nov. 1716, Hannah Ingram. Children—*Jonathan*, b. July 28, 1717; *David*, b. June 6, 1719; *Hannah*, b. June 26, 1723; *John*.

9. DANIEL, s. of John, (3) resided in So. Had. until about the time of the American Revolution, when he removed to Shelburne, and d. Aug. 24, 1791, in 84th yr. He m. Abigail ——, who d. in Conway, Sept. 6, 1803, ae. 93.

Children—*Marah*, b. July 7, 1731, m. June 22, 1751, Samuel Kellogg of So. Had., and d. June, 1811, ae. 80; *Joseph*, b. March 1, 1734, res. in So. Had. and Rowe, and d. Dec. 23, 1799, ae. 68. He m. Abigail Cooper; *Abigail*, b. Feb. 17, 1740, m. Jan. 5, 1762, Azariah Alvord, and d. in So. Had. March 31, 1782; *Daniel*, b. March 22, 1742, settled in Great Barrington, and d. May 6, 1794. He m. May 3, 1770, Abigail Dewey; *Eunice*, b. Oct. 8, 1744, m. Enoch Chapin of So. Had., and d. Nov. 27, 1802; *Azubah*, b. June 24, 1747, m. 1771, Joshua Abbott of Conway; *Benjamin*, b. July 3, 1750, rem. from So. Had. to Shelburne, and d. June 17, 1797, ae. 47. He m. Jan. 1, 1778, Lydia, dau. of Aaron Skinner of Colchester, Ct.; *Elihu*, b. Sept. 16, 1752, d. unm.

10. ENOS, s. of John, (3) blacksmith, deacon in Church, d. Aug. 28, 1768, ae. 54. He m. Feb. 18, 1736, Joanna Barnard, who d. March 10, 1788, in 73d yr. Children—*Joanna*, b. Jan. 1, 1737, d. 1740; *Enos*, d. young; *Rebecca*, m. Sept. 4, 1766, Nehemiah Gaylord; *Enos*; *Josiah*, b. Aug. 27, 1749.

11. TIMOTHY, s. of Ephraim, (5) resided in Granby and Shutesbury. He m. Oct. 15, 1736, Experience Kellogg. Children—*Joanna*, b. Dec. 29, 1737, m. 1768, Jacob Hastings of Warwick; *Samuel*, b. Jan. 29, 1739, settled in Lunenburgh, Vt.; *Timothy*, b. Oct. 15, 1740, m. Mary Powers, and settled in Lunenburgh, Vt.; *Experience*, b. Dec. 14, 1743, m. 1764, George Wheeler; *Mary Crouch*, b. May 20, 1747, m. 1768, James Lyman of Northfield, and d. March 23, 1777, ae. 29.

12. AARON, s. of Ephraim, (5) removed, about 1774, from Granby to Brattleboro', Vt. He m. Dec. 2, 1736, Damaris, dau. of William Wait, Jr., of Nh. She was b. Feb. 26, 1717. Children—*Damaris*, b. Nov. 19, 1737, m. Rev. Titus Smith of West Suffield, Ct., and d. Aug. 1779, ae. 41; *Phebe*, b. March 22, 1739, m. William Williams of Brattleboro', Vt., and d. 1798; *Aaron*, b. March 24, 1741, rem. from Brattleboro', to Ellisburg, N. Y., and d. Jan. 17, 1827, ae. 85. He m. Hannah, dau. of Dea. David Nash of So. Had.; *Sarah*, b. Dec. 27, 1744, m. John Ellis of Brattleboro', Vt., and d. Jan. 7, 1827, ae. 82; *Moses*, b. Nov. 10, 1750, rem. to Brattleboro', and d. June 25, 1821, ae. 70. He m. 1772, Grace McCune; *Oliver*, b. Aug. 20, 1752, res. in Brattleboro' and Ellisburg, N. Y., and d. Nov. 20, 1835, ae. 83. He m. June 2, 1777, Mary Hooker; *Ebenezer*, b. July 20, 1756, d. unm. in Brattleboro', Vt.

13. MARTIN, s. of Ephraim, (5) Granby, d. Oct. 9, 1749, ae. 31. He m. Oct. 20, 1743, Elizabeth, dau. of William Wait, Jr., of Nh. She was b. June 25, 1712, and d. in Brattleboro', Vt., May 6, 1799, ae. 86. Children— *Elizabeth*, b. Sept. 30, 1744, m. April 15, 1766, Elisha Moody of Gr., and d. July 3, 1833, ae. 88; *Chloe*, b. Feb. 26, 1746, m. Daniel Warriner of Brattleboro', Vt., and d. July 4, 1800, ae. 54; *Miriam*, b. Nov. 26, 1747, rem. to State of New York; *Martin*, b. April 9, 1749, rem. to the West.

14. ELEAZER, s. of Ephraim, (5) Granby, d. May 19, 1775, ae. 55. He m. Nov. 9, 1749, Phebe, dau. of Nathaniel Kellogg, Jr. Children—*Lucy*, b. Sept. 18, 1750, m. (1) March 5, 1789, Azariah Alvord; (2) Oct. 31, 1813, John Stickney, and d. Dec. 24, 1836, ae. 86; *Joanna*, b. abt. 1752, d. unm. May 16, 1816, in 64th yr.; *Ephraim*, b. March, 1754, rem. to Brattleboro', Vt., and d. Dec. 18, 1816. He m. Feb. 2, 1786, Hannah Wells; *Eleazer*, b. Aug. 1755, res. in Granby, and d. June 9, 1836, ae. 80. He m. April 6, 1795,

Abigail Brown of Amh.; *Nathaniel*, b. 1757, d. unm. July 8, 1834, ae. 77; *Phebe*, b. Jan. 14, 1768, m. July 15, 1789, [1790?] Josiah Smith of So. Had., and d. Jan. 11, 1847, ae. 78.

15. ELISHA, s. of Ephraim, (5) Granby, d. March, 1814, ae. 84. He m. Lois Frost, who d. Nov. 1820, ae. 83. Children—*Samuel*, b. Feb. 1, 1760, d. in Dover, Athens Co., Ohio, Sept. 5, [9?] 1823, ae. 63. He m. (1) Vashti Pierre; (2) Jan. 1, 1822, Lucy Goodenow; *Rebecca*, b. Nov. 7, 1762, d. unm. March 23, 1796, ae. 34; *Lois*, b. Jan. 15, 1765, prob. d. unm.; *Elisha*, b. Sept. 11, 1766, settled in Williamsburgh, and d. 1827. He m. Elizabeth Ludden; *Justin*, b. April 25, 1768, settled in North East, Erie Co., O., and d. March 15, 1851, ae. 82. He m. (1) Ruth Hopkins; (2) May 18, 1743, Betsey Nettleton; *Adonijah*, b. March 1, 1770, d. in Argyle, N. Y., June 9, 1849, ae. 79. He m. 1801, Sarah Breck; *Dorcas*, b. Feb. 18, 1772, m. 1797, Joel White of So. Had., and d. April 5, 1837, ae. 65; *Simeon*, b. Sept. 8, 1776, res. in So. Had., and d. July 15, 1850, ae. 73. He m. (1) 1801, Amy White; (2) March 29, 1827, Mrs. Naomi Chapin; (3) May 26, 1830, Elizabeth Chapin.

16. JONATHAN, s. of Dea. John, (8) Amh., d. Sept. 28, 1796, ae. 79. He m. Mary, dau. of Samuel Hawley of Amh. Children—*Jonathan*, bapt. Aug. 19, 1744, res. in Amh., m. Anna Hastings, and d. 1796; *Joseph*, bapt. April 5, 1747, res. in Whately, m. March 15, 1770, Lucy Allis, and d. May 15, 1804; *Amos*, bapt. 1750, res. in Amh., m. Eunice Pomeroy; *Reuben*, bapt. Nov. 1, 1752, res. in Amh., m. April, 1780, Lydia Edwards, and d. Jan. 24, 1831; *Abner*, bapt. April 10, 1757, m. (1) Hannah Dickinson; (2) 1813, Sarah Munson, and d. in Earlville, N. Y., Aug. 22, 1837; *Mary*, bapt. July 6, 1760, d. unm.; *Abigail*, m. Dec. 16, 1784, Stoughton Dickinson of Amh.; *Samuel*, d. unm. in Pelham.

17. DAVID, s. of Dea. John, (8) Amh. and So. Had., d. April 26, 1803, ae. 82. He m. (1) Sept. 29, 1742, Jemima, dau. of Samuel Boltwood of Amh.; (2) May 9, 1754, Elizabeth Smith. She d. 1765; (3) Experience, wid. of Amos Loomis of Southampton, and dau. of Nathaniel Parsons of Nh. She was b. Aug. 9, 1729, and d. Feb. 1817, ae. 87. Children—*Samuel*, bapt. Sept. 8, 1745, prob. d. young; *David*, bapt. Aug. 9, 1747, d. Sept. 25, 1750; *Hannah*, m. Aaron Nash, and d. Feb. 24, 1825; *David*, b. Feb. 10, 1755, m. Lois Alvord, res. for many years in Granby, but rem. before his death to Watervliet, N. Y., where he d. Oct. 6, 1832, ae. 77; *Abigail*, b. June 1, 1757, m. July 2, 1789, Daniel Moody of Granby, and d. June 4, 1802, ae. 45; *Jonathan*, b. Nov. 5, 1760, grad. D. C. 1789, was ord. as pastor of (Cong.) church in Middlefield, Oct. 31, 1792, and dismissed July 11, 1832. He m. (1) Oct. 30, 1793, Eunice, dau. of Edward Taylor of Montgomery; (2) June 22, 1803, Rebecca, wid. of Alpheus Russell, and dau. of Isaac Clark. He d. Aug. 31, 1834, ae. 73; *Asa*, b. Dec. 1, 1763, res. in So. H. He m. (1) Oct. 21, 1792, Kezia Eastman; (2) March 31, 1808, Lydia Bodurtha, and d. May 25, 1814, ae. 50; *Elizabeth*, b. March 19, 1765, d. young.

18. JOHN, s. of Dea. John, (8) Amh. He m. (1) Mary Graves of Hat.; (2) April 23, 1778, Sarah, wid. of Ebenezer Kellogg of Amh., and dau. of Preserved Clapp of Amh. Children—*Levi*, d. unm., ae. abt. 20; *Judith*, m. Samuel Boltwood of Amh., and d. April 28, 1832, ae. 76; *Miriam*, m. June 15, 1779, Samuel Field; *Mary*, bapt. Dec. 9, 1759, m. (1) 1779, Firmin Wood;

(2) David Stockbridge, and d. June 20, 1832, ae. 75; *Child*, bapt. Sept. 27, 1761, prob. d. young; *Lucretia*, bapt. April 17, 1763, d. in youth; *Martha*, bapt. Sept. 16, 1764, d. unm. Oct. 5, 1836; *Moses*, bapt. Dec. 20, 1767, res. in Amh., m. Sally Lewis, and d. Sept. 28, 1841.

19. ENOS, s. of Enos, (10) d. March 30, 1796, ae. 49. He m. (1) Nov. 27, 1771, Martha, dau. of Samuel Gaylord. She d. Sept. 25, 1788, ae. 41; (2) April 28, 1794, Eleanor Stebbins of Springfield. She was b. Sept. 3, 1755, and d. in Enfield, Ct. Children—*Martha*, b. June 5, 1773, m. Eli Smith, and d. July 28, 1817, ae. 44; *Enos*, b. Feb. 10, 1775; *Cotton*, b. Sept. 27, 1776; *Erastus*, b. Feb. 12, 1780; *Lemuel*, b. Nov. 18, 1782, d. unm., in U. S. service in Burlington, Vt., Dec. 11, 1812, ae. 30; *Sarah*, b. Aug. 12, 1785, d. unm. July 10, 1824, ae. 38; *Peggy*, b. Oct. 11, 1787, d. Dec. 8, 1787.

20. JOSIAH, s. of Enos, (10) blacksmith, d. March 4, 1814, ae. 64. He m. Jan. 30, 1772, Eunice, dau. of Simeon Knight of Ware, Mass , and Rockingham, Vt. She was b. July 24, 1751, and d. Feb. 14, 1814, ae. 62. Children—*Samuel*, b. Nov. 13, 1772, d. April 20, 1787, ae. 15; *Josiah*, b. March 2, 1775, killed by the kick of a horse, May, 1793, ae. 18; *John*, b. Nov. 29, 1776; *Elijah*, b. Dec. 16, 1778; *Timothy*, b. July 6, 1781; *Eunice*, b. Nov. 5, 1783, d. unm. April 5, 1812, ae. 38; *Oliver*, b. Oct. 24, 1785; *Samuel*, b. Nov. 29, 1788, d. March 5, 1789; *Lois*, b. Dec. 8, 1789, d. unm.; *Joanna*, b. Jan. 29, 1792, m. Jan. 27, 1814, Enos Dickinson of Amh., and d. March 19, 1818, ae. 26; *Sarah*, b. March 25, 1794, m. Jan. 1823, Andrew Scott, and d. in Cleveland, O., Jan. 21, 1847, ae. 52; *Submit*, b. June 25, 1797, m. Jan. 31, 1838, Dea. John Tolman of Ware.

21. ENOS, s. of Enos, (19) Hat., d. Nov. 3, 1823, ae. 48. He m. Feb. 21, 1797, Sarah Wells of Hatfield. She d. Aug. 1848. Children—*Martha*, b. Sept. 10, 1797, prob. d. Oct. 1798; *Abel Wells*, b. May, 1799, m. July 13, 1820, Mary Mosher, and res. in Whately; *Enos*, b. March 3, 1801, d. Aug. 13, 1802; *Patty Gaylord*, b. May, 1803, m. Aug. 17, 1818, Simeon Dickinson; *Sally*, b. April 4, 1805, d. 1805; *Sally Chapin*, b. June 6, 1806, m. William Blake; *Daughter*, b. Dec. 21, 1807, d. 1807; *Enos Barnard*, b. July, 1809, res. in Rushville, Ill., m. Nov. 6, 1838, Katherine Keller; *Mary Stebbins*, b. Oct. 27, 1811, m. Oct. 20, 1831, Samuel Shipman of Had.

22. COTTON, s. of Enos, (19) d. in Had. He m. Nov. 18, 1804, Phebe, dau. of Joseph Smith. Children—*Aminta Day*, b. April 13, 1808, d. Aug. 28, 1811, ae. 3; *Nancy*, b. March 22, 1811, m. April 19, 1832, Wyman Smith; *Lorenzo S.*, b. July 4, 1814, m. Nov. 21, 1838, Permelia Smith, and res. in Granby.

23. ERASTUS, s. of Enos, (19) joiner, d. Sept. 20, 1849, ae. 69. He m. June 4, 1804, Penelope Gaylord. Children—*Elizabeth Worthington*, b. Dec. 10, 1804, d. Sept. 27, 1807, ae. 2; *Martha*, b. Jan. 3, 1807, d. Aug. 26, 1807; *Erastus*, b. Nov. 4, 1808; *Edwin*, b. Nov. 24, 1810, d. Aug. 9, 1824; *Lucius*, b. Jan. 21, 1813, d. Nov. 7, 1813; *Lucius*, b. Oct. 25, 1814; *George Williams*, b. May 23, 1817, d. Dec. 4, 1831, ae. 14; *Elizabeth Worthington*, b. Oct. 16, 1818, m. May 19, 1841, Enos E. Cook; *Cotton Gaylord*, b. Sept. 10, 1820; *Martha Smith*, b. April 9, 1823, m. Oct. 20, 1843, Addington Daniels.

24. JOHN, s. of Josiah, (20) followed the business of boating down the Conn. river to Hartford, until the building of the Conn. River R. R. in 1849

changed the mode of transportation, when he sold out his boats and gave up the business. He d. Jan. 10, 1858, ae. 81. He m. Lephe Packard, b. Feb. 19, 1777. She d. of disease of the heart, June 7, 1850, ae. 73. Children—*Josiah*, b. May 17, 1799; *Eliza*, b. Jan. 20, 1801, m. Nov. 20, 1823, Henry Hodge; *Walter*, b. Dec. 5, 1802, d. Sept. 23, 1804; *Mary*, b. Nov. 27, 1804, m. June 29, 1826, Lester W. Porter; *Lephe*, b. Aug. 30, 1807; *Lucinda*, b. April 3, 1811, m. Dec. 3, 1835, Theodore Clark; *John Walter*, b. Nov. 26, 1814; *Joanna D.*, b. Sept. 3, 1818, m. Jan. 22, 1837, Frederick Dickinson.

25. ELIJAH, s. of Josiah, (20) joiner and farmer, m. (1) Nov. 15, 1803, Electa Morton of Hat. She was b. Oct. 25, 1779, and d. Feb. 21, 1813; (2) Ruth, dau. of Josiah Cowls of Leverett. She d. June 22, 1846. Children—*Harriet*, b. March 29, 1804, m. Nov. 23, 1820, Levi Hawley; *Lucy*, b. Feb. 16, 1806, m. Aug. 30, 1843, Josiah Rice of Leverett; *Electa*, b. Nov. 19, 1807, d. unm. Jan. 13, 1829; *Samuel*, b. March 13, 1810; *Hiram*, b. April 16, and d. June 6, 1812.

26. TIMOTHY, s. of Josiah, (20) was a truckman in Boston, where he d. March 16, 1822. He m. —— ——. Children—*Matilda*, bapt. June 20, 1816; *Charles*, b. Oct. 1, 1811, m. Rachel Robbins, and res. in Amh.; *Julia*, bapt. Jan. 20, 1816, m. (1) Charles Jones; (2) Orrin Hammond.

27. OLIVER, s. of Josiah, (20) rem. in 1836 to Amh., and there d. 1856. He m. (1) 1810, Hannah Dickinson of Amh., who d. May 22, 1832; (2) Dec. 27, 1832, Sally, wid. of —— Kennan, and dau. of —— Whitcomb. She was b. in Princeton, March 21, 1798. Children—*Louisa*, b. Dec. 10, 1810, d. Oct. 1, 1824; *Eunice Knight*, b. May 25, 1813, m. May 7, 1840, Moses M. Brown of Springfield; *Lucretia Montague*, b. Aug. 11, 1815; *Oliver*, b. Aug. 4, 1818, m. Roxana Houghton, and d. in Boston, Feb. 7, 1851; *Hannah Submit*, b. June 6, 1823, m. Frederick Wells; *Timothy*, b. Oct. 20, 1833; *Horace*, b. July 2, 1836; *Sarah Louisa*, b. Aug. 9, 1839.

28. LORENZO S., s. of Cotton, (22) resides in Gr., is a deacon in the (Cong.) church, and was in 1859 a Representative to the General Court for the District embracing the towns of Amherst, Granby and Pelham. He m. Nov. 21, 1838, Permelia, dau. of Dr. Enos Smith of Gr. She was b. Sept. 20, 1817. Children—*Henry Smith*, b. Oct. 22, 1840, d. Sept. 14, 1841; *Sarah Hawkes*, b. Aug. 20, 1842.

29. ERASTUS, s. of Erastus, (23) m. (1) April 9, 1832, Achsah W., dau. of Jonathan Warner. She d. April 26, 1842; (2) April 19, 1843, Susan, dau. of Elisha Hubbard. Children—*Maria Williams*, b. April 11, 1833; *Edwin Smith*, b. Feb. 21, 1835; *Francis Lewis*, b. May 9, 1838; *Arthur Henry*, b. July 1, 1840, d. Aug. 20, 1841; *Isabella Susan*, b. April 22, 1844; *Margaret Louisa*, b. May 10, 1846; *Erastus Hall*, b. May 12, 1848.

30. LUCIUS, s. of Erastus, (23) m. (1) May, 1844, Margaret, dau. of Joseph Marsh. She d. May, 1846; (2) Nov. 14, 1846, Elizabeth, dau. of Moses Marsh. She d. Feb. 28, 1856, ae. 38; (3) Cornelia Johnson. Children—*George Williams*, b. May 10, 1845; *Henry Barnard*, b. Dec. 8, 1847, d. June 14, 1849.

31. JOSIAH, s. of John, (24) m. Nov. 20, 1823, Almira Colt, who d. Jan. 31, 1832. Child—*Catherine*, b. Nov. 16, 1825, m. April 8, 1846, Charles D. Hodge.

32. JOHN WALTER, s. of John, (24) m. May 2, 1837, Almira Bartlett· Children—*Almira*, b. March 16, 1843; *Sarah J.*, b. July 5, 1848; *Helen E.*' b. Aug. 13, 1849, d. Aug. 21, 1855, ae. 6.

33. SAMUEL, s. of Elijah, (25) was a farmer, surveyor, Representative to General Court 1844, deacon in North Hadley (Cong.) church, and d. 1861. He m. May 1, 1834, Lurintha Ball of Leverett. Children—*Laura E.*, b. July 9, 1835; *Martin Samuel*, b. March 20, 1838; *Jay Elijah*, b. March 29, 1843; *Jane Lurintha*, b. Sept. 23, 1845; *John*, b. Oct. 17, 1847; *Sarah E.*, b. May 15, 1850, d. May 23, 1851.

1. NEWTON, FRANCIS. Children—*Elizabeth*, m. Nov. 6, 1783, Moses Kellogg, Jr.; *Eleanor*, m. 1783, Jonathan Cook, Jr.; *Tryphena*, m. Jan. 3, 1790, Solomon Cooke; *Sally*, m. May 18, 1798, Daniel Russell, Jr.; *Francis*.

2. FRANCIS, s. of Francis, (1) m. July 21, 1794, Abigail, dau. of John Dickinson. Children—*Son*, bapt. July, 1796; *Theodocia*, bapt. Dec. 1, 1801; *Obed*, bapt. Feb. 21, 1802; *John*, bapt. Feb. 21, 1802.

NORTHAM, SAMUEL, s. of James of Hartford, Ct., carpenter, rem. before 1686 to Deerfield, and thence as early as 1709, to Colchester, Ct. He m. Mary Dickinson. Children—*Samuel*, b. May 4, 1675; *Mary*, b. Jan. 7, 1676; *Elizabeth*, b. April 11, 1680; *Jonathan*, b. May 18, 1682.

OSBORN, RICHARD, m. Dec. 15, 1796, Lucinda Gaylord. Children— *Chester*, bapt. Dec. 24, 1797; *Fanny Gaylord*, bapt. May 4, 1800.

1. PANTON or PANTHERN, ALEXANDER, m. June 30, 1689, Mary Moody. She m. (2) June 29, 1698, James Munn. Child—*Philip*, b. April 16, 1689.

2. PHILIP, s. of Alexander, (1) d. s. p., April 7, 1717. He m. March 27, 1712, Elizabeth, dau. of John Ingram. She m. (2) Dec. 13, 1716, Ebenezer Kellogg.

PARKER, ELI, Amh., d. Nov. 9, 1829, ae. 93. He m. Elizabeth, dau. of John Hubbard. She d. Oct. 13, 1813, ae. 74. Children—*Eli*, b. abt. 1763, m. (1) Salome Dickinson; (2) Fanny Woodward; *Levi*, bapt. June 14, 1767, d. ae. abt. 18; *Samuel*, bapt. Sept. 24, 1769; *Deborah*, bapt. Jan. 19, 1772, m. Sylvanus Dickinson; *Hannah*, m. (1) Thomas Goodale; (2) Simeon Pomeroy; *Elizabeth*, m. Aug. 29, 1776, Moses Hastings.

1. PARSONS, REV. DAVID, s. of Rev. David, was b. in Malden, March 24, 1712, grad. H. C. 1729, was ord. as first pastor of the Amh. (Cong.) Church, Nov. 7, 1739, and d. Jan. 1, 1781, ae. 68. He m. Eunice, dau. of Gideon Wells of Wethersfield, Ct. She was b. Aug. 6, 1723, and d. Sept. 20, 1796, ae. 73. Children—*Eunice*, bapt. July 19, 1747; *David*, bapt. Jan. 28, 1749; *Eunice*, bapt. July 28, 1751, m. Solomon Stoddard, Esq., of Nh., and d. Jan. 22, 1797, ae. 45; *Salome*, bapt. Feb. 28, 1753, d. unm. Aug. 22, 1839, ae. 84; *Mary*, bapt. March 27, 1757, m. Nov. 1, 1790, Ezekiel Belding of Wethersfield, Ct., and d. 1845, ae. 88; *Gideon*, bapt. June 28, 1759, d. Oct. 14, 1761, ae. 2; *Gideon*, bapt. Nov. 22, 1761, m. April 16, 1787, Huldah Rowe, and d. 1805, in Esopus, N. Y.; *Leonard Chester*, bapt. Nov. 11, 1764, d. while a member of the Junior Class in Yale College, Nov. 30, 1785, ae. 24.

2. DAVID, D. D., s. of David, (1) grad. H. C. 1771, was ord. Oct. 2, 1782, as successor of his father, over the 1st Cong. Church in Amh., dis. at his own request, Sept. 1, 1819, and d. May 18, 1823, ae. 74, while on a visit in Wethersfield, Ct. He received in 1800 from Brown Univ. the degree of Doctor of Divinity. He m. Nov. 5, 1785, Harriet, dau. of Ezekiel Williams, Esq., of Wethersfield, Ct. She was b. June 26, 1764, and d. June, 1850, ae. 85. Children—*Ezekiel Williams*, b. Feb. 16, 1787, m. June, 1822, Sally Clark, and is a physician in Colchester, Ct.; *David*, b. June 10, 1788, res. in Amh., m. (1) Jan. 21, 1816, Elizabeth Williams; (2) Dec. 16, 1845, Wid. Lucy Howell of Hartford, Ct.; *Prudence Stoddard*, b. Dec. 24, 1789, m. Oct. 7, 1823, Rev. Marcus Smith; *Thomas*, b. Oct. 10, 1791, m. March 18, Frances Catharine Chappel, res. in New London, Ct., but d. in Colchester, Ct., Aug. 21, 1832, ae. 41; *Harriet*, b. Aug. 6, 1793, m. (1) Rev. Royal Washburn of Amh.; (2) May 16, 1844, Hon. David Mack of Amh.; *Francis*, b. Feb. 16, 1795, grad. Y. C., was a lawyer in Hartford, Ct., m. Dec. 23, 1829, Clarissa Brown, and d. 1861; *Mary*, b. Dec. 8, 1796, m. Sept. 1, 1821, Rev. William Williams of Salem; *Caroline*, b. Sept. 15, 1798, d. unm. in Wethersfield, Ct., Jan. 5, 1820, ae. 21; *Sophia*, b. Aug. 8, 1800, m. May 17, 1837, Rev. Silas Aiken, D. D., then of Boston, but now of Rutland, Vt.; *William*, b. Oct. 30, 1802, a physician, d. unm. in Canaan, Ct., April 18, 1830, ae. 27; *James*, b. Nov. 4, 1804, grad. Amh. Col. 1830, m. March, 1832, Mary Eliza Lewis, and d. on Staten Island, N. Y., Sept. 3, 1833, ae. 28.

1. PARTRIDGE, WILLIAM, came from Berwick upon Tweed, Eng., was an early settler of Hartford, Ct., whence he rem. to Had., where he d. June 27, 1668. He m. Dec. 12, 1644, Mary Smith of Hartford. She was sister of Christopher of Northampton, Joseph of Hartford, Simeon and William, and d. July 20, [28?] 1680, ae. 55. Children—*Samuel*, b. Oct. 15, 1645; *Mary*, m. (1) Nov. 12, 1663, John, s. of Lieut. Samuel Smith; (2) Sept. 1679, Peter Montague, and d. May 20, 1680, ae. abt. 55.

2. COL. SAMUEL, s. of William, (1) was Representative 1685 and 1686, Colonel of the Regiment, Judge of Probate, and one of his Majesty's Council, and the most important man, after the death of Col. Pynchon, 1703, in all the western part of the Province. About 1687 he removed to Hat., where he d. Dec. 25, 1740, ae. 95. He m. (1) Sept. 24, 1668, Mehitable, dau. of John Crow; (2) —— Atwater, wid. of John of Salem, and dau. of Rev. Seaborn Cotton. Children—*William*, b. Nov. 16, 1669, grad. H. C. 1689, a preacher, d. in Wallingford, Ct., Sept. 1693; *Samuel*, b. Jan. 21, 1672; *Mehitable*, b. May 1, 1674, d. May 16, 1674; *Mehitable*, b. Aug. 26, 1675, m. Dec. 9, 1693, Nathaniel Dwight; *Child*, b. 1677, d. young; *Mary*, b. 1678, m. Dec. 4, 1695, Josiah Dwight; *Jonathan*, b. April 5, 1681, d. Sept. 11, 1684; *Edward*, b. April 26, 1683, res. in Hat.; *Jonathan*, b. Sept. 18, 1685, d. Jan. 24, 1686; *John*, b. 1686, grad. H. C. 1705, and d. in Spr. 1717; *Elizabeth*, b. Oct. 7, 1688, m. (1) May 9, 1709, John Hamlin, Jr.; (2) —— Hamlin; (3) —— Johnson of Woodstock, Ct.; (4) —— Payson of Middletown, Ct.

3. SAMUEL, s. of Col. Samuel, (2) d. betw. 1735 and 1738. He m. 1695, Mrs. Mary Atwater, dau. of Rev. Seaborn Cotton. She was b. 1670, and d. June 23, 1729, ae. 59. Children—*William*, b. Jan. 9, 1696, d. March 16,

1698; *Samuel*, b. June 1, 1696; *Mary*, b. June 15, 1698, m. Isaac Mattoon of Northfield; *Elizabeth*, b. Sept. 22, 1701, m. Ezekiel Kellogg of New Salem; *Dorothy*, b. March 2, 1703, d. March, 1703; *Cotton*, b. Oct. 13, 1705; *Mehetable*, b. Oct. 8, 1707, m. Thomas Barnard of Tolland, Ct.; *William*, b. Sept. 15, 1710, prob. grad. Y. C. 1729, and rem. to Nova Scotia, where he was Secretary of State.

4. EDWARD, s. of Col. Samuel, (2) Hat., d. Dec. 26, 1757, ae. 74. He m. May 14, 1707, Martha, dau. of Rev. William Williams of Hat. She d. Nov. 26, 1766. Children—*Elizabeth*, b. Oct. 14, 1708; *Martha*, b. Oct. 9, 1710; *Oliver*, b. June 13, 1712.

5. COTTON, s. of Samuel, (3) d. Sept. 28, 1733, ae. 27. He m. Margaret, dau. of Moses Cook. She m. (2) Samuel Gaylord. Children—*Samuel*, b. July 3, 1730; *Sybil*, b. Oct. 7, 1732, m. Josiah Dickinson.

6. OLIVER, s. of Edward, (4) Hat., d. July 21, 1792, ae. 80. He m. 1734, Anna, dau. of William Williams of Weston. She d. Dec. 21, 1802, ae. 85. Children—*William*, b. Aug. 15, 1735, d. Aug. 30, 1735; *Anna*, b. July 27, 1736, m. —— Bull; *Oliver*, b. Aug. 19, 1738, d. Sept. 9, 1738; *Martha*, b. Nov. 8, 1739; *Mercy*, b. Feb. 15, 1742; *Elizabeth*, b. March 15, 1744; *Sophia*, b. Aug. 3, 1746; *Samuel*, b. Sept. 5, 1748; *Oliver*, b. April 15, 1751, unm., was a physician in Stockbridge; *William*, b. April 30, 1753, a farmer in Pittsfield; *John*, b. May 1, 1755; *Pamela*, b. Sept. 21, 1757, d. Jan. 10, 1759; *Pamela*, b. Jan. 15, 1761.

7. SAMUEL, s. of Cotton, (5) Hat., m. Jan. 18, 1754, Abigail Dwight. Children—*Esther*, b. March 26, 1761, m. John Allis of Hat., and d. Dec. 22, 1834; *Cotton*, b. Dec. 1, 1765; *Samuel*, b. Nov. 4, 1767, d. young; *Samuel*.

8. COTTON, s. of Samuel, (7) Hat., m. (1) May 4, 1788, Sophia, dau. of Dea. —— Arms of Deerfield; (2) June 23, 1796, Hannah, dau. of Rev. Jonathan Lyman, D. D. of Hat. Children—*Dwight*, b. 1789, m. April 5, 1807, Elizabeth Sabin, and d. in Phelps, N. Y., ae. 32; *Theodore*, b. 1791, res. in Newark, N. J.; *Sophia Arms*, b. 1798, m. Moses Morton; *Eunice*, b. 1800; *Hannah Huntington*, b. 1802, m. David S. Whitney of Nh.; *Joseph Lyman*, b. 1804, grad. W. C. 1828; *Abigail Dwight*, m. (1) Aug. 26, 1835, Rev. Levi Pratt of Medford; (2) Lebbeus Ward; *Fanny*, b. March 22, 1811, m. —— Brainerd of St. Albans, Vt.; *George Cotton*, grad. A. C. 1833, a clergyman in Ill.; *Harriet*, m. Alfred Woodruff.

PARTRIDGE, SAMUEL, Hat., m. Feb. 21, 1792, Caroline Adams of West Springfield. She d. Jan. 19, 1798. Children—*Clarissa*, b. 1793, m. —— Sergeant of Stockbridge; *Caroline*, b. July 31, 1795, m. Harvey Ely of Rochester, N. Y.

1. PERKINS, ELISHA, d. abt. 1720. He m. Feb. 27, 1713, Sarah, dau. of Samuel Smith. She m. (2) May 29, 1724, Benjamin Church. Children—*Son*, b. and d. 1713; *Son*, b. and d. 1715; *Elisha*, b. Jan. 5, 1716; *John*, b. Sept. 9, 1719.

2. ELISHA, s. of Elisha, (1) m. Eunice ——, who d. Oct. 7, 1744. Children—*Sarah*, b. Aug. 28, 1741; *Eunice*, b. Sept. 12, 1742; *Sibil*, b. Feb. 28, 1744.

PERRY, JOHN, rem. after 1745, to Amh., m. April 1, 1737, Rebecca Warner; (2) 1743, Elizabeth Meacham of New Salem. Children—*Rebecca*, b. May 5, 1738; *Mary*, b. Jan. 26, 1740.

PETTY, JOHN, res. in Amh., and d. abt. 1790, m. ——, dau. of Benjamin Rhodes. Children—*Mary* and *Thankful*, (twins,) bapt. Aug. 31, 1760; *Joseph*, m. —— Wales; *Lucretia*, bapt. July 31, 1768, m. Joseph Robbins of Amh.; *Rachel*, bapt. Aug. 19, 1770.

1.   PHELPS, CHARLES, s. of Nathaniel, was b. in Northampton, Aug. 15, 1717, rem. to Had. in 1743 or 1744, and thence to New Marlboro', Vt. He d. April, 1789. He m. (1) April 24, 1740, Dorothy, dau. of Hezekiah Root. She d. Sept. 11, 1777; (2) abt. 1779, —— ——. Children—*Solomon*, b. 1742, grad. H. C. 1762, a preacher, became deranged, and d. unm. 1785 or 1786; *Dorothy*, m. July 9, 1772, Lemuel Warner; *Abigail*, m. June 6, 1776, John Williams of Wethersfield, Vt.; *Charles*, b. 1744; *Timothy*, b. Jan. 25, 1747, m. June 6, 1776, Zipporah Williams, res. in Halifax, Vt., and d. July 3, 1817, ae. 70; *Joseph*, d. Dec. 18, 1749, ae. 3 weeks. *Experience*, m. (1) March 11, 1784, Caleb Cooley; (2) Aaron Dickinson of Whately; *John*, d. Dec. 14, 1761, ae. 5; *Lucy*, d. Jan. 27, 1757, ae. 3.

2.   CHARLES, s. of Charles, (1) d. Dec. 3, 1814, in 72d yr. He m. June, 1770, Elizabeth, dau. of Dr. Moses Porter. She d. Nov. 11, 1817, ae. 70. Children—*Moses Porter*, afterwards called Charles Porter, b. Aug. 8, 1772, grad. H. C. 1791, d. Dec. 21, 1857, ae. 85; *Charles*, b. Dec. 1, 1776, d. Dec. 8, 1776; *Elizabeth Whiting*, b. Feb. 4, 1779, m. Rev. Dan Huntington.

PIERCE, JOHN, m. Bathsheba.   Child—*John*, b. June 24, 1748.

PIERCE, JONATHAN, m. abt. 1751, [pub. Dec. 21,] Experience Montague. She m. (2) 1757, Philip Ingram of Amh.   Child—*John*, b. July 8, 1752.

1.   PIERCE, JOSIAH, s. of Samuel, s. of Samuel, s. of Thomas, b. in Woburn, grad. H. C. 1735, rem. first to Mansfield, and thence to Had., where he was town clerk and teacher. He sometimes preached, though he does not appear to have been ordained.   He d. Feb. 10, 1788, ae. 79.   He m. Nov. 17, 1743, Miriam Cook, who d. June 27, 1795, in 79th yr. Children—*Josiah*, b. Oct. 11, 1745; *Hannah*, b. Nov. 19, 1747, d. unm. Jan. 31, 1841, ae. 93; *Samuel*, b. Nov. 11, 1749, m. April 3, 1794, Anna Cook, and d. s. p., Jan. 12, 1796, ae. 46. His wife d. March 1, 1825, ae. 67; *William*, b. June 21, 1752, d. unm. Jan. 11, 1832, ae. 79; *David*, b. Sept. 27, 1754, went with Arnold to Canada, and there d. unm. Dec. 28, 1775, ae. 21; *Miriam*, b. March 1, 1757, m. 1783, her cousin Josiah Pierce of Charlemont.

2.   JOSIAH, s. of Josiah, (1) d. March 22, 1834, ae. 88.   He m. 1771, Lucy, dau. of Walter Fairfield.   She was b. Feb. 26, 1745, and d. April 6, 1845, ae. 100. Children—*Lucy*, b. July 1, 1773, d. Sept. 26, 1775, ae. 2; *Dolly*, b. Oct. 29, 1774, m. Oct. 21, 1794, Rufus Shumway; *Anne*, b. May 17, 1776, m. Oct. 10, 1798, Andrew Dunakin; *Lucy*, b. April 26, 1778, m. Dec. 24, 1799, Elijah White; *David*, b. March 3, 1780; *Elihu*, b. Jan. 27, 1782; *Job*, b. July 8, 1785.

3.   DAVID, s. of Josiah, (2) d. March 6, 1850, ae. 70.   He m. May 9, 1825, Miriam, dau. of Samuel Cook.   Children—*Eliza*, b. Feb. 13, 1826; *William*

Martin, b. Dec. 30, 1827, grad. A. C. 1853; *Sarah*, b. Nov. 23, 1829; *John Nelson*, b. Dec. 8, 1833; *Almira*, b. April 1, 1835, d. April 6, 1836; *Charles*, b. Aug. 19, 1839, d. May 26, 1841.

PIXLEY, WILLIAM, removed in 1668 to Nh., and thence abt. 1680, to Westfield, where he d. Oct. 9, 1689. He m. (1) Nov. 24, 1663, Sarah Lawrence; (2) 1681, Sarah, who d. Dec. 25, 1713. Children—*Sarah*, b. Jan. 11, 1665, m. Dec. 9, 1680, John Lee of Westfield; *Thomas*, b. June 6, 1667, d. in Westfield, 1731; *William*, b. June 27, 1669; *Joseph*, b. Nov. 18, 1671; *Joseph*, b. March 9, 1676, res. in Westfield and Housatonnuck; *Ebenezer*, b. May 3, 1678, d. in Westfield, 1716; *Anthony*, b. July 4, 1681, d. April 25, 1697· *Mary*, d. 1735.

PLIMPTON or PLYMPTON, PETER, s. of John, bapt. in Dedham, March 16, 1652, rem. to Deerfield, thence as early as 1679 to Hatfield and still later to Marlborough, where he d. March 27, 1717. He m. July 2, 1677, Mary Mundan. Children—*Hannah*, b. March 28, 1679; *Mary*, b. March 8, 1681.

1. POMEROY, EBENEZER, b. May 1, 1723, s. of Ebenezer, Jr. of Nh., d. in 1800 or 1801. He m. Mindwell, dau. of Capt. John Lyman. She d. Oct. 9, 1797, in 77th yr. Children—*Ethan; Eunice*, m. Jan. 6, 1774, Ebenezer Clark; *Abigail*, m. Capt. John Woods: *Elizabeth*, bapt. Dec. 23, 1753, m. (1) June 1, 1780, Dr. Timothy Lyman; (2) Ebenezer Clark; *Mindwell*, bapt. April 11, 1756, m. (1) Joseph Marsh; (2) 1793, Ebenezer Clark; *Ebenezer*, bapt. Nov. 19, 1758; *Solomon*, bapt. Feb. 8, 1761; *Hannah*, m. 1786, John Colton; *Rhoda*, m. 1793, Daniel Warren.

2. ETHAN, s. of Ebenezer, (1.) Children—*Dau.*, b. March 9, 1779; *Esther*, bapt. April 4, 1779; *Jacob Parsons*, b. 1780; *Ethan*, bapt. Oct. 14, 1787.

POMEROY, SIMEON, s. of Samuel, was b. in Nh., June 5, 1725, settled in Amh., and d. June 22, 1812, ae. 87. He m. March 27, 1747, Abigail Smith, who d. Dec. 10, 1820, ae. 94. Children—*Abigail*, b. Nov. 22, 1747, m. Justus Williams of Amh., and d. Nov. 20, 1832, ae. 85; *Eunice*, b. Nov. 24, 1749, m. Amos Nash; *Lucy*, b. Jan. 22, 1752, m. (1) Sept. 15, 1774, Samuel Hastings; (2) Martin Kellogg, and d. Dec. 23, 1839, ae. 87; *Simeon*, b. April 24, 1754, m. Dec. 30, 1779, Mary Hastings; (2) Hannah, wid. of Thomas Goodale; *Mary*, b. Sept. 10, 1756, d. young; *Jerusha*, b. Feb. 6, 1760, m. Jan. 23, 1783, Philip Edwards; *David*, b. March 12, 1762, m. Sabra, dau. of David Blodgett of Amh., and d. Aug. 6, 1825, ae. 63; *Mary*, b. Aug. 12, 1764, m. Jan. 16, 1794, Nathaniel Edwards of Amh., and d. 1795; *Dorcas*, b. Oct. 13, 1767, m. Oct. 26, 1794, Justus Clark of Amh., and d. July 22, 1849, ae. 81; *Samuel*, b. Nov. 19, 1769, d. Sept. 1, 1777; *Moses*, b. April 10, 1773, d. Sept. 2, 1777.

1. PORTER, SAMUEL, s. of John of Windsor, Ct., was among the first settlers of Had., where he d. Sept. 6, 1689. He m. Hannah, dau. of Thomas Stanley of Hartford, Ct. She d. Dec. 18, 1708. Children—*Samuel*, b. April 6, 1660; *Child*, b. and d. April 26, 1662; *Thomas*, b. April 17, 1663, d. May 27, 1663; *Hezekiah*, b. Jan. 7, 1665; *John*, b. Dec. 12, 1666; *Hannah*, b.

1670, m. March 29, 1689, John Nash; *Mehitable*, b. Sept. 15, 1673, m. Nathaniel Goodwin of Hartford, Ct., and d. Feb. 6, 1726, ae. 52; *Experience*, b. Aug. 5, 1676; *Ichabod*, b. June 17, 1678; *Nathaniel*, b. Nov. 15, 1680; *Thomas*, b. abt. 1683.

2. HON. SAMUEL, s. of Samuel, (1) at one time Representative, an extensive trader with England, and afterwards Judge and Sheriff of the County, d. July 29, 1722, leaving to his family an immense estate of over £10,000. He left upwards of £534 in goods including 196£ shipped for him at London, and sixteen hundred and forty two acres of land in Brookfield, valued at £518. He had bills of credit on hand to the amount of £403. He m. (1) Feb. 22, 1683, Joanna, dau. of Capt. Aaron Cook. She d. Nov. 13, 1713, ae. 49; (2) ———— ————, who survived him. Children—*Samuel*, b. May 25, 1685; *Joanna*, b. Dec. 24, 1689, [1687?] m. 1704, John Marsh; *Aaron*, b. July 19, 1689; *Moses*, b. June 28, 1690, was living in 1709; *Sarah*, b. Dec. 12, 1692, m. Dec. 5, 1711, Josiah Goodrich of Wethersfield, Ct., and d. July, 1726, ae. 33; *Mehitable*, b. Sept. 12. 1694, m. Sept. 24, 1713, Job Marsh, and d. July 13, 1739, ae. 44; *Miriam*, b. Aug. 3, 1696, d. Oct. 15, 1703, ae. 7; *Eleazar*, b. Feb. 25, 1698; *Hannah*, b. July 2, 1699, d. Aug. 12, 1699; *Nathaniel*, b. July 12, 1700, d. Nov. 1700; *Ruth*, b. Nov. 10, 1701, m. 1720, Rev. Stephen Steel of Tolland, Ct.; *Mary*, b. Nov. 4, 1703, prob. m. Rev. Solomon Williams of Lebanon, Ct.; *Daughter*, b. and d. Oct. 20, 1705; *Son*, b. and d. Dec. 5, 1706.

3. HEZEKIAH, s. of Samuel, (1) rem. abt. 1707 to East Hartford, Ct., and d. Jan. 3, 1752, ae. 88. He m. (1) May 20, 1686, Hannah Cowles, probably dau. of Samuel Cowles of Farmington, Ct. She d. Sept. 5, 1701; (2) Hannah ————, who d. Dec. 18, 1708; (3) 1714, Esther, wid. of Nathaniel Smith, and dau. of Thomas Dickinson. Children—*Hezekiah*, b. June 10, 1687; *Timothy*, b. April 12, 1689; *Hannah*, b. July 20, 1691; *Abigail*, b. Aug. 27, 1693; *James*, b. Feb. 24, 1696; *Isaac*, b. Nov. 24, 1698; *Jonathan*, b. Nov. 30, 1701, d. Jan. 15, 1702; *Mary*, b. Oct. 20, 1703; *Joseph*, b. Oct. 11, 1704; *David*, b. Sept. 27, 1706; *Sarah*, b. 1708; *Mabel*, b. 1710.

4. JOHN, s. of Samuel, (1) res. in Hat., Lebanon, Ct., and Hebron, Ct., and d. Jan. 4, 1747. He m. April 3, 1690, Mary, dau. of Thomas Butler of Hartford, Ct. Children—*John*, b. Jan. 26, 1691; *Mary*, b. May 4, 1692; *Joseph*, b. 1702; *Daniel*, b. 1706, d. 1707.

5. EXPERIENCE, s. of Samuel, (1) rem. abt. 1725 to Mansfield, Ct., where he d. Aug. 28, 1750, ae. 74. He m. May 26, 1698, Abigail, dau. of Samuel Williams of Roxbury. She was b. July 12, 1674, and d. April 20, 1765, ae. 90. Children—*Theoda*, b. Aug. 15, 1699, m. 1719, ———— Walbridge; *Hannah*, b. March 25, 1701, m. (1) 1722, William Marsh; (2) May, 1735, Joseph Storrs of Mansfield, and d. Aug. 28, 1741; *Experience*, b. Dec. 15, 1702, m. Nov. 29, 1725, Abigail Safford, and d. Oct. 28, 1744, ae. 41; *John*, b. Dec. 27, 1704, m. Jan. 13, 1732, Abigail Arnold; *Abigail*, b. March 19, 1707, m. Oct. 18, 1742, Nehemiah Estabrook, and d. July 31, 1770; *Nathaniel*, b. Aug. 26, 1709, m. Sept. 10, 1730, Elizabeth Storrs, and rem. to Lebanon, N. H., but d. in Hatfield, Nov. 4, 1779, ae. 70; *Martha*, b. Jan. 11, 1712, d. Feb. 18, 1712; *Eunice*, b. Dec. 30, 1712, m. Nov. 12, 1731, Huckins Storrs; *Mehitable*, b. July 30, 1715, m. April 30, 1741, Thomas Barrows, and d. March 25, 1742; *Martha*, b. Nov. 21, 1717, m. Sept. 4, 1738, Cornelius Storrs.

6. Ichabod, s. of Samuel, (1) Hat., m. July 4, 1700, Dorcas Marsh. Children—*Dorcas*, b. 1703; *Mehitable*, b. July 20, 1706; *Son*, b. and d. April 28, 1707; *Hannah*, b. July 21, 1708; *Mary*, b. April 24, 1711; *James*, b. Sept. 19, 1714; *Sarah*, b. Feb. 2, 1718.

7. Samuel, s. of Samuel, (2) d. Nov. 16, 1748, ae. 63. He m. 1708, Anna Colton of Springfield. She d. May 11, 1761, ae. 81. Children—*Samuel*, b. Dec. 2, 1709, grad. H. C. 1730, minister of (Cong.) church in Sherburn, Mass., where he d. 1758, ae. 49; *Anna*, b. May 13, 1712, m. 1754, Jonathan Mills, and d. 1755; *Joanna*, b. Jan. 2, 1716, m. 1737, Joseph Hubbard; *Sarah*, b. Feb. 9, 1718, m. 1740, Rev. Samuel Cook; *Phebe*, b. Jan. 19, 1720, m. 1745, Samuel Marsh; *Moses*, b. Jan. 13, 1722; *Miriam*, b. Jan. 30, 1724.

8. Aaron, s. of Samuel, (2) grad. H. C. 1708, was ordained Feb. 11, 1713, pastor of (Cong.) church in Medford, where he d. Jan. 23, 1722. He m. Oct. 22, 1713, Susanna, dau. of Major Stephen Sewall of Salem. Children —*Aaron*, b. July 9, 1714, d. young; *Susanna*, b. March 1, 1716, m. Aug. 4, 1739, Rev. A. Cleveland; *Margaret*, b. July 18, 1717; *Joanna*, b. March 22, 1719, m. Jan. 1, 1735, Josiah Cleveland.

9. Eleazar, s. of Samuel, (2) d. Nov. 6, 1757, ae. 59. He m. Sarah Pitkin, prob. dau. of William Pitkin, Jr., and if so, b. Dec. 9, 1702. She d. June 6, 1784, ae. 82. Children—*Jerusha*, b. Feb. 24, 1722, d. Aug. 5, 1726, ae. 4; *Eleazar*, b. Oct. 28, 1723, d. Aug. 6, 1726, ae. 2; *Sarah*, b. April 18, 1726, m. (1) Aug. 23, 1744, Rev. Chester Williams; (2) Feb. 17, 1756, Rev. Samuel Hopkins, D. D., and d. Feb. 5, 1774; *Eleazar*, b. June 27, 1728; *Jerusha*, b. Aug. 11, 1730, m. 1758, Col. Ebenezer Williams of Pomfret, Ct.; *Elizabeth*, b. Nov. 15, 1732, d. Sept. 14, 1755, ae. 22; *Mary*, b. May 2, 1736, d. Sept. 4, 1736; *William*, b. April 13, 1738, d. Nov. 28, 1738; *Mehitable*, b. Dec. 13, 1739, d. Nov. 7, 1755, ae. 15; *Elisha*, b. Jan. 29, 1742; *William*, b. April 13, 1746, d. Oct. 5, 1755, ae. 9; *Mary*, b. Sept. 16, 1748, m. Oct. 4, 1770, Rev. Jonathan Edwards, D. D. of New Haven, Ct.

10. James, s. of Ichabod, (6) Hat., d. April 25, 1792, ae. 78. He m. (1) Feb. 22, 1737, Hannah Wait, who d. Nov. 10, 1740; m. (2) Eunice. Children—*Hannah*, b. Nov. 2, 1740; *Hannah*, b. Nov. 23, 1745, m. Abel Allis of Somers, Ct.; *Jonathan*, b. June 5, 1747, d. July 5, 1747; *Jonathan*, b. April 16, 1752, m. Ruth Chapin of Somers, Ct.; *Submit*, b. March 15, 1754, m. ———— Chapin; *David*, b. July 5, 1757, rem. to Williamsburgh; *Silas*, b. Aug. 18, 1759, res. in Hat.

11. Moses, s. of Samuel, (7) was slain at Lake George, Sept. 8, 1755, ae. 33. He m. Elizabeth, dau. of Nathaniel Pitkin of Hartford, Ct. She was b. Oct. 4, 1719, and d. Oct. 2, 1798, ae. 78. Child—*Elizabeth*, b. Nov. 15, 1747, m. June, 1770, Charles Phelps.

12. Hon. Eleazar, s. of Eleazar, (9) grad. Y. C. 1748, was a Justice of the Peace 1779, Judge of Probate 1779, and d. May 27, 1797, ae. 68. He m. (1) Aug. 6, 1754, his cousin Anne Pitkin, who d. Nov. 7, 1758, ae. 24; (2) Sept. 17, 1761, Susanna, dau. of Rev. Jonathan Edwards of Northampton. She was b. June 20, 1740, and d. May 2, 1803, ae. 62. Children—*Elizabeth*, b. Aug. 29, 1755, d. Oct. 14, 1755; *Anne*, b. Sept. 25, 1756, m. Selah Norton, and d. 1850; *Elizabeth*, b. Oct. 17, 1758, m. Jan. or June 25, 1777, Elisha Hills of Hartford, Ct.; *Eleazar*, b. June 14, 1762; *William*, b. Dec. 9, 1763;

114   PORTER.

Jonathan Edwards, b. May 17, 1766, grad. H. C. 1786; *Moses,* b. Sept. 19,
1768; *John,* b. July 27, 1772, d. Aug. 7, 1772; *Pierpont,* b. June 12, 1775.

13. ELISHA, s. of Eleazar, (9) grad. H. C. 1761, Sheriff of Hampshire
Co., d. May 29, 1796, ae. 54. He m. (1) May 13, 1762, Sarah, dau. of Rev.
David Jewett of Rowley. She was b. Aug. 25, 1741, and d. April 5, 1775;
(2) March 19, 1778, Abigail, dau. of Hon. Jóhn Phillips of Boston. She was
b. Feb. 14, 1743, and d. March 2, 1791, ae. 48. Children—*Sarah,* b. April 29,
1763, m. Oct. 7, 1781, David Hillhouse, and d. March 19, 1831; *Samuel,* b.
April 15, 1765; *David,* b. June 13, 1767, drowned June 8, 1775, ae. 7; *Mary,*
b. April 8, 1769; *Lucy,* b. Oct. 18, 1770; *Patience,* b. April 19, 1773.

14. ELEAZAR, s. of Eleazar, (12) rem. first to Hartford, Ct., and thence to
Sturbridge, where he d. May 2, 1849, ae. 86. He m. 1783, Sarah Keyes, b.
1760, who d. March 26, 1837, ae. 76. Children—*David Keyes,* b. Feb. 25,
1784, res. at Sturbridge; *Susanna,* b. Dec. 20, 1785, d. unm.; *Sarah,* b. March
4, 1788, m. Samuel Pettis; *Edwin,* b. June 11, 1790, res. in Richmond, Va.;
Henry, b. Aug. 3, 1793, d. ae. 33; *Sidney,* b. Sept. 29, 1795, res. in Sturbridge;
Maria, b. July 2, 1797, m. Dr. —— Woodward; *Eleazar,* b. Aug. 26, 1799,
res. in Stamford, Ct.; *Horace,* b. June 11, 1802 or 1803, d. ae. 27.

15. WILLIAM, s. of Eleazar, (12) a physician, d. Nov. 6, 1847, ae. 88. He
m. (1) Dec. 9, 1788, Lois, dau. of Dea. John Eastman. She d. Dec. 12, 1792,
ae. 28; (2) June 10, 1794, Charlotte, dau. of Hon. William Williams of
Dalton, Mass. She d. Nov. 13, 1842, ae. 72. Children—*Daughter,* b. Oct. 14,
1789, d. in infancy; *John,* b. Oct. 24, 1790; *William,* b. Nov. 14, 1792, grad.
W. C. 1813, a lawyer at Lee, Mass., where he d.; *Eleazar Williams,* b. May
29, 1795, d. Feb. 29, 1797, ae. 1; *Caroline Williams,* b. May 19, 1797; *Mary
Edwards,* b. Dec. 11, 1799, d. May 13, 1803; *Lois Eastman,* b. Feb. 8, 1801;
James Bayard, b. Feb. 10, 1803, a merchant; *Jeremiah,* b. Dec. 27, 1805,
grad. W. C. 1825, a (Cong.) clergyman in Chicago, Ill.; *Charles,* b. July 28,
1808, d. July 30, 1808.

16. MOSES, s. of Eleazar, (12) d. May 22, 1854, ae. 85. He m. Aug. 30,
1791, Amy, dau. of Benjamin Colt. She d. Feb. 14, 1843, ae. 71. Children—
Benjamin Colt, b. June 8, 1792, d. June 3, 1793; *Elizabeth,* b. June 2, 1794;
Benjamin, b. Oct. 25, 1795; *Sophia,* b. Nov. 6, 1797; *Moses,* b. Oct. 13, 1799;
Amy, b. Sept. 20, 1801; *Susannah Edwards,* b. Jan. 18, 1804, d. Nov. 20,
1805; *Eleazar,* b. Jan. 21, 1806; *Susannah,* b. Jan. 30, 1808, m. Rev. Luther
Farnum, and d. in Batavia, Ill., Jan. 27, 1849, ae. 40; *Lucretia Colt,* b.
May 15, 1810; *Delia Dwight,* b. July 7, 1812; *Jonathan Edwards,* b. April 6,
1815.

17. PIERPONT, s. of Eleazar, (12) d. Jan. 15, 1805, ae. 29. He m. 1796,
Hannah Wiggins of East Windsor, Ct. Children—*Jerusha,* b. July 22, 1797;
Lucretia, b. Nov. 23, 1798; *Frederic,* b. Dec. 30, 1800; *Lester,* b. 1803.

18. HON. SAMUEL, s. of Elisha, (13) State Senator, 1817, d. April 23,
1841. He m. Oct. 26, 1786, Lucy Hubbard. She d. Jan. 23, 1848, ae. 83.
Children—*Margaret,* b. Feb. 9, 1787, m. Oct. 11, 1810, Rev. Seth Smith of
Genoa, N. Y.; *Abigail,* b. Oct. 18, 1788; *Lucy,* b. April 13, 1791, m. Nov. 11,
1812, Nathaniel Coolidge, and d. June, 1825; *Elisha,* b. May 27, 1794, unm.;
Polly, b. April 4, 1796, d. Dec. 13, 1847; *Pamela,* b. May 7, 1797, m. Dec.
5, 1822, Dudley Smith.

POTTER, EPHRAIM, s. of Ephraim, b. in Marlboro', March 6, 1807, m. Oct. 6, 1835, Delia, dau. of Enos Smith, Jr. Children—*Ellen Augusta*, b. Oct. 12, 1836; *Ephraim Henry*, b. March 2, 1839; *Mary Louisa*, b. Dec. 16, 1842; *Abby Jane*, b. July 26, 1845; *Eugene Emerson*, b. Dec. 31, 1847; *Martha Everlyn*, b. June 2, 1852, in New Salem.

1. PRESTON, JOHN, alive in 1728, m. March 25, 1678, Sarah Gardner, who was living in 1728. Children—*Sarah*, b. Dec. 10, 1678, d. Dec. 21, 1678; *Sarah*, b. July 10, 1681, d. May 29, 1683; *Child*, b. and d. April 20, 1683; *Mercy*, b. June 6, 1684, d. March 11, 1692; *John*, b. July 31, 1686; *Daughter*, b. and d. April 25, 1688; *Samuel*, b. Feb. 27, 1690, d. Jan. 19, 1711; *Sarah*, b. Nov. 8, 1693, m. March 4, 1714, Nathaniel Kellogg.

2. JOHN, s. of John, (1) rem. to So. Had., and d. March 2, 1728. He was "the first person buried on the south side of Mount Holyoke." He m. Dec. 2, 1714, Mary, dau. of Luke Smith. Children—*Samuel*, b. Oct. 29, 1715; *John*, b. Dec. 26, 1716; *Mary*, b. Jan. 29, 1718, m. Ephraim Smith of So. Had.; *Jonathan*, b. April 2, 1720; *Hannah*, b. March 26, 1722, d. March 26, 1745, ae. 23; *Sarah*, b. June 16, 1724, m. 1749, Silas Smith of So. Had.; *Benoni*, b. Oct. 1, 1728, m. Nov. 24, 1757, Mary Cook, res. in So. Had., and d. abt. 1803.

3. SAMUEL, s. of John, (2) So. Had., d. Jan. 18, 1799, ae. 83. He m. Tryphena Woodbridge, who d. Aug. 18, 1777, ae. 46. Children—*Samuel*, b. April 21, 1759; *Emereniana*, b. Dec. 5, 1760, d. young; *Tryphena*, b. Nov. 29, 1762, d. young; *John*, b. Dec. 26, 1764; *Mary*, b. Sept. 21, 1767.

4. JOHN, s. of John, (2) Granby, d. Feb. 2, 1759. He m. Hannah. Children—*Mary*, b. Dec. 27, 1743; *John*, b. May 25, 1746; *James*, b. June 25, 1748, m. Martha ———, who d. Nov. 4, 1835. He d. in Gr., Jan. 28, 1801, ae. 52; *Hannah*, b. June 18, 1751; *Sarah*, b. June 2, 1754; *Moses*, b. Sept. 20, 1756; *Jabez*, b. Sept. 10, 1759.

5. JONATHAN, s. of John, (2) So. Had., d. 1792, in 73d yr. He m. Eunice, dau. of William Wait, Jr. of Northampton. She was b. May 21, 1722. Children—*Jonathan*, b. Sept. 9, 1743; *Hannah*, b. July 4, 1746, m. ——— Church, and d. 1833, ae. 87; *Gardner*, b. Sept. 15, 1749, d. in So. Had., May 26, 1834, ae. 85; *Eunice*, b. May 25, 1752; *Job*, b. June 18, 1756; *Lucina*.

6. JOHN, s. of John, (4) Gr., d. July 9, 1815, ae. 69. He m. Martha, who d. Sept. 29, 1811, ae. 66. Children—*John*, b. Oct. 25, 1767; *Joel*, b. Sept. 9, 1769; *Jeriel*, b. July 26, 1771; *Clarina*, b. Nov. 2, 1773; *Rachel*, b. July 31, 1776; *Sophia*, b. Oct. 21, 1778; *Roxa*, b. March 12, 1781; *Justin*, b. June 21, 1783; *Azubah*, b. Nov. 17, 1787.

PRIOR, NATHANIEL COLLINS, s. of Frederick of East Windsor, Ct., was b. Jan. 21, 1804, and d. Nov. 29, 1857, ae. 53. He m. April, 1835, Mary, dau. of Enos Smith. Children—*Enos Parsons*, b. Oct. or Nov. 14, 1836; *Cynthia Rebecca*, b. Oct. 6, 1840; *Frederick Smith*, b. July 26, 1842; *Helen Adelaide*, b. June 1, 1845.

PRUTT, ARTHUR, a negro, said to have been the slave of Rev. Isaac Chauncy, m. Joan. Children—*George*, b. Aug. 1722, d. in Whately, 1794, ae. 72; *Elenor*, b. Aug. 1724; *Ishmael*, b. Jan. 1726; *Cæsar*, b. June, 1727, lived with Josiah Chauncy, Esq.; *Abner*, b. Aug. 1729; *Zebulon*, b. Aug. 15, 1731, was the slave of Oliver Warner, and d. in Amh., Dec. 2, 1802; *Chloe*, b. July 20, 1738.

RAULF, BENJAMIN. Child—*Azubah*, b. April 7, 1802.

RAWSON, REV. GRINDAL, b. Sept. 6, 1707, s. of Rev. Grindal of Mendon, grad. H. C. 1728, was ord. Oct. 3, 1733, first pastor of the church in So. Had., resigned in 1741, and was inst. Sept. 18, 1745, as pastor of the church in Hadlyme, Ct., where he d. March 29, 1777. He m. May 19, 1738, Dorothy, dau. of Rev. Isaac Chauncy. She d. 1780. Children—*Grindall*, b. Feb. 7, 1739, grad. Y. C. 1759, was a preacher, m. 1768, Sarah Holmes; *Charles*, b. Nov. 11, 1740, a physician, d. in R. I., ae. 23; *Wilson*, b. Dec. 4, 1742, d. young; *Hooker; Chauncy*, d. young; *Dorothy*, d. young.

RAYMOND, JOSIAH, m. Eunice, dau. of Dea. Noah Cook of Nh. She was b. June 4, 1721. Children—*Abigail*, b. Feb. 10, 1748; *Josiah*, b. May 8, 1750; *Eunice*, b. June 3, 1753; *Dau.*, b. Sept. 16, 1755; *Jonathan*, b. Jan. 18, 1761; *Jonathan*, b. July 2, 1763.

REYNOLDS, SAMUEL. Child—*Joanna*, bapt. 1805.

REYNOLDS, THOMAS. Children—*Sophia*, bapt. May 22, 1803; *Edwin*, bapt. July 17, 1806; *Mary*, bapt. April 1, 1810.

RICHMOND, DAVID, came from Dighton. Child—*Thankful*, b. Dec. 22, 1777, m. Oct. 9, 1796, Enos, s. of David Hitchcock of Brookfield. Enos Hitchcock, b. Jan. 16, 1774, res. in Brookfield, and d. July 14, 1814. His widow d. in Had., June 27, 1853, ae. 76.

RIDER, STEPHEN, m. 1795, Thankful Montague. Children—*Charles*, b. Jan. 8, 1796; *Ansel*, b. Oct. 28, 1797; *Stephen*, b. Sept. 1, 1799; *Matilda*, b. Sept. 8, 1801; *Thankful*, b. Aug. 17, 1803.

ROOD, SIMEON, m. March 5, 1767, Ruth Hawley, and rem. as early as 1789, to Brookfield, Vt. Children—*Simeon*, b. Feb. 25, 1768; *John*, b. June 4, 1770; *Ruth*, b. April 19, 1772; *Samuel*, b. Feb. 25, 1775, d. Nov. 7, 1776; *Samuel*, b. Nov. 18, 1776; *Mary*, b. Jan. 22, 1779; *Giles*, b. April 24, 1781; *Solomon*, b. Aug. 22, 1783; *Sarah*, b. Oct. 1, 1785; *Betsey*, b. Sept. 15, 1787.

ROOKER, WILLIAM, d. abt. 1705. He m. May 30, 1687, Dorothy, dau. of Samuel Smith. Children—*Daughter*, b. and d. March 28, 1687; *William*, b. Feb. 10, 1688; *Samuel*, b. June 24, 1692; *William*, b. April 8, 1695, d. abt. 1739, leaving neither wife nor child; *Sarah*, b. Jan. 24, 1698; *Dorothy*, b. Sept. 27, 1703, m. Dec. 21, 1727, Joseph Taylor.

ROSEVELT, JACOB. Children—*Susanna; Jacob; Sarah*.

ROWE, JOHN, Granby, m. Mehitable. Children—*John*, b. Feb. 24, 1754; *Lois*, b. July 24, 1756; *Elijah*, b. Nov. 7, 1758.

1. RUGG, SAMUEL, from Lancaster, m. Hannah. Children—*Gideon*, b. Feb. 11, 1718, d. in S. H.; *Phineas*, b. May 17, 1721; *Lydia*, b. Jan. 1, 1723, m. Feb. 6, 1745, Jonathan White; *John*, b. Feb. 7, 1725; *Hannah*, b. March 1, 1727, m. Dec. 25, 1746, Eleazar Goodman; *Thankful* b. Sept. 21, 1729.

2. JOHN, s. of Samuel, (1) rem. from So. Had. to Bennington, Vt. He m. 1750, Sarah Holliday, who d. June 17, 1765, in 40th yr. Children—*Thankful*, b. April 2, 1753; *Hannah*, b. June 10, 1755; *Moses*, b. Feb. 1, 1758; *Miriam*, b. Feb. 1, 1758; *Sarah*, b. Feb. 12, 1761; *Phineas*, b. July 11, 1763.

1. RUSSELL, JOHN, b. abt. 1597, glazier, Cambridge, freeman March 3, 1636, town clerk in 1645, constable in 1648, rem. early to Wethersfield, and thence to Hadley, where he d. May 8, 1680, ae. 83. He m. (1) ——— ———; (2) Dorothy, wid. of Rev. Henry Smith of Wethersfield, Ct. She d. 1694. Children—*John*, b. abt. 1626; *Philip*.

2. JOHN, s. of John, (1) grad. H. C. 1645, ord. abt. 1649, as pastor of the church in Wethersfield, Ct., and there remained until the settlement of Hadley, when he removed and was pastor of said church until his death, Dec. 10, 1692, in the 66th yr. of his age. He m. (1) June 28, 1649, Mary Talcott; (2) Rebecca, dau. of Thomas Newbury of Windsor, Ct. She d. Nov. 21, 1688, in 57th yr.; (3) Rebecca, wid. of Rev. John Whiting of Hartford, Ct. She d. Sept. 19, 1730. Children—*John*, bapt. Sept. 23, 1650, d. Jan. 20, 1670; *Jonathan*, b. abt. 1655, grad. H. C. 1675, m. Martha ———, was ord. Sept. 19, 1683, pastor of the church in Barnstable, and d. Feb. 21, 1711, ae. 56; *Samuel*, b. Nov. 4, 1660, grad. H. C. 1681, m. Abigail, dau. of Rev. John Whiting of Hartford, Ct., was in 1687 ord. as pastor of the church in Branford, Ct., and d. June 25, 1731, ae. 70; *Eleazar*, b. Nov. 8, 1663, was alive in 1687; *Daniel*, b. Feb. 8, 1666, d. Dec. 17, 1667.

3. PHILIP, s. of John, (1) glazier, Hat., d. May 19, 1693. He m. (1) Feb. 4, 1664, Joanna, dau. of Rev. Henry Smith, who d. Dec. 29, 1664; (2) Jan. 10, 1666, Elizabeth, dau. of Stephen Terry. She was slain by the Indians, Sept. 19, 1677; (3) Dec. 25, 1679, Mary, dau. of Edward Church. She d. in Sunderland, May 1, 1743. Children—*Joanna*, b. Oct. 31, 1664, d. Dec. 29, 1664; *John*, b. Jan. 2, 1667; *Samuel*, b. abt. 1669, slain 1677, while on the way to Canada; *Philip*, b. Jan. 24, 1671; *Stephen*, b. Oct. 12, 1674, slain by the Indians, Sept. 19, 1677; *Samuel*, b. Dec. 31, 1680, was of New York in 1720; *Thomas*, b. Feb. 12, 1683, slain Aug. 1704 in Deerfield; *Mary*, b. Feb. 10, 1685, d. March ———; *Mary*, b. May 21, 1686, m. Joseph Root, and d. in Sunderland, Jan. 23, 1738; *Philip*, b. June 21, 1688; *Daniel*, b. Oct. 8, 1691.

4. DANIEL, s. of Philip, (3) was an early settler of Sunderland, where he d. June 28, 1737. He m. Jerusha, dau. of John Dickinson. She m. (2) 1744, Simon Cooley of Sunderland. Her estate was divided in 1782. Children—*Jonathan*, b. Aug. 2, 1714; *Mary*, b. Nov. 1, 1716; *Philip*, b. 1722, d. young; *Jerusha*, m. Ebenezer Clark; *Mary*, b. 1725, m. 1743, David Ballard; *Sarah*, b. 1730, m. Jedediah Clark; *Martha*, b. 1734, d. young.

5. JONATHAN, s. of Daniel, (4) Sunderland, m. 1743, Mary, dau. of Nathaniel Smith. Children—*Daniel*, b. 1744; *Jonathan*, b. 1746; *Martha*, b. 1748, m. ——— Cooley; *Mary*, b. 1750, m. ——— Ashley; *Philip*, b. 1752; and prob. also, *Israel; Samuel; John; Spencer; Persis*.

SAMPSON, PHINEHAS. Child—*Eliza*, bapt. June 22, 1800.

SCOTT, EDWARD, m. Nov. 22, 1670, Elizabeth Webster, who d. May 16, 1689, ae. abt. 40. Children—*Elizabeth*, b. Oct. 11, 1671; *Sarah*, b. Jan. 14,

1674; *Thomas*, b. Sept. 10, 1675; *John*, b. Jan. 13, 1677; *Ebenezer*, b. June 11, 1681; *Bridget* and *Ann*, (twins,) b. July 16, 1682; *Hannah*, b. March 14, 1689.

1.   SCOTT, WILLIAM, Hatfield, m. Jan. 28, 1670, Hannah, dau. of William Allis.   Children—*Josiah*, b. June 18, 1671; *Richard*, b. Feb. 22, 1673; *William*, b. Nov. 24, 1676; *Hannah*, b. Aug. 11, 1679; *Joseph*, b. March 21, 1682; *John*, b. July 6, 1684, d. Feb. 8, 1692; *Mary*, b. 1686; *Mehitable*, b. Sept. 9, 1687, d. Sept. 18, 1687; *Jonathan*, b. Nov. 1, 1688, d. Nov. 15, 1688; *Abigail*, b. Nov. 23, 1689.

2.   JOSIAH, s. of William, (1) Hat., m. Sarah Barrett.   Children—*Josiah*, b. Nov. 29, 1699, settled in Whately; *Sarah*, b. Sept. 9, 1701; *Hannah*, b. May 30, 1704; *Benjamin*, b. May 31, 1708, m. Jemima ——, res. in Whately, and d. 1792; *Mehitable*, b. May 4, 1711; *Moses*, b. Feb. 3, 1713; *Ruth*, b. Nov. 25, 1715.

3.   RICHARD, s. of William, (1) rem. after 1713, from Hat. to Sunderland. He m. Jan. 15, 1702, Elizabeth, dau. of Stephen Belding.   Children—*Mary*, b. April 29, 1703; *Jonathan*, b. Aug. 11, 1705; *Elizabeth*, b. Oct. 9, 1707; *Rachel*, b. July 3, 1710; *Experience*, b. Oct. 27, 1713; *Reuben*, b. 1719; *Mehitable*, b. 1722; *Stephen*, b. 1725.

4.   WILLIAM, s. of William, (1) rem. after 1717, from Hat. to Sunderland. He m. (1) Mary ——, who d. Dec. 7, 1711; (2) 1715, Elizabeth ——. Children—*William*, b. Jan. 16, 1702, res. in Sunderland; *John*, b. June 3, 1704, res. in Sunderland; *Samuel*, b. March 3, 1707, res. in Sunderland; *Mary*, b. Oct. 23, 1709; *Esther*, b. Sept. 12, 1715, m. Dea. Noah Wright; *Absalom*, b. April 28, 1717, res. in Sunderland and Leverett, and d. 1797; *Joshua*, b. 1719, m. 1747, Elizabeth Cooley, and res. in Sunderland; *Jerusha*, b. 1723; *Abigail*, b. 1729.

5.   JOSEPH, s. of William, (1) Hat., m. Feb. 13, 1707, Lydia Leonard. Children—*Lydia*, b. Feb. 24, 1708, m. John Allis; *Miriam*, b. Dec. 14, 1713, m. (1) —— Allis; (2) —— Benton of Hartford, Ct., and d. May 26, 1715; *Ebenezer*, b. June 15, 1716, d. Dec. 25, 1735; *David*, b. Aug. 18, 1717, m. Dec. 13, 1739, Esther Belding; *Hepzibah*, b. Jan. 12, 1719; *Joseph*, b. abt. 1722, m. Margaret ——; *Martha; Leonard*, (dau.,) b. abt. 1726; *Submit*.

SCOVIL, EBENEZER, b. Nov. 27, 1707, s. of John of Middletown, Ct., kept the upper ferry, and d. Nov. 26, 1731, ae. 24.

SELDEN, JOSEPH, bapt. Nov. 2, 1651, s. of Thomas of Hartford, settled about 1678, in Hadley, whence he removed about 1684 to Deerfield, but prior to 1689 returned to Hadley, and before 1700 removed to Lyme, Ct., where he d. July 14, 1724, ae. 72.   He m. Feb. 11, 1677, Rebecca, dau. of Edward Church.   She d. June 9, 1726, ae. 65.   Children—*Rebecca*, b. Feb. 12, or March 5, 1678, m. James Wells of Haddam, Ct.; *Hester*, b. April 11, 1680, d. July 21, 1681; *Joseph*, b. May 10, 1682, res. in Haddam, and d. April 3, 1729, in 47th yr.; *Thomas*, b. 1684, res. in Haddam, and d. Sept. 12, 1754, in 70th yr.; *Mary*, b. March 5, 1689; *Esther*, b. May 2, 1691, m. Jabez Chapman of Haddam; *Samuel*, b. May 17, 1695, res. in Lyme, Ct.; *Sarah*, bapt. July 20, 1712.   Mr. Savage says that he had dau. Mercy, who m. Isaac Spencer.   It may be that Mercy and Mary are the same.

1. SELDEN, THOMAS, bapt. Aug. 30, 1645, s. of Thomas of Hartford, d. Nov. 24, 1734, ae. 89. He m. Felix, dau. of William Lewis of Farmington, Ct. She was alive in 1738. Children—*John*, b. June 16, 1675; *Thomas*, b. Nov. 12, 1677, slain at Deerfield Feb. 29, 1704; *Ebenezer*, b. March 2, 1679.

2. JOHN, s. of Thomas, (1) d. Dec. 3, 1744, ae. 69. He m. March 24, 1698, Sarah Harrison. Children—*John*, b. April 16, 1699, d. Aug. 21, 1703; *Isaac*, b. July 14, 1701; *Mary*, b. Sept. 27, 1703, m. (1) July 23, 1723, John Taylor; (2) March 22, 1728, William White; *Joseph*, b. March 17, 1706, d. April 11, 1706; *Obadiah*, b. March 17, 1706, d. April 8, 1706; *Sarah*, b. June 29, 1709, m. Jan. 20, 1737, Abel Stockwell of Springfield; *Jonathan*, b. May 20, 1711.

3. EBENEZER, s. of Thomas, (1) d. 1740, ae. 61. He m. Elizabeth, dau. of John Clark of Middletown, Ct. She was b. 1685, and was alive in 1746. Children—*Joseph*, b. Aug. 4, 1711, d. Aug. 12, 1711; *Elizabeth*, b. Feb. 9, 1713, m. Jan. 1, 1736, Diodatus Curtis; *Esther*, b. May 27, 1715, unm. in 1745; *Ruth*, b. Sept. 23, 1717, m. May 20, 1741, Aaron Warner of Amh.; *Ebenezer*, b. May 17, 1720, m. Nov. 15, 1753, Jerusha Pomeroy, res. in 1754, in Agawam; *Joseph*, b. July 20, 1722, res. in 1754, in Agawam; *Mary*, b. Sept. 3, 1725, d. April 28, 1745, ae. 19; *Hannah*.

4. ISAAC, s. of John (2) d. May 27, 1764. He m. Oct. 14, 1725, Esther Ingram. She d. June 28, 1766. Children—*Child*, b. and d. Aug. 5, 1726; *Abigail*, b. Sept. 10, 1727, m. 1755, Oliver White; *Azariah*, b. July 8, 1730, m. Feb. 19, 1752, Lavinia Wood; *Thomas*, b. Sept. 22, 1732, m. Nov. 13, 1760, Jane Farrand; *Rhoda*, b. Feb. 8, 1735, m. Aug. 28, 1758, John Montague; *Jabez*, b. March 27, 1737, m. 1769, Anne Parish; *Martha*, b. Jan. 16, 1742, m. Jan. 7, 1761, Asa Wood.

5. JONATHAN, s. of John, (2) Granby, d. May 30, 1776. He m. Oct. 6, 1732, Mercy Ingram. She d. July 29, 1780. Children—*Mercy*, b. Jan. 20, 1733, m. 1754, Eliph. Green; *Bitterne*, (dau.) b. Aug. 3, 1735; *Sarah*, b. May 20, 1737; *Child*, b. March, 1739, d.; *Jonathan*, b. July 15, 1740; *Martha*, b. Jan. 9, 1742; *John*, d. Sept. 23, 1746.

1. SEYMOUR, NATHAN, removed to Vt. He m. April 27, 1780, Elizabeth, dau. of Orange Warner. Children—*Mary*, b. Nov. 11, 1780; *William*, b. Aug. 19, 1782; *Samuel*, b. Feb. 3, 1785; *Horace*, b. Jan. 22, 1787; *Fanny*, b. July 17, 1789; *Nathan*, b. March 31, 1792; *Henry*, b. March 25, 1797.

2. SAMUEL, s. of Nathan, (1) d. Jan. 22, 1854. He m. (1) 1810, Mary Clary of Leverett; (2) 1820, Sarah Clark of Deerfield; (3) Dec. 1828, Lucinda Montague. She d. Oct. 15, 1831; (4) June 2, 1833, Asenath, dau. of Silas Smith of So. Had. She was b. March 3, 1787. Children—*Elizabeth*, b. June 1, 1813, m. Sept. 1840, Samuel C. Wilder; *Samuel*, b. April 15, 1818, d. June 12, 1853; *Sarah*, b. Sept. 26, 1827, m. 1847, Isaac Woodruff.

3. HORACE, s. of Nathan, (1) d. May 22, 1829. He m. 1813, Mary Standish of Preston, Ct. She d. July 11, 1829. Children—*Lovisa Cooley*, b. Jan. 16, 1814, m. Edwin Cook, and res. in Mich.; *Sarah Ann*, b. June 12, 1815, d. Aug. 5, 1834; *Henry*, b. Oct. 20, 1816, grad. A. C. 1838, Union Theo. Sem. in N. Y. City, 1842, settled over Orthodox church in Deerfield, March 1, 1843, dis. March 14, 1849, inst. over church in East Hawley, Oct. 3, 1849. He m. (1) May 9, 1844, Laura Isabella Fisk of Shelburne; (2) Aug. 11,

1851, Sophia Williams of Ashfield; *Levi Dwight*, b. April 26, 1819, pursued medical studies in Pittsfield, and res. in Greenfield. He m. Nov. 14, 1842, Lucy Ann Clark of New York City; *Susan Elvira*, b. Nov. 23, 1822, m. Jan. 21, 1848, James M. Hosford, Esq. of Genesee, Ill.; *Rebecca Elvira*, b. Oct. 13, 1824, m. Edwin Bliss of Kendall, N. Y., and d. Nov. 30, 1827.

4. HENRY, s. of Nathan, (1) Children—*Maria Sophia*, b. July 10, 1821; *Rebecca Moore*, b. March 20, 1823, d. Aug. 15, 1828; *Edwin Henry*, b. Feb. 11, 1826; *Harriet Rebecca*, b. Oct. 1, 1829; *Caroline Mary*, b. Oct. 18, 1833; *Horace Dwight*, b. July 14, 1836.

SMITH, ELEAZAR, m. Agnes. Children—*Rebecca*, d. June 20, 1745; *Dorothy*, b. June 13, 1746; *Rebecca*, b. April 11, 1748.

SMITH, ELIAKIM, d. in the army at Watertown, Aug. 27, 1775, ae. 40. He m. (1) June 17, 1760, Mehitable Smith, who d. April 16, 1770, ae. 30; (2) Nov. 14, 1771, Jerusha Kellogg. She d. Sept. 22, 1823, ae. 84. Children —*Rebecca*, b. Sept. 17, 1763, d. Sept. 8, 1766; *Eliakim*, b. Sept. 13, 1767; *Rebecca*, b. April 6, 1770, m. Aug. 9, 1792, Timothy Hopkins.

1. SMITH, JOSEPH, sergeant, b. March, 1657, eldest s. of Joseph of Hartford, Ct., rem. abt. 1680, to Hadley, was freeman 1690, and d. Oct. 1, 1733, ae. 76. He m. Feb. 11, 1681, Rebecca, dau. of John Dickinson. She d. Feb. 16, 1731, ae. 73. Children—*Joseph*, b. Nov. 8, 1681; *John*, b. Oct. 24, 1684, d. Aug. 27, 1686; *John*, b. Jan. 5, 1687; *Rebecca*, b. June 11, 1689, m. Feb. 1712, Joseph Smith; *Jonathan*, b. Oct. 28, 1691; *Lydia*, b. Sept. 15, 1693, m. Dec. 26, 1720, Joseph Chamberlain; *Benjamin*, b. Jan. 22, 1696, m. Elizabeth Crafts. She was b. April 17, 1691, and d. Feb. 9, 1764, ae. 72. He d. July 1, 1780, ae. 84; *Elizabeth*, b. Dec. 22, 1701, d. Feb. 15, 1728.

2. JOSEPH, s. of Joseph, (1) d. Oct. 21, 1767. He m. 1715, Sarah Alexander. She d. Jan. 31, 1768. Children—*Alexander*, b. Oct. 11, 1717; *Edward*, b. March 26, 1719; *Reuben*, b. April 2, 1721; *Sarah*, b. Nov. 9, 1722, m. Dec. 3, 1747, Windsor Smith, and d. Sept. 1, 1772, ae. 49; *Thomas*, b. Dec. 6, 1725.

3. JOHN, s. of Joseph, (1) deacon, rem. in 1711 to Hat., and in 1736 to Belchertown, where he d. 1777, ae. 90. He m. 1709, Elizabeth, dau. of Thomas Hovey. She d. 1758, ae. 70. Children—*John*, b. Dec. 21, 1710; *Abner*, b. Sept. 10, 1712, m. (1) Oct. 2, 1736, Martha Warner; (2) Mary Pomeroy, rem. to Springfield, and d. Nov. 19, 1766, ae. 54; *Elizabeth*, b. Sept. 19, 1714, m. April 20, 1736, Walter Fairfield of Belchertown; *Daniel*, b. prob. 1716, m. 1742, Abigail Sacket, and d. in Belchertown, May 31, 1800, ae. 84; *Miriam*, b. Oct. 30, 1718, m. Oct. 3, 1739, Jesse Warner; *Samuel*, b. 1721; *Joseph*, m. Eunice Bascom, and d. in 1803, in Lyme, N. H.; *Elijah*, b. 1723; *Rachel*, b. Jan. 4, 1727, m. Aaron Hannum of Belchertown, and d. 1811, ae. 85; *Sarah*, b. Sept. 27, 1729, m. Abner Dickinson of Whately; *Rebecca*, b. May 4, 1732, m. Oliver Graves of Whately.

4. JONATHAN, s. of Joseph, (1) made his will Nov. 1768, which was proved 1778. He left all his estate to Dea. David Nash. He m. 1718, Abigail, dau. of Nathaniel Alexander of Nh. Children—*Jonathan*, b. Aug. 27, 1719, alive in 1738; *Abigail*, b. July 19, 1723; *Elizabeth*, b. Feb. 17, 1729, m. May 9, 1754, Dea. David Nash of So. Had.

5. ALEXANDER, s. of Joseph, (2) Amherst, d. Sept. 21, 1787, ae. 69. He m. 1743, [pub. April,] Rebecca Warner of Westfield, who d. Nov. 26, 1801, ae. 87. Children—*Nathaniel Alexander*, b. Feb. 22, 1744; *Hannah*, b. Jan. 12, 1746, m. Oliver Lovell of Rockingham, Vt.; *Joseph*, b. Jan. 4, 1748, d. Jan. 22, 1748; *Joseph*, b. April 11, 1750; *Rebecca*, b. March 4, 1751, d. March 10, 1752; *Rebecca*, b. Dec. 3, 1753, m. (1) Lemuel Childs of Deerfield; (2) Martin Cooley of Sunderland, and d. Aug. 29, 1809, ae. 55; *Elias*, b. Feb. 11, 1756; *Samuel*, b. Sept. 4, 1758.

6. EDWARD, s. of Joseph, (2) Amherst, d. 1795, ae. 76. He m. Hamutal, dau. of Benjamin Ellsworth of E. Windsor, Ct. She was b. Jan. 11, 1726. Children—*Benjamin*, b. March 26, 1750; *Timothy*, b. Aug. 10, 1752; *Hewitt*, bapt. Oct. 13, 1754, d. unm., in Amh., Jan. 30, 1823, ae. 70; *Tryphena*, bapt. April 24, 1757, m. —— Locke of Williamson, N. Y.; *Sarah*, bapt. April 5, 1761, m. Nov. 29, 1787, Thomas Munsell of E. Windsor, Ct.; *Roxana*, bapt. Oct. 7, 1764, m. William Rice of Amh.; *Lucy*, bapt. May 1, 1768, d. unm. 1797.

7. REUBEN, s. of Joseph, (2) So. Had. He m. (1) Jan. 19, 1749, Miriam Moody, who d. Feb. 16, 1770; (2) Sibil, wid. of Elijah Smith of Belchertown, and dau. of Daniel Worthington of Colchester, Ct. Children—*Jonathan*, b. Oct. 16, 1749; *Reuben*, b. March 1, 1752, d. 1759; *Abigail*, b. March 1, 1754; *Miriam*, b. Aug. 31, 1756; *Reuben*, b. Feb. 21, 1759; *Persis*, b. July 24, 1761; *Selah*, b. May 21, 1764.

8. THOMAS, s. of Joseph, (2) rem. to Williamstown. He m. Oct. 15, 1754, Rhoda Worthington of Colchester, Ct. She was b. Sept. 25, 1730, and d. May 8, 1784, ae. 53. Children—*Rhoda*, b. Feb. 8, 1755; *Lydia*, b. Feb. 27, 1757, m. Nov. 10, 1779, Seth Smith, and d. Aug. 23, 1828, ae. 72; *Daniel*, b. Oct. 26, 1759, m. Lucy Cook, and rem. to Williamstown; *Thomas*, b. Dec. 3, 1761; *Ephraim*, b. Sept. 27, 1764; *Mehitable*, bapt. Feb. 1, 1767, d. Sept. 1775; *Loomis*, bapt. Aug. 17, 1769, d. Sept. 14, 1779.

9. JOHN, s. of John, (3) Hatfield, d. 1751. He m. Mary. Children— *Caleb*, b. July 9, 1733; *Benjamin*, b. March 15, 1735; *Mary; Elizabeth*, m. 1758, Paul Smith; *John*, rem. to the West; *Joel*, d. unm. in Hat.; *Edward*, b. 1747, rem. abt. 1793, from Belchertown, where he was deacon, to Shelburne; *Submit*, m. Asa Wait; *Hannah*, m. 1779, Elihu Dickinson.

10. ELIJAH, s. of John, (3) Belchertown, d. April 21, 1770, ae. 47. He served as captain in French war in 1756, and was deacon in Belchertown. He m. 1751, Sibyl, dau. of Daniel Worthington of Colchester, Ct. She m. (2) Reuben Smith, and d. May 26, 1828, ae. 101. Children—*Asa*, b. 1752, d. 1835, in Halifax, Vt.; *Sibyl*, m. Jan. 1774, Dea. Joseph Bardwell of So. Had.; *Sarah W.*, m. Dec. 1777, Elijah Bardwell of Goshen; *Elijah*, b. 1758, d. in Greenfield, in 1843; *Elizabeth*, m. April, 1778, John Cowles, Jr.; *Ethan*, b. Dec. 19, 1762, grad. D. C. 1790, was a (Cong.) minister in Haverhill, N. H., Hopkinton, N. H., Hebron, N. Y., Poultney, Vt., Hanover, and d. in Boylston, Sept. 1849, ae. 86. He m. Bathsheba, dau. of Rev. David Sanford of Medway; *Jacob*, b. 1764, res. in Hadley, was deacon in the church, and d. April 5, 1852; *William*, b. 1766, rem. to Scipio, N. Y.; *Josiah*, rem. to Scipio, N. Y.

11. NATHANIEL ALEXANDER, s. of Alexander, (5) Amherst, d. April 4, 1839, ae. 95. He m. (1) Jan. 17, 1771, Sarah, dau. of Thomas Hastings of Amh. She d. Oct. 7, 1810, ae. 66; (2) Oct. 13, 1811, Irene, wid. of —— Lovell, and dau. of —— Chapin of E. Windsor, Ct. She d. July 23, 1835, ae. 83. Children—*Sally*, b. July 17, 1776, m. April 2, 1801, Thomas Reed of Amh.; *Nathaniel Alexander*, b. March 17, 1781, d. Oct. 10, 1781, ae. 6 mos.

12. JOSEPH, s. of Alexander, (5) m. Eunice, dau. of Nathan Goodman of Hat. Children—*Nathan*, b. Dec. 4, 1776; *Sereno*, b. March 27, 1779; *Docia*, b. Sept. 16, 1783; *Parks*, b. Sept. 2, 1788; *Chester*, b. Oct. 12, 1791; *Joseph*, b. Feb. 12, 1796.

13. ELIAS, s. of Alexander, (5) Amherst, d. March 2, 1826, ae. 70. He m. Jan. 1, 1788, Philothea Debell. Children—*Alexander; Rodney*, d. Feb. 3 1809, ae. 19; *Fanny*, bapt. April 1, 1792, d. unm. in Milwaukee, Wis., July 28, 1850; *Prudence*, bapt. June 21, 1795, d. unm. in Milwaukee, Wis., July 24, 1850; *Elias*, bapt. Aug. 27, 1797, d. Dec. 20, 1804; *Philothea*, bapt. Sept. 15, 1799, m. Charles Ripley; *Sidney*, bapt. Sept. 19, 1802; *Clarinda*, bapt. July 29, 1804, m. —— Keeler.

14. SAMUEL, s. of Alexander, (5) Amh., d. Nov. 8, 1834, ae. 76. He m. Feb. 10, 1782, Sabra, dau. of John Debell of Rockingham, Vt. She was b. Jan. 24, 1759, and d. Sept. 28, 1849, ae. 90. Children—*Melinda*, b. March 18, 1784, d. July 23, 1801; *John*, b. Jan. 14, 1786, d. Jan. 7, 1791; *Laurana*, b. May 9, 1788, m. John Russell of Northampton; *John Debell*, b. Oct. 25, 1790, m. June 11, 1813, Relief Thayer, and d. May 5, 1836; *Sibyl Kilbourn*, b. Feb. 3, 1793, m. Cotton Smith of Amh.; *Hannah*, b. Aug. 18, 1796, m. Frederick A. Palmer of Amherst; *Samuel*, b. Jan. 2, 1801, d. June 17, 1829.

15. BENJAMIN, s. of Edward, (6) Amh., d. July 14, 1819, ae. 69. He m. Dec. 26, 1783, Elizabeth Rush. Children—*Elizabeth*, bapt. June 2, 1785, d. unm. Sept. 28, 1839, ae. 54; *Spenser*, b. July 5, 1787, m. (1) Jan. 16, 1816, Betsey Rust, who d. May 30, 1823, ae. 30; (2) Wid. Lydia Kellogg, who d. Nov. 25, 1830, ae. 45; (3) Oct. 9, 1843, Mary Mack. He d. in Amh., Dec. 31, 1849, ae. 62.

16. TIMOTHY, s. of Edward, (6) Amherst, d. Oct. 24, 1814, ae. 62. He m. (1) Eunice Munsell. She d. abt. June, 1788; (2) Sabra Munsell. She d. Jan. 17, 1815. Children—*Timothy*, bapt. May 18, 1788, m. Mary Bissell, and res. in Amherst; *Daniel*, bapt. Jan. 1, 1792, m. Nancy Williams of Ashfield; *Hervey*, bapt. Sept. 28, 1795, m. Eliza Ferry of Amherst, and d. in Amh., Nov. 6, 1830.

17. THOMAS, s. of Thomas, (8) m. Catharine. Children—*Mehitable*, b. Dec. 24, 1785; *Eunice*, b. June 12, 1787, d. June 12, 1787; *Roswell*, b. June 24, 1788, d. July 31, 1802; *Stephen*, b. Jan. 3, 1790; *Susanna*, b. Oct. 16, 1791; *Patty*, b. Nov. 28, 1793; *Walter*, b. Dec. 15, 1795, d. April 18, 1797; *Christopher*, b. June 9, 1798; *Salome*, b. July 1, 1800, d. Aug. 19, 1802.

18. BENJAMIN, s. of John, (9) was drowned abt. 1803, while crossing the Conn. river. Children—*Caleb*, b. Sept. 24, 1760; *Erastus; Rachel*, b. Jan. 31, 1764; *Daughter; Daughter; Benjamin*, bapt. March 17, 1771, kept tavern in Nh. and Had.

19. SERENO, s. of Joseph, (12) m. Jan. 29, 1807, Betsey, dau. of David Stockbridge, and d. Jan. 22, 1852, ae. 72. Children—*Edmund*, b. Dec. 19,

1808; *Theodocia*, b. May 26, 1810, m. George Allen; *Chester*, b. March 22, 1811; *Maria*, b. Feb. 19, 1813, m. Francis Forward of Belchertown; *Elizabeth*, b. May, 1816, d. July 16, 1819, ae. 3; *Hinsdale*, b. March 2, 1819; *Rufus* d. ae. 4 mos.

20. HON. JOSEPH, s. of Joseph, (12) was a State Senator, 1853 and 1854. He m. Jan. 28, 1818, Sophia, dau. of Caleb Smith. Children— *Nathan Emilius*, b. Nov. 15, 1818, d. Oct. 15, 1820; *Edward Chester*, b. June 1, 1820; *Mary Wilson*, b. April 10, 1822; *Joseph Emilius*, b. June 3, 1824, d. Nov. 8, 1832; *William Parks*, b. April 4, 1826, d. Sept. 16, 1836; *Harriet Cornelia*, b. Nov. 30, 1827; *Julia Maria*, b. April 28, 1830; *Charles Porter*, b. April 10, 1832; *Sophia Louisa*, b. March 17, 1834; *Joseph Henry*, b. Oct. 22, 1835; *James William*, b. June 1, 1838.

21. CALEB, s. of Benjamin, (18) m. Nov. 25, 1784, Olive Hibbard. Children—*Elizabeth*, b. Feb. 5, 1785; *Chester*, b. Oct. 17, 1786; *Cotton*, b. March 5, 1790; *John*, b. Feb. 19, 1792; *Melinda*, b. July 15, 1794; *Sophia*, b. Oct. 8, 1796, m. Jan. 28, 1818, Joseph Smith; *Olive*, b. Feb. 7, 1799; *Caleb*, b. July 5, 1801.

22. ERASTUS SMITH, s. of Benjamin, (18) m. Aug. 17, 1791, Lydia Hibbard. Children—*Clarissa; Sophia; Lydia; Erastus; Sarah; Zebina; Thaddeus*, Representative, 1860; *Elizabeth*, bapt. April 6, 1806; *Catharine Amelia*, bapt. Sept. 20, 1807; *Child*, bapt. April 24, 1793, d. ae. 4 days.

23. EDMUND, s. of Sereno, (19) m. June 5, 1833, Sarah C., dau. of Elihu Smith. Children—*Elizabeth*, b. July 7, 1835; *Martha Hitchcock*, b. June 28, 1837; *Henry Parks*, b. Aug. 21, 1839, grad. A. C. 1860, and d. Dec. 17, 1861, ae. 22; *Sarah Maria*, b. Oct. 19, 1841; *Edmund Hubbard*, b. Dec. 10, 1843, d. Feb. 2, 1844; *Edwin Clapp*, b. July 8, 1845; *George Edmund*, b. March 18, 1847; *William Hubbard*, b. Dec. 27, 1849, d. Jan. 27, 1859, ae. 9; *Joseph Chester*, b. Oct. 11, 1852, d. Feb. 6, 1859, ae. 6.

24. CHESTER, s. of Sereno, (19) m. May 29, 1844, Mary Ann Warner, dau. of Sylvester Smith. Children—*Edward Warner*, b. Sept. 3, 1847; *Enos*, b. Feb. 19, 1849; *Mary Elizabeth*, b. Nov. 11, 1851; *Rufus May*, b. Feb. 6, 1855; *Helen Maria*, b. Nov. 25, 1857.

SMITH, SAMUEL, Lieut., with wife Elizabeth and children, Samuel, ae. 9, Elizabeth, ae. 7, Mary, ae. 4, and Philip, ae. 1, sailed for New England, the last day of April, 1634, in the Elizabeth of Ipswich. He and his wife were each then called thirty two years of age. He came from Wethersfield, Ct., where he was a leading man, to Hadley, where he held important offices both in church and state. He is supposed to have died in 1680, ae. abt. 78. His inventory was taken Jan. 17, 1681. He m. Elizabeth, who d. March 16, 1686, ae. 84. Children—*Samuel*, b. abt. 1625, prob. rem. to New London, Ct., and thence prior to 1664 to Va., and if so, m. Elizabeth, dau. of Rev. Henry Smith of Wethersfield; *Elizabeth*, b. abt. 1627, m. abt. 1646, Nathaniel Foote; (2) William Gull; *Mary*, b. abt. 1630, m. (1) John Graves; *Philip*, b. abt. 1633; *Chileab*, b. abt. 1635; *John*.

2. PHILIP, s. of Samuel, (1) was one of the first men of his time, in the town of his adoption, a lieutenant, deacon, and representative, and d. Jan. 10, 1685, "murdered with an hideous witchcraft," according to Cotton Mather.

He m. Rebecca, dau. of Nathaniel Foote of Wethersfield. She m. (2) Oct. 2, 1688, Maj. Aaron Cook, and d. April 6, 1701. Children—*Samuel*, b. Jan. 1659; *Child*, d. Jan. 22, 1661; *John*, b. Dec. 18, 1661; *Jonathan; Philip; Rebecca*, m. abt. 1686, George Stillman of Had. and Wethersfield, and d. Oct. 7, 1750; *Nathaniel; Joseph; Ichabod*, b. April 11, 1675.

3. CHILEAB, s. of Samuel, (1) was freeman 1673, and d. March 7, 1731, ae. 95. He m. Oct. 2, 1661, Hannah, dau. of Luke Hitchcock of Wethersfield. She d. Aug. 31, 1733, ae. 88. Children—*Hannah*, b. July 7, 1662, m. March 23, 1681, John Montague; *Samuel*, b. March 9, 1665; *Luke*, b. April 16, 1666; *Ebenezer*, b. July 11, 1668; *Nathaniel*, b. Jan. 2, 1670, d. Jan. 1670; *John*, b. Oct. 8, 1671, m. 1691, Martha Golding, and d. s. p. abt. 1750; *Son*, d. 1673; *Hester*, b. March 31, 1674, m. Oct. 20, 1696, Nathaniel Ingram; *Daughter*, d. March, 1677; *Elizabeth*, b. Feb. 2, 1679, m. Oct. 26, 1698, James Smith; *Mary*, b. Aug. 16, 1681, m. (1) Dec. 15, 1697, Preserved Smith; (2) April 22, 1721, Peter Montague; *Chileab*, d. Aug. 1682; *Chileab*, b. Feb. 18, 1685; *Sarah*, b. April 26, 1688, m. April 13, 1710, Jonathan Morton.

4. JOHN, s. of Samuel, (1) was slain by the Indians in Hatfield meadow, May 30, 1676. He m. Nov. 12, 1673, Mary, dau. of William Partridge. She m. (2) Sept. 1679, Peter Montague, and d. May 20, 1683. Children—*John*, b. May 15, 1665; *Samuel*, b. Dec. 7, 1667, killed by falling from a horse, June 19, 1681; *Joseph*, b. Nov. 16, 1670; *Benjamin*, b. 1673, settled in Wethersfield, Ct.; *Marah*, b. 1677, m. March 10, 1696, John Day.

5. SAMUEL, s. of Philip, (2) deacon, purchased in 1706, property in East Hartford, Ct., and d. Aug. 28, 1707, ae. 48. He m. (1) Nov. 16, 1682, Mary, dau. of Samuel Church of Hartford, Ct. She d. June 18, 1700; (2) Jan. or June 24, 1701, Mary Smith. Children—*Samuel*, b. April 9, 1687; *Mary*, b. Dec. 28, 1689, m. John Keeney; *Rebecca*, b. Nov. 20, 1691; *Samuel*, b. Dec. 18, 1694, idiot, was alive in 1721; *Mehitable*, b. May 9, 1696, m. Ebenezer Taylor of Granby; *Benoni*, b. June 10 or 12, 1700; *Timothy*, b. June 1, 1702; *Edward*, b. Nov. 17, 1704; *Mercy*.

6. JOHN, s. of Philip, (2) deacon, d. April 16, 1727, ae. 66. He m. Nov. 29, 1683, Joanna, dau. of Joseph Kellogg. She survived her husband. Children—*John*, b. Dec. 3, 1684; *Joanna*, b. Sept. 1, 1686, m. Jan. 10, 1705, Ephraim Nash; *Rebecca*, b. Aug. 5, 1688, m. Jan. 11, 1710, Samuel Crow; *Joseph*, b. July 19, 1690; *Martin*, b. April 15, 1692, m. 1715, Sarah Wier, and res. in Wethersfield, Ct.; *Eleazer*, b. Sept. 25, 1694, d. Oct. 3, 1721, ae. 27; *Sarah*, b. Nov. 18, 1696, d. Dec. 28, 1697; *Sarah*, b. Nov. 9, 1698, m. (1) May 22, 1724, Samuel Kellogg; (2) Jan. 1749, William Montague; *Prudence*, b. March 15, 1701, m. (1) March 1, 1722, Timothy Nash of Longmeadow; (2) Dea. Ichabod Hinckley, and d. April 18, 1774, ae. 72; *Experience*, b. April 19, 1703, m. Aug. 11, 1727, James Kellogg, and d. Aug. 23, 1762, ae. 59; *Elizabeth*, b. Oct. 12, 1705, m. May 22, 1728, Stephen Nash of Westfield, and d. 1790; *Mindwell*, b. May 25, 1708, m. May 3, 1732, Benoni Sacket.

7. JONATHAN, s. of Philip, (2) Hatfield, d. Oct. or Nov. 1737. He m. Nov. 14, 1688, Abigail, dau. of Joseph Kellogg. She survived her husband, and was living in Amherst in 1742. Children—*Jonathan*, b. Aug. 10, 1689; *Daniel*, b. March 3, 1692, deranged, d. in Amh., Nov. 16, 1760, ae. 68; *Abigail*, b. April 20, 1695, m. Jonathan Parsons; *Stephen*, b. Dec. 5, 1697;

Prudence, b. May 16, 1700; *Moses*, b. Sept. 8, 1702, m. Nov. 1726, Mary Marsh, prob. moved to Ware River, and d. abt. 1749. Administration on his estate was granted July 4, 1749; *Elisha*, b. July 10, 1705, and d. in Whately in 1784; *Elizabeth*, b. May 8, 1708, m. Nov. 6, 1728, [1729?] Richard Chauncy, and d. in Whately, May 22, 1790, ae. 82; *Ephraim*, b. March 24, 1711, m. Martha, dau. of Joseph Scott, and settled in Athol; *Aaron*, b. Feb. 7, 1715, m. Abigail, dau. of Joseph Scott, and settled in Athol.

8. PHILIP, s. of Philip, (2) rem. first to Springfield, and thence abt. 1704, to E. Hartford, Ct., and d. Jan. 25, 1725. He m. (1) July 9, 1687, Mary, dau. of Samuel Bliss of Springfield. She d. Dec. 23, 1707, in 57th yr.; (2) Sept. 1708, Mary Robinson, who d. May 17, 1733, in 60th yr. Children— *Philip*, b. May 1, 1689, d. unm. 1712; *David*, b. April 23, 1691; *Daughter*, b. June 11, and d. June 12, 1693; *Daughter*, b. June 11, and d. June 16, 1693; *Martha*, b. Sept. 27, 1694, m. Thomas Wiard; *Aaron*, b. Feb. 14, 1697; *Mary*, b. Feb. 23, 1699; *Samuel*, b. abt. 1702, d. in East Hartford, Aug. 28, 1777, ae. 75; *Rebecca; Ebenezer*, b. Jan. 1, 1707; *Nehemiah*, b. July 17, 1709; *Hannah*, b. Nov. 20, 1711.

9. NATHANIEL, s. of Philip, (2) Hatfield, d. 1740 or 1741, as appears from the fact, that his will made 1740, was proved Jan. 1741. He m. Feb. 6, 1696, Mary, dau. of Nathaniel Dickinson. She d. Aug. 16, 1718, ae. 45. Children—*Nathaniel*, b. Jan. 1, 1698; *Mary*, b. Dec. 11, 1700, m. Jonathan Dickinson; *Joshua*, b. Nov. 2, 1702; *Rebecca*, b. April 4, 1705, m. Jonathan Wells; *Hannah*, b. March 7, 1707, m. —— Wright; *Martha*, b. Jan. 31, 1709, m. Benjamin Wait, and d. 1794; *Lydia*, b. March 16, 1711, m. Samuel Morton; *Jerusha*, b. Jan. 9, 1713; m. Simeon White, and d. abt. 1809.

10. JOSEPH, s. of Philip, (2) grad. H. C. 1695, teacher in Hopkins Grammar School, also in Springfield and Brookfield, was ord. May 10, 1709, pastor of the church in Cohanzy, N. J., and Jan. 15, 1715, pastor of the 2d church in Upper Middletown, Ct. He d. Sept. 8, 1736, ae. 62. He m. Esther Parsons, b. Dec. 24, 1672, who d. May 30, 1760, in 89th yr. Children—*Martha*, b. Sept. 17, 1699, m. Nov. 30, 1721, Richard Hamlin; *Joseph*, m. Dec. 20, 1726, Elizabeth Buckley; *Mary*, m. Dec. 10, 1729, Rev. Samuel Tudor of East Windsor, Ct., and d. June 15, 1785, ae. 76.

11. ICHABOD, s. of Philip, (2) d. Sept. 6, 1746, ae. 70 or 71. He m. July 19, 1698, Elizabeth, dau. of Capt. Aaron Cook. She d. Oct. 10, 1751, ae. 73. Children—*Philip*, b. May 2, 1699; *Aaron*, b. Sept. 20, 1700; *Nathaniel*, b. Feb. 16, 1702; *Rebecca*, b. Nov. 9, 1703, m. Oct. 21, 1726, William Smith; *Moses*, b. April 30, 1706; *Bridget*, b. March 15, 1708, m. Nov. 20, 1730, Jonathan Moody of Amherst; *Miriam*, b. Aug. 22, 1710, m. Nov. 16, 1738, David Moody; *Elizabeth*, b. Sept. 10, 1712, m. (1) Dec. 4, 1735, Noadiah Lewis; (2) Aug. 14, 1743, Elisha Ingram of Amh.; *Samuel*, b. Aug. 4, 1715, m. Rebecca, and in 1759 res. in Sandisfield; *Experience*, b. Jan. 27, 1717; *Elisha*, b. Jan. 23, 1721, was of Amh. 1761, and Had. 1770.

12. SAMUEL, s. of Chileab, (3) shoemaker, d. Aug. 4, 1724, ae. 60. He m. March 9, 1687, Sarah Bliss, who was alive in 1742. Children—*Samuel*, b. Nov. 25, 1687, d. Jan. 18, 1688; *Sarah*, b. April 10, 1689, m. Feb. 27, 1713, E. Perkins; *Samuel*, b. Aug. 11, 1691; *Peletiah*, b. March 8, 1694; *William*; b. Dec. 21, 1696; *Lydia*, b. Nov. 30, 1699, m. June 12, 1724, Samuel Smith, *Hannah*, b. Oct. 18, 1701, unm.; *Elizabeth*, b. Jan. 23, 1704, d. March 18,

1712; Esther, b. June 14, 1706, m. Feb. 22, 1727, Daniel Belding of Deer-field; *Margaret*, b. Jan. 24, 1710, m. March 6, 1734, Samuel Church.

13. LUKE, s. of Chileab, (3) captain. His will made 1736, was proved Jan. 1748. He m. 1690, Mary Crow, who d. June 19, 1761, ae. 89. Children—*Luke*, b. Feb. 12, 1691, d. June 15, 1693; *Son*, b. April 5, 1692, d. ae. 4 days; *Mary*, m. Dec. 2, 1714, John Preston; *Hannah*, b. March 1, 1694, m. Nathaniel Dickinson; *Luke*, b. May 21, 1697; *Samuel*, b. May 23, 1699; *Jonathan*, b. March 4, 1702; *Ruth*, b. April 8, 1703, m. Feb. 13, 1724, Israel Dickinson; *David*, b. July 7, 1707; *Joseph*, b. March 22, 1710; *Sarah*, b. May 5, 1713, m. Aug. 9, 1734, James Smith, a Baptist minister of Granby.

14. EBENEZER, s. of Chileab, (3) a weaver, d. abt. 1716. His inventory was presented 1716, and his estate settled 1717. He m. Oct. 1691, Abigail Broughton. Children—*Abigail*, b. Oct. 10, 1692, m. March 15, 1711, Joseph Kellogg; *Martha*, b. Nov. 10, 1694, m. —— Read; *Ebenezer*, b. March 20, 1697, settled in Norwalk, Ct.; *John*, b. May 1, 1699; *Nathan*, b. Aug. 14, 1701, settled in Norwalk, Ct.; *Eliakim*, b. Jan. 13, 1704, settled in Norwalk, Ct.; *Eunice*, b. June 9, 1706, m. —— Olmsted; *Joseph*, b. Sept. 18, 1708; *Ephraim*, b. Jan. 27, 1730, settled in Stamford, Ct.; *Dinah*, b. July 8, 1713, m. —— Hoyt.

15. CHILEAB, s. of Chileab, (3) d. Nov. 8, 1746, ae. 61. He m. Dec. 19, 1710, Mercy Golding. She d. Aug. [6?] 1756, in 69th yr. Children—*Peter*, b. Oct. 31, 1711; *Chileab*, b. Sept. 27, 1713, d. Aug. 14, 1715; *Mercy*, b. May 25, 1715, m. March 24, 1739, Nathaniel Coleman of Hat. and Amh., and d. May 16, 1798, ae. 83; *Phinehas*, b. June 5, 1717, m. Mary; *Martha*, b. Jan. 16, 1719, m. Feb. 18, 1742, Thomas Meekins; *Windsor*, b. Nov. 12, 1720; *Thankful*, b. July 12, 1722, m. Moses Dickinson of Amh., and d. Oct. 18, 1802, ae. 80; *Chileab*, b. May 25, 1724, d. before 1730; *Mary*, b. Dec. 1. 1725, m. May 31, 1748, Moses Billings of Sunderland; *Chileab*, b. July 8, 1730, d. Oct. 24, 1752, ae. 22.

16. JOHN, s. of John, (4) called "Orphan John," d. Jan. 20, 1724, ae. 58. He m. 1687, Mary, dau. of John Root of Westfield. She survived her husband. Children—*Son*, b. 1688, d. same day; *Mary*, b. May 7, 1689, m. June 19, 1712, Thomas Sheldon of N. H., and Suffield, Ct., and d. 1771, ae. 82; *Abigail*, b. Oct. 26, 1691, m. Sept. 29, 1714, John Montague; *Mercy*, b. July 3, 1694, m. Nov. 22, 1711, Joseph Eastman; *John*, b. Feb. 1, 1697; *Rachel*, b. Aug. 4, 1699, m. Aug. 14, 1724, John Smith, s. of Ebenezer of Granby, and d. Sept. 20, 1724, ae. 25; *Hezekiah*, b. Dec. 21, 1702; *Noah*, b. May 16, 1707.

17. JOSEPH, s. of John, (4) Hatfield, d. Feb. 6, 1752, ae. 81. He m. Dec. 15, 1696, Canada Waite. She d. May 5, 1749, ae. 72. Children—*Mary*, b. Sept. 24, 1697, m. Joseph Field of Sunderland; *Martha*, b. Oct. 19, 1699, m. Thomas Nash; *Benjamin*, b. Nov. 17, 1701, slain June 18, 1724; *John*, b. Dec. 26, 1703, d. abt. the middle of July, 1705; *Sarah*, b. Oct. 14, 1707, m. Elisha Smith; *Esther*, b. June 2, 1710, m. Jonathan Field of Sunderland; *Hannah* or *Anna*, b. July 22, 1712, m. Moses Dickinson; *Eleanor*, b. Dec. 9, 1717, m. Jonathan Morton; *Joseph*, b. Nov. 21, 1720; *Samuel*, m. Mary, res. in Hat., and d. abt. 1779 or 1780.

18. JOHN, s. of Dea. John, (6) d. Dec. 25, 1761, ae. 77. He m. Esther, dau. of Ephraim Colton of Longmeadow. She d. ae. abt. 84. Children—

Philip, b. Oct. 12, 1712, m. 1743, Alice Jones, and d. s. p., abt. 1800; *Ephraim*, b. Nov. 17, 1714; *John*, b. Jan. 20, 1717; *Phinehas*, b. April 12, 1719; *Silas*, b. Feb. 2, 1722; *Eleazar*, b. Jan. 27, 1725; *Esther*, b. Nov. 27, 1726; *Josiah*, rem. to Brookfield, Vt., and d. ae. abt. 66.

19.   JOSEPH, s. of Dea. John, (6) rem. to Sunderland, but returned to Hadley, and there d. He m. Feb. 1712, Rebecca, dau. of Joseph Smith. Children—*Joseph*, b. Jan. 22, 1715, d. Dec. 29, 1735; *Rebecca*, b. May 29, 1717; *Joanna*, b. Aug. 27, 1719, m. (1) June 17, 1737, Joshua Olds; (2) May 19, 1743, Benjamin Wright; *Lydia*, b. Feb. 28, 1722; *Elisha*, bapt. Oct. 3, 1726, d. Aug. 27, 1744; *Elisha*, b. Oct. 3, 1726, d. 1810, ae. 84.

20.   JONATHAN, s. of Jonathan, (7) captain, rem. from Hat. to Amherst, and d. abt. 1778. He m. June 6, 1722, Hannah, dau. of Benoni Wright of Hatfield. Children—*Jonathan*, b. abt. 1728; *Martin; David; Noah*, b. Oct. 8, 1742; *Hannah*, m. 1753, David Dickinson; *Abigail*, b. abt. 1723, m. Jan. 2, 1755, Joseph Church of Amh., and d. March 22, 1815, ae. 92; *Rebecca*, m. June 16, 1757, Elijah Baker of Amh.; *Jerusha*, perhaps, who m. —— May.

21.   STEPHEN, s. of Jonathan, (7) rem. to Amh., and thence to Sunderland, where he d. abt. 1760. Children—*Stephen; Joel; Titus*, res. in Leverett; *Mary*, b. abt. 1727, m. 1753, Daniel Shattuck of Hinsdale, N. H., and d. Sept. 3, 1788, in 61st yr.

22.   PHILIP, s. of Ichabod, (11) Hatfield, m. Jan. 11, 1722, Sarah White, per. dau. of John White of Hat.; (2) 1734, John Burk. Children—*Simeon*, killed by the fulling mill wheel, April 25, 1735; *Oliver*, b. Jan. 18, 1727, d. April 26, 1728.

22½.   AARON, s. of Ichabod, (11) was of Amh. 1739, but d. in Shutesbury, July 5, 1759, ae. 58. He m. Nov. 26, 1724, Mehitable, dau. of John Ingram, and perhaps m. (2) Abigail, for it appears from Records of 1st Chh. of Amherst, that Aaron and Abigail Smith had baptized to them, there, Abner, Aug. 16, 1747. Children—*Son*, b. Sept. 16, and d. Sept. 17, 1725; *Jemima*, b. Aug. 18, 1726, prob. m. —— Whiton, and d. Feb. 14, 1774; *Philip*, b. 1729, d. in Shutesbury, Nov. 21, 1759, ae. 30; *Aaron*, b. 1732. An old family record says he was missing in a battle March, 1758, ae. 25 yrs. and ten mos. He was in Maj. Roger's Rangers, and taken near Ticonderoga, March 13, 1758.

23.   NATHANIEL, s. of Ichabod, (11) was the first physician of Amh., whither he removed as early as 1731, and d. July 21, 1789, ae. 84. He m. Nov. 11, 1726, Mehitable, dau. of John Ingram. She d. July 21, 1789, ae. 84. Children—*Nathaniel*, b. Aug. 23, 1727, d. Sept. 9, 1727, ae. 17 days; *Dorothy*, b. Feb. 23, 1729, m. 1747, (pub. June 14,) Ebenezer Mattoon of Amh., and d. June 3, 1756, ae. 27; *Rebecca*, b. July 1, 1731, m. April 8, 1756, Jonathan Smith, Jr. of Amh., and d. Sept. 5, 1807, ae. 76.

24.   MOSES, s. of Ichabod, (11) Amh., d. May 12, 1781, ae. 75. He m. 1732, Hannah, dau. of Samuel Childs of Deerfield. She d. Jan. 26, 1778, ae. 67. Children—*Moses*, b. Dec. 10, 1733; *Simeon*, b. Aug. 26, 1735; *Hannah*, b. July 18, 1737, m. Oct. 6, 1774, Daniel Church; *Catharine*, b. Aug. 13, 1739, m. Robert Emmons, and d. April 1, 1779, ae. 39; *Azubah*,

b. Sept. 30, 1741, d. Oct. 10, 1743; *Elizabeth*, b. Sept. 10, 1743, m. Aug. 13, 1767, Elisha Nash of Hatfield, and d. April 29, 1782, ae. 38; *Amasa*, b. April 23, 1746, res. in Deerfield; *Samuel*, b. June 19, 1748, went to sea, and d. early in Kingston, Jamaica; *Noadiah*, b. Sept. 26, 1751; *Oliver*, b. Nov. 7, 1755, d. of measles, during the revolution, in White Plains, N. Y.

25. EXPERIENCE, s. of Ichabod, (11) Granby, m. Mercy Eastman. Children—*Mercy*, b. Aug. 19, 1746, d. 1748; *Mercy*, b. Sept. 27, 1748; *Asa*, b. Sept. 29, 1750; *Rebeckah*, b. Jan. 22, 1753; *Ruth*, b. April 22, 1755; *Martha*, b. Oct. 5, 1757; *Jemima*, b. Oct. 18, 1758.

26. SAMUEL, s. of Samuel, (12) deacon, Sunderland, d. 1755 or 1756. He m. (1) 1716, Esther, dau. of Eleazar Warner; (2) Jan. 16, 1724, Sarah, dau. of Samuel Billings of Hatfield.   Children—*Esther*, b. 1719, m. Nehemiah Church; *Nathan*, b. 1721; *Miriam*, b. 1723; *Moses*, b. 1724, settled in Leverett; *Margaret*, b. 1727, d. 1745; *Rebekah*, b. 1730, m. Jonathan Church; *Lydia*, b. 1731; *Caleb*, b. 1733.

27. PELETIAH, s. of Samuel, (12) Amherst, m. 1721, Abigail, dau. of William Wait of Nh. Children—*Elizabeth*, b. May 19, 1722, m. Moses Smith; *Peletiah*, b. Feb. 14, 1724; *Abigail*, b. Sept. 14, 1726, m. March 27, 1747, Simeon Pomeroy of Amh., and d. Dec. 10, 1820, ae. 94; *Lucy*, b. Nov. 7, 1728, d. May 8, 1737.

28. WILLIAM, s. of Samuel, (12) South Hadley, d. 1770. In his will made and proved 1770, he names his wife Elizabeth, the heirs of his daughter Elizabeth, deceased, grandchild Charles Chapin and his wife Silence. Children—*Jerusha*, b. June 25, 1727; *Rebecca*, b. Sept. 21, 1731; *Elizabeth*, b. July 10, 1734, m. March 27, 1755, William Negus, and d. prior to 1770. One of his daughters probably d. June 25, 1740.

29. LUKE, s. of Luke, (13) rem. to Sunderland, but before his death, returned to Had. He m. (1) Sarah; (2) April 14, 1739, Sarah Hamilton. Children—*Sarah*, b. 1721; *Hannah*, b. 1723; *Eleazar*, b. 1725; *Abigail*, b. 1729, m. Joseph Cook of South Had. and Had.; *Asahel*, b. 1731; *Abiel*, (dau.) b. 1735, was of South Hr l., 1756.

30. SAMUEL, s. of Luke, (13) d. Aug. 22, 1763, ae. 64. He m. June 12, 1724, Lydia Smith. She d. Feb. 6, 1786, in 85th yr. Children—*Samuel*, b. Sept. 7, 1724, d. 1746; *Lydia*, b. April 7, 1728, m. Nov. 17, 1750, Gad Alvord, and d. prior to 1786; *Josiah*, b. Aug. 26, 1729, m. Dec. 26, 1751, Abigail Eastman, res. in So. Had., and d. Aug. 29, 1779, ae. 50; *Mary*, b. March 3, 1733, [Rec.] m. March 16, 1749, Josiah White; *Reuben*, b. Sept. 23, 1733, d. Nov. 11, 1733; *Rebecca*, b. March 25, 1740, m. Job Alvord, and was living in 1833; *Phebe*, b. March 25, 1742, m. —— Dickinson, and d. before 1786.

31. JONATHAN, s. of Luke, (13) deacon, d. April 4, 1774. He m. (1) Dec. 16, 1725, Rebecca, dau. of Nehemiah Dickinson. She d. Oct. 3, 1726, ae. 27; (2) Jan. 31, 1734, Mehitable Cook. She d. Nov. 3, 1766. Children— *Oliver*, b. Sept. 23, 1726; *Enos*, b. Nov. 19, 1734, d. Feb. 11, 1738, ae. 3; *Rebecca*, b. Oct. 27, 1736, m. Jan. 24, 1760, John Cook, and d. July 30, 1761; *Seth*, b. Feb. 6, 1738, d. Feb. 15, 1738, ae. 9 days; *Mehitable*, b. March 24, 1740, m. June 17, 1760, Eliakim Smith; *Anne*, b. June 22, 1742, m. Nov. 15, 1770, Timothy Eastman, and d. Dec. 7, 1777, ae. 35; *Enos*, b. June 28, 1745;

Jonathan, b. Jan. 28, 1747; *Seth,* b. June 24, 1751; *Ebenezer,* b. and d. June 24, 1751; *Perez,* b. Sept. 20, 1754.

32. DAVID, s. of Luke, (13) deacon, resided for a few years in Amh., but after a short absence returned to Had., where he d. Aug. 6, 1771, ae. 64. He m. Hannah, dau. of Josiah Willard of Wethersfield, Ct. She d. in Westhampton, Jan. 27, 1809, ae. 87. Children—*Elizabeth,* bapt. April 8, 1741, m. (1) Sept. 16, 1762, Josiah Smith; (2) Jan. 4, 1770, John Cook; *Hannah,* m. Jan. 31, 1771, Coleman Cook; *Theoda,* m. Aug. 13, 1769, Nathaniel Dickinson of Amh.; *Mary,* b. July 21, 1754, m. Feb. 24, 1778, Peter Montague; *Eunice,* b. Oct. 11, 1756, m. 1792, Reuben Wright of Nh.; *Naomi,* m. —— Wallace; *Willard,* b. Oct. 30, 1761; *Jerusha,* m. Oliver Atwell.

33. JOSEPH, s. of Luke, (13) d. June or July, 1797, ae. 88. He m. May 24, 1739, Miriam, dau. of Benjamin Church. She d. abt. 1794. Children— *Gideon,* b. April 12, 1740; *Miriam,* b. Jan. 12, 1742, d. unm., Sept. 1794, ae. 52; *John,* b. Jan. 17, 1744; *Joseph,* b. April 19, 1751.

34. JOHN, s. of Ebenezer, (14) deacon, Granby, d. June 17, 1774, ae. 75. He m. (1) Aug. 14, 1724, Rachel, dau. of "Orphan John" Smith. She d. Sept. 20, 1724, ae. 25; (2) April 6, 1727, Mary, dau. of William Dickinson. She d. March 5, 1781, in 78th yr. Children—*Nathan,* b. abt. 1731; *Abigail,* m. Dr. Samuel Vinton of So. Had., and d. Aug. 11, 1793.

35. PETER, s. of Chileab, (15) Amh., d. abt. 1787, as appears from the fact, that his will dated 1771, was proved 1787. He m. Amy Bissell of Windsor, Ct., who d. Aug. 1796. Children—*Chileab,* b. Oct. 27, 1747; *Elisha,* b. March 14, 1749; *Child,* bapt. Dec. 24, 1751.

36. WINDSOR, s. of Chileab, (15) d. Dec. 31, 1788, ae. 68. He m. (1) Dec. 3, 1747, Sarah, dau. of Joseph Smith. She d. Sept. 1, 1772, in 50th yr.; (2) Oct. 20, 1773, Lydia, wid. of Hopestill Hastings. Children—*Martha,* b. Oct. 11, 1749, m. (1) April 16, 1795, Dea. Hezekiah Belding of Amh.; (2) July 6, 1815, Col. Asaph White of Erving's Grant; *Sarah,* b. Dec. 30, 1751, m. Nov. 16, 1775, Perez Cook; *Chileab,* b. May 21, 1754; *Mercy,* b. Oct. 26, 1756, m. Sept. 23, 1779, Timothy Marsh; *Windsor,* b. Dec. 22, 1758; *Electa,* b. Nov. 17, 1761, d. March 20, 1763; *Electa,* b. Feb. 13, 1764, m. May 16, 1782, Holcomb Granger; *Naomi,* b. June 28, 1767, d. Dec. 18, 1775, ae. 8.

37. JOHN, s. of "Orphan" John, (16) m. Elizabeth. Children—*Elizabeth,* b. Feb. 14, 1728, m. Phinehas Smith; *Timothy,* b. Dec. 6, 1729; *Benjamin,* b. May 16, 1732, of Granby, 1761, became a tory, and went to Halifax, N. B.; *Titus,* b. June 23, 1734, grad. H. C. 1764, a tory, went to Halifax; *Seth,* b. Aug. 21, 1736, m. Thankful; *Israel,* b. April 2, 1739; *Lucy,* b. 1746, d. 1763; *Ruth,* (?) m. John Ayres.

38. HEZEKIAH, s. of "Orphan" John, (16) Granby, made his will 1780, which was proved Dec. 1790. He m. May 10, 1728, Dorcas Dickinson. Children—*Rachel,* b. Aug. 13, 1729, m. Nov. 22, 1748, Thomas Wait; *Esther,* m. —— Dickinson, and was alive in 1812; *Hezekiah,* b. Sept. 17, 1751.

39. NOAH, s. of "Orphan" John, (16) d. 1767. He m. Mary ——. Children—*Noah,* b. Feb. 8, 1732, m. (1) 1756, Mary Kilbourne of Newfane, Vt.; (2) 1754, Sarah Stephenson of Spr.; *Warham,* b. March 19, 1735; *Josiah,* b. June 26, 1737, d. Oct. 8, 1765; *John,* b. Jan. 18, 1740; *Mary,* m. James Hunt, to whom she was pub. June 16, 1769.

40. EPHRAIM, s. of John, (18) So. Hadley, m. Mary, dau. of John Preston of So. Had. Children—*Ephraim*, m. Thankful Goodman; *Eli; Darius; Simeon; Luther; Joanna*, m. Samuel Goodman; *Lois*, m. William Taylor.

41. JOHN, s. of John, (18) d. March 24 or 25, 1795, ae. 78. He m. Elizabeth, dau. of Nathaniel Edwards of Nh. She was b. Nov. 29, 1723, and d. March 12, 1795, ae. 72. Children—*Beriah*, rem. to Woodstock, Vt.; *Joel*, res. for a time in Greenfield, but rem. thence to the West; *John*, b. abt. 1751; *Elizabeth*, m. Reuben Judd of So. Had., and d. March 31, 1781; *Martha*, m. —— Thayer, and rem. to State of N. Y.; *Lucy*, m. Enos Pomeroy of Had. and Buckland; *Sabra*, m. —— Badger.

42. PHINEHAS, s. of John, (18) rem. to Wilmington, Vt. He m. 1754, Eleanor Bell. Children—*Medad*, b. Feb. 2, 1755; *Esther*, b. Dec. 22, 1756; *Phinehas*, b. 1761, d. 1767.

43. SILAS, s. of John, (18) m. (1) 1749, Sarah, dau. of John Preston; (2) Rebecca Allen. Children—*Philip*, m. Achsah Chapin, (see the Chapin genealogy) d. in Springfield; *Perez*, b. 1753; *Silas*, b. Nov. 30, 1754; *Sarah*, m. Hugh McMaster of Palmer.

44. ELEAZAR, s. of John, (18) deacon, res. in Longmeadow and Amherst, and d. Jan. 4, 1816, ae. 90. He m. (1) Lydia Thomas of Lebanon, Ct. She was b. Jan. 29, 1725; (2) Abigail, dau. of Thomas Hale of Longmeadow. She was b. Feb. 9, 1735, and d. June 24, 1812, in 77th yr. Children, all but youngest, by 1st wife—*Lydia*, b. June 8, 1750, d. Nov. 7, 1774; *Lucina*, b. Feb. 11, 1752; m. Chileab Brainerd Merrick of Wilbraham; *Eleazar*, b. Feb. 28, 1754, d. Oct. 22, 1757; *Ithamar*, b. June 13, 1756, m. Lucy Nevers of Springfield, and d. Sept. 1, 1844, ae. 88; *Eleazar*, b. June 20, 1758, d. March 14, 1759; *Sarah*, b. Sept. 10, 1760, m. Dec. 4, 1783, Medad Dickinson of Amh., and d. Oct. 11, 1784, ae. 24; *Ethan*, b. April 24, 1763, m. Nov. 7, 1785, Tabitha, dau. of Thomas Hastings, and d. March 22, 1821, ae. 57; *Achsah*, b. Aug. 20, 1765, m. April 27, 1786, Levi Cook of Amh. and Ashfield, and d. June 5, 1809, ae. 43; *Eleazar*, b. Oct. 25, 1767, m. Mabel Bartlett; *Justin*, b. Aug. 12, 1770, m. Experience Clark of Nh.; *Seth*, b. July 12, 1775.

45. JONATHAN, s. of Jonathan, (20) Amherst, d. April 20, 1814, ae. 86. He m. April 8, 1756, Rebecca, dau. of Dr. Nathaniel Smith of Amh. She d. Sept. 5, 1807, ae. 76. Child—*Jerusha*, b. April 27, 1764, m. June 13, 1780, Col. Elijah Dickinson of Amh., and d. April 6, 1853, ae. 88.

46. MARTIN, s. of Jonathan, (20) Amherst, d. 1780. He m. Jan. 4, 1760, Lucy, dau. of Preserved Clapp of Amh. She m. (2) Daniel Shattuck of Hinsdale, N. H., and d. in Randolph, Vt. Children—*Levi*, m. —— Holland of Pelham; *Josiah*, m. Sally, dau. of John Field; *Solomon; Jonathan*, bapt. Nov. 6, 1768; *Martin*, bapt. Oct. 7, 1770, rem. to Massena, N. Y.; *Stephen*, bapt. March 21, 1773; *Wright*, bapt. Feb. 19, 1775; *Phineas*, rem. to Randolph, Vt.

47. DAVID, s. of Jonathan, (20) Amherst, d. Nov. 23, 1807. He m. Mary, dau. of Moses Warner of Amh. She d. July 25, 1826. Children—*Elijah*, m. Martha Burt, and d. in Amh., Sept. 12, 1848; *Mary*, m. Lucius Wait of Hat.; *David*, m. Jan. 5, 1804, Anna Nash, and d. in Amh., Oct. 31, 1833, ae. 70; *Martha*, bapt. Nov. 26, 1769, m. April 7, 1791, Ephraim Kellogg of Amh.; *Moses*, m. Nov. 20, 1794, Tamar Pettis; *Oliver; Eli*, per. m. Oct. 7, 1802, Thankful Dickinson.

48. NOAH, s. of Jonathan, (20) Amherst, d. Feb. 22, 1830, ae. 87. He
m. abt. 1766, Mary, dau. of Edward Elmer. She d. Sept. 4, 1833, ae. 88.
Children—*Hannah*, b. Jan. 3, 1767, m. Jan. 28, 1785, Martin Cook, and d.
1846, ae. 79; *Jonathan*, b. Dec. 17, 1768, m. Feb. 7, 1799, Ruth Jurdon, and
d. Dec. 27, 1843, ae. 75; *Reuben*, b. Sept. 14, 1770, m. April 14, 1796, Margaret Carpenter, and still (1862) resides in Goshen; *Noah*, b. June 6, 1772,
m. Jerusha Cowls; *Andrew*, b. April 20, 1774, m. Rachel McClary of Massena,
N. Y.; *Polly*, b. April 17, 1776, m. July 6, 1797, Martin Baker of Amh.;
Rebecca, b. Jan. 2, 1779, m. Dec. 3, 1809, John Strong of Amh.; *Sarah*,
b. Dec. 4, 1782, m. Feb. 9, 1806, Jonathan Hubbard of Amh., and d. March 21,
1828, ae. 46; *Abigail*, b. Dec. 4, 1782, m. Simeon Smith of Amh., and d.
Dec. 1838, ae. 56.

49. STEPHEN, s. of Stephen, (21) Amh., d. Aug. 9, 1813. He m. Dorothy, dau. of Ebenezer Mattoon of Amh. Children—*Dorothy*, m. Nov. 21,
1793, Enos Baker of Amh.; *Prudence; Arad; Perez*, rem. to Massena, N. Y.;
Gideon.

50. MOSES, s. of Moses, (24) rem. from Amherst to Waitesfield, Vt.
Children—*Moses; Elijah; Selah; Samuel; Hannah*.

51. SIMEON, s. of Moses, (24) Amherst, d. March 23, 1777. He m. 1763,
Rachel, dau. of Nathaniel Strong of Nh. She was b. Feb. 5, 1732, and d. Sept. 1,
1797, ae. 65. Children—*Simeon*, b. May 5, 1764, m. Jerusha Cooley; *Asa*,
b. Sept. 6, 1766, m. July 3, 1788, Sarah Moody; *Electa*, b. Jan. 21, 1769,
m. Sept. 10, 1794, Seth Montague of So. Had.; *Rachel*, b. Dec. 14, 1772,
m. Jan. 27, 1791, Elijah Moody; *Sylvanus*, b. June 28, 1775, res. in Hat.

52. NOADIAH, s. of Moses, (24) Amherst, d. Sept. 23, 1799, ae. 48. He
m. Nov. 3, 1779, Sarah Lee. Children—*Sarah*, b. July 26, 1780, d. July 10,
1797, ae. 16; *Catharine*, b. May 21, 1782, m. Nov. 1805, Ira Edwards, and
rem. to Morristown, Vt.; *Moses*, b. May 11, 1784, grad. W. C. 1811, m. April,
1816, Lois Lee, and d. in Amh.; *Samuel*, b. March 9, 1786, m. May 7, 1807,
Mary Hastings, and rem. to Marion, N. Y.; *Oliver*, b. March 30, 1788, grad.
W. C. 1812, d. unm. in New York City; *Martin*, b. Aug. 9, ——, d. unm. in
Johnson, Vt., July 27, 1855; *Calvin*, b. Aug. 12, 1792, rem. to Johnson, Vt.;
Abel, b. April 28, 1794, m. Achsah Edwards, and d. in Amh., Jan. 12, 1840,
ae. 46; *Mary*, b. June 1, 1796, m. April 2, 1820, Dexter Dickinson, and d.
Sept. 25, 1839, ae. 43.

53. PELETIAH, s. of Peletiah, (27) rem. after 1773, from Amh. to Charlemont. He m. April 24, 1755, Rhoda Morgan. Children—*Reuben*, bapt.
March 14, 1756; *Rhoda*, b. Aug. 3, 1760; *Sarah*, bapt. Sept. 19, 1762; *Mary*,
bapt. Oct. 25, 1765; *Aaron*, bapt. Dec. 2, 1770; *Phinehas*, bapt. Dec. 26,
1773; *Samuel*.

54. OLIVER, s. of Jonathan, (31) deacon, d. July 22, 1808, ae. 81. He
m. June 2, 1757, Elizabeth Eastman. She d. Aug. 13, 1811, in 79th yr.
Children—*Elizabeth*, b. Dec. 29, 1758, m. Sept. 10, 1783, Doct. Job Marsh,
and d. June 7, 1823; *Elihu*, b. Oct. 3, 1761; *Joanna*, b. July 12, 1764, m.
Dec. 14, 1792, Gad Cook; *Naomi*, b. Feb. 5, 1767, d. Dec. 7, 1787, ae. 20;
Oliver, b. Oct. 29, 1769; *Timothy Eastman*, b. Jan. 22, 1773, d. April 8, 1776,
ae. 3; *Rebeckah*, b. Dec. 9, 1775, m. Rev. John Smith of Haverhill, N. H.

55. ENOS, s. of Jonathan, (31) d. March 14, 1836, ae. 90. He m. Nov. 15, 1770, Mary, dau. of John Dickinson. She d. Feb. 7, 1815, ae. 64. Children —*Mehitable*, b. Sept. 13, 1771, d. Sept. 5, 1776, ae. 4; *Mary*, b. Aug. 20, 1773, d. Jan. 12, 1777, ae. 3; *Enos*, b. Sept. 13, 1775, d. Jan. 18, 1777, ae. 1; *Enos*, b. Nov. 7, 1777; *Mehitable*, b. Jan. 24, 1780; *William*, b. March 5, 1782; *Jonathan*, b. Dec. 27, 1784; *Sylvester*, b. April 15, 1789; *Elijah*, b. Feb. 17, 1791, d. Feb. 27, 1791; *Mary*, b. Nov. 15, 1793, m. Rufus Kellogg of Amh.

56. JONATHAN, s. of Jonathan, (31) prob. grad. H. C. 1768, was settled, Jan. 23, 1788, over church in Chilmark, dis. Feb. 4, 1827, and d. in Had., April 14, 1829, ae. 81. He m. Oct. 25, 1789, Anna, dau. of Rev. Abraham Williams of Sandwich. She d. in Chilmark, Oct. 26, 1807. Children— *Eloisa*, b. Jan. 13, 1791, d. unm. in Greenfield, July 5, 1855, ae. 64; *Erastus*, b. Nov. 1, 1794, unm.

57. SETH, s. of Jonathan, (31) deacon, d. June 30, 1828, ae. 75. He m. Nov. 10, 1779, Lydia, dau. of Thomas Smith. She d. Aug. 23, 1828, ae. 71. Children—*Ebenezer*, b. Aug. 4, 1781, d. June 15, 1782; *Ebenezer*, b. Jan. 21, 1783, d. Jan. 22, 1783; *Seth*, b. July 4, 1785; *Ephraim*, b. June 17, 1787, d. Jan. 8, 1788; *Ephraim*, b. Oct. 8, 1788; *Elijah*, b. Oct. 24, 1791; *Worthington*, b. Oct. 11, 1795; *Lydia*, b. March 12, 1795, m. July 3, 1826, William Owen Gadcomb of St. Albans, Vt., and d. Feb. 13, 1856, ae. 60.

58. PEREZ, s. of Jonathan, (31) d. Nov. 1, 1824, ae. 70. He m. Feb. 15, 1786, Lovisa, dau. of Stephen Noble of Westfield. She d. June 19, 1823, ae. 69. Children—*Anna*, b. Dec. 19, 1786, m. Ashley Williams, and d. Oct. 11, 1828; *Lovisa*, b. Oct. 12, 1790, m. David Smith, and d. March 31, 1842, ae. 51.

59. GIDEON, s. of Joseph, (33) rem. to Vt. He m. (1) May 20, 1763, Margaret Church. She d. Jan. 1, 1781; (2) March 3, 1784, Sarah Fairfield. Children—*Lucy*, b. March 26, 1764, d. Oct. 12, 1775, ae. 11; *Irene*, b. June 22, 1768; *Samuel*, b. Oct. 18, 1770, d. ae. 5; *Sophia*, b. March 29, 1773; *Lucy*, b. Nov. 11, 1777.

60. JOHN, s. of Joseph, (33) d. Feb. 1818, ae. 78. He m. Dec. 5, 1764, Marah, dau. of Westwood Cook. She d. Dec. 22, 1822, ae. 79. Children— *Martha*, b. May 25, 1765, m. (pub. Aug. 20,) 1791, Timothy Stockwell, and d. Aug. 20, 1793; *William*, bapt. April 5, 1767; *Eli*, b. Nov. 25, [22?] 1769; *Stephen*, b. June 19, 1774, a blacksmith, rem. to Williamstown, and d. May, 1838, ae. 64; *Mary*, b. March 6, 1784, m. David Smith, and d. Aug. 23, 1823, ae. 39.

61. JOSEPH, s. of Joseph, (33) d. Sept. 13, 1842, ae. 91. He m. June 10, 1775, Nancy Day of Springfield. She was b. May 22, 1754, and d. Aug. 27, 1845, ae. 91. Children—*Hannah*, b. Aug. 28, 1775, m. Nov. 18, 1814, Andrew Holt, and d. July 25, 1855, ae. 79; *Phebe*, b. Dec. 8, 1777, m. Nov. 18, 1804, Cotton Nash; *Samuel*, b. Aug. 13, 1780; *Anson*, b. June 27, 1787.

62. NATHAN, s. of John, (34) deacon in Granby, d. Aug. 21, 1811, ae. 80. He m. Eunice, dau. of James Smith. She d. Sept. 19, 1822, ae. 87. Children —*Mary*, b. Sept. 18, 1754; *Ebenezer*, b. Feb. 4, 1756; *Nathan*, b. April 1, 1757; *John*, b. March 11, 1758, d. March, 1758; *Jared*, b. March 17, 1759; *Martha*, b. Feb. 7, 1761; *John*, b. Sept. 14, 1762, unm., killed by the fall of a tree; *James*, b. March 14, 1764; *Sarah*, b. Oct. 20, 1765; *Elisha*, b. July

11, 1767, drowned at So. Hadley Canal, 1789; *Eunice*, b. June 24, 1769; *William*, b. April 29, 1771, d. unm.; *Abigail*, b. Nov. 24, 1772, d. 1776; *Samuel*, b. Aug. 4, 1775; *Elihu*, b. March 21, 1777, educated (prob. graduated D. C. 1801) minister in Castleton, Vt.; *Benoni Mandeville*, b. Jan. 26, 1779.

63. ELISHA, s. of Peter, (35) Amherst, d. March 25, 1823, ae. 74. He m. Feb. 1782, Ursula, dau. of Dea. John Billings. She d. Aug. 30, 1832. Children—*Jerusha*, bapt. Jan. 26, 1783, m. July 27, 1809, Jonathan Bridgman of Amherst; *Lucretia*, bapt. March 21, 1784; *Achsah*, bapt. Oct. 1, 1786, m. March 1, 1809, David Moody of Amh.; *Peter*, bapt. March 31, 1788; *Polly*, bapt. Oct. 25, 1789, d. Aug. 16, 1796, ae. 6 yrs.; *Elisha*, bapt. Nov. 6, 1791, rem. to China, Mich., and d. March 20, 1846, ae. 54.

64. CHILEAB, s. of Windsor, (36) d. Aug. 25, 1804, ae. 50. He m. March 2, 1775, Tabitha Clark, who d. Sept. 12, 1817, in 67th yr. Children—*Erastus*, b. May 29, 1775, m. Sarah Williams, and d. March 5, 1832, ae. 57; *Lucretia*, b. Feb. 5, 1777, m. (1) Samuel Gaylord; (2) Samuel D. Ward of Brimfield; *Cotton*, b. April 22, 1779, d. April 20, 1780; *Son*, b. and d. March 25, 1781; *Lucinda*, b. April, 1782, m. Col. Sylvester Goodman; *Joanna*, b. Dec. 1784, m. Hon. Estes Howe; *Cotton*, bapt. May 20, 1787, d. in Amh.

65. WINDSOR, s. of Windsor, (36) d. Jan. 1835, ae. 76. He m. Elizabeth. Children—*Abigail*, b. Feb. 3, 1781; *Elizabeth*, b. Dec. 1783; *Obadiah*, bapt. May, 1787; *Melinda*, b. March 11, 1789, m. Rev. Cyrus W. Gray of Stafford, Ct.; *Henry*, b. Nov. 1791; *Electa*, bapt. Feb. 23, 1794; *Roger Robbins*, bapt. Feb. 14, 1797; *Horace*, bapt. Oct. 1798; *Charles*, bapt. May 16, 1802; *Frederic*, bapt. May 27, 1804; *Miranda*, bapt. Jan. 5, 1806.

66. TIMOTHY, s. of John, (37) Granby, d. Feb. 13, 1794. He m. Hannah, who d. Nov. 6, 1802. Children—*Lucy*, b. Aug. 19, 1764, d. unm. 1838; *Hannah*, b. Sept. 9, 1766, d. ae. 9; *Joel*, b. July 28, 1769, res. in Granby; *Timothy*, b. April 27, 1771, d. in Granby, 1837; *Moses*, b. Feb. 21, 1775; *John*, b. July 10, 1777, res. in Granby; *Hannah*, b. Aug. 12, 1780, d. Oct. 1846.

67. ISRAEL, s. of John, (37) Granby, m. Abigail. Children—*Chloe*, b. Nov. 10, 1762; *Israel*, b. Dec. 15, 1764; *Simeon*, b. Dec. 5, 1766.

68. WARHAM, s. of Noah, (39) d. Oct. 30, 1802. He m. Martha, who d. Jan. 22, 1802. Children—*Josiah*, b. July 11, 1766; *Patty*, b. July 24, 1768; *Lois*, b. Nov. 8, 1770; *Justin*, b. May 26, 1775, m. Anna.

69. JOHN, s. of John, (41) d. Aug. 11, 1840, ae. 89. He m. (1) Dec. 8, 1774, Ruth, dau. of Jonathan Cook. She d. July 10, 1785, ae. 33; (2) May 10, 1787, Maria, dau. of Josiah Dickinson. She d. May 21, 1808, ae. 46; (3) Sept. 21, 1808, Betsey, wid. of Lemuel Brown, and dau. of John Dickinson. She d. June 22, 1832, ae. 57. Children—*David*, b. Jan. 4, 1775, d. Sept. 12, 1779; *Alethea*, b. June 12, 1782, m. Doct. Reuben Bell, and d. 1861; *David*; b. Nov. 3, 1783, m. (1) Mary, dau. of John Smith; (2) *Lovisa*, dau. of Perez Smith; *Infant*, b. and d. July, 1785; *Ruth*, b. May 30, 1788, m. Jan. 29, 1812, Ephraim Smith, and d. April 27, 1857; *Orlando*, b. Dec. 10, 1789, m. Nov. 7, 1814, Dorothy Arms, was a merchant, post-master, and town clerk, and d. Sept. 1857; *Dudley*, b. Nov. 4, 1793; *Maria*, b. Nov. 28, 1795, m. Dec. 3, 1817, Elijah Smith; *Elizabeth Edwards*, b. March 27, 1798, m. April 6, 1819, Sylvester Smith; *Clarissa Cook*, b. Aug. 5, 1804, m. Charles C. May of New York City.

70. SILAS, s. of Silas, (43) deacon in South Hadley, d. March 23, 1813.
He m. 1780, (pub. March 18,) Asenath, dau. of Phinehas Chapin of Spring-
field. She d. Nov. 31, 1835, ae. 85. Children—*Horace*, b. Feb. 16, 1781;
Rufus, b. March 2, 1782; *Allen*, b. Dec. 8, 1783; *Child*, b. and d. Aug. 29, 1785;
Asenath, b. March 3, 1787, m. Jan. 2, 1833, Col. Samuel Seymour; *Laura*, b.
March 10, 1789, m. Nov. 23, 1812, Zebina Judd of So. Had.; *Warren*. b. Sept.
25, 1790, d. April 2, 1820; *Hiram*, b. Sept. 23, 1793.

71. ELIHU, s. of Oliver, (54) d. March 9, 1821. He m. (1) Jan. 15, 1792,
Lucretia, dau. of Jonathan Cook. She d. March 6, 1793, ae. 31; (2) Eliza-
beth, dau. of Edmund Hubbard Children—*Lorenzo*, b. Feb. 11, 1790;
Naomi, b. Nov. 8, 1792, m. William Stall; *Lucretia*, b. Dec. 24, 1794, m.
Salmon Morton Dickinson of Amh.; *Giles*, b. Jan. 22, 1797, d. Feb. 26, 1797;
Giles Eastman, b. Jan. 14, 1798; *Sophia*, b. March 15, 1800; *David*, b. Aug.
8, 1802; *Sarah*, b. Nov. 21, 1805.

72. OLIVER, s. of Oliver, (54) d. Aug. 13, 1851, ae. 81. He m. June 4,
1806, Anna, dau. of Nathan Dickinson, Jr., of Amh. Children—*Thankful D.*,
b. April 4, 1807; *Oliver Eastman*, b. Feb. 21, 1809, d. Nov. 13, 1810; *Margaret Prentiss*, b. June 6, 1813, m. Sept. 6, 1838, Rev. E. W. Bullard of
Fitchburg, and d. Dec. 2, 1841, ae. 28; *Oliver Eastman*, b. Sept. 20, 1815;
James Fowler, b. Aug. 24, 1819, d. Oct. 10, 1852, ae. 33.

73. ENOS, s. of Enos, (55) d. Jan. 24, 1822, ae. 45. He m. Dec. 10,
1804, Polly, dau. of Elisha Dickinson. She d. Nov. 9, 1849. Children—
Roswell, b. Nov. 30, 1805, d. Aug. 30, 1807; *Mary*, b. Sept. 23, 1807, m. April
31, 1835, Nathaniel Collins Prior; *Hannah*, b. June 23, 1809, m. Joseph
Enterton; *Delia*, b. June 22, 1812, m. Ephraim Potter; *Roswell*, b. April 5,
1815; *Enos Dickinson*, b. July 25, 1817; *Lucius*, b. June 5, 1819, d. Oct. 22,
1819; *Mehitable Morgan*, b. Dec. 28, 1821, m. Joseph Howe.

74. WILLIAM, s. of Enos, (55) d. June 12, 1840, ae. 58. He m. Dec. 17,
1805, Elizabeth, dau. of Dr. Job Marsh. She d. Dec. 18, 1856, ae. 72.
Children—*Elizabeth Marsh*, b. Oct. 15, 1806, d. unm.; *William Dickinson*,
b. Sept. 5, 1808; *Julia*, b. July 17, 1810, d. unm. May 23, 1829, ae. 18;
Charles, b. May 17, 1812; *Ethelinda*, b. March 11, 1814, m. Nov. 2, 1842,
Stephen Lawrence; *Theodore*, b. Feb. 15, 1817, d. Jan. 16, 1819; *Sarah Ann*,
b. Jan. 10, 1820; *Caroline*, b. Feb. 13, 1823.

75. JONATHAN, s. of Enos, (55) d. Dec. 2, 1856, ae. 61. He m. Dec. 15,
1814, Cynthia, dau. of Moses White. Children—*Jonathan Dwight*, b. Feb. 11,
1818; *George*, b. Aug. 4, 1820, d. Nov. 29, 1821; *George*, b. Nov. 13, 1823,
d. April 19, 1824; *Jane*, b. Nov. 13, 1823, d. Dec. 1825; *Sophia*, b. Aug. 4,
1825, m. April 3, 1851, Ebenezer Watson Dickinson; *Jane*, b. April 9, 1827;
George Barlow, b. Aug. 9, 1831.

76. SYLVESTER, s. of Enos, (55) deacon in 1st church, is the person, by
whose solicitations Mr. Judd was induced to commence the History of Hadley,
and from whom he obtained ten-fold more information and assistance in the
prosecution of the work, than from any one beside. He m. (1) Jan. 1, 1812,
Polly, dau. of Lemuel Warner. She d. Aug. 19, 1817, ae. 24; (2) April 6,
1819, Elizabeth Edwards, dau. of John Smith. Children—*Rodney*, b. Aug. 6,
1812; *Henry*, b. Dec. 14, 1814, d. Nov. 3, 1815; *Mary Ann*, b. April 23, 1817,
m. May 29, 1844, Chester Smith.

77. SETH s. of Seth, (57) grad. Y. C. 1803, was a clergyman in Genoa, N. Y., where he d. Jan. 30, 1849, ae. 63. He m. Nov. 29, 1810, Margaret, dau. of Gen. Samuel Porter. Children—*Samuel Porter*, b. June 20, 1812; *Margaret*, b. Feb. 15, 1814, d. Feb. 18, 1814; *Margaret*, b. May 21, 1815, m. Sept. 13, 1842, Isaac Peck of Genoa, N. Y., and d. Dec. 28, 1849; *Lydia*, b. April 17, 1817, d. Sept. 14, 1831; *Lucy*, b. Aug. 3, 1821, d. Feb. 12, 1844; *Julia*, b. Aug. 11, 1823, d. unm. Aug. 9, 1851; *Abigail*, b. April 17, 1825, res. in Had.; *Harriet*, b. Jan. 31, 1827, d. May 16, 1831; *Susan Hubbard*, b. Nov. 6, 1828, m. Nov. 23, 1852, Daniel H. Dickinson.

78. EPHRAIM, s. of Seth, (57) m. Jan. 29, 1812, Ruth, dau. of John Smith. She d. April 27, 1857. Children—*Theodore Worthington*, b. Oct. 30, 1812; *Ephraim Orlando*, b. Aug. 11, 1814; *Lydia Maria*, b. June 2, 1816; *Mehitable Worthington*, b. July 3, 1818; *John Edwards*, b. Sept. 26, 1821; *George Dickinson*, b. Jan. 16, 1824; *Seth Pomeroy*, b. Aug. 11, 1830.

79. ELIJAH, s. of Seth, (57) d. June, 1861. He m. Dec. 3, 1817, Maria, dau. of John Smith. Children—*Susan Partridge*, b. Sept. 17, 1818; *Mary Ann*, b. July 5, 1821, d. Aug. 10, 1828; *Lydia*, b. Oct. 16, 1824; *Mary Ann*, b. Jan. 8, 1829; *Maria Dickinson*, b. Nov. 23, 1831.

80. REV. WORTHINGTON, D. D., s. of Seth, (57) grad. W. C. 1816, was for many years pastor of the (Cong.) church in St. Albans, Vt., and at the time of his decease, President of Vermont University. He d. in St. Albans, Feb. 30, 1856, ae. 60. He m. July 1, 1823, Mary Ann Little of St. Albans, Vt. Children—*Mary Ann*, b. Oct. 26, 1825; *Julia Elizabeth*, b. May 22, 1827, d. June 9, 1828; *Jane Worthington*, b. May 3, 1829; *Ellen Maria*, b. Jan. 9, 1830; *Edward Worthington*, b. Dec. 16, 1832; *Arthur Hampden*, b. Nov. 3, 1834; *Alfred Little*, b. Nov. 3, 1836; *Sarah Elizabeth*, b. Sept. 19, 1838, d. March 17, 1840; *Elisabeth Little*, b. July 14, 1840; *Robert Leighton*, b. Aug. 7, 1841; *Charles Sidney*, b. Dec. 26, 1843; *Anna Porter*, b. Jan. 3, 1845; *William Kingman*, b. June 12, 1847; *Sarah Lydia*, b. Sept. 25, 1851.

81. WILLIAM, s. of John, (60) a blacksmith, rem. to Williamstown, and d. Sept. 1803, ae. 37. He m. Nov. 7, 1787, Persis, dau. of Aaron Cook. She d. Aug. 30, 1847, ae. 85. Children—*Joanna*, b. Feb. 9, 1788, m. 1805, Amasa Shattuck of Williamstown, and d. Sept. 1, 1847, ae. 59; *Dennis*, b. Feb. 7, 1790, d. unm. 1852; *Pamelia*, b. March, 1792, m. (1) Daniel Cook; (2) Lucius Crane; *Martha*, b. April, 1794, m. Nathan B. Towne of Williamstown.

82. ELI, s. of John, (60) d. Oct. 4, 1839, ae. 70. He m. (1) Nov. 17, 1791, Martha, dau. of Enos Nash. She d. July 28, 1817, ae. 44; (2) Sept. 10, 1818, Hannah, dau. of Timothy Stockwell. Children—*Lorinda*, b. Oct. 13, 1792, m. John, s. of Caleb Smith, and d. Aug. 17, 1829; *Martha*, b. Sept. 23, 1794, d. unm. Dec. 20, 1821; *Joanna*, b. April 28, 1797, m. Horace Judd; *Almira*, b. Sept. 17, 1799, d. unm. Sept. 23, 1848; *Edwin*, b. June 23, 1802; *Sophronia*, b. Sept. 13, 1804, d. unm.; *John*, b. March 29, 1809, m. July 7, 1836, Harriet Ellis; *William*, b. Jan. 5, 1811, m. Laura Fuller; *Mary*, b. May 13, 1820; *Jeriah Stockwell*, b. June 11, 1822; *George*, b. Jan. 11, 1825.

83. SAMUEL, s. of Joseph, (61) a physician, rem. to Williamstown, and d. June 9, 1852, ae. 72. He m. Jan. 1800, Betsey Towner. She was b. 1784, and d. March 17, 1850, ae. 66. Children—*Albert Gallatin*, b. Jan. 12, 1800;

136   SMITH.

Sally, b. Nov. 19, 1801; *Betsey*, b. 1802, d. in infancy; *Betsey Adeline*, b. Nov. 3, 1803, m. Rev. Wm. Bradley of Newark, N. J.; *Samuel*, b. June 8, 1805, d. 1810, ae. 5; *Daughter*, b. and d. 1807; *Nancy Emeline*, b. Jan. 1808, d. May 17, 1845, ae. 37; *Francis Towner*, b. 1810, m. Doct. James Wilson of Washington, D. C.; *Hannah E.*, b. Sept. 3, 1812, m. Rev. Samuel Day of Bellows Falls, Vt.; *Mary A.*, b. Aug. 1814, m. Gilman Darling of Holden; *Samuel Augustus*, b. April, 1816, d. Oct. 3, 1834; *Sarah Augusta*, b. April, 1816, m. Doct. Jonathan Ford, and d. Dec. 1843, ae. 27; *Henry*, b. 1814, d. Aug. 1831, ae. 17; *Harriet*, b. 1814, d. in infancy; *Andrew Murray*, b. Nov. 1826, m. Laura Hosford of Williamstown.

84. ANSON, s. of Joseph, (61) m. May, 1810, Betsey Mead, who d. July 14, 1814, ae. 28; (2) March 2, 1816, Sally Purdy, who d. April 20, 1856, ae. 69. Children—*William*, b. June 14, 1817; *George Purdy*, b. April 18, 1819, m. Oct. 4, 1847, Florence Rogers; *Caroline*, b. Jan. 17, 1821, d. Feb. 11, 1856, ae. 35; *Albert Douglass*, b. March 10, 1823, m. 1849, Adeline Hurd; *Orlando*, b. May 2, 1825, m. July 30, 1848, —— Andrews; *Anson*, b. July 30, 1827; *Joseph*, b. Sept. 17, 1830, m. 1852, Sarah Snow.

85. JUSTIN, s. of Warham, (68) m. Anna. Children—*Flavia Ann*, b. Oct. 10, 1797; *Cordelia*, b. Jan. 19, 1800; *Oliver*, b. Jan. 20, 1802; *Calvin*, b. May 28, 1804; *Wareham*, b. Jan. 22, 1806, d. Feb. 1, 1806.

86. DUDLEY, s. of John, (69) merchant, d. May 27, 1858, ae. 64. He m. Dec. 5, 1822, Pamela, dau. of Elisha Porter. Children—*Samuel Porter*, b. June 26, 1824, d. Aug. 26, 1825; *Lucy*, b. Sept. 18, 1826, d. Aug. 16, 1828; *Dudley Porter*, b. Aug. 31, 1828, d. Oct. 29, 1828; *John*, b. Oct. 11, 1829, grad. A. C. 1849; *Sarah Hillhouse*, b. Aug. 7, 1831; *Abby Phillips*, b. Aug. 26, 1833; *Clarissa*, b. Jan. 11, 1836; *Lucy*, b. May 8, 1839; *Samuel Dudley*, b. May 30, 1843.

87. HORACE, s. of Silas, (70) deacon and Colonel, res. in Amh., and d. Nov. 11, 1862, ae. 81. He m. (1) March 5, 1805, Rebecca Moody. She was b. March 28, 1783, and d. Nov. 30, 1821, ae. 38; (2) —— King of Suffield, Ct. Children—*Mary Berintha*, b. Dec. 2, 1806, m. Dec. 2, 1824, James B. Wood, and d. Aug. 11, 1841, ae. 34; *Cordelia*, b. Aug. 15, 1808, m. May 25, 1830, Joseph Fuller of Suffield, Ct.; *Silas Moody*, b. May 8, 1810; *Asenath*, b. July 8, 1812; *Josiah White*, b. June 3, 1819.

87½. RUFUS, s. of Silas, (70) Huntington, m. Jan. 31, 1808, Salome Clark, b. Sept. 17, 1786. Children—*Philetus*, b. Nov. 10, 1808, m. Sept. 29, 1836, Mary E. Bates of Springfield, and d. Nov. 21, 1853; *Almena*, b. Oct. 3, 1810, m. Oct. 7, 1847, Daniel F. Lyman of Easthampton; *Bethia Chapin*, b. July 10, 1814, m. June 6, 1843, Franklin Burt of Chesterfield, *Phinehas Clark*, b. Oct. 19, 1816, m. May 24, 1848, Amanda Sadler of Ludlow, and d. Aug. 14, 1853, ae. 36; *Paulina*, b. Sept. 14, 1819, m. Nov. 6, 1847, Ezra H. Corning of Chicopee Falls; *Warren*, b. Aug. 13, 1822, d. Sept. 4, 1823; *Minerva*, b. Jan. 17, 1825, m. Oct. 7, 1853, Elbridge Hazen.

88. ALLEN, s. of Silas, (70) So. Hadley, d. Sept. 2, 1848, ae. 64. He m. Jan. 1811, Polly Bartlett. She was b. Oct. 1, 1786, and d. May 8, 1850, ae. 63. Children—*Silas Allen*, b. Dec. 11, 1813, m. Nov. 5, 1835, Olive, dau. of Col. Eliphaz Moody; *Mary Bartlett*, b. July 30, 1816, d. Dec. 30, 1836, ae. 20; *Luna Chapin*, b. April 21, 1819, m. Dec. 30, 1846, Horace Rice, Jr. of Chicopee;

Clarissa Delphia, b. April 3, 1822, m. Oct. 1, 1848, John Beckwith; *Frances Eliza*, b. Jan. 3, 1825, m. Dec. 15, 1848, Elisha Pomeroy, Jr.

89. HIRAM, s. of Silas, (70) So. Hadley, was for many years engaged in boating on the Conn. river, but of late has devoted his attention to agriculture. He has been much employed in town business, and has been Representative to the General Court. He m. June 2, 1817, Mary, dau. of Col. Eliphaz Moody of So. Had. She was b. Aug. 13, 1796. Children— *Rebecca Allen*, b. April 7, 1819, m. Oct. 6, 1842, Moses Gaylord; *Child*, b. Jan. 7, 1821, d. young; *Edwin*, b. June 26, 1822, a farmer in So. Hadley, m. Feb. 26, 1851, Sarah Jane, dau. of Dr. Lucius Wright of Westfield. She was b. Feb. 24, 1814. No children; *Hiram*, b. July 24, 1824; *Mary Jane*, b. Dec. 26, 1826, m. Feb. 23, 1848, William Stacy; *Julia Avis*, b. Feb. 7, 1831, m. Sept. 5, 1850, John Lyman; *Eliza Augusta*, b. Dec. 8, 1832; m. Dec. 15, 1853, Jotham Graves; *Emily Wright*, b. June 8, 1834; *Josiah Moody*, b. Nov. 21, 1837, d. Sept. 8, 1839.

90. LORENZO, s. of Elihu, (71) d. Feb. 20, 1827, ae. 37. He m. Hannah, dau. of Medad Dickinson of Amh. She was b. March 10, 1788. Children— *Medad D.*, b. July 21, 1818, d. Dec. 19, 1820; *Pliny Edwards*, b. July 1, 1820, d. Nov. 7, 1820; *Medad*, b. Nov. 2, 1822; *Lorenzo*, b. Sept. 20, 1825, d. Aug. 29, 1828.

91. GILES EASTMAN, s. of Elihu, (71) m. Sept. 25, 1821, Martha K., dau. of Enos Hitchcock. Children—*David R.*, b. Dec. 3, 1822, d. July 31, 1827, ae. 4; *Charles Hitchcock*, b. July 7, 1825, m. Sarah Eliza, dau. of William Cushman; *Francis*, b. Jan. 31, 1828, d. Jan. 8, 1846, ae. 17.

92. ROSWELL, s. of Enos, (73) m. (1) Nov. 28, 1843, Louisa, dau. of Henry Tuttle of West Springfield. She was b. April 3, 1824, and d. May 2, 1844, ae. 20; (2) Nov. 10, 1846, Elizabeth Ely of Charlestown, N. H. She was b. Oct. 14, 18—. Child—*Emma Elizabeth*, b. Nov. 19, 1849.

93. ENOS DICKINSON, s. of Enos, (73) m. Nov. 25, 1840, Adeline, dau. of Elihu Cook. Children—*Lucius*, b. Nov. 22, 1842; *Clara Adeline*, b. June 25, 1845, d. July 30, 1849, ae. 4; *Orra Louisa*, b. Sept. 13, 1847, d. Aug. 6, 1849, ae. 1; *George Ely*, b. May 12, 1851; *Lucy Jane*, b. April 17, 1855.

94. WILLIAM DICKINSON, s. of William, (73) m. Oct. 9, 1844, Louisa, dau. of Isaac Sylvester Taylor of Nh. She was b. April 29, 1812. Children— *Henry Dwight*, b. Aug. 31, 1845; *Horace William*, b. Feb. 9, 1847; *Job Marsh*, b. Aug. 11, 1849, d. Dec. 13, 1849; *Edward Taylor*, b. Nov. 21, 1851, d. Sept. 15, 1855.

95. CHARLES, s. of William, (74) m. Dec. 6, 1838, Eliza Maria French, b. Aug. 26, 1818. Children—*Charles Frederick Harrington*, b. March 7, 1840; *Theodore French*, b. Dec. 13, 1841.

96. GEORGE BARLOW, s. of Jonathan, (75) m. Nov. 20, 1851, Maria Mann, b. Oct. 5, 1832. Children—*Francis Dwight*, b. Sept. ——; *Charlotte Carrina*, b. Feb. 12, and d. March 16, 1854; *Eugene Jonathan*, b. Nov. 28, 1856, d. Feb. 23, 1859, ae. 2; *Cynthia Maria*, b. March 27, 1859.

97. RODNEY, s. of Sylvester, (76) entered A. C. in Class of 1833, but remained only a short time. He m. Oct. 20, 1841, Rebecca, dau. of Elijah Kilbourn of Walpole, N. H. She was b. Aug. 21, 1815. Children—*Elizabeth Rebecca*, b. Nov. 7, 1842, d. Feb. 23, 1847, ae. 4; *Mary Ellen*, b. March 4,

1845; *William Henry*, b. July 23, 1848, d. Aug. 17, 1848; *Maria May*, b. Nov. 27, 1850; *Arthur* b. Sept. 18, 1852; *Sylvester*, b. Oct. 23, 1854, d. Sept. 15, 1857, ae. 2; *John Kilbourn*, b. May 18, 1857, d. July 16, 1857.

98. EDWIN, s. of Eli, (82) m. Jan. 1, 1839, Mary Ann, dau. of Noah Edson. Children—*Eliza Ann*, b. Nov. 29, 1839; *Henry Edson*, b. Sept. 12, 1843.

99. JERIAH STOCKWELL, s. of Eli, (82) m. Oct. 1, 1845, Sophia Lewis, dau. of Winthrop Cook. Children—*Mary*, b. Sept. 4, 1846; *George Franklin*, b. July 17, 1848; *Ebenezer Dennis*, b. Aug. 21, 1851; *Louisa Hannah*, b. March 30, 1858.

100. GEORGE, s. of Eli, (82) m. (1) May 27, 1852, Catherine Mary, dau. of Benjamin Carlisle. She d. Jan. 27, 1856, ae. 28; (2) April 13, 1858, Mary, dau. of Rufus Dickinson of Amh. Children—*Frances Mary*, b. April 16, 1853; *Julia Catharine*, b. July 20, 1855; *Herman Kellogg*, b. March 23, 1860.

101. SILAS MOODY, s. of Horace, (87) is a cabinet-maker in Northampton. He m. Jan. 6, 1832, Theodocia, dau. of Abner Hunt of Nh. She was b. May 19, 1811. Children—*Watson Loud*, b. July 28, 1834, res. in Nh., in company with his father. He m. Oct. 28, 1856, Eunice A. Brewster of Cummington; *Thomas Hunt*, b. Aug. 21, and d. Dec. 3, 1836; *Harriet Louisa*, b. March 16, 1838, d. Sept. 8, 1839; *Louisa Helen*, b. March 25, 1841; *George Hunt*, b. Oct. 25, 1844; *Mary Jane*, b. Sept. 16, 1850.

102. JOSIAH WHITE, s. of Horace, (87) Nh., was by trade a printer, for several years publisher of the Northampton Courier, but at the time of his death, a clerk in the office of Superintendent of the Conn. River Rail Road. He d. May 1, 1854. He m. May 27, 1841, Jane S. Damon of Nh. Children—*Isaac Damon*, b. Aug. 6, 1845; *Jane*, b. April 13, 1853.

103. HIRAM, s. of Hiram, (89), is a merchant in So. Hadley Falls. He m. Jan. 17, 1848, Harriet Sophia Coney. Children—*Ellis Dwight*, b. July 10, 1849, d. April 22, 1851; *Harriet Victoria*, b. July 11, 1850, d. Oct. 10, 1852, ae. 2; *Jenne Belle*, b. Nov. 21, 1858.

1. SMITH, SAMUEL, b. Jan. 27, 1639, s. of Rev. Henry Smith of Wethersfield, resided from 1666 to about 1679, in Nh., and then rem. to Hadley, where he d. Sept. 10, 1703, ae. 64. He m. Mary, dau. of James Ensign. Children—*Samuel*, m. Nov. 18, 1685, Joanna McLathlin, res. in Nh. and Suffield, Ct., and d. Sept. 1, 1723; *Sarah*, m. Oct. 16, 1684, John Lawrence; *Dorothy*, bapt. 1667, m. May 30, 1687, William Rooker; *Ebenezer*, bapt. 1668; *Ichabod*, b. Jan. 24, 1670; *Mary*, b. Jan. 18, 1673, m. Aug. 20, 1696, William Barnes; *James*, b. June 12, 1675; *Preserved*, b. Aug. 1677.

2. EBENEZER, s. of Samuel, (1) rem. abt. 1698 from Had. to Suffield, and d. Sept. 15, 1728. He m. Sarah, wid. of James Barlow, and dau. of Thomas Huxley of Suffield. She m. (2) Oct. 5, 1732, Martin Kellogg of Suffield. Children—*Sarah*, b. Sept. 17, 1694, m. 1714, John Barber of Springfield; *Dorothy*, b. Dec. 21, 1696; *Ebenezer*, b. April 2, 1699; *Nathaniel*, b. March 3, 1702; *Joanna*, b. June 8, 1703; *Jonathan*, b. Aug. 1, 1705; *Dorcas*, b. Nov. 19, 1707; *Mary*, b. March 26, 1710, d. 1711; *Mary*, b. May 24, 1713, d. 1716.

3. ICHABOD, s. of Samuel, (1) deacon, rem. abt. 1699 to Suffield. He m. Mary Huxley. Children—*Child*, b. Feb. 1, 1693, d. Feb. 13, 1693; *Mary*, b. May 20, 1696; *Hannah*, b. Jan. 21, 1698; *Samuel*, b. Nov. 5, 1700, m. Nov. 8, 1725, Jerusha Mather, and d. Aug. 25, 1767, ae. 66; *Ichabod*, b. Jan. 1, 1708, m. Jan. 1, 1731, Elizabeth Stedman, and d. Feb. 26, 1749, ae. 41; *James*, b. March 15, 1711; *Joseph*, b. Jan. 1, 1717.

4. JAMES, s. of Samuel, (1) rem. abt. 1706, to East Haddam, Ct. He m. Oct. 26, 1698, Elizabeth, dau. of Chileab Smith. Children—*Elizabeth*, b. July 26, 1699; *James*, b. Dec. 30, 1700; *Noah*, b. Aug. 24, 1702; *Samuel*, b. April 28, 1704; *Chileab*, b. Feb. 11, 1706; *Hannah*, b. July 3, 1708; *Ebenezer*, b. Feb. 26, 1710; *Mindwell*, b. April 22, 1714.

5. PRESERVED, s. of Samuel, (1) d. 1713. He m. Dec. 15, 1697, Mary, dau. of Chileab Smith. She m. (2) April 22, 1721, Peter Montague, and was living in 1746. Children—*Mary*, b. Jan. 3, 1699, d. 1714; *Ebenezer*, b. Nov. 9, 1700, d. young; *Preserved*, b. Nov. 9, 1700; *Ebenezer*, b. Feb. 4, 1703; *Samuel*, b. Oct. 1, 1705, d. in Northfield, Dec. 21, 1799; *Chileab*, b. May 21, 1708; *James*, b. Sept. 23, 1710, m. Aug. 9, 1734, Sarah Smith; *Moses*, b. Oct. 30, 1712, d. 1726.

6. EBENEZER, s. of Preserved, (5) was killed at the raising of Ebenezer Moody's house in So. Hadley, June, 1729, ae. 26. He m. Nov. 9, 1726, Hannah, dau. of Samuel Boltwood. She d. Oct. 23, 1733, ae. 28. Children —*Preserved*, b. March 13, 1728, d. at Cape Breton, Oct. 29, 1745, ae. 17; *Hannah*, b. Feb. 11, 1730, per. m. July 7, 1748, Moses Cook of Amh.

7. CHILEAB, s. of Preserved, (5) So. Hadley and Ashfield, was at the age of eighty years, by his sons ordained as a Baptist minister. He d. Aug. 19, 1800, ae. 92. He m. (1) Jan. 28, 1732, Sarah Moody. She d. Dec. 23, 1789, ae. 87; (2) Jan. 5, 1792, Rebecca Butler. Children—*Mary*, b. Jan. 22, 1732; *Ebenezer*, b. Oct. 4, 1734; *Moses*, b. Aug. 10, 1736; *Sarah*, b. Aug. 24, 1738; *Jemima*, b. March 15, 1740, m. Jan. 19, 1764, Dea. Isaac Shepard of Ashfield, and d. in Stockton, Chautauque Co., N. Y.; *Chileab*, b. Oct. 24, 1742, d. May 25, 1843, ae. 100; *Enos*, b. July 31, 1744, d. 1746; *Miriam*, b. and d. 1746; *Miriam*, b. May 21, 1747, m. Ephraim Jennings; *Enos*, b. July 24, 1749; *Son*, b. and d.; *Eunice*, b. 1757, m. —— Randall.

8. JAMES, s. of Preserved, (5) Granby, was a Baptist preacher, and appears to have been alive in 1799. He m. Aug. 9, 1734, Sarah, dau. of Luke Smith. Children—*Eunice*, b. Sept. 28, 1735; *Sarah*, b. Oct. 26, 1737; *Sarah*, b. Aug. 8, 1742; *Mary*, b. Dec. 9, 1747.

SMITH, SIMON, b. in Hartford, Aug. 2, 1662, s. of Joseph, m. May 1, 1689, Hannah, wid. of John Haley, and dau. of Samuel Bliss. Children— *Hannah*, b. Jan. 31, 1690; *Lydia*, b. Aug. 7, 1691; *Simon*, b. 1693; *Elizabeth*, b. 1697; *Margaret*, b. 1699. In addition to the above, perhaps he had in Hartford, *Ebenezer*, b. 1703; *Margaret*, b. 1705, d. young; *Elisha*, b. 1706; *Jemima*, b. 1708; *Martha*, b. 1710.

1. SNOW, JOSIAH, from Norwich, Ct., m. Mary, who m. (2) Dec. 15, 1748, Ebenezer Kellogg of So. Had. Children—*Ebenezer*, b. Aug. 14, 1738; *Josiah*; *Jabez*, b. March 11, 1743.

2. JOSIAH, s. of Josiah, (1) So. Hadley, m. (1) Dec. 8, 1757, Azubah Dickinson; (2) —— ——. Children, by second wife—*Josiah*, b. June 18, 1762; *Azubah*, b. March 8, 1764; *Josiah*, b. July 26, 1766; *Lucy*, b. Sept. 2, 1768; *Lydia*, b. May 18, 1772; *Elizabeth*, b. Aug. 17, 1774.

1. STANLEY, THOMAS, was at Hartford, 1636, whence he removed to Had. in the first settlement of the town, and was there buried Jan. 30, 1663. He m. Bennett ——, who subsequently m. Gregory Wolterton, and d. 1665. Children—*Nathaniel*, b. abt. 1638; *Hannah*, m. Samuel Porter, and d. Dec. 18, 1708; *Mary*, m. John Porter of Windsor, Ct.; *Sarah*, m. John Wadsworth of Farmington.

2. NATHANIEL, s. of Thomas, (1) rem. prior to 1669, to Hartford, Ct., and d. Nov. 14, 1712, in 74th yr. He m. 1659, Sarah Boosey. She was b. abt. 1640, and d. Aug. 8, 1716, ae. 76. Children—*Nathaniel*, b. Jan. 5, 1665; *Sarah*, b. Aug. 24, 1669, d. Nov. 28, 1689; *Joseph*, b. Feb. 20, 1671, d. March 18, 1676, ae. 5; *Hannah*, b. Sept. 30, 1674, d. Oct. 31, 1681, ae. 7; *Mary*, b. Oct. 8, 1677; *Susanna*, b. April 13, 1681, d. Sept. 18, 1683, ae. 2; *Nathaniel*, b. July 9, 1683.

STICKNEY, JOHN, b. in Stoughton, abt. 1742 or 1743, while a butcher's boy, learned of one Dunbar, near Boston, the new style of music, and came up into the Connecticut valley, and taught the same in Northampton, South Hadley, Hartford, Wethersfield, New Haven, and other places. In the face of not a little opposition, he persevered, until he had banished the old and introduced the new method of singing. He finally settled in South Hadley, worked on the farm in summer and in winter taught singing school, in most of the towns in the region, until he was about sixty-five years of age. He d. in 1826 or 1827, ae. 84. He m. (1) Elizabeth Howard of Stoughton; (2) Lucy, wid. of Azariah Alvord. Children—*Jonas*, b. June 10, 1769, d. July 23, 1771; *John*, b. April 3, 1772, a physician in Canada; *Chester*, b. July 3, 1779, d. Nov. 1779; *Caleb Howard*, b. April 2, 1785, d. Jan. 26, 1786; *Caleb H.*, b. 1787; *Walter*, b. Aug. 1790.

STILLMAN, GEORGE, a merchant of enterprise and wealth, Representative in 1698, removed in 1704 or 1705, to Wethersfield, Ct., and d. Nov. 17, 1728, in 74th yr. He m. abt. 1685, Rebecca, dau. of Lt. Philip Smith. She d. Oct. 7, 1750. Children—*George; Rebecca*, b. Jan. 14, 1688; *Mary*, b. July 12, 1689, m. Feb. 5, 1713, Deliverance Blinn of Wethersfield, and d. June 30, 1735, ae. 46; *Nathaniel*, b. July 1, 1691, m. (1) March 3, 1715, Anna Southmayd; (2) Sarah Allyn, and d. in Wethersfield, Jan. 1, 1770, ae. 78; *John*, b. Feb. 19, 1693; *Sarah*, b. Dec. 28, 1694; *Martha*, b. Nov. 28, 1696; *Ann*, b. April 6, 1699, m. April 27, 1721, Hezekiah May of Wethersfield, and d. Nov. 7, 1767, ae. 68; *Elizabeth*, b. Oct. 19, 1700, m. —— Blinn; *Hannah*, b. Nov. 7, 1702; *Lydia*, b. Nov. 7, 1702, m. Nov. 13, 1728, Rev. Daniel Russell of Wethersfield, and d. Sept. 3, 1750, ae. 47; *Benjamin*, b. July 29, 1705, m. (1) Aug. 29, 1727, Sarah Doty; (2) Catharine Chauncey.

STOCKWELL, QUINTAN, rem. from Hat. to Deerfield, and thence to Suffield, Ct. He was captured Sept. 19, 1677, at Deerfield, and carried to Canada, but returned the subsequent year. He m. Abigail. Children—*John*, b. Oct. 8, 1676; *Eleazar*, b. in Branford, Ct. 1679.

STOCKWELL, Timothy, from Conn., d. June 8, 1807, in 66th yr. He
m. (1) Aug. 8, 1771, Hannah Goodman, who d. March 9, 1799, in 61st yr.;
(2) Sept. 12, 1799, Submit, dau. of Elisha Cook. She m. (2) —— Wallis.
Children—*Josiah*, b. March 8, 1772, d. Aug. 15, 1776, ae. 4; *Anne*, b. May
12, 1774, d. Aug. 31, 1775; *Jeriah*, b. Sept. 30, 1776; *Hannah*, b. Oct. 2,
1781. "Old Mrs. Stockwell," mother of Timothy, "d. Oct. 8, 1788, ae.
over 80."

1. STRONG, Nehemiah, b. 1694 or 1695, s. of Samuel of Nh., rem. abt.
1741, to Amherst, and d. Feb. 28, 1772, ae. 78. He m. (1) Hannah, wid. of
Nathaniel Edwards, and dau. of Jonathan French of Nh. She was b. March
4, 1697, and m. (1) Sept. 3, 1719, Nathaniel Edwards, who was slain by
Indians, Aug. 26, 1724. She d. Aug. 31, 1761, ae. 64; (2) April 24, 1764,
Wid. Catharine Barrett of Sunderland. Children—*Nehemiah*, b. Feb. 24,
1730, grad. Y. C. 1755, settled Jan. 21, 1761, as pastor of (Cong.) church in
Turkey Hills, (Granby,) Ct., and in Dec. 1770, entered on his duties as the
first Professor of Mathematics and Natural Philosophy in Yale College.
After resigning his professorship at Yale College, he studied law, but practiced little. He resided for a time in New Milford, Ct., whence he removed
to Bridgeport, Ct., where he d. Aug. 12, 1807; *Mary*, b. Feb. 21, 1732,
m. Aug. 29, 1751, Solomon Boltwood of Amh., and d. Aug. 1, 1814, ae. 82;
Simeon, b. March 6, 1736.

2. Hon. Simeon, s. of Nehemiah, (1) Amh., grad. Y. C. 1756, Representa-
tive, 1767 and 1769, Senator, 1793, a lawyer of great eminence, was in 1800
appointed one of the Judges of the Supreme Court of Mass., and d. in office
Dec. 14, 1805, ae. 69. He received from H. C. in 1805, the degree of LL.D.
He m. (1) Jan. 12, 1763, Sarah, dau. of Stephen Wright of Nh. She was
bapt. March 9, 1740, and d. Dec. 3, 1783, ae. 43; (2) 1787, Mary, wid. of Wm.
Barron of Petersham, and dau. of —— Whiting of Concord. She d. in West
Springfield, Feb. 12, 1808, ae. 65. Children—*Simeon*, b. Feb. 22, 1764, grad.
Y. C. 1786, was a lawyer in Conway and Amh., and d. in Amh., Sept. 2, 1841,
ae. 78. He m. Louisa C., dau. of Rev. John Emerson, and was Representative, 1809, 1812, 1813, 1814; *Sally*, b. Oct. 20, 1766, d. Feb. 26, 1777, ae. 10;
Hezekiah Wright, bapt. Jan. 1, 1769, m. Martha Dwight, was a lawyer in
Deerfield and Amh., and afterwards for several yrs. Post Master in Amh. He
d. in Troy, N. Y., Oct. 7, 1848, ae. 80; *Polly*, bapt. June 11, 1775, d. Feb. 28,
1777; *John*, b. Aug. 4, 1778, grad. W. C. 1798, m. Dec. 3, 1809, Rebecca,
dau. of Noah Smith of Amh., and d. in Amh., July 5, 1849, ae. 70; *Solomon*,
b. March 2, 1780, grad. W. C. 1798, practiced law in Royalston, Athol,
Westminster, and Leominster, was a member of Congress, 1815—1819, and in
1818, was appointed Judge of the Circuit Court of Common Pleas, and in
July, 1821, Judge of the Court of Common Pleas, and retained said office
until his resignation in Sept. 1842. He d. Sept. 16, 1850, ae. 70. He m.
Nov. 20, 1803, Sally Sweetser; *Lemuel*, bapt. Aug. 10, 1783, d. Dec. 13, 1783.

1. TAYLOR, John, d. Oct. 17, 1713. He m. Dec. 12, 1666, Mary, dau.
of Thomas Selden. She d. Jan. 7, 1713. Children—*Hester*, b. Dec. 9, 1667,
m. May 29, 1689, Eleazar Warner; *John*, b. Jan. 6, 1670; *Thomas*, b. June 5,
1672, m. March 30, 1720, Elizabeth Prest, and d. in So. Had. She d. May,

1741; *Stephen*, b. 1674; *Mary*, b. Oct. 12, 1676; *Thankful*, b. 1680, m. May 10, 1710, Nathaniel Warner of Suffield, Ct., and d. March 4, 1756; *Jacob*, b. 1685; *Samuel*, b. Dec. 3, 1688; *Ebenezer*, b. March 1, 1697.

2. JOHN, s. of John, (1) rem. to So. Had., and was alive in 1744. He m. Feb. 9, 1694, Hannah Gillet, who was living in 1743. Children—*John*, b. May 3, 1695; *Joseph*, b. March 20, 1697, d. Aug. 6, 1698; *Joseph*, b. Dec. 6, 1698; *Hannah*, b. Jan. 24, 1701, m. April 16, 1730, Nathaniel Hitchcock; *Samuel*, b. Nov. 17, 1703; *Twins*, b. and d. 1704; *Joshua*, b. April 14, 1706; *Mary*, b. May, 1708, m. April 16, 1730, James Brownson; *Moses*, b. May, 1709, res. in So. Had., 1770, and had Oliver, Reuben, and John; *Aaron*, b. Oct. 1712.

3. STEPHEN, s. of John, (1) res. in Hartford, Ct. He m. (1) Oct. 6, 1703, Esther Richards of Hartford, Ct. She d. 1705; (2) Sept. 1, 1709, Violet Bigelow. Children—*Moses*, b. June 3, 1710; *Violet*, b. Sept. 10, 1712; *Stephen*, b. Jan. 9, 1715; *Jonathan*, b. March 3, 1720; *Esther*, b. Oct. 23, 1725.

4. SAMUEL, s. of John, (1) rem. as early as 1731, to So. Had., and d. 1735. He m. Dec. 17, 1719, Hannah Kellogg, who m. (2) James Dewey. Children—*Samuel*, b. Oct. 30, 1721; *Joanna*, b. Oct. 9, 1723; *Jonathan*, b. Nov. 21, 1726; *Ruth; Paul; Silas.*

5. EBENEZER, s. of John, (1) rem. as early as 1731, to Granby, and was alive in 1756. He m. Mehitable, dau. of Dea. Samuel Smith of East Hartford, Ct. Children—*Jacob*, b. July 10, 1718; *Ebenezer*, b. March 24, 1723, m. Experience; *Lois; Mary.*

6. JOHN, s. of John, (2) d. 1725. He m. July 23, 1723, Mary Selding, She m. (2) March 22, 1728, William White. Children—*John*, b. Nov. 14, 1724, d. in infancy; *John*, b 1725.

7. JOSEPH, s. of John, (2) So. Hadley, was alive in 1764. He m. Dec. 21, 1727, Dorothy Rooker. Children—*Joseph*, b. April 2, 1732; *William*, b. April 18, 1735; *Twins*, b. May 9, 1737; *Eunice*, b. April 30, 1741; *Joseph*, b. June 6, 1744.

8. SAMUEL, s. of John, (2) So. Hadley, was alive in 1770. He m. May 25, 1730, Elizabeth Warner of Suffield. Children—*Elisha*, b. July 10, 1732; *Elizabeth*, b. March 2, 1735; *Samuel; Daniel*, d. in the army, Jan. 21, 1762.

9. JOSHUA, s. of John, (2) So. Hadley, was a soldier in 1759, and d. 1760. He m. Nov. 2, 1737, Mercy Rowe of Suffield. Children—*Hannah*, b. Jan. 17, 1739, d. prior to 1764; *Huldah*, b. April 14, 1741, *Sarah*, b. Dec. 14, 1743; *Lois.*

10. AARON, s. of John, (2) was in 1763, warned out of South Hadley. He m. Katharine. Children—*Phebe; Catharine; Dinah; Eunice.*

11. JACOB, s. of Ebenezer, (5) perhaps resided in Granby. He m. (1) Elizabeth Lane, to whom he was pub. Sept. 28, 1751; (2) Wid. Ruth White, dau. of —— Rood. Children—*Ithamar*, b. 1752, res. in Granby; *Susanna*, b. 1754; *Samuel*, b. 1756; *Shubael*, b. 1759, d. in Granby, in 1834; *Benoni*, b. 1761.

1. TAYLOR, STEPHEN, Hatfield, was buried Sept. 3, 1665. He m. Sarah, dau. of John White. She m. (2) Oct. 15, 1666, Barnabas Hinsdale; (3) Feb. 3, 1679, Walter Hickson, and d. Aug. 10, 1702. Child—*Stephen.*

2. STEPHEN, s. of Stephen, (1) rem. in 1713, from Hat. to Colchester, Ct. He m. Nov. 27, 1700, Patience Brown of Deerfield. Children—*Elizabeth*, b. Sept. 12, 1701, d. Sept. 29, 1701; *Abigail*, b. Oct. 20, 1705, d. Nov. 2, 1705; *Stephen*, b. Aug. 4, 1708; *Mercy*, b. Sept. 12, 1711.

TEMPLE, THOMAS, rem. to Shutesbury, where he was living in 1758. He m. Aug. 12, 1730, Sarah Barnard. Children—*Sarah*, b. Dec. 23, 1730; *Elijah*, b. July 2, 1732; *Thomas*, b. Jan. 22, 1734; *Archelaus*, b. Dec. 10, 1735; *Beulah*, b. Nov. 11, 1737; *William; John; Mary; Dorcas; Silas; Rosina; Frederick*.

TERRY, STEPHEN, was of Dorchester, 1630, whence he rem. to Windsor, and thence to Hadley, where he d. Sept. 1668. His wife d. June, 1647. [Elizabeth, per. his mother, d. Aug. 11, 1683, ae. 90.] Children—*Mary*, b. Dec. 31, 1633, m. Dec. 8, 1659, Richard Goodman, and d. 1692; *John*, b. March 6, 1638, m. Nov. 27, 1662, Elizabeth Wadsworth, and res. in Windsor, Ct.; *Elizabeth*, bapt. Jan. 9, 1641, m. Jan. 10, 1666, Philip Russell, and was slain by Indians, Sept. 1667; *Abigail*, bapt. Sept. 27, 1646, m. May 9, 1667, Joseph Kellogg.

THOMAS, JOSEPH, removed after 1677, from Hat. to Springfield. He m. Mary. Children—*Child*, b. and d. Feb. 6, 1675; *Joseph*, b. Dec. 10, 1676, d. Dec. 21, 1676; *Samuel*, b. Nov. 9, 1677.

TILTON, HON. PETER, came here from Windsor, Ct., was Recorder of Hadley from 1661 to 1693, Representative in General Court, 1665-6, 1668, 1670—1679, one of the commissioners, or Associate Judges of the County Court, and at a later period one of the "most worshipful Assistants of the colony," and last, though not least, a deacon, if not an elder in the church. He d. July 11, 1696. He m. (1) May 10, 1641, Elizabeth ——; (2) Mary, who d. April 16, 1689; (3) Nov. 3, 1690, Sarah, wid. of Dea. Benjamin Parsons of Springfield. She had been wid. of John Leonard of Springfield. She d. Nov. 23, 1711. Children—*Elizabeth*, bapt. June 19, 1642, d. 1655; *Mary*, bapt. Feb. 18, 1643, m. (1) Joseph Eastman of Suffield; (2) Feb. 17, 1693, James Guernsey; *Peter*, bapt. Dec. 5, 1647, imbecile, was living in 1707.

TRAYNER, FRANCIS, m. Feb. 25, 1768, Mary, dau. of John Clark. Children—*Nelly*, b. Nov. 20, 1769; *Daughter*, b. Aug. 1, and d. Aug. 2, 1771; *Jane*, b. July 1, 1772; *Elizabeth*, b. Nov. 18, 1774; *Isabel*, b. Dec. 2, 1776, d. Sept. 12, 1777; *James*, b. Aug. 5, 1778; *Mary*, b. Feb. 13, 1781; *William*, b. June 30, 1784; *Son*, b. and d. April, 1786; *Sarah*, b. June 17, 1787.

1. VINTON, ABIATHAR, s. of Abiathar, b. in Leicester, Sept. 18, 1732, res. in Charlton until abt. 1772, when he removed to Granby, where he d. subsequent to 1800. He m. (1) April 14, 1757, Rhoda Wheelock; (2) Rachel Caswell; (3) Wid. —— Smith of Gr. Children—*Abiathar*, b. May 20, 1764; *Tamar*, b. July 30, 1766, m. (1) Asa Newton; (2) Jonas Belknap; *Simeon*, b. Nov. 17, 1768, d. before 1776; *Hannah*, b. Jan. 25, 1771, m Feb. 7, 1797, Ichabod Damon of Chesterfield; *Samuel*, b. May 17, 1773, m. Jan. 27, 1811, Florinda Hinckley, and rem. in 1803, from Granby to Coventry, N. Y., and thence in 1825, to South Bainbridge, N. Y.; *John*, m.

Emma Wares of Hartford, Ct., and d. in Michigan; *Simeon*, b. Feb. 25, 1776; *Rhoda*, b. Sept. 4, 1778, m. April 7, 1803, Joseph Dickinson of Granby.

2. ABIATHAR, s. of Abiathar, (1) resided in South Had. until within a few years of his death, when he rem. to Amherst, and there d. July, 1833, ae. 69. He m. Dec. 22, 1791, Sarah, dau. of Ezra Day, of So. Had. Children —*Samuel Finley*, b. Sept. 25, 1792, grad. W. C. 1814, an eminent lawyer, rem. in 1816 to Gallipolis, Ohio, was member of Congress from 1822 to 1837 and from 1843 to 1849. He m. June, 1824, Romaine Madelaine Bureau, and d. in Washington, D. C., May 11, 1862, ae. 69; *Abigail Smith*, b. Feb. 5, 1794, m. June 19, (Sept. 12?) 1815, Giles Chapin, rem. to Milan, Erie Co., Ohio, and d. Nov. 18, 1852, ae. 58; *Medad*, b. Dec. 4, 1795, m. (1) Jan. 29, 1829, Eliza, dau. of Nathan Franklin of Amh.; (2) Jan. 21, 1836, Mary, dau. of Ebenezer White, and wid. of Dr. Chester Johnson, res. until 1838 in Amh., when he rem. to Port Washington, O., where he d. Sept. 29, 1847, ae. 51; *Plin*, b. June 14, 1799, m. Feb. 21, 1828, Lydia P. Wilmarth, and res. in Port Washington, O.; *Sarah Eliza*, b. April 2, 1801, m. (1) May 10, 1825, Rev. Abner Towne; (2) May 28, 1831, Dr. Robert Safford of Putnam, O.; *Clarissa*, b. Sept. 17, 1803, m. Nov. 28, 1822, Augustus Eastman of Gr., and d. March 4, 1840, ae. 36; *Alvin*, b. Aug. 23, 1807, m. Nov. 24, 1836, Fanny Sweet Heydon, and res. in New Philadelphia, O.

3. SIMEON, s. of Abiathar, (1) Granby, d. June 25, 1824, ae. 48. Children—*Rachel*, b. Aug. 12, 1802, d. March 1, 1815; *Lydia*, b. Aug. 27, 1804, m. May, 1826, Ephraim R. Barker; *David*, b. Feb. 12, 1807, m. 1827, Cynthia Moody; *Ursula*, b. March 10, 1809; *Simeon*, b. Nov. 22, 1811; *Rachel*, b. Dec. 6, 1814, m. May 25, 1833, William Cooley of So. Had. Falls and Chicopee.

VINTON, Dr. SAMUEL, s. of Abiathar, b. in Leicester, abt. 1737, m. (1) Abigail, dau. of —— Smith. She d. in So. Had., Aug. 11, 1793; (2) Sybil, dau. of —— Miller, and wid. of —— Brewer, was for many years a physician in So. Had., where he d. 1800 or 1801.

1. WAIT, BENJAMIN, Hatfield, was slain in Deerfield, Feb. 29, 1704. He m. June 8, 1670, Martha, dau. of John Leonard of Springfield. She, together with her daughters, Martha, Mary and Sarah, was in 1677, carried captive to Canada, and there her daughter Canada was born. Children— *Mary*, b. Feb. 25, 1672, m. Dec. 4, 1690, Ebenezer Wells; *Martha*, b. Jan. 23, 1673; *Sarah*, b. abt. 1675, m. John Belding; *Canada*, b. Jan. 22, 1678, m. Dec. 15, 1696, Joseph Smith, and d. May 5, 1749; *John*, b. Jan. 17, 1680; *Joseph*, b. July 17, 1682, d. Jan. 21, 1686; *Jeremiah*, b. Sept. 24, 1684; *Joseph*, b. Nov. 11, 1688.

2. JOHN, s. of Benjamin, (1) Hatfield, made his will 1743, which was proved July, 1744. He m. Feb. 12, 1702, Mary, dau. of Stephen Belding. Children—*John*, b. Dec. 3, 1703, m. Sept. 19, 1723, Submit Hastings, and d. in Whately, 1776; *Martha*, b. Feb. 20, 1706, m. Nathaniel Hawks; *Mary*, b. June 22, 1708; *Lydia*, b. Oct. 7, 1710, d. young; *Lydia*, b. July 14, 1712, m. July 15, 1756, Israel Graves; *Eunice; Benjamin*, b. Jan. 11, 1718; *Eleanor*, b. Dec. 10, 1722; *Elisha*, b. Oct. 10, 1725, m. Martha Wells of Hardwick, and d. June, 1816; *Sarah*.

2. JEREMIAH, s. of Benjamin, (1) Hatfield. His inventory was dated Dec. 1733. He m. April 4, 1706, Mary Graves. Children—*Benjamin*, b. April 8, 1707, m. Bathsheba; *Mary*, b. Nov. 17, 1708, m. —— Morton; *Nathan*, b. Feb. 15, 1711, m. Hannah, dau. of Richard Billings, and d. in Whately, 1798; *Gad; Reuben*, slain abt. 1756, prob. unm.; *Simeon; Miriam*.

3. JOSEPH, s. of Benjamin, (1) Lieut., Hatfield, d. abt. 1780. He m. (1) Nov. 19, 1713, Hannah Billings, prob. dau. of Samuel. She d. July 15, 1716; (2) Sept. 22, 1720, Mary, dau. of Daniel Warner, Jr. She d. Aug. 18, 1792, ae. 98, leaving 6 children, 45 grandchildren, 98 great-grandchildren, and 1 great-great-grandchild, making in all 120 descendants. Children—*Moses*, b. Sept. 23, 1714, m. (1) Hepzibah; (2) Miriam Graves, and d. abt. 1784; *Hannah*, b. July 8, 1716, m. Dec. 22, 1737, James Porter; *Rhoda*, b. Aug. 21, 1721; *David*, b. Dec. 7, 1722, m. Martha Bardwell, and d. abt. 1805; *Martha*, b. Oct. 7, 1724; *Lucy*, b. Sept. 27, 1727, m. (1) —— Bardwell; (2) Asahel Wright; *Mary*, b. Oct. 17, 1730.

WALKER, ISRAEL, m. Abigail. Children—*Isaiah; Israel; Hannah; Elijah; Walter; Susanna; Ephraim*, b. June 1, 1764; *Ebenezer*, b. March 30, 1766.

1. WALLIS, DANIEL, m. (1) Ruth, who d. Nov. 1791; (2) Oct. 18, 1795, Amy Smith. Children—*William; Polly; David; Addi; Elijah*, bapt. 1800; *Amy Saxton*, bapt. Feb. 21, 1802.

2. ADDI, s. of Daniel, (1.) Children—*Ruth Sexton*, b. Sept. 26, 1818; *David*, b. Jan. 1, 1820, d. Jan. 21, 1823, ae. 3; *Sarah*, b. May 18, 1823, d. Aug. 28, 1824; *David*, b. July 28, 1825; *William*, b. July 13, 1827; *Sarah Sumner*, b. Sept. 2, 1830.

WARD, ISAAC, b. March, 1707, s. of Obadiah of Watertown, res. after his marriage in Petersham, whence he rem. to Amherst, and about 1775 to Leverett, where he d. Oct. 1777. He m. Sybil. Children—*Sarah*, b. 1735, m. Joseph Clary of Leverett, and d. 1815, ae. 80; *Isaac*, b. 1738, d. unm. in the army, 1757; *Betsey*, b. 1740, m. John Adams, and d. in Rowe, 1837, ae. 97; *Sybil*, b. 1742, m. 1768, Nathan Adams of Leverett, and d. Oct. 29, 1839, ae. 96; *Lucy*, b. 1746, m. Gideon Lee, and d. in Leverett, Feb. 17, 1817, ae. 71; *Mary*, b. 1750, m. John Woodbury of Leverett, and d. 1829, ae. 78; *Grace*, b. 1752, m. Nov. 1, 1771, Asa Adams of Shutesbury; *Susanna*, b. 1755, m. (1) Noah Dickinson of Amh.; (2) Nathaniel Wilder of Wendell; (3) John Dickinson of Amh., and d. 1838, ae. 83; *Nahum*, b. 1757, m. 1781, Joanna Hubbard of Leverett, and rem. to White Creek, N. Y.; *Lois*, b. 1759, m. 1807,——Cady; *Lucretia*, b. 1761, m. —— Marsh, and res. in Adams, N. Y.

WARD, NATHANIEL, an early settler of Hartford, and a gentleman of good standing in the colony of Conn., was one of the first settlers of Had., where he was made freeman, March 26, 1661. He d. childless, naming in his will, dated May 27, 1664, and proved Sept. 1664, his kinsman William Markham, kinswoman Elizabeth Hawks, sister Cutting, sister Allen, and her son Daniel, and kinsman Noyes. He was buried June 1, 1664. He m. Jane, wid. of John Hopkins of Hartford.

WARD, Samuel Dexter, m. Jan. 6, 1799, Wid. Lucretia Gaylord. Children—*Mary Dexter*, bapt. Jan. 6, 1800; *Samuel Gaylord*, bapt. March 7, 1802.

1. WARNER, Andrew, Cambridge, 1632, and Hartford, 1639, was one of the first settlers of Hadley, where he d. Dec. 18, 1684. He m. (1) ——; (2) Esther, wid. of Thomas Selden, who d. 1693, as is inferred from the fact, that, her inventory was taken Dec. 1, 1693. Children—*Andrew*, m. Rebecca Fletcher, and d. in Middletown, Jan. 26, 1681; *Robert*, m. (1) Feb. 1654, Elizabeth Grant; (2) Mrs. Deliverance Rockwell, and d. in Middletown, Ct., April 10, 1690; *Jacob; Daniel; Isaac*, b. abt. 1645; *Ruth*, living in 1677, and presented to the Court, for wearing silk; *Dau.*, m. John, or Daniel Pratt; *Mary*, m. (1) John Steel; (2) William Hills; *John*, res. in Middletown, Ct.

2. Jacob, s. of Andrew, (1) d. Nov. 29, 1711, acc. to town records, but Sept. 29, acc. to grave stone. He m. (1) Rebecca, who d. April 10, 1687; (2) Elizabeth, dau. of Richard Goodman. She prob. m. (2) —— Picket. Children—*Jacob*, b. Nov. 5, 1687, d. 1687 or 1688; *Rebecca*, b. March 31, 1690; *Jacob*, b. Sept. 29, 1691; *Mary*, b. July 22, 1694, m. April 17, 1720, Benjamin Graves of Sunderland; *Elizabeth*, b. July 20, 1696, d. young; *John*, b. June 10, 1698, d. June, 1698; *John*, b. March 10, 1700, rem. to New Milford, Ct.; *Joseph*, b. April 30, 1707, rem. to New Milford, Ct.; *David*, b. June 4, 1710, unm., was alive in 1794.

3. Daniel, s. of Andrew, (1) Hatfield, d. April 30, 1692. He m (1) Mary, who d. Sept. 19, 1672; (2) April 1, 1674, Martha, dau. of Robert Boltwood. She d. Sept. 22, 1710. Children—*Mary*, b. Feb. 24, 1663; *Daniel; Sarah*, m. Nov. 25, 1685, Isaac Sheldon of Nh.; *Andrew*, b. June 24, 1667; *Anna*, b. Nov. 17, 1669, m. Isaac Hubbard; *Mary*, b. Sept. 19, 1672, per. m. Samuel Sheldon; *Hannah*, b. Jan. 24, 1675, m. Oct. 14, 1696, Samuel Ingram of Hat.; *John*, b. April, 1677, rem. to Wethersfield, Ct., and d. 1714, ae. 38; *Abraham*, b. Dec. 20, 1678; *Samuel*, b. April 13, 1680; *Ebenezer*, b. Nov. 5, 1681; *Mehitable*, b. Oct. 1, 1683, m. Jan. 21, 1703, Preserved Clapp; *Elizabeth*, m. Dec. 26, 1705, Thomas Wells of Haddam, Ct.; *Esther*, b. Dec. 15, 1686, m. June 26, 1707, Samuel Henry; *Martha*, b. April 3, 1688, d. Nov. 25, 1689; *Nathaniel*, b. Oct. 15, 1690.

4. Isaac, s. of Andrew, (1) rem. abt. 1686, to Northfield, and thence to Deerfield, where he d. 1691. He m. May 31, 1666, Sarah, dau. of Robert Boltwood. She m. (2) Dec. 30, 1696, Dea. John Loomis of Windsor, Ct. Children—*Sarah*, b. May 2, 1668, m. —— French, per. Jonathan French of Nh.; *Isaac*, b. Jan. 13, 1670; *Mary*, b. Jan. 6, 1672, m. —— Crowfoot, prob. dau. of Samuel of Had.; *Andrew*, b. Feb. 24, 1673, per. rem. to Saybrook, Ct.; *Hannah*, b. Nov. 14, 1674; *Ebenezer*, b. 1676; *Daniel*, b. Feb. 25, 1677; *Samuel*, b. March 14, 1681, m. Nov. 8, 1702, Sarah Field; *Ruth*, b. Oct. 18, 1682; *Mercy*, b. Sept. 25, 1685, m. Samuel Gilbert of Hebron, Ct.; *Ichabod*, settled in Mansfield, Ct.; *Lydia*, m. Dec. 8, 1698, Joseph Brooks; *Thankful*, m. —— Loomis; *Mehitable*, m. 1715, Samuel Hitchcock of Springfield.

5. Jacob, s. of Jacob, (2) d. Oct. 3, 1747. He m. Mary, who d. March 20, 1756. Children—*Moses*, b. Sept. 30, 1715; *Jacob*, b. Nov. 1716; *Aaron*, b. March, 1717; *Jonathan*, b. July 10, 1718; *Orange*, b. Oct. 5, 1720; *Gideon*,

b. May 15, 1721; *Oliver*, b. Aug. 10, 1723, d. s. p., May 15, 1786, ae. 56. He
m. (1) 1754, Hannah Jones of Stockbridge; (2) Nov. 28, 1771, Eunice, dau.
of Dea. Jonathan Church of Springfield. She m. (2) June 27, 1785, Dr.
Seth Coleman of Amh., and d. Aug. 8, 1822, ae. 81; *Noadiah*, b. Nov. 3,
1726, d. 1748, while a member of Yale College; *Mary*, b. Jan. 21, 1731,
d. young.

6. DANIEL, s. of Daniel, (3) resided in Hat., West Hartford and Hardwick, and d. March 12, 1754, ae. 88. He m. Dec. 12, 1688, Mary Hubbard.
Children—*Mary*, b. Aug. 31, 1689, d. Feb. 24, 1692; *Daniel*, b. March 1,
1693, settled in Hat., and prob. m. (1) Thankful Billings, and (2) Dec. 29,
1719, Elizabeth Adams of Suffield, Ct.; *Mary*, b. Aug. 17, 1694, m. Sept. 22,
1720, Joseph Wait; *Hannah*, b. 1700, m. Samuel Belding; *Jonathan*, d.
May 28, 1763, ae. 59; *Sarah*, b. Oct. 11, 1707; *Joseph*, b. Jan. 18, 1710,
m. Mary, dau. of John Hubbard.

7. SAMUEL, s. of Daniel, (3) Hatfield. He m. (1) May 1, 1715, Hannah
Sacket; (2) Elizabeth, dau. of Joseph Morton. Children—*Rebecca*, b. May 6,
1716; *Jesse*, b. May 6, 1718, res. in Belchertown and Conway; *Samuel*, b.
Oct. 27, 1722; *Nathan; David*, b. Feb. 15, 1732; *Joshua*, b. Dec. 12, 1733,
settled in Williamsburgh; *Hannah; Elizabeth*, m. Israel Chapin; *Abraham*,
lost at sea; *Sarah*, m. Elijah Wait.

8. EBENEZER, s. of Daniel, (3) rem. from Hat. to Belchertown. He m.
Dec. 15, 1709, Ruth Ely. Children—*Ruth*, b. July 31, 1712, d. Dec. 17, 1730,
ae. 18; *Martha*, b. June 27, 1715, m. Abner Smith; *Moses*, b. May 13, 1717,
m. Jan. 24, 1739, Sarah Porter, and d. in Belchertown; *Lydia*, b. Feb. 15,
1720; *Eli*, b. Aug. 14, 1722; *John*, b. Jan. 28, 1727; *Ebenezer*, b. July 29,
1729, m. Dinah Phelps, and d. 1812, in Belchertown.

9. ISAAC, s. of Isaac, (4) rem. as early as 1730 to Northfield, and d. Sept.
8, 1754, ae. 84. He m. Jan. 24, 1694, Hope, dau. of Timothy Nash. Children—*Isaac*, b. Nov. 12, 1694, d. Feb. 18, 1711; *Daniel*, b. Oct. 10, 1697,
d. April 7, 1698; *Sarah*, b. April 3, 1699; *Rebecca*, b. Sept. 5, 1701; *Israel*,
b. Dec. 1, 1703, d. unm. in Northfield, Nov. 12, 1772, ae. 68; *Ruth*, b. Feb. 14,
1706; *Ebenezer*, b. Jan. 26, 1709, d. in Northfield, Oct. 19, 1768; *Ruth*, b.
July 13, 1713.

10. DANIEL, s. of Isaac, (4) d. Dec. 21, 1711. He m. April 13, 1704,
Sarah Golding. She m. (2) Jan. 6, 1714, Thomas Horton. Children—
Martha, b. Oct. 25, 1706, m. June 2, 1727, William White, and d. Oct. 3,
1787, ae. 81; *Comfort*, (dau.) b. Dec. 1, 1711, d. Jan. 25, 1728.

11. MOSES, s. of Jacob, (5) Amherst, d. May 3, 1772, ae. 58. He m.
May 18, 1738, Mary Field, who d. 1796. Children—*Mary*, bapt. May 18,
1738, m. David Smith of Amh.; *Moses*, m. Sarah Sellon, and res. in Amh.

12. JACOB, s. of Jacob, (5) Amherst, d. 1795. He m. Ann. Children—
Wareham; Jacob, bapt. Dec. 15, 1745, m. —— Hulet, from Belchertown;
Anna, bapt. Feb. 23, 1752; *Abigail*, bapt. Oct. 13, 1754; *Esther*, bapt. June
1, 1760; *Reuben*, prob. m. Nov. 18, 1787, Olive Payne; *Sarah*.

13. AARON, s. of Jacob, (5) Amherst, was a blacksmith, and d. abt. 1787,
as is inferred from the fact that his inventory was taken on the 6th Dec. of
that year. Children—*Maribee*, b. Feb. 23, 1742, m. Aug. 27, 1761, Eli Colton
of Rowe; *Ruth*, b. May 23, 1745; *Aaron*, bapt. Jan. 10, 1748, res. in Amherst,

148

m. Hannah Dickinson, and d. Oct. 12, 1776, ae. 26; *Lucy*, bapt. 1749, m. May 21, 1778, John Emerson of Wendell; *Noadiah*, bapt. 1751; *David*, bapt. May 27, 1753, d. July 18, 1753; *Hannah*, bapt. June 30, 1754, m. Jeremiah Cady; *David*, bapt. 1756, m. Mrs. Lucy Orchard, and d. in Amh., Dec. 10, 1828, ae. 72; *Jonathan*, m. Dec. 2, 1779, Margaret Elizabeth Sewall; *Elisha*, bapt. 1761, m. Sarah Peck, and d. in Amh., Dec. 10, 1823, ae. 62.

14.   JONATHAN, s. of Jacob, (5) d. Dec. 23, 1791, ae. 73. He m. 1745, Mary Graves. Children—*Lemuel*, m. (1) Dorothy Phelps, and d. Aug. 11, 1829, in 82d yr.; *Noadiah*, b. 1749; *Dau.*, b. June 29, 1752, d. Aug. 16, 1752; *Lucy*, b. July 4, 1754, d. May 14, 1778.

15.   ORANGE, s. of Jacob, (5) maltster, d. abt. Jan. 1811, ae. abt. 90. He m. (1) 1749, Elizabeth, dau. of Benjamin Graves of Sunderland; (2) Mrs. Lydia Wait, or Coleman of So. Had.   Children—*William*, b. Oct. 9, 1750, d. April 24, 1751; *Daughter*, b. and d. Sept. 25, 1752; *Elizabeth*, b. Dec. 29, 1753, m. April 27, 1780, Nathan Seymour; *Martha*, b. Sept. 11, 1756, m. John Crafts of Whately; *Elihu*, b. Oct. 29, 1758.

16.   GIDEON, s. of Jacob, (5) resided in Durham, Ct. and Hadley, and d. abt. 1789.   Adm. on his estate was granted March 19, 1789.   He m. 1749, Mary Parsons of Durham, Ct. She d. Dec. 9, 1786.   Children—*Gideon*, rem. to Windsor, Vt.; *Roxelana*, m. (1) Dec. 17, 1772, David White; (2) May 20, 1779, Joseph Crafts of Whately; *Olive; Gideon*, d. Dec. 1766, ae. 12.

17.   LEMUEL, s. of Jonathan, (14) d. Aug. 11, 1829, in 82d yr. He m. (1) July 9, 1772, Dorothy Phelps.   Children—*Jonathan*, b. Dec. 16, 1773; *Polly*, b. Nov. 22, 1775, d. young; *Dorothy*, b. March 19, 1777, m. Nov. 15, 1795, Dea. Wm. Dickinson; *Oliver*, b. June 27, 1789; *Polly*, b. Sept. 29, 1792, m. Jan. 1, 1812, Sylvester Smith, and d. Aug. 19, 1817, ae. 24.

18.   NOADIAH, s. of Jonathan, (14) m. 1783, Martha Hunt.   She was b. July 17, 1750, and d. Oct. 25, 1787, ae. 37.   Children—*Lucy*, b. Nov. 15, 1784, m. 1814, Giles Crouch Kellogg, Esq.; *Patty Hunt*, b. Oct. 9, 1787, m. (1) Robert Cook; (2) Abel Warner.

19.   ELIHU, s. of Orange, (15) m. Oct. 31, 1784, Elizabeth Freeman, who d. July 25, 1834, in 68th yr.   Children—*Abigail*, b. Dec. 20, 1785, m. Samuel Wood; *Dau.*, b. and d. Oct. 21, 1787; *Hannah*, b. May 1, 1789, m. John H. Jones; *John*, b. Aug. 5, 1791, d. Oct. 21, 1801; *Harriet*, b. July, 1793, m. Jonathan Marsh; *Elizabeth*, b. Aug. 16, 1795; *William Freeman*, b. April 1, 1797, d. unm. July 9, 1846, ae. 49; *Abel*, b. Feb. 28, 1799, d. s. p. July 19, 1831; *John*, b. Jan. 1, 1802, d. while a member of the Junior Class in Dart. Col., Jan. 11, 1822, ae. 20; *Giles*, b. Sept. 24, 1803, d. Sept. 15, 1804; *Lydia*, b. Nov. 17, 1805, d. Jan. 4, 1841, ae. 35; *Sophia*, b. Aug. 22, 1807, d. Dec. 30, 1809.

1.   WARNER, JOHN, supposed to have been the son of William of Ipswich, rem. from Ipswich to Brookfield, and thence to Had.   He was living as late as May 17, 1692, and then gave his real and personal property to his three sons, Mark, Eleazar and Nathaniel.   He m. Priscilla, dau. of Mark Symonds.   Children—*Mark; John; Nathaniel*, b. abt. 1655; *Joseph*, b. Aug. 15, 1657, d. 1658; *Mehitable*, b. April 16, 1659, d. June 12, 1678; *Daniel*, b. April 16, 1661, res. in Ipswich, and d. 1688; *Eleazar*, b. Nov. 13, 1662; *Priscilla*, m. 1688, Thomas Cummings.

2. MARK, s. of John, (1) rem. abt. 1687, from Had. to Nh., and d. May 3, 1738, ae. 92. He m. (1) Dec. 8, 1671, Abigail, dau. of Richard Montague. She d. Feb. 6, 1705; (2) 1713, Mary Root of Westfield, who d. 1732. Children—*Abigail*, b. Aug. 18, 1675, m. May 4, 1695, Charles Ferry, Jr. of Springfield; *Mark*, b. Feb. 20, 1678.

3. NATHANIEL, s. of John, (1) a weaver, freeman 1683, d. Jan. 15, 1714. He m. Feb. 3, 1681, Joanna, dau. of Samuel Gardner. She d. March 18, 1729. Children—*Nathaniel*, b. Sept. 28, 1681, slain at Deerfield, 1704; *John*, b. Sept. 3, 1683, rem. to Stafford, Ct.; *Samuel*, b. and d. Jan. 15, 1687; *Samuel*, b. Jan. 24, 1688, rem. to Stafford, Ct.; *Daniel*, b. Aug. 7, 1690, rem. to Stafford, Ct.; *Elizabeth*, m. Nov. 22, 1709, Samuel Pease of Enfield; *Israel*, b. April 16, 1696, rem. to Springfield, and d. abt. 1746.

4. ELEAZAR, s. of John, (1) d. May 8, 1729, ae. 66. He m. May 27, 1689, Hester, dau. of John Taylor. She d. Dec. 28, 1748, ae. 82. Children— *Hester*, b. Aug. 3, 1692, m. May 23, 1716, Samuel Smith of Sunderland; *Eleazar*, b. July 29, 1694; *Stephen*, b. Nov. 3, 1698; *Marah*, b. Oct. 30, 1699; *Joanna*, b. Sept. 22, 1706, m. Ebenezer Moody; *Ruth*, b. abt. 1712, d. unm. Aug. 16, 1755, ae. 43.

5. MARK, s. of Mark, (2) Northampton, d. Aug. 3, 1766, ae. 88. He m. April 16, 1701, Lydia Phelps, who d. Nov. 19, 1765, in 83d yr. Children— *Lydia*, b. Feb. 9, 1702, m. abt. 1726, Abner Lyman; *Abigail*, b. Feb. 6, 1704, m. Elisha Noble of Sheffield; *Elizabeth*, b. April 9, 1706, m. 1737, Joseph Bridgman of Belchertown; *Mehitable*, b. Aug. 9, 1708, m. 1731, Noah Bridgman; *Downing*, b. Dec. 14, 1710, d. Feb. 8, 1729, ae. 18; *Mark*, b. Dec. 21, 1712; *Mary*, b. May 24, 1715, m. 1735, Israel Rust; *Daniel*, b. 1717; *Naomi*, b. Sept. 26, 1719, m. 1741, Israel Sheldon of Southampton; *Elisha*, b. Oct. 5, 1722, m. Mrs. Spaulding, and lived in Chesterfield; *Lucy*, b. Sept. 25, 1724, m. Ebenezer Edwards.

6. ELEAZAR, s. of Eleazar, (4) Sunderland, d. abt. 1777, as appears from the fact, that, his will made 1770, was proved Nov. 1777. He m. Martha. Children—*Seth*, b. 1729, m. Martha, and d. before his father, leaving wid. Martha, and four children, viz., Eleazar; Gideon; Jonathan; and Martha; *Eleazar*, b. 1733; *Jonathan*, b. 1736, d. in Albany, 1759; *Martha*.

7. STEPHEN, s. of Eleazar, (4) Granby, d. Sept. 12, 1782, ae. 85. He m. 1723, Rebecca Ferry of Springfield. Children—*Stephen*, b. Dec. 16, 1726; *Eleazar*, b. Jan. 15, 1731; *Esther*, Sept. 26, 1732.

8. STEPHEN, s. of Stephen, (7) Granby, d. Sept. 16, 1796, ae. 69. He m. (1) Mary; (2) Rachel, dau. of Peter Montague. Children—*Mary*, b. March 4, 1750; *Rachel*, b. Sept. 12, 1754; *Ruth*, b. June 16, 1756; *Sewall*, b. June 22, 1758; *Rebecca*, b. Nov. 15, 1760; *Miriam*, b. May 15, 1764; *Eli*, b. Dec. 7, 1766; *Adonijah*, b. May 24, 1769; *Jehiel*, b. March 27, 1771; *Nathan*, b. Sept. 3, 1774.

9. ELEAZAR, s. of Stephen, (7) Granby, d. June 19, 1810, ae. 79. He m. 1752, Mary Chapin, who d. Feb. 14, 1813, ae. 87. Children—*Mary*, b. May 28, 1753; *Eleazar*, b. Jan. 22, 1755; *Samuel*, b. Dec. 26, 1757, [1756?] *Violet*, b. Aug. 5, 1759; *Elisha*, b. Aug. 3, [23?] 1761; *Asher*, b. Oct. 16, 1763; *Esther*, b. Oct. 3, 1765; *Jeremiah Chapin*, b. Sept. 17, 1767, [Sept. 18, 1766?]; *Eunice*, b. May 26, 1769; *Seth*, b. May 30, 1771.

150   WARRINER—WELLS.

WARRINER, Joseph, b. in Springfield, Feb. 6, 1645, s. of William Warriner, rem. after 1686, from Had. to Enfield, and d. 1697, ae. 52. He m. (1) Nov. 25, 1668, Mary, dau. of Richard Montague. She d. July 22, 1689 ae. 47; (2) July 12, 1691, Sarah, wid. of Daniel Collins. After his death she m. Obadiah Abbee. Children—*Mary*, b. Nov. 17, 1669, m. 1691, Zechariah Booth; *Joseph*, b. Jan. 16, 1671, d. Nov. 1, 1672; *Joseph*, b. Jan. 6 1672; *Hannah*, b. Sept. 10, 1674, m. 1691, Robert Pease, Jr.; *Ebenezer*, b. Jan. 18, 1676; *Dorcas*, b. June 27, 1678; *Abigail*, b. Aug. 23, 1680, d. July 21, 1689; *Joanna*, b. Nov. 8, 1682, m. 1708, Thomas Colton; *Elizabeth*, b. Sept. 30, 1686; *Abigail*, b. May 4, 1692; *Mary*, b. May 4, 1692.

WAY, Ralph, Jr., negro, m. (1) 1765, Phillis Smith; (2) Nov. 16, 1769, Margaret Gregory. Children—*Philip*, b. Aug. 7, 1766, d. July 11, 1768; *Nancy*, b. July 20, 1768; *Ebenezer*, b. Aug. 31, 1770; *Philip*, b. Oct. 3, 1775.

1. **WEBSTER, Hon. John**, probably came into Connecticut in 1636, or 1637, of which colony he was one of the fathers. He was there a magistrate, Deputy Governor, Governor, and one of the Commissioners of the United Colonies. He was an influential member of the church in Hartford, took a deep interest in the controversy which agitated that and other churches, and was one of the leaders of the Hadley company. He was buried in Hadley, April 5, 1661. He m. Agnes. Children—*Matthew*, res. in Farmington, Ct., and d. July 16, 1655; *William; Thomas; Robert*, res. in Middletown and Hartford, and d. 1676. He m. abt. 1652, Susannah Treat;*Anne*,m. John Marsh, and d. June 9, 1662; *Elizabeth*, prob. m. William Markham; *Dau.*, name unknown, m. Jonathan Hunt of Nh.

2. **William**, s. of John, (1) d. s. p. in Hadley, abt. 1688. He m. Feb. 17, 1670, Mary, dau. of Thomas Reeve of Springfield. She d. 1696.

3. **Thomas**, s. of John, (1) res. in Nh., Had. and Northfield, and d. 1686. He m. June 16, 1663, Abigail, dau. of George Alexander of Nh. She d. before March, 1690. Children—*Abigail*, b. Jan. 9, 1668, d. in infancy; *Abigail*, b. Jan. 10, 1669; *George*, b. Nov. 7, 1670, m. 1696, Sarah Bliss of Spr.; *John*, b. Feb. 26, 1673; *Elizabeth*, b. Nov. 26, 1676; *Thankful*, b. Jan. 12, 1679, m. 1700, John Bascom; *Mary*, b. May 25, 1681.

1. **WELLS, John**, rem. prob. from Stratford, Ct. to Hatfield, and d. Oct. 18, 1692. He m. Sarah, who d. abt. 1743. Children—*Sarah; Mary; Abigail; Hannah*, b. Nov. 12, 1665, d. Nov. 24, 1676; *Hester*, b. April 26, 1668; *John*, b. Sept. 15, 1670; *Elizabeth*, b. June 21, 1675; slain Sept. 20, 1677; *Jonathan*, b. Dec. 14, 1682; *Elizabeth*, b. Jan. 10, 1686.

2. **John**, s. of John, (1) Hatfield, d. April 21, 1720, ae. 49. He m. Rachel, dau. of Samuel Marsh. Children—*John*, b. March 12, 1700, res. in Amherst, and prob. in Hardwick, and d. 1746; *Joseph*, b. March 4, 1702, res. in Amh. and Sunderland; *Samuel*, b. Nov. 19, 1704, res. in Hatfield; *Aaron*, b. Sept. 2, 1707, d. Aug. 9, 1778, ae. 71; *Sarah*, b. Jan. 21, 1710; *Jonathan*, b. April 4, 1713, res. in Shutesbury; *Noah*, b. Jan. 18, 1719; *Abigail*.

1. **WELLS, Thomas** b. abt. 1620, s. of Wid. Frances Wells, who m. Thomas Coleman, came from Wethersfield, and d. between Sept. 30 and Dec. 14, 1676, ae. abt. 56. He m. Mary. She m. (2) June 25, 1678, Samuel

Belding of Hatfield, and d. before 1691. Children—*Thomas*, b. June 10, 1652; *Mary*, b. Oct. 1, 1653, d. young; *Sarah*, b. May 5, 1655, m. David Hoyt, April 3, 1673; *John*, b. Jan. 14, 1657, d. in infancy; *Jonathan*, b. abt. 1658; *John*, b. April 3, 1660, drowned Jan. 20, 1680; *Samuel*, b. abt. 1662; *Mary*, b. Sept. 8, 1664, m. (1) Aug. 16, 1682, Stephen Belding; (2) Jan. 2, 1723, Capt. Joseph Field; *Noah*, b. July 26, 1666; *Hannah*, b. July 4, 1668, m. July 7, 1687, John White of Hat., and d. Dec. 17, 1733, ae. 65; *Ebenezer*, b. July 20, 1669, *Daniel*, b. Dec. 11, 1669, (record,) d. June 11, 1670; *Ephriam*, b. abt. 1671, m. Jan. 23, 1696, Abigail, dau. of John Allis of Hat., res. in New London and Colchester, Ct.; *Joshua*, b. Feb. 18, 1673.

2. THOMAS, s. of Thomas, (1) rem. abt. 1684 to Deerfield, and there d. 1691. He m. (1) Jan. 12, 1673, Hepzibah, dau. of Peter Buell of Windsor, Ct. She with three of her daughters was in June, 1693, knocked on the head and scalped by the Indians, but she and one dau. recovered from their injuries. She m. (2) Feb. 17, 1699, Daniel Belding. Children—*Mary*, b. Nov. 12, 1673; *Sarah*, b. 1676; *Thomas*, res. in Deerfield, m. March 29, 1700, Sarah Barnard, and d. s. p. 1750; *Eleazar*, a sailor, d. in Middletown, Ct., 1723; *John*, sent to Canada, 1706, slain May, 1709; *Daniel; David; Hepzibah*, m. John Dickinson.

3. JONATHAN, s. of Thomas, (1) captain, res. in Deerfield, and d. Jan. 3, 1739. He m. (1) Dec. 13, 1682, Hepzibah, dau. of Geo. Colton. She d. Aug. 27, 1697; (2) Sept. 23, 1698, Sarah, wid. of Joseph Barnard and dau. of Elder John Strong. She d. Feb. 10, 1733; (3) Lucy. Children—*Jonathan*, b. 1684, m. Mary, and d. abt. 1735; *David*, b. Jan. 31, 1700, d. 1700.

4. SAMUEL, s. of Thomas, (1) Hatfield, d. Aug. 9, 1690. He m. Dec. 11, 1684, Sarah, dau. of Nathaniel Clark of Northampton. She m. 1693 or 1695, Thomas Meekins, and rem. to Hartford, Ct. Child—*Samuel*, b. July 7, 1688, m. 1709, Rachel Caldwell, and rem. to Hartford.

5. NOAH, doubtless s. of Thomas, (1) was in New London, Ct., 1691, Colchester, Ct., 1709, and there d. 1712. He m. Mary [per. White, dau. of Daniel.] Children—*Noah*, b. Aug. 5, 1686; *Mary*, b. Dec. 10, 1687; *Sarah*, b. Oct. 30, 1692; *John; Jonathan; Samuel; Hannah*.

6. EBENEZER, s. of Thomas, (1) Hatfield. He m. (1) Dec. 4, 1690, Mary, dau. of Benjamin Waite; (2) 1705, Sarah, wid. of John Lawrence. Children—*Ebenezer*, b. Sept. 13, 1691, m. 1720, Abigail Barnard, and d. s. p. in Deerfield, 1758; *Thomas*, b. Sept. 25, 1693; *Joshua*, b. Aug. 31, 1695; *Martha*, b. Sept. 18, 1697, m. Feb. 4, 1720, Edward Allen; *John*, b. June 9, 1700; *Jonathan*, b. Sept. 26, 1702; *Mary*, b. Oct. 24, 1707, m. Aaron Graves.

7. THOMAS, s. of Ebenezer, (6) physician, d. in Deerfield, 1744. He m. 1736, Sarah Hawks, who d. in Whately, 1783, ae. 82. Children—*Eleazar*, b. 1728; *Ebenezer*, b. 1730; *Joseph*, b. 1731; *Thomas*, an apprentice of Dea. Ebenezer Hunt, d. in Nh., 1747; *Augustus*, b. 1734; *Sarah*, b. 1736, m. Col. William Williams of Pittsfield; *Agrippa*, b. 1738; *Mary*, b. 1741, m. Lucius Allis of Conway; *Rufus*, b. Sept. 29, 1743, grad. H. C. 1764, was ord. Sept. 25, 1771, pastor of (Cong.) church in Whately, and d. Nov. 8, 1834, ae. 91.

8. JOSHUA, s. of Ebenezer, (6) d. in Greenfield, 1768, in 73d yr. He m. 1720, Elizabeth Smead. Children—*Joshua*, b. Sept. 16, 1721; *Ebenezer*,

b. 1723; *Martha*, b. 1725, m. 1750, Daniel Nash of Greenfield; *Elizabeth*, b. 1726, d. 1737; *Simeon*, b. 1728, killed, in Johnson's fight, Sept. 8, 1755; *Asa*, b. 1730; *Elisha*, b. 1731, m. —— Graves, and d. in Hat., 1792; *Mary*, b. 1733, m. —— Holland; *Joel*, b. 1735; *Esther*, b. 1736, m. Seth Hawks.

9. JOHN, s. of Ebenezer, (6) Deerfield and Greenfield, d. abt. 1747, as is inferred from the fact, that, adm. on his estate was granted March, 1747. He m. Sarah Allen of Windsor. She m. (2) Michael Metcalf, and d. as early as April, 1761. Children—*Samuel*, b. Oct. 28, 1729, m. Margaret McCullis, (grandfather of Hon. Daniel Wells of Greenfield, Judge of the Court of Common Pleas, and Samuel Wells, Esq. of Northampton, Clerk of the Courts;) *Sarah*, b. 1732, m. Col. Isaac Lyman of Keene, N. H.; *John*, b. 1734, m. Tamar Rice; *Daniel*, b. 1735, killed in Johnson's fight, 1755; *Susanna*, b. 1737, d. young; *Elijah*, b. 1740, m. Hannah Billings; *Susanna*, b. 1743, m. —— Phelps of Suffield, Ct.; *Thomas*, b. 1745, m. —— Allen of Windsor, and res. in Keene, N. H.

10. JONATHAN, s. of Ebenezer, (6) Deerfield, d. May 7, 1735. He m. (1) 1718, Rebecca Barnard. She was b. Dec. 25, 1686, and d. Nov. 14, 1718; (2) 1723, Mary Hoyt, who d. Nov. 22, 1750. Children—*Jonathan*, b. 1724, d. Oct. 30, 1750; *David*, b. 1726, d. unm. 1802; *Mary*, b. 1728, m. —— Childs; *Samuel*, b. 1730, a Colonel in the militia, res. in Brattleboro', Vt. He m. May 20, 1751, Hannah Sheldon; *Oliver*, b. 1732; *Rebecca*, b. 1734.

WEST, DAN, m. June 13, 1771, Mary Cook. She m. (2) —— Bryant. Children—*Dan*, b. Jan. 10, (16?) 1772; *Thomas*, b. Nov. 1773, d. Sept. 22, 1775; *Dau.*, b. July 19 and d. July 24, 1776; *Thomas*, bapt. Feb. 1, 1778; *Polly*, b. Nov. 13, 1779, d. Sept. 18, 1781; *Rebekah*, b. May, 1782; *Polly*, b. May 2, 1784; *Mary*, b. May, 1785; *Roswell*, bapt. Oct. 26, 1788, d. April, 1790; *Roswell*, bapt. March 31, 1790; *Hannah*, b. June 18, 1792, m. Chester Gray; *Jerusha*, bapt. March, 1795.

WESTCARR, JOHN, physician, came to Had. abt. 1665, and d. Sept. 1675, in 31st yr. He m. Oct. 17, 1667, Hannah, dau. of Francis Barnard, who m. (2) Oct. 9, 1680, Simon Beaman.

WESTWOOD, WILLIAM, together with Bridget, his wife, sailed from England, in ship Francis, the last of April, 1634, he ae. 28, and his wife 32. He was made freeman of Mass., March 4, 1635. He removed in 1636, with Mr. Hooker and his company to Hartford, or rather arrived in Hartford before Mr. Hooker, and when the first Court was holden at Hartford in April, 1636, was one of the six men (two from each town) who composed it. One of the wealthiest and most prominent of the first settlers of Hartford, he took the same position in Hadley, where he d. April 9, 1669, ae. abt. 63. He m. Bridget, who d. May 12, 1676, ae. abt. 74. Child—*Sarah*, b. abt. 1644, m. May 30, 1661, Aaron Cook, and d. March 24, 1730, ae. 86.

1. WHITE, JOHN, came from England, in the ship Lyon, which sailed from London, June 22, 1632, and arrived in New England, Sept. 16, following. He settled in Cambridge, was adm. freeman, March 4, 1633, and rem. prob. in June, 1636 to Hartford, of which town he was an original proprietor. He was one of the first settlers of Hadley, and Representative, 1664 and 1669. About 1670, he returned to Hartford, where he was an Elder in the

South Church, and d. betw. Dec. 17, 1683 and Jan. 23, 1684. He m. Mary, who was living in March, 1666. Children—*Mary*, m. Jan. 29, 1646, Jonathan Gilbert of Hartford; *Nathaniel*, b. abt. 1629; *John; Daniel; Sarah*, m. (1) Stephen Taylor of Hat.; (2) Oct. 15, 1666, Barnabas Hinsdale of Hat.; (3) Feb. 3, 1679, Walter Hickson of Hat., and d. Aug. 10, 1702; *Jacob*, b. Oct. 8, 1645, m. Elizabeth Bunce, res. in Hartford, Ct., and d. abt. 1701.

2. NATHANIEL, s. of John, (1) deacon, res. in Middletown, Ct., was eighty-five times Representative to the General Court, and d. Aug. 27, 1711, "ae. abt. 82." He m. (1) Elizabeth, who d. 1690, ae. abt. 65; (2) Martha, wid. of Hugh Mould of New London, Ct., and dau. of John Coit. She d. April 14, 1730, ae. abt. 86. Children—*Nathaniel*, b. July 7, 1652; *Elizabeth*, b. March 7, 1655, m. John Clark of Middletown, and d. Dec. 25, 1711, ae. 56; *John*, b. April 9, 1657, m. Mary [Pierce?] res. in Hartford, Ct., and d. July, 1748, ae. 91; *Mary*, b. April 7, 1659, m. (1) Jan. 16, 1678, Jacob Cornwall of Middletown; (2) April 13, 1710, John Bacon, Sen. of Middletown, and d. Nov. 15, 1732, ae. 73; *Daniel*, b. Feb. 23, 1662, m. March, 1683, Susannah Mould, res. in Middletown, and d. Dec. 18, 1739, ae. 78; *Sarah*, b. Jan. 22, 1664, m. John Smith of Haddam, Ct.; *Jacob*, b. May 10, 1665, m. (1) Feb. 4, 1692, Deborah Shepard; (2) Dec. 16, 1729, Rebecca, wid. of Thomas Ramney, and dau. of —— Willett, res. in Middletown, Ct., and d. March 29, 1738, ae. 72; *Joseph*, b. Feb. 20, 1667, m. April 3, 1693, Mary, dau. of Hugh Mould, res. in Middletown, Ct., and d. Feb. 28, 1725, ae. 58.

3. JOHN, s. of John, (1) res. in Hatfield, where he was buried Sept. 15, 1665. He m. Sarah, dau. of Thomas Bunce. She m. (2) Nicholas Worthington of Hat., and d. June 20, 1676. Children—*Sarah*, m. Feb. 12, 1678, John Graves of Hatfield; *John*, b. 1663.

4. DANIEL, s. of John, (1) lieutenant, res. in Hatfield, freeman 1690, and d. July 27, 1713. He m. Nov. 1, 1661, Sarah, dau. of John Crow. She d. June 26, 1719, ae. 72. Children—*Sarah*, b. Oct. 15, 1662, m. (1) March 31, 1680, Thomas Loomis of Hatfield; (2) Nov. 12, 1689, John Bissell of Windsor and Lebanon, Ct.; *Mary*, d. Sept. 5, 1664; *Mary*, b. Aug. 5, 1665, m. (1) —— Wells; (2) —— Barnard; *Elizabeth*, b. Nov. 13, 1667, m. July 2, 1688, Dea. Samuel Loomis of Windsor and Colchester, Ct., and d. Feb. 18, [25?] 1736, ae. 68; *Daniel*, b. July 4, 1671; *Esther*, d. Feb. 1675; *Hannah*, b. July 4, 1674, d. in infancy; *John*, b. Nov. 16, 1676, d. Aug. 1677; *Esther*, m. Dec. 7, 1696, Lt. John Ellsworth of Windsor, Ct. and Ellington, Ct., and d. Sept. 7, 1766, ae. abt. 89; *Hannah*, b. Sept. 1679, m. Dea. Nathaniel Dickinson of Hatfield; *Mehitable*, b. March 14, 1683, m. Dec. 18, [19?] 1705, Jeremiah Bissell of Windsor, Ct.

5. NATHANIEL, s. of Dea. Nathaniel, (2) deacon, rem. abt. 1678 from Middletown, Ct. to Hadley, and settled upon the original homelot of his grandfather, Elder John White, and there took the oath of allegiance, February, 1679. He d. Feb. 15, 1742, ae. 89. He m. March 28, 1678, Elizabeth, dau. of John Savage. She was b. June 3, 1655, and d. Jan. 30, 1742, ae. 86. Children—*Elizabeth*, b. Jan. 13, 1679, d. young; *Nathaniel*, b. Nov. 4, 1680; *John*, b. Nov. 28, 1682; *Sarah*, prob. d. young; *Joseph*, b. Feb. 28, 1687; *Daniel*, b. March 1, 1690; *Jacob*, b. Dec. 5, 1691, d. June, [1692?]; *Mary*, b. Oct. 16, 1693, m. Jan. 28, 1719, Israel Dickinson; *Elizabeth*, b. Nov. 8, 1695, m. Jan. [June?] 24, 1716, Dea. Samuel Montague of Sunderland, and d. 1753, ae. 57; *William*, b. Aug. 15, 1698; *Ebenezer*, b. April 9, 1701.

6. JOHN, s. of John, Jr., (3) deacon, Hatfield, in his old age, prob. 1742, removed to Bolton, Ct., and thence to Hardwick, Mass., where he d. Nov. 13, 1750, ae. 87. He m. July 7, 1687, Hannah, dau. of Thomas Wells. She d. Dec. 17, 1733, ae. 65. Children—*John*, b. Sept. 26, 1689, m. (1) 1717, Sarah, wid. of Thomas Barber, and dau. of Jonathan Ball of Springfield. She was b. Aug. 6, 1685, and d. Nov. 3, 1744, ae. 59; (2) 1746, Hannah, dau. of John Meekins. He settled in West Springfield, and d. 1759, ae. abt. 70; *Mary*, b. Jan. 3, 1692, d. in infancy; *Hannah*, b. March 26, 1695, m. July 14, 1720, John Hastings of Hatfield; *Mary*, b. 1697, prob. d. young; *Jonathan*, b. Sept. 18, 1700, m. (1) Esther ——, who d. March 25, 1727; (2) Anna ——, who d. March 2, 1747; (3) Oct. 6, 1747, Mrs. Anna Wright, who d. Sept. 30, 1777. He res. in Hat., until 1731, when he rem. to Hebron, Ct., where he d. March 28, 1776, ae. 75; *Sarah*, m. (1) Jan. 11, 1722, Philip Smith of Hat.; (2) 1734, John Burk of Hat.; (3) Sept. 5, 1739, Daniel Griswold of Bolton, Ct.; *Elizabeth*, m. Jan. 19, 1726, Daniel White of Hat., and d. July 4, 1770, ae. abt. 65; *Martha*, b. March 14, 1708, m. Oct. 31, [Nov. 1?] 1732, Joseph Olmsted of Bolton, Ct. and Enfield, Ct.; *David*, b. July 1, 1710.

7. DANIEL, s. of Daniel, (4) settled in Hatfield, whence in 1704 or 1705, he rem. to Windsor, Ct., and d. June 22, 1726, ae. 55. He m. (1) Sarah, dau. of Thomas Bissell of Windsor, Ct. She was b. Jan. 8, 1672, and d. July 18, 1703, ae. 31; (2) July 6, 1704, Anna, dau. of John Bissell, Jr. of Windsor. She was b. April 28, 1675, and d. in Windsor, April 21, 1709, ae. 34; (3) April 25, 1710, Elizabeth, dau. of Samuel Bliss of Windsor, Ct. She was b. Feb. 28, 1687, and d. July 2, 1757, ae. 70. Children—*Sarah*, b. 1693, d. Feb. 24, 1693; *Sarah*, b. Aug. 20, 1694, m. Sept. 5, 1716, Daniel Griswold, Jr. of Windsor and Bolton, and d. in B., Feb. 1, 1738, ae. 43; *Daniel*, b. Sept. 5, 1698; *Thomas*, b. July 10, 1701, grad. Y. C. 1720, was ord. pastor of church in Bolton, Ct., Oct. 26, 1725, where he d. Feb. 22, 1763, ae. 61. He m. June 17, 1725, Martha, dau. of Jonathan Hunt of Northampton; *Joel*, b. April 6, 1705, m. (1) Ruth, who d. Sept. 4, [15?] 1735, ae. 32; (2) Jan. 22, 1736, Ruth, dau. of Daniel Dart of Bolton, Ct.; (3) April 8, 1761, Eunice, wid. of Roger Wolcott, Jr. of East Windsor, Ct., and dau. of John Colton of Longmeadow; (4) 1778, Sarah, wid. of [Shubael?] Conant of Mansfield, Ct., res. in Bolton, Ct., where he d. June 28, 1789, ae. 84; *Elisha*, b. Nov. 11, 1706, settled in Bolton, Ct., whence he rem. abt. 1744, to East Guilford, (now Madison,) Ct., and thence abt. 1749, to Killingworth, Ct., where he d. abt. 1778. He m. Aug. 31, 1732, Ann, dau. of Ebenezer Field of East Guilford, Ct.; *Simeon*, b. March 11, 1708; *Seth*, b. March 6, 1713, m. Elizabeth ——, settled in Providence, R. I., but rem. abt. 1748, to Plainfield, Ct., where he d. Jan. 1758, ae. 44; *Lucy*, b. June 16, 1715, m. (1) Joseph French of Norwich and Coventry, Ct.; (2) April 23, 1741, Josiah Wolcott of Coventry, Ct.; *Elizabeth*, b. May 18, 1717, m. Nov. 4, 1734, Samuel French of Norwich, Ct.; *Oliver*, b. March 26, 1720, m. Feb. 21, 1745, res. in Bolton and Saybrook, Ct., and d. Sept. 13, 1801, ae. 81.

8. NATHANIEL, s. of Nathaniel, (5) settled in Hadley, whence abt. 1727, he removed to South Hadley, and d. May 28, 1762, ae. 81. He m. May 10, 1709, Esther, dau. of Samuel Strong of Northampton. She was b. April 30, 1685, and d. Aug. 11, 1756, ae. 71. Children—*Nathaniel*, b. April 10, 1710; *Samuel*, b. Oct. 22, 1711, d. Nov. 22, 1711, *Timothy*, b. Aug. 9, 1712, d.

Aug. 15, 1712, *Submit*, b. Aug. 21, 1713, m. (1) July 4, 1753, William Judd of Nh.; (2) Dec. 4, 1760, Dea. John Clark of Southampton; *Esther*, b. Dec. 4, 1715, m. Samuel Dickinson of Granby; *Jonathan*. b. Jan. 29, 1717; *Christian*, b. June 6, 1720, d. July 13, 1720; *Child*, b. and d. Jan. 2, 1722; *Christian*, b. May 9, 1723, d. Dec. 11, 1732, ae. 9; *Samuel*, b. Oct. 1, 1725, d. Oct. 25, 1745, ae. 20; *Child*, b. and d. March 17, 1728.

9. JOHN, s. of Nathaniel, (5) prob. d. prior to 1766. He m. (1) Jan. 5, 1715, Martha Church; (2) Feb. 27, 1722, Abigail Atherton, who prob. d. May 10, 1766. Children—*Martha*, b. March 18, 1716, m. Nov. 14, 1734, Henry Bartlett; *Abigail*, m. Feb. 16, [Jan. 19?] 1749, John Brooks of Hat.; *Ruth*, m. (1) Nov. 1, 1748, Daniel Rood; (2) 1764, Jacob Taylor of So. Had.; *Oliver*.

10. JOSEPH, s. of Nathaniel, (5) deacon, res. in Had. and So. Had., and d. before 1770. He m. Feb. 3, 1709, Abigail, dau. of Thomas Craft, or Croft. She d. Nov. 15, 1770, ae. 82. Children—*Moses*, b. Feb. 7, 1710; *Abigail*, b. Aug. 20, 1713, m. July 17, 1734, John Alvord, Jr. of So. Had., and d. Nov. 19, 1757, ae. 44; *Thomas*, b. July 20, 1715; *Joseph*, b. Oct. 4, 1718; *Mary*, b. Oct. 15, 1721, d. July 8, 1726; *Rebecca*, b. March 11, 1724, m. Jan. 17, 1745, Josiah Moody of Had. and So. Had., and d. Sept. 15, 1751, ae. 27; *Mary*, b. June 25, 1727, m. Dec. 11, 1744, William Eastman of Granby, and d. Nov. 19, 1752, ae. 25; *Josiah*, b. 1729.

11. WILLIAM, s. of Nathaniel, (5) d. May 30, 1774, ae. 75. He m. (1) March 22, 1728, Mary, wid. of John Taylor, and dau. of John Selden. She d. Aug. 10, 1735, ae. 32; (2) June 2, 1737, Martha, dau. of Daniel Warner. She d. Oct. 3, 1787, ae. 81. Children—*Mary*, b. Feb. 2, 1729, m. Ebenezer Dodd of New Haven and Guilford, Ct.; *Sarah*, b. Oct. 6, 1730, m. 1764, Thomas Chamberlain of Coos, N. H., and d. before 1788; *William*, b. Oct. 4, 1732; *Daniel*, b. Aug. 10, 1734, d. Dec. 10, 1738; *Nathaniel*, b. Nov. 12, 1738; *Daniel*, b. Sept. 1, 1740; *Martha*, b. Aug. 3, 1742, m. April 26, 1770, William Cooke, and d. Oct. 14, 1816, ae. 74; *Ebenezer*, b. March 16, 1744, m. March 13, 1766, Abigail, dau. of Abraham Porter of Hartford, Ct., settled in Pittsfield, and d. May 15, 1794, ae. 50; *John*, b. March 28, 1746, d. unm. May 22, 1819, ae. 73; *David*, b. Feb. 18, 1748.

12. EBENEZER, s. of Nathaniel, (5) d. March 23, 1733, ae. 31. He m. Oct. 28, 1730, Ruth Atherton, who d. April 29, 1785, in her 85th yr. Children—*Rachel*, b. abt. 1731, d. unm. May 25, 1815, ae. 83; *Ebenezer*, b. abt. 1733.

12½. DANIEL, s. of Daniel, (7) captain, rem. with his father's family from Hat. to Windsor, Ct., but returned as early as 1719 to Hat. In 1731, he rem. to Bolton, Ct., whence in 1742 he again returned to Hat. and there d. Dec. 15, 1786, ae. 88. He m. (1) Oct. 7, 1719, Mary Dickinson of Hat., who d. July 8, 1721; (2) Jan. 19, 1726, Elizabeth, dau. of Dea. John White. She d. July 4, 1770, ae. abt. 65. Children—*Salmon*, b. June 22, 1721, d. in infancy; *Daniel*, b. Dec. 28, 1726; *Mary*, b. Aug. 30, 1729, m. Dr. Elijah Paine of Hat. and Williamsburgh, and d. April 19, 1804, ae. 74; *Salmon*, bapt. Oct. 31, 1731; *Elihu*, bapt. April 21, 1734; *Elizabeth*, bapt. Sept. 5, 1736, m. Gen. Seth Murray of Hat., and d. Feb. 4, 1814, ae. 77; *Hannah*, b. Oct. 26, 1740, prob. d. young.

156 WHITE.

[Omission here in First Edition.]

retained her physical and mental powers, in a good degree, almost to the close of life. Children—*Simeon*, b. 1745, m. Aug. 2, 1770, Hannah, dau. of Elisha Hubbard of Hatfield, res. in Williamsburgh, and Rutland, N. Y., and d. Aug. 20, 1820, ae. 75; *Asa*, b. 1747, m. Jan. 20, 1785, Zilpah Hayes of Granby, Ct., settled in Williamsburgh, and there resided till his death, except a few years, from 1812 to 1816, when he lived in Chesterfield. He d. Sept. 15, 1829, ae. 82; *Jerusha*, b. 1751, m. Jan. 6, 1789, Arnold Mayhew of Williamsburgh, and d. Dec. 1, 1839, ae. 88.

14. NATHANIEL, s. of Nathaniel, (8) South Hadley, d. March 23, 1787, ae. 77. He m. Nov. 24, 1741, Martha, dau. of Thomas Bascom of Northampton. She was b. Sept. 16, 1713, and d. Dec. 6, 1796, ae. 83. Children— *Timothy*, b. 1743, d. unm. Feb. 21, 1789, ae. 46; *Samuel*, b. Oct. 3, 1747, m. Sept. [Oct.?] 1771, Mary Collins, res. in So. Had., and d. Jan. 22, 1817, ae. 69; *Nathaniel*, b. Nov. 28, 1749, res. in So. Had. until abt. 1794, when he rem. to Easthampton, where he d. Oct. 15, 1828, ae. 72. He m. May 14, 1778, Huldah, dau. of Eliakim Clark; *Christian*, b. 1751, d. unm. May 5, 1801, ae. 50; *Ezekiel*, b. 1754, was a physician in So. Had. where he d. unm. Nov. 3, 1789, ae. 35; *Ebenezer*, b. May 6, 1756, m. Sept. 26, 1793, Ruth, dau. of Benjamin Lyman, res. in So. Had. and Ludlow, and d. March 29, 1829, ae. 73; *Ezra*, b. 1758, d. unm. April 7, 1790, ae. 32.

15. JONATHAN, s. of Nathaniel, (8) South Hadley, d. Aug. 2, 1789, ae. 72. He m. (1) Dorcas Alvord, who d. Nov. 24, 1744, ae. 24; (2) Feb. 6, 1745, Lydia, dau. of Samuel Rugg. She was b. Jan. 1, 1723, and d. Nov. 18, 1802, ae. 80. Children—*Enoch*, b. Nov. 8, 1744, d. Nov. 15, 1744; *Enoch*, b. Feb. 1747, m. Susannah, dau. of Thomas Goodman of So. Had., res. in So. Had., where he was a deacon, selectman and representative, and d. Jan. 10, 1813, ae. 65; *Phineas*, b. 1748, d. in New Haven, Ct., Sept. 5, 1769, while a member of Yale College; *Thankful*, m. Enos Goodman of So. Had.; *Lydia*, b. 1759, m. Darius Smith of So. Had. and Susquehannah, N. Y., and d. March, 1837, ae. 78; *Phebe*, m. Gad Alvord of Granby.

16. OLIVER, s. of John, (9) d. June 28, 1789, ae. abt. 65. He m. (1) Feb. 17, 1752, Elizabeth Charter, who d. June 29, 1752; (2) 1755, (pub. Jan. 18,) Abigail Selden. Children—*Son*, b. June 6, 1752, d. Aug. 15, 1752; *Oliver*, b. Dec. 19, 1755; *Elizabeth*, b. Nov. 29, 1757, m. Phinehas Clark of Easthampton, and d. March 25, 1847, ae. 89; *Moses*, b. Dec. 3, 1759; *Jerusha*, b. March 5, 1762, m. Aug. 1781, Seth Kellogg; *Eunice*, b. March 18, 1764; m. March 2, 1784, George Wells, and rem. abt. 1800, to N. Y. or Vt.; *Elihu*, b. March 8, 1766, d. March 27, 1766; *Esther*, b. April 2, 1768, m. Jan. 1, 1789, William Ingram, who rem. to N. Y.; *Abigail*, b. Sept. 24, 1770, m. Feb. 11, 1789, Green Wells of Mapletown, and rem. to Vt. or N. Y.

17. MOSES, s. of Dea. Joseph, (10) South Hadley, a trader, d. prob. in 1783, ae. 73. He m. July 29, [1738?] Lydia Bellows. Children—*Lydia*, b. March 30, 1739, d. April 19, 1739; *Child*, b. and d. March 30, 1739; *Elizabeth*, b. 1741, m. Reuben Judd of So. Had., and d. May 9, 1765, ae. 24.

18. THOMAS, s. of Dea. Joseph, (10) South Hadley, d. July 18, 1795, ae. 80. He m. Mindwell Alvord, who d. Aug. 25, 1764, ae. 59. Children— *Joel*, prob. m. Anna, and d. 1771; *Mindwell*, b. 1739, m. (1) —— Looman; (2) Lt. Thomas White, 2d, of So. Had., and d. Oct. 10, 1768, ae. 29; *Abigail*, m. Caleb Ely of So. Had. and Norwich; *Aaron*, b. May 29, 1744, m. March 6,

1770, Thankful, dau. of Jonathan White, and d. in So. Had., Feb. 8, 1810, ae. 65; *Job*, b. abt. 1752, m. (1) Charity, dau. of Benoni Chapin of Springfield; (2) Oct. 6, 1785, Mindwell Clapp, res. principally in Northampton, and d. Feb. 12, 1807, ae. 54; *Mary*, b. July 1, 1754, m. Dec. 3, 1780, Perez Smith of So. Had., and d. March, 10 1835, ae. 80; *Simeon*.

19. JOSEPH, s. of Dea. Joseph, (10) South Hadley, d. Nov. 1795, ae. 77. He m. Oct. 23, 1746, Editha Moody, prob. dau. of Ebenezer Moody of So. Had. She d. July, 1793. Children—*Editha*, b. Jan. 27, 1748, m. —— Chamberlain; *David*, b. Oct. 14, 1749, d. unm. Sept. 1811, ae. 62; *Moses*, b. April 10, 1751, m. Abigail, and d. in So. Had., Sept. 15, 1777, ae. 26; *Rebecca*, b. Jan. 14, 1753, m. Eleazer Goodman, and rem. to the vicinity of Lake George, N. Y.; *Joseph*, b. Dec. 13, 1754, m. Dec. 14, 1788, Sally Yoemans of Colchester, Ct., res. in So. Had., and d. July 30, 1829, ae. 74; *Lois*, b. Oct. 20, 1756; *Miriam*, b. Aug. 2, 1758, m. Samuel Alvord of So. Had., and d. Feb. 25, 1844, ae. 85; *Reuben*, b. Oct. 1, 1761, m. May 18, 1797, Mabel, dau. of Nathaniel White, rem. in 1818, from So. Hadley to Belchertown, and d. Feb. 27, 1856, ae. 94.

20. JOSIAH, s. of Dea. Joseph, (10) deacon, South Hadley, d. March 29, 1809, ae. 80. He m. March 16, 1749, Mary, dau. of Samuel Smith of So. Had. She d. Sept. 21, 1818, ae. 85 or 86. Children—*Maria*, b. Aug. 13, 1749, d. unm. Aug. 29, 1772, ae. 23; *Mary*, b. Feb. 13, 1752, m. Phineas Smith; *Irene*, b. March 30, 1755, d. Sept. 12, 1757; *Josiah*, b. Feb. 22, 1759, d. Feb. 12, 1760; *Josiah*, b. March 30, 1761, m. Nov. 22, 1787, Mabel, dau. of David Mitchell of So. Had. He was a farmer in So. Had., and d. Feb. 26, 1829, ae. 88; *Irene*, b. Feb. 26, 1763, d. Oct. 2, 1775, ae. 12; *Keziah*, b. March 30, 1766, m. Dec. 31, 1799, Joel Clark of So. Had., and d. Nov. 28, 1810, ae. 44; *Eldad*, b. March 31, 1768, m. March 31, 1789, Hannah, dau. of Ezra Day of So. Had., and d. in So. Had., April 11, 1823, ae. 55; *Medad*, b. Sept. 5, 1771, d. Oct. 10, 1771; *Medad*, b. Nov. 25, 1774, d. Sept. 26, 1775.

20½. WILLIAM, s. of William, (11) resided in Hinsdale, N. H., in Northfield and Springfield, Mass., and d. in Had., Dec. [30?] 1810, ae. 78. He m. (1) April, 1757, Lydia, dau. of Elizur Patterson of Northfield. She was b. 1737; (2) Nov. 14, 1765, Martha Chapin of Springfield. Children—*Giles*, m. Sarah Dodd, and rem. to Cobleskill, N. Y., as early as 1797; *Sarah*; *Mary; William; Samuel; Gad*, m. Flavia.

21. NATHANIEL, s. of William, (11) kept tavern on the "Bay Road," and d. March 12, 1821, ae. 82. He m. (1) Nov. 5, 1761, Sarah, dau. of Abel Stockwell of Springfield. She was b. March 10, 1742, and d. March 4, 1802, ae. 60; (2) Rebecca Shepard of Hartford, Ct. Children—*Jarib*, b. April 27, 1763; *Sarah*, b. March 27, 1765, m. Nov. 16, 1791, Orange Hart Warren of Williamsburgh, and d. Dec. 1828, ae. 63; *Lydia*, b. March 27, 1765, m. Jan. 8, 1800, Benjamin Burr of So. Had., and d. Feb. 28, 1834, ae. 69; *Mabel*, b. Sept. 1, 1767, m. May 18, 1797, Reuben White of So. Had. and Belchertown, and d. Sept. 20, 1855, ae. 88; *Lois*, b. July 20, [22?] 1770, m. Jan. 16, 1794, Cotton Mather Warren of Williamsburgh, and d. July 19, 1842, ae. 72; *Tirzah*, b. Aug. 13, 1772, m. Nov. 8, 1797, Phineas Thompson of Palmer.

22. DANIEL, s. of William, (11) captain, d. Nov. 17, 1815, ae. 75. He m. June 11, 1772, Sarah, dau. of Aaron Goodrich. She was b. Oct. 10, 1747, and d. 1837, ae. 90. Children—*Zenas*, b. Oct. 10, 1773, a farmer, d. unm.

Sept. 16, 1844, ae. 71; *Judith*, b. March 27, 1775, m. March 10, 1806, Eli Graves, and d. June 2, 1837, ae. 62; *Bethene*, b. Feb. 14, 1777, m. Jan. 10, 1798, Eli Graves, and d. Aug. 12, 1802, ae. 25; *Sarah*, b. Jan. 26, 1779, m. Jan. 22, 1799, John Cook; *Permelia*, b. Nov. 2, 1780, m. Jan. 23, 1805, Roswell Wells of Had. and Waterbury, Vt.; *Grace Grant*, b. Oct. 18, 1782, m. Nov. 28, 1802, Stephen Montague; *Silva*, b. April 20, 1785, m. Aug. 8, 1813, John Baker of Westhampton; *Daniel*, b. Nov. 6, 1789.

23.   DAVID, s. of William, (11) was a lieutenant in the Expedition to Canada, early in 1776, and d. abt. 1778.   He m. Dec. 17, 1772, Roxcellany Warner.   She m. (2) May 20, 1779, Joseph Crafts of Whately.   Children— *Cotton*, bapt. July 10, 1774; *Luther*, bapt. Sept. 10, 1775, m. and rem. to the South.

24.   EBENEZER, s. of Ebenezer, (12) d. Oct. 11, 1817, ae. 84.   He m. Sarah, dau. of Samuel Church of Amh.   She d. abt. 1802, ae. abt. 66.   Children—*Sarah*, b. 1770, m. Nov. 1787, John Sumner of Had. and Belchertown; *Jonathan*, b. Oct. 29, 1774; *Elijah*, b. June 28, 1778.

25.   DANIEL, s. of Daniel, (12½) Hatfield, d. Aug. 13, 1805, ae. 78.   He m. 1754, Submit Morton of Hat., who d. July 21, 1798, ae. 71.   Children—*Sarah*, b. March 6, 1755, m. March 24, 1780, Lt. Samuel Smith of Hat., and d. Dec. 7, 1843, ae. 88; *Lucy*, b. Aug. 23, 1757, m. Jan. 26, 1779, Elijah Smith of Hat., and d. June 9, 1839, ae. 81; *Hannah*, b. June 8, 1759, m. June 22, 1780, Elisha Hubbard of Hat. and Williamsburgh, and d. March 27, 1824, ae. 64; *Eunice*, b. Oct. 10, 1761, m. March 1, 1789, Amasa Wells of Hat., and d. April 28, 1824, ae. 62; *Submit*, b. March 28, 1764, m. Feb. 19, 1783, Nathan Bliss of Hat., and d. Aug. 8, 1840, ae. 76; *Daniel*, b. March 17, 1766, m. (1) March 8, 1796, Lucy Allis; (2) Sept. 27, 1815, [1814?] Lucy Burt; (3) Sept. 2, 1834, Elizabeth, wid. of Cotton White; (4) Sarah, wid. of Moses Burt, and dau. of Ebenezer Fitch of Hat.   He was a physician, res. for several yrs. in Whitestown, N. Y., but returned to Hat., and d. Jan. 26, 1848, ae. 81; *Elijah*, b. April 26, 1768; *John*, b. and d. Feb. 27, 1775.

26.   SALMON, s. of Daniel, (12½) res. in that part of Hatfield which became Whately, was a member of the third Provincial Congress in Mass., and deacon of the church in Whately.   He d. June 21, 1815, ae. 83.   He m. Mary Wait, who d. June 22, 1821, ae. 90 or 91.   She was perhaps dau. of Joseph Wait of Hat.   Children—*Salmon*, b. Sept. 22, 1760, m. (1) Lydia Amsden of Deerfield; (2) Nov. 27, 1799, Anna, wid. of Josiah Allis, was a farmer in Whately, where he d. May 1, 1822, ae. 61; *John*, b. Jan. 9, 1762, m. Feb. 7, 1796, Elizabeth, dau. of Samuel Brown of Worcester, was a farmer, representative, and deacon in Whately, and d. April 2, 1836, ae. 74; *Mary*, b. Jan. 24, 1764, m. March 24, 1785, Ebenezer Arms of Greenfield, and d. in Prattsburg, Steuben Co., N. Y., Dec. 26, 1837, ae. 73; *Elizabeth*, b. Feb. 18, 1766, m. Oct. 31, 1787, Perez Hastings of Hatfield; *Mercy*, b. March 3, 1768, m. Nov. 14, 1798, Asahel Wright, Jr. of Deerfield, and d. Aug. 25, 1842, ae. 74; *Judith*, b. Dec. 29, 1770, was for more than twenty years a highly successful teacher in Whately, and d. unm. April 18, 1824, ae. 53; *Thomas*, b. April 12, 1773, m. Aug. 30, 1795, Hannah, dau. of Nathan Harwood of Windsor, was a farmer and blacksmith in Ashfield, where he d. Aug. 17, 1848, ae. 75; *Electa*, b. Sept. 22, 1775, m. Nov. 27, 1800, Elijah Allis of Whately, and d. April, 1859, ae. 83.

26½. ELIHU, s. of Daniel, (12½) Hatfield, was in May, 1775, chosen with John Dickinson to represent the town in the Provincial Congress, to be held at Watertown, on the 31st of May. He d. Dec. 23, 1793, ae. 60. He m. Zeruiah, dau. of Ebenezer Cole of Hat. She m. (2) Feb. 19, 1795, Capt. Perez Graves of Hat. She was b. Nov. 30, 1741, and d. Dec. 13, 1820, ae. 79. Children—*Electa*, b. June 4, 1764, m. June 26, 1783, Benjamin Morton of Hat., and d. abt. 1835; *Ebenezer*, b. Feb. 28, 1766, m. Jan. 10, 1793, Mary Dickinson, was a farmer in Hat., and d. Jan. 6, 1826, ae. 60; *Elihu*, b. Dec. 17, 1767, m. July 5, 1792, Sarah Smith, and d. in Hat., June 26, 1816, ae. 48; *Lois*, b. Oct. 14, 1769, m. Feb. 19, 1789, Joseph Smith, 2d, of Hat., and d. Oct. 10, 1829, ae. 60; *Anna*, b. Dec. 14, 1771, m. Dec. 30, 1790, Elias Lyman of Hartford, Vt., and d. Feb. 11, 1844, ae. 72; *Patty*, b. Dec. 14, 1773, m. (1) March 24, 1795, Elihu Robbins of Hat.; (2) Elisha Clapp of Deerfield, and d. abt. 1856; *Betsey*, b. Jan. 28, [27?] 1776, m. June, 1798, Wyllys J. Cadwell of Montpelier, Vt., and d. Sept. 30, 1849, ae. 73; *Nabby*, b. April 30, 1778, m. Aug. 1804, Isaac Freeman of Montpelier, Vt.; *Jonathan Cole*, b. Feb. 17, 1780, m. Cynthia Parkhurst, was a hatter, settled in Hartford, Vt., and d. Aug. 17, 1844, ae. 64.

27. OLIVER, s. of Oliver, (16) rem. abt. 1800 to Vt. or N. Y. Children— *Eunice*, bapt. in Had., Feb. 6, 1795; *Anne*, bapt. in Had., Feb. 6, 1795.

28. MOSES, s. of Oliver, (16) d. Nov. 10, 1823, ae. 64. He m. Jan. 17, 1788, Chloe Peck. Children—*David*, b. Sept. 24, 1788; *Cynthia*, b. Jan. 14, 1792, m. Dec. 15, 1814, Jonathan Smith; *Elihu*, b. Sept. 22, 1794.

29. JARIB, s. of Nathaniel, (21) a farmer in Amherst, d. Feb. 2, 1821, ae. 57. He m. Feb. 24, 1794, Ruth, dau. of Thomas Sherman of Bridgewater. She was b. July 10, 1763. Children—*Jay*, b. Jan. 8, 1795, m. June 29, 1823, Caroline Wood, was a merchant in Amh., and d. April 1, 1825, ae. 29; *Orra*, b. March 8, 1796, m. June 1, 1821, Rev. Edward Hitchcock, D. D., LL. D. of Amherst College; *Bela*, b. Feb. 23, 1798, m. (1) Feb. 1, 1832, Julia Ann Stratton; (2) Harriet Hoppin, and res. near Omaha City, Nebraska; *Perez*, b. Aug. 14, 1799, d. July 31, 1800; *Mabel*, b. May 8, 1801, d. Aug. 16, 1803; *Rebecca*, b. Feb. 13, 1803, d. Aug. 19, 1803; *George*, b. July 5, 1806, grad. A. C. 1825, a physician, d. unm. in Carlinville, Macoupin Co., Ill., Sept. 1, 1834, ae. 28.

30. DANIEL, s. of Daniel, (22) is a farmer, m. Sept. 25, 1816, Dorcas, dau. of Eleazar Barrows of Barre. She was b. Sept. 29, 1790. Children— *Sarah Jane*, b. Oct. 2, 1817, m. April 22, 1840, Enos Foster Cook of Amh.; *Daniel Sherman*, b. Aug. 25, 1819, d. Sept. 20, 1819; *Pamela Wells*, b. March 3, 1824, d. Aug. 25, 1832, ae. 8; *George*, b. Dec. 2, 1825; *Daniel Sherman*, b. Aug. 10, 1827; *Charles*, b. July 3, 1831, is a physician in Chicago, Ill.; *John Baker*, b. Dec. 4, 1833, is a druggist in New York.

31. COTTON, s. of David, (23) res. in Hat. and Had., and d. in Hat., May 19, 1826, ae. 52. He m. (1) Oct. 9, 1799, Demis Dickinson, who d. Dec. 20, 1801; (2) Feb. 19, 1807, Elizabeth Bancroft of Westfield. She m. (2) Sept. 2, 1834, Dr. Daniel White of Hat. She was b. in Westfield, Nov. 8, 1787, and d. May 20, 1843, ae. 55. Children—*Sarah*, b. Aug. 20, 1800, m. —— Taylor; *David*, b. July 5, 1809; *Elizabeth*, b. April, 1816, m. Rev. Mr. McKee of New York.

32. JONATHAN, s. of Ebenezer, (24) d. April 13, 1846, ae. 71. He m. (1) May 30, 1799, Lydia Atwood, who d. abt. 1811; (2) Phebe, dau. of Isaac Rider. She d. May 15, 1856, ae. 69. Children—*Thankful; Pamela*, m. Charles Warner; *Sarah; Ruth*, m. Nov. 22, 1824, Samuel Dunakin; *Lydia*, m. John Miller; *Susan*, m. Nov. 28, 1833, James Wilbur of Hat.; *Olive*, m. —— Stacey of Davenport, Iowa; *Phebe*, m. (1) Sept. 1841, Samuel Hager of Enfield; (2) June 25, 1857, Stoddard Meekins; *Jonathan*, b. Dec. 21, 1817; *Emeline*, m. Levi Ramsdell of Westfield; *Elijah*, b. June 23, 1821, d. July 2, 1821.

33. ELIJAH, s. of Ebenezer, (24) d. Nov. 24, 1856, ae. 78. He m. Dec. 24, 1799, Lucy, dau. of Josiah Pierce, Jr. She d. Oct. 18, 1855, ae. 77. Children—*Josiah*, b. Aug. 1, 1800, m. Hannah Cushing of Chesterfield, and res. in Dover, Wis.; *Samuel Sumner*, b. May 10, 1803; *Ebenezer*, b. Sept. 11, 1805, m. 1829, Mary Ann Coon, and res. in Dover, Wis.; *Delia*, b. Jan. 20, 1808, m. March 28, 1827, Isaac Stall; *Margaret Smith*, b. March 20, 1811, m. April, 1828, Lewis Tower.

34. DAVID, s. of Moses, (28) d. April 18, 1851, ae. 62. He m. (1) Jan. 15, 1815, Mary Bumps of Pelham, who d. 1836, ae. 34; (2) Sept. 1836, Celinda D., dau. of Abial Bragg of Enfield. She was b. July 4, 1805. Children—*Cynthia*, m. (1) Stephen Atwood; *Zenas*, m. and lives in Wisconsin; *Oliver; Sarah Ann*, b. April 22, 1822, m. Oct. 18, 1843, Lyman Stocking of Chicopee; *James Porter; Reuben*, b. Feb. 1830; *Sylvester*, b. Nov. 28, 1832; *Harvey*, b. June 2, 1836; *Albert Rensselaer*, b. Dec. 1837; *Mary Bumps*, b. March 26, 1843.

35. ELIHU, s. of Moses, (28) d. Sept. 5, 1850, ae. 56. He m March 21, 1820, Ruth, dau. of Isaac Rider of Enfield. She was b. Feb. 27, 1797. Children—*Eliza Ann*, d. ae. 1 yr.; *George Smith; Henry*, b. Feb. 1824, d. unm. Jan. 12, 1854, ae. 30; *Eliza Ann*, b. June 11, 1826, m. June 3, 1846, Lewis H. Wilder; *Moses*, m. Sept. 1848, Jane Berditt; *David; Elijah*, b. Jan. 3, 1830.

36. GEORGE, s. of Daniel, (30) m. March 14, 1851, Elizabeth S., dau. of William Judd of So. Had. She was b. Sept. 12, 1831. Child—*Ellen Jane*, b. Dec. 10, 1855.

37. DANIEL SHERMAN, s. of Daniel, (30) m. Feb. 24, 1854, Elizabeth W., dau. of Chester Powers of New Salem. Child—*Edward Sherman*, b. Jan. 27, 1858.

WILLIAMS, CHARLES, prob. removed to Colchester, Ct. He m. Elizabeth. Children—*Charles*, b. Oct. 1691; *Weeks*, b. Feb. 13, 1693; *John*, b. June 13, 1695; *Abraham*, b. April 28, 1696, d. 1697; *Abraham*, b. May 20, 1698.

1. WILLIAMS, REV. CHESTER, s. of Rev. Ebenezer of Pomfret, Ct., grad. Y. C. 1735, was ord. Jan. 21, 1741, third pastor of the church in Had., and d. Oct. 13, 1753, in 36th yr. He m. Aug. 23, 1744, Sarah Porter. She m. (2) Feb. 17, 1756, Rev. Samuel Hopkins, and d. Feb. 5, 1774. Children—*Penelope*, b. July 18, 1745, m. Nov. 15, 1770, Samuel Gaylord; *John Chester*, b. March 6, 1747; *Nehemiah*, b. Jan. 27, 1749, grad. H. C. 1769, m. 1775, Percy Keyes, was ord. Feb. 9, 1775, pastor of church in Brimfield, where he

d. Nov. 26, 1796, ae. 47. He possessed to a great extent the confidence of his people. As a public speaker, he was universally acceptable. His preaching was evangelical and plain. A volume of his sermons was published after his death; *Martha*, b. Nov. 27, 1750, m. Nov. 4, 1779, Rev. Nathaniel Emmons, D. D., of Franklin; *Sarah*, b. Aug. 10, 1752, d. unm. June 9, 1836, ae. 83.

2. JOHN CHESTER, s. of Rev. Chester, (1) grad. Y. C. 1765, rem. to Randolph, Vt., and d. May 18, 1819, ae. 72. He m. Nov. 14, 1770, Lois, dau. of Obadiah Dickinson. She d. Sept. 7, 1787. Children— *Henry Dickinson*, b. Oct. 6, 1771, a carpenter, res. in Randolph, Vt.; *Emily*, b. May 31, 1773, d. in Northfield, July 13, 1789, ae. 16; *Mary*, b. Aug. 17, 1775; *Sarah*, b. July 17, 1778; *Child*, b. and d. May 10, 1780; *Chester*, b. June 15, 1781, a hatter; *Horace*, b. Sept. 27, 1785, rem. to Black River, N. Y.

1. WILLIAMS, REV. WILLIAM, was b. in Newton, 1666, grad. H. C. 1683, was settled over the church in Hatfield, about 1686, and d. Aug. 29, 1741, in 76th yr. He m. (1) Elizabeth, dau. of Rev. Seaborn Cotton. She was b. Sept. 13, 1665, and d. Aug. 7, 1698, ae. 32; (2) Aug. 9, 1699, Christian Stoddard, who d. April 23, 1764, ae. 87. Children—*William*, b. April 30, 1687, d. May 5, 1687; *William*, b. May 11, 1688, m. —— Stoddard, and was minister of Weston; *Martha*, b. Oct. 10, 1690, m. Edward Partridge; *Elisha*, b. Aug. 26, 1694, Rector of Yale Col., d. in Wethersfield, Ct.; *Solomon*, b. June 4, 1700, minister of Lebanon, Ct.; *Elizabeth*, b. June 1, 1707; *Israel*, b. Nov. 30, 1709; *Dorothy*, b. June 20, 1713, m. Rev. Jonathan Ashley of Deerfield.

2. ISRAEL, s. of Rev. William, (1) d. Jan. 9, 1788, ae. 78, having broken his skull by falling down his cellar stairs. He m. Sarah, dau. of John Chester of Wethersfield, Ct. She d. Sept. 18, 1770, ae. 63. Children—*John*, b. May 26, 1732, grad. H. C. 1751, and d Nov. 7, 1751, ae. 19; *William*, b. June 10, 1734, d. in Dalton, March 1, 1808, ae. 74; *Israel*, d. April 11, 1823, ae. 79; *Sarah*, m. —— Marsh, and res. in Ashuelot, N. H.; *Eunice*, m. Israel Stoddard; *Jerusha*, m. William Billings; *Elizabeth*, m. Feb. 9, 1780, Elisha Billings; *Lucretia*, m. Feb. 15, 1786, John C. Williams, and d. 1834, ae. 81.

1. WOODBRIDGE, REV. JOHN, was b. in West Springfield, Dec. 25, 1702, s. of Rev. John Woodbridge, grad. Y. C. 1732, was settled over the church in So. Had., April 21, 1742, and retained that connection until his death, which occurred Sept. 10, 1783, ae. 80. He m. (1) Tryphena, dau. of Rev. Benjamin Ruggles. She was b. 1707, and d. Jan. 10, 1749, in 42d yr.; (2) Wid. Martha Strong, dau. of —— Clark of Nh. She d. Aug. 20, 1783, in 58th yr. Children—*Tryphena*, b. July 31, 1731, m. S. Preston; *John*, b. July 24, 1732; *Benjamin Ruggles*, b. Oct. 16, 1733; *Jahleel*, b. Sept. 13, 1751, d. Dec. 31, 1825; *Æneas*, b. 1752, d. Jan. 6, 1832, ae. 79; *Sylvester*, b. May 10, 1754; *Caroline*, b. Dec. 14, 1756, d. Feb. 27, 1785; *Sophia*, b. 1761, m. Rev. Joseph Strong.

2. JOHN, s. of Rev. John, (1) So. Hadley, a trader, was for eight years in the French war as captain, and a major in the Revolutionary war. He d. Dec. 27, 1782, ae. 50. He m. Mary Whitney of Watertown. Children— *Dorothy*, b. May 2, 1763; *Lucy*, b. Jan. 6, 1765; *John*, b. July 12, 1769, d. Dec. 2, 1835; *Martha*, b. Jan. 8, 1771; *Ruggles*, b. June 1, 1775.

WOODBRIDGE, Rev. John, was b. in Southampton, Dec. 2, 1784, s. of Dr. Timothy Woodbridge, grad. W. C. 1804, was ord. as pastor of the church in Hadley, June 20, 1810, and remained in that connection until Sept. 15, 1830, when he was dismissed to take the pastorate of the Bowery Presbyterian Church in New York City. After a short ministry over the last named church, Dr. W. was settled in Bridgeport, and New Hartford, Ct., and on the 16th of Feb. 1842, became the first pastor of the Russell Society in Hadley. He was dis. July 15, 1857 from his charge, and has since resided in Hadley. He m. Mary Ann, dau. of Thomas Y. Seymour of Hartford, Ct. She d. June 16, 1858. Children—*Mindwell*, b. March 20, 1815, m. Oct. 5, 1847, George A. Gibbs, Esq., of Chicago, Ill., and d. Oct. 3, 1849, ae. 34; *Mary Ann*, b. July 13, 1817, m. (1) Aug. 11, 1840, Aaron Hawley, who d. Aug. 19, 1847; (2) July 20, 1850, Rev. Parsons Cook, D. D., of Lynn; *Susan Augusta*, b. Aug. 30, 1819; *Emeline*, b. Nov. 23, 1821, m. Feb. 2, 1848, William P. Dickinson, and rem. to Chicago, Ill.; *Charlotte*, b. March 6, 1824, m. Aug. 4, 1842, Elisha S. Wadsworth of Chicago, Ill.; *Rebecca*, b. March 22, 1826, m. Oct. 2, 1850, Erastus S. Williams, Esq., of Chicago, Ill.; *John*, b. March 3, 1829, m. July 10, 1851, Elizabeth Butler, and is a lawyer in Chicago, Ill.; *Louisa Christmas*, b. Sept. 10, 1831; *Elizabeth Octavia*, b. Jan. 10, 1836, m. Sept. 10, 1853, Rev. Richard H. Richardson of Chicago, Ill.

WOODWARD, Samuel, m. Sarah. Children—*Sarah Smith; George Douglass*, b. Nov. 4, 1800; *Sophronia Williams*, b. Jan. 17, 1803; *Abigail Willard*, bapt. Oct. 1807; *Samuel Williams*, bapt. Feb. 4, 1810.

1. WORTHINGTON, Nicholas, Hatfield, d. Sept. 6, 1683. He m. (1) Sarah, wid. of John White, and dau. of Thomas Bunce of Hartford, Ct. She d. June 20, 1676; (2) Susanna ——. She m. (2) 1684, Capt. Jonathan Ball of Springfield, and d. March 9, 1727. Children—*Elizabeth*, m. —— Morton; *William*, b. abt. 1670, m. Wid. Mehitable Morton, and d. in Colchester, Ct., May 22, 1753; *Mary*, b. Jan. 24, 1674; *Jonathan; John*, b. Aug. 17, 1679; *Margaret*, d. April 8, 1682.

2. DANIEL, s. of Daniel, gr. s. of William, and gr. grandson of Nicholas, (1) bapt. Aug. 19, 1733, m. 1772, Margaret Parsons of Palmer. Children— *Amasa*, b. May 9, 1773; *Daniel*, b. March 1, 1775; *Elijah*, b. Oct. 22, 1776; *Child*, b. Aug. 1782, d. Sept. 19, 1782, ae. 40 days; *Elizabeth*, b. May 22, 1784, d. May 24, 1784; *Son*, b. Aug. 24, 1785, d. Oct. 24, 1785; *Son*, b. and d. Oct. 4, 1786.

WRIGHT, Charles, b. in Northampton, Jan. 5, 1719, s. of Samuel, res. in Amherst for many years, but prior to 1762 rem. to Pownal, Vt., where he d. Dec. 23, 1793. He m. Oct. 19, 1742, Ruth, dau. of Solomon Boltwood of Amherst. She d. April 15, 1806, ae. 83. Children—*Solomon*, b. June 27, 1743, d. young; *Samuel*, b. Feb. 8, 1745; *Dorcas*, b. Dec. 31, 1750, m. Ebenezer Woolcott; *Josiah*, b. April 9, 1752, res. in Pownal, Vt., and at the date of his death, which occurred Jan. 2, 1817, ae. 64, was Chief Judge of the Bennington Co. Court, and a member of the Executive Council; *Sarah*, b. July 18, 1757, m. Abel Russell, and d. in Salem, N. Y.; *Esther*, b. Nov. 13, 1760, m. (1) —— Bates; (2) —— Kingsley, and d. in Scipio, N. Y.; *Solomon*, b. Dec. 28, 1762, res. in Pownal, Vt., m. Nov. 19, 1782, Eunice, dau. of

Thomas Jewett of Bennington, Vt., held various important offices, among others, that of Chief Judge of Bennington Co., and d. March 24, 1837, ae. 73.

1. WRIGHT, SAMUEL, b. in Northampton, s. of Samuel, m. (1) May 11, 1757, Penelope Leonard; (2) Nov. 11, 1772, Elizabeth Stevens. Children— *Paul; Silas*, b. May 17, 1760; *Ozias*, rem. to Maine; *Esther*, m. Sept. 21, 1800, Dea. Jason Stockbridge.

2. SILAS, s. of Samuel, (1) res. in Amh. until Feb. 1796, when he rem. to Weybridge, Vt., where he d. May 13, 1843, ae. 72. He m. Sept. 26, 1780, Eleanor, dau. of Isaac Goodale of Amh. Children—*Samuel*, b. Aug. 18, 1785, m. Feb. 15, 1810, Electa Langdon; *Orinda*, b. March 19, 1788, m. May 31, 1810, Josiah Parker; *Lucretia*, b. March 16, 1790, m. Chester Elmer; *Eleanor*, b. Sept. 22, 1792, m. Sept. 21, 1813, Alpheus Bigelow; *Silas*, b. May 24, 1795, grad. Mid. Col. 1815, m. Sept. 11, 1833, Clarissa Moody, settled as an Attorney in Canton, N. Y., was State Senator and Comptroller, Representative and Senator in Congress, Gov. of the State, and d. Aug. 27, 1847, ae. 52; *Daniel L.*, b. April 10, 1799, m. April 26, 1826, Martha Williamson; *Pliny*, b. Dec. 14, 1805.

WYATT, ISRAEL, removed from Hatfield to Colchester, Ct. He m. Dec. 10, 1690, Sarah Pratt. Children—*Sarah*, b. July 8, 1691; *Israel*, b. Sept. 26, 1696; *Susannah*, b. Sept. 26, 1696; *Israel*, b. Nov. 26, 1700; *Hannah*, b. April 10, 1703.

YOUNGLOVE, JOHN, removed as is supposed from Ipswich to Brookfield, where he was a preacher, though not ordained. About 1675, he came to Hadley, and for several years taught the Grammar School. He afterwards preached in Suffield, where he d. June 3, 1690. He m. Sarah, who d. Jan. 17, 1710. Children—*John; Samuel*, b. Feb. 10, 1676, m. July 28, 1696, Abilene Hunter; *James*, b. Oct. 6, 1701, m. Hannah Phelps, and d. in Suffield, Oct. 21, 1723; *Joseph*, b. Nov. 26, 1682, m. Anna, and res. in Suffield, Ct.; *Sarah*, m. Sept. 25, 1682, John Taylor of Suffield, and d. June 19, 1683; *Mary*, m. Dec. 2, 1689, Thomas Smith of Suffield, and d. June 24, 1743; *Hannah*, m. Dec. 11, 1695, George Norton of Suffield, and d. Nov. 23, 1715; *Lydia*, m. April 26, 1693, George Granger of Suffield.

ADDENDA

BASS, SAMUEL. Children—*Elizabeth*, bapt. April 30, 1781; *Seth*, bapt. March 23, 1783.

BEAMAN, REV. WARREN HARRISON, m. April 27, 1841, Elizabeth Lydia, dau. of Rev. Samuel Worcester, D. D. of Salem. She was b. Dec. 19, 1814. Children—*Mary Elizabeth*, b. Feb. 19, 1842; *Emma W.*, b. Oct. 4, 1843; *John Warren*, b. Dec. 28, 1845; *Anna Jane*, b. Jan. 10, 1848, d. 1849; *Mina D.*, b. 1853.

BLAKE, WILLIAM, m. Sarah Chapin, dau. of Enos Nash. Children— *Francis*, b. Sept. 1827, d. 1828; *Emily*, b. Jan. 11, 1829; *Mary Shipman*, b. June 10, 1834; *Sarah Jane*, b. Aug. 6, 1837; *Catharine Shipman*, b. Jan. 15, 1842.

COOLEDGE, NATHANIEL, Jr., deacon, merchant, Representative 1828, d. April 9, 1835. He m. Nov. 7, 1827, Lois Eastman, dau. of William Porter.

COWLES, SILAS, b. Nov. 4, 1779, s. of David, (10) p. 30, d. He m. Dec. 22, 1805, Zilpha Shumway. Children—*Myra*, bapt. 1811, m. May 21, 1829, Simeon Clark, of Amherst; *Daniel*, bapt. 1811, m. Mary Henderson; *Lewis*, bapt. 1815, m. (1) Nov. 14, 1833, Pamela E. Bolles; (2) May 18, 1854, Eliza Henderson; *Elijah*, bapt. 1812; *David S.*, bapt. 1816; *Emily*, bapt. 1818; *Asa*, d.; *Elijah*, bapt. 1824; *Zilpha Gilbert*, bapt. 1829.

CURTIS, REV. JOSEPH W., d. March 16, 1857. He m. for his second wife, Nov. 27, 1836, Lois Eastman, wid. of Dea. Nathaniel Cooledge, Jr., and dau. of William Porter. Children—*Charlotte Porter*, b. Nov. 21, 1838, d. Sept. 10, 1840; *William Porter*, b. March 23, 1843, d. March 2, 1844; *James Edwards*, b. Jan. 23, 1845, d. March 2, 1845.

DOWNING, JOHN, Braintree, 1673, rem. to Hat. He m. July 20, 1676, Mary, widow of Thomas Meekins, Jr. Children—*Jonathan*, b. Jan. 1677; *John*, b. Oct. 29, 1678.

DRURY, JOHN. Child—*Abel*, b. 1780.

DUNAKIN, ANDREW, m. Oct. 10, 1798, Anna Pierce. Children—*Henry*, bapt. 1803; *Dolly*, bapt. 1803; *Anna*, bapt. 1809.

DWIGHT, NATHANIEL, s. of Timothy, was b. in Dedham, Nov. 25, 1666, settled in Hatfield, whence about 1695, he removed to Nh. He d. in Springfield, Nov. 7, 1711, ae. 44. He m. Dec. 9, 1693, Mehitable, dau. of Col. Samuel Partridge of Hat. She d. Oct. 19, 1756, ae. 82. Children—*Timothy*, b. Oct. 19, 1694, m. Aug. 16, 1716, Experience King, and res. in Nh.; *Samuel*, b. June 28, 1696; *Mehitable*, b. Nov. 11, 1697, d. Dec. 22, 1697; *Daniel*, b. April 29, 1699, grad. Y. C. 1721; *Seth*, b. Oct. 3, 1702, d. Sept. 12, 1703; *Elihu*, b. Feb. 17, 1704; *Abia*, b. Feb. 17, 1704, m. Samuel Kent of Suffield, Ct.; *Mehitable*, b. Nov. 2, 1705, m. abt. 1728, Abraham Burbank; *Jonathan*,

b. March 14, 1708; *Ann*, b. July 2, 1710, m. 1731, Abel Caldwell of Hartford, Ct.; *Nathaniel*, b. June 20, 1712, m. Jan. 1735, Hannah Lyman, rem. to Belchertown, and d. 1784.

FOX, JOEL, m. April 19, 1801, Lucinda Cook, and had besides those children mentioned on page 53, *Amy Smith*, bapt. April 6, 1806; and *Calvin*, bapt. Aug. 21, 1808.

HAWLEY, LEVI, b. Nov. 28, 1798, s. of Chester, who was s. of Zechariah, who was s. of Samuel, (2) p. 67, m. Nov. 23, 1820, Harriet, dau. of Elijah Nash, and d. Feb. 16, 1844. Children—*Mary*, b. May 23, 1822, m. July 3, 1845, Joseph Vincent, of Ashfield; *Caroline R.*, b. Nov. 6, 1824, m. Nov. 27, 1845, Enos D. Williams, of Amh.; *Harriet W.*, b. Nov. 3, 1826, m. Zebulon Taylor; *Levi Parsons*, b. Oct. 12, 1828, d. May, 1829; *Levi Parsons*, b. July 19, 1830 m. Abigail J. Boise; *Julia Electa*, b. Feb. 3, 1833, d. Oct. 1851; *Henry Elijah*, b. Aug. 1, 1836, d. March 2, 1837; *Elbertine Maria*, b. July 24, 1838; *Ellen R.*, b. Oct. 21, 1839; *Elijah Knights*, b. May 15, 1844.

HOOKER, JOSEPH, rem. from Had. to Watertown, N. Y., where he d. He m. (1) —— Spur; (2) Mary, dau. of Nathan Seymour. Children by second wife—*Nancy Spur*, m. William Wood of Watertown, N. Y.; *Mary*, m. O. B. Brainerd of Watertown, N. Y.; *Sarah R.*, m. Rev. M. L. R. P. Thompson, D. D., of Cincinnati, O.; *Joseph*, b. 1815, grad. at West Point, 1837, served with distinction in Mexico as aid-de-camp to Brig. Gen. Hamer, was for a few years in U. S. service in California and Oregon, resigned his commission in 1853, and became a farmer in Sonora, on the Bay of San Francisco. At the breaking out of the Rebellion in 1861, he tendered his services to the Government, and was soon appointed Brigadier General of Volunteers, and later on account of his valor at the battle of Antietam, was made Major General.

HODGE, JOHN, b. Oct. 19, 1760, s. of George, p. 70, m. March 19, 1789, Sarah Dickinson. Children—*Son*, b. April, 1789; *Son*, b. April, 1791; *Child*, b. July, 1793.

JOHNSON, STEPHEN, m. April 14, 1791, Sarah, dau. of Israel Lyman. She d. Sept. 19, 1835, ae. 65. Children—*Betsey; Roxy; Alfred; Chester*, bapt. March 10, 1798; *Sally*, bapt. Dec. 29, 1799; *Stephen*, bapt. May 9, 1802; *Rachel*, bapt. June 3, 1804; *Letha*, bapt. Oct. 12, 1806; *Emeline*, b. Feb. 1809.

LYMAN, ZADOC, prob. s. of Israel, p. 90, and b. March 26, 1774. He prob. d. Dec. 8, 1849. Children—*Samuel; Watson; Lucretia; William; Horace*, bapt. Dec. 5, 1802; *Zadoc*, bapt. 1804; *Rodney*, bapt. Aug. 3, 1806; *Charles*, b. Nov. 6, 1808.

MARSH, CALVIN, m. Oct. 7, 1800, Anna Smith. Children—*Orsamus*, m. Harriet Smith; *Hiram*, bapt. Aug. 30, 1804, m. Betsey, dau. of Jason Stockbridge, and res. in Boston; *Chapman*, bapt. 1806; *Calvin*, bapt. 1808; *Oliver; Elizabeth; Ann; Elihu; Merriam*.

MARSH, TIMOTHY, b. Oct. 5, 1751, s. of Ebenezer, (11) p. 92, d. Oct. 19, 1796, ae. 45. He m. Sept. 23, 1779, Mary Smith. Children—*Child*, b. and d. Oct. 25, 1780; *Mary*, b. Nov. 1781; *Sarah*, bapt. Oct. 26, 1783; *Clarissa*, bapt. April 9, 1786; *Lois*, b. June, 1788.

PORTER, JAMES BAYARD, s. of William, (15) p. 114, is a merchant. He m. Jan. 6, 1836, Susan Parsons. Children—*Edward Clarke*, b. Dec. 3, 1836, grad. Y. C. 1858, delivered the poem at the Bi-Centennial Celebration; *Charlotte Williams*, b. Oct. 6, 1840; *William Parsons*, b. March 9, 1844.

PORTER, JONATHAN EDWARDS, b. May 17, 1766, s. of Eleazar, (12) p. 113, grad. H. C. 1786, and m. Fidelia, dau. of Timothy Dwight of Nh., was by profession a lawyer. Children—*Dau.*, b. Aug. 13, 1793; *Julia*, bapt. May 7, 1797; *Timothy Dwight*, bapt. May 7, 1797; *Theodore W.*, bapt. Oct. 20, 1799.

PORTER, *Mary*, dau. of Elisha, (13) p. 114, d. May 13, 1769; *Lucy*, of do., d. Oct. 18, 1770; *Patience*, of do., d. April 20, 1773.

Lucretia, first wife of Elihu Smith, (No. 71) p. 134, d. May 7, 1810. *Lucretia*, dau. of do., d. May 7, 1810; *Sophia*, dau. of do., m. Park Smith of Nelson, N. Y.; *David*, s. of do., d. Aug. 31, 1825; *Sarah C.*, dau. of do., d. Jan. 1, 1810. By his second wife, Elizabeth Hubbard, whom he m. July, 1811, and who d. Oct. 14, 1854, Elihu Smith had *Sarah Cook*, b. May 20, 1812, m. June 5, 1833, Edmund Smith; *Elizabeth Eastman*, b. Nov. 1813, m. Fordyce M. Knapp of Cummington; *Margaret Gaylord*, b. Jan. 1, 1816, m. Abel D. Forrest of Morrisville, N. Y.

SHIPMAN, SAMUEL, s. of Samuel, d. in Had. He m. Oct. 20, 1831, Mary Stebbins, dau. of Enos Nash. Children—*Sarah Wells*, b. Nov. 7, 1832, d. Sept. 23, 1848; *George Smith*, b. June 6, 1836; *Mary Warner*, b. Aug. 23, 1838; *Lucy Miller*, b. Aug. 23, 1838; *Ellen Elizabeth*, b. March 8, 1845.

STOCKBRIDGE, CALEB, s. of David, m. (1) 1795, Sarah Allis of Hatfield; (2) April 6, 1805, Mrs. Achsah Fairbanks. Children—*Caleb; Eber; Allis; David.*

STOCKBRIDGE, JASON, s. of David, deacon in No. Had. church, Representative, 1835, d. 1860. He m. (1) Sept. 21, 1800, Esther, dau. of Samuel Wright; (2) Oct. 26, 1815, Abigail, dau. of John Montague of Sunderland. Children by first wife—*Samuel*, bapt. Aug. 30, 1804; *Betsey*, bapt. April 25, 1805, m. Hiram Marsh, and res. in Boston; *Jason*, b. April 5, 1806. By second wife—*Levi*, Representative, 1855; *Henry Smith*, grad. A. C. 1845, is a lawyer in Baltimore, Md.; *Elvira*, d.

SUMNER, JOHN, from Belchertown, d. July, 1804. He m. Nov. 1787, Sarah, dau. of Ebenezer White. She d. Aug. 1803, ae. 33. Children— *Zebina*, b. April, 1788, d. 1792; *Susan*, b. July, 1790, d. Dec. 1811, ae. 21; *Margaret*, b. March 29, 1792, m. Nov. 19, 1816, Addi Wallis; *Samuel*, b. April, 1794, d. Aug. 1800; *John*, bapt. Aug. 27, 1795, d. 1795.

WARNER, JONATHAN, b. Dec. 16, 1773, s. of Lemuel, (17) p. 148, m. June 22, 1796, Sally Shipman. Children—*Elizabeth*, bapt. Aug. 17, 1796; *Emily*, bapt. Nov. 5, 1797; *Charles*, bapt. Feb. 3, 1799; *Elizabeth*, bapt Jan. 18, 1801; *Dorothy*, bapt. 1803; *Sally Shipman*, bapt. June 2, 1805; *Henry Phelps*, bapt. June 28, 1806; *Henry Phelps*, bapt. Sept. 18, 1808.

INDEX

TO THE GENEALOGIES.

NOTE:— Dash (———) indicates given name unknown.

Graves, Isaac, 18, 51, 54, 59, 60, 61, 64, 75, 100.
Israel, 60, 144.
Jemima, 59, 60, 61, 87.
Jerusha, 61.
Joel, 61.
John, 5, 54, 59, 60, 61, 123, 153.
John Judd, 27.
Jonathan, 59, 60, 61, 62.
Joseph, 59, 60, 61, 62.
Josiah Dwight, 62.
Jotham, 137.
Judith, 60.
Kellogg, 62.
Levi, 62.
Lucius, 60.
Lucy, 60, 61, 62.
Lydia, 60, 61.
Margaret, 62.
Martin, 61, 62.
Martha, 29, 31, 45, 59, 60, 61, 62, 66, 102.
Mary, 54, 59, 60, 61, 62, 104, 145, 148.
Matthew, 61, 101.
Mehitable, 59, 60, 61, 100.
Miriam, 60, 145.
Moses, 59, 60, 62, 78, 92.
Nancy, 62.
Naomi, 62.
Nathan, 61.
Nathaniel, 5, 59, 60, 61.
Noah, 60, 61, 62.
Oliver, 60, 120.
Patience, 62.
Penelope, 61.
Perez, Capt., 159.
Perez, 56, 59, 60, 61, 62.
Phinehas, 61.
Randall, 62.
Rebecca, 59, 60, 61, 102.
Reuben, 61, 62.
Rhoda, 61.
Rufus, 61.
Ruth, 60.
Sally, 62.
Samuel, 59, 60, 61, 62.
Sarah, 31, 59, 60, 61, 62, 96.
Selah, 62.
Seth, 60.
Silas, 52, 60, 61.

Graves, Simeon, 61, 74.
Solomon, 62.
Submit, 61, 62, 75, 78.
Susanna, 62.
Sybil, 62.
Thankful, 61.
Thomas, 59, 60.
Timothy, 61, 62.
Walter, 62.
William, 62.
William Morton, 45.
Zebadiah, 61.
Zeruiah, 62.
———, 37, 152.
Gray, Chester, 152.
Cyrus W., Rev., 133.
Green, Clark, 62, 66.
David, 62.
Eliph, 119.
Eliphalet, 62.
Elizabeth, 62.
Eunice, 62.
Hepzibah, 62.
Jared, 62.
Joel, 62.
Judith, 62.
Lucina, 62.
Lucretia, 62.
Mercy, 62.
Phebe, 62.
Philomela, 62.
Polly, 62.
Rhoda, 62.
Rufus, 14, 62.
Sybil, 62.
Timothy, 21, 62.
Timothy, Jr., 65.
Zera, 62.
Gregory, Margaret, 150.
Grey, James, 63, 92.
John, 63.
Gridley, Timothy J., 94.
Grimes, ———, 52.
Griswold, Azubah, 53.
Daniel, 154.
Mercy, 56.
Nathaniel, 53.
Grout, Susan, 45.
Grover, Dorcas, 97.
Hosea, 63.
Diadema, 63.
Josiah, 63, 97.
Leonard, 63.
Phineas, 63.
Ruth Marilla, 63.
Gubtill, Benjamin, 14.
Guernsey, Isaac, 32, 164.
James, 47, 143.
Gull, Anna, 63.
Elizabeth, 63.

Gull, Esther, 56, 63.
Mary, 63.
Mercy, 63.
William, 8, 63, 123.
Gunn, Abel, 63.
Christian, 63, 74.
Daniel, 22.
Editha, 63.
Elizabeth, 63.
John, 63.
Lucretia, 46.
Mary, 63, 74.
Moses, 63, 76, 95.
Nathaniel, 11, 63, 87.
Perly, 40.
Rufus, 63.
Samuel, 63, 74.
Samuel, Dea., 74.
Sarah, 22, 35, 63, 87.
———, 91.

HADLOCK, Josiah, 64.
Hager, Samuel, 160.
Hale, Abigail, 130.
John, 63.
Joseph, 63.
Martha, 63.
Priscilla, 63.
Samuel, 63.
Thomas, 63, 90, 130.
William, 63.
Haley, Hannah, 63.
John, 32, 55, 63, 139.
Hall, Erastus, 75.
Rebecca, 48.
Samuel, 69.
Sybil, 97.
Halsted, Matthew O., 49.
Hamer, Brig. Gen., 165.
Hamilton, Calvin, 65.
Chauncey, 65.
James, 78.
Jude, 45.
Lydia F., 65.
Mary, 45.
Norman, 27.
Sarah, 128.
———, Wid., 36.
Hamlin, Giles, 32.
John, Jr., 108.
Richard, 125.
———, 108.
Hammond, Azubah, 42.
Hannah, 63.
Martha, 63.
Martha, Mrs., 83.
Molly, 63.
Nathaniel, 63.

Sherman, Thomas, 159.
Shipman, Elizabeth, 29.
Ellen Elizabeth, 166.
George Smith, 166.
John, 29, 33.
Lucy Miller, 166.
Mary Warner, 166.
Sally, 166.
Samuel, 105, 166.
Sarah Wells, 166.
Shumway, Betsey, 40.
Rufus, 110.
Zilpha, 31, 164.
Sikes, John, 25.
Nathaniel, 94.
Sarah, 57.
———, 78.
Skinner, Aaron, 103.
Lydia, 103.
Smead, Ebenezer, 61.
Elisha, 84.
Elizabeth, 151.
John, 6.
Joseph, 51.
Judith, 67.
Rachel, 78.
Thankful, 61.
William, 67.
Smith, Aaron, 76, 125, 127, 131.
Abby Phillips, 136.
Abel, 131.
Abial, 58, 128.
Abigail, 25, 49, 74, 82, 95, 111, 120, 121, 124, 126, 127, 128, 129, 130, 131, 133, 135, 144.
Abner, 120, 127, 147.
Achsah, 130, 133.
Adeline, 137.
Agnes, 120.
Albert Douglass, 136.
Albert G., 135.
Alethea, 11, 133.
Alexander, 120, 121, 122.
Alfred Little, 135.
Allen, 134, 136.
Almena, 136.
Almira, 86, 135
Amasa, 128.
Amy, 145.
Andrew, 131.
Andrew Murray, 136.
Anna, 37, 48, 66, 124, 132, 133, 134, 136, 165.
Anne, 128, 133.
Ann Porter, 135.
Anson, 132, 136.
Arad, 131.

Smith, Aristobulus, 84.
Arthur, 138.
Arthur Hampden, 135.
Asa, 121, 128, 131.
Asahel, 128.
Asenath, 9, 119, 134, 136.
Aurelia, 29.
Azubah, 127.
Bathsheba, 121.
Benjamin, 31, 80, 120, 121, 122, 123, 124, 126, 129.
Benoni, 124.
Benoni Mandeville, 133.
Beriah, 130.
Bethia Chapin, 136.
Betsey, 122, 133, 136.
Betsey Adeline, 136.
Bridget, 99, 125.
Caleb, 121, 122, 123, 128, 135.
Calvin, 131, 136.
Caroline, 134, 136.
Catherine, 127, 131.
Catherine Amelia, 123.
Catherine Mary, 138.
Charles, 133, 134, 137.
Charles Frederick Harrington, 137.
Charles Hitchcock, 137.
Charles Porter, 123.
Charles Sidney, 135.
Charlotte Carrina, 137.
Chester, 122, 123, 134.
Chileab, 39, 56, 95, 100, 123, 124, 125, 126, 129, 133, 139.
Chloe, 133.
Christopher, 108, 122.
Clarinda, 122.
Clarissa, 79, 123, 136.
Clarissa Cook, 133.
Clarissa Delphia, 137.
Clement, 27.
Cordelia, 136.
Cotton, 58, 97, 122, 123, 133.
Cynthia Maria, 137.
Daniel, 25, 120, 121, 122, 124.
Darius, 130, 156.
David, 25, 38, 84, 125, 126, 127, 129, 130, 132, 133, 134, 147, 166.
David R., 37.
Delia, 115, 134.
Dennis, 135.
Dinah, 126.
Docia, 122.
Dorcas, 138.

Smith, Dorothy, 93, 116, 117, 120, 127, 131, 138.
Dudley, 114, 133, 136.
Dudley Porter, 136.
Ebenezer, 13, 36, 81, 82, 124, 125, 126, 129, 132, 138, 139.
Ebenezer Dennis, 138.
Edmund, 122, 123, 166.
Edmund Hubbard, 123.
Edward, 120, 121, 122, 124.
Edward Chester, 123.
Edward Taylor, 137.
Edward Warner, 123.
Edward Worthi., 135.
Edwin, 135, 137, 138.
Edwin Clapp, 123.
Eleanor, 100, 126.
Eleazar, 120, 124, 127, 128, 130.
Eleazar, Dea., 25.
Electa, 129, 131, 133.
Eli, 37, 79, 105, 130, 132, 135, 138.
Eliakim, 56, 72, 82, 120, 126, 128.
Elias, 121, 122.
Elihu, 24, 74, 123, 131, 133, 134, 137, 166.
Elijah, 120, 121, 130, 131, 132, 133, 135, 158.
Elisha, 20, 125, 126, 127, 129, 132, 133, 139.
Elisha, Dea., 12, 125,
Eliza Ann, 138.
Eliza Augusta, 137.
Elizabeth, 9, 25, 35, 63, 76, 78, 93, 102, 104, 120, 121, 122, 123, 124, 125, 128, 129, 130, 131, 133, 134, 139, 166.
Elizabeth Edwards, 133.
Elizabeth Little, 135.
Elizabeth Marsh, 134.
Elizabeth, Mrs., 83.
Ellen Maria, 135.
Eloisa, 132.
Emily Wright, 137.
Emma Elizabeth, 137.
Enos, 38, 41, 115, 123, 128, 132, 134, 137, 139.
Enos, Dr., 106.
Enos Dickinson, 134, 137.

202   GENEALOGICAL INDEX.

Vinton, Rhoda, 144.
Samuel, 143.
Samuel, Dr., 129, 144.
Samuel Farley, 15.
Samuel Finley, 144.
Sarah Eliza, 144.
Simeon, 143, 144.
Tamar, 143.
Ursula, 144.

WADE, Sally, 30.
Wait, Asa, 121, 125.
Bathsheba, 145.
Benjamin, 11, 125, 144, 145.
Canada, 144.
Damaris, 103.
Daniel, 65.
David, 145.
Dolly, 67.
Eleanor, 101, 144.
Elijah, 147.
Elisha, 52, 84, 144.
Elizabeth, 103.
Esther, 101.
Eunice, 115, 144.
Gad, 145.
Hannah, 113, 145.
Hepzibah, 145.
Jeremiah, 59, 144, 145.
John, 11, 12, 54, 64, 65, 144.
Joseph, 144, 145, 147, 158.
Lucius, 130.
Lucy, 145.
Luke, 85.
Lydia, 20, 144, 148.
Martha, 144, 145.
Martin, 56, 76.
Mary, 7, 66, 144, 145, 158.
Miriam, 145.
Moses, 145.
Nathan, 12, 145.
Rachel, 78.
Reuben, 145.
Rhoda, 145.
Samuel, 66, 145.
Sarah, 11, 144.
Simeon, 145.
Thomas, 129.
William, 103, 115, 128.
Waite, Benjamin, 151.
Canada, 126.
Mary, 151.
Wakefield, John, 58.
Hannah, 58.
Walbridge, ———, 112.

Wales, Anna, 68, 110.
Jemima, 39.
Walker, Ebenezer, 145.
Elijah, 145.
Ephraim, 145.
Hannah, 145.
Isaiah, 145.
Israel, 145.
John, 23.
Nathan, 15.
Susanna, 145.
Walter, 145.
Walkup, Beulah, 31.
Wallace, ———, 129.
Wallis, Addi, 145, 166.
Amy Saxton, 145.
Daniel, 145.
David, 145.
Elijah, 145.
Polly, 145.
Ruth, 145.
Ruth Sexton, 145.
Sarah, 145.
Sarah Sumner, 145.
William, 26, 141, 145.
Ward, Betsey, 145.
Grace, 145.
Isaac, 145.
Lebbeus, 109.
Lois, 145.
Lucretia, 67, 145.
Lucy, 145.
Mary, 53, 145.
Mary Dexter, 146.
Nahum, 74, 145.
Nathaniel, 90, 145.
Obadiah, 145.
Samuel D., 133.
Samuel Dexter, 56, 146.
Samuel Gaylord, 146.
Sarah, 145.
Susan, 45.
Susanna, 145.
Sybil, 145.
Wardsworth, Elisha S., 162.
Elizabeth, 143.
John, 140.
William, 89.
———, 72.
Ware, Samuel, Rev., 14.
Wares, Emma, 144.
Warner, Andrew, 146.
Aaron, 39, 98, 119, 146, 147.
Abel, 148.
Abigail, 147, 148, 149.
Abraham, 146, 147.
Achsah W., 106.
Adonijah, 149.

Warner, Andrew, 32, 146.
Ann, 73, 147.
Anna, 90, 146, 147.
Asher, 149.
Charles, 160, 166.
Comfort, 147.
Daniel, 13, 56, 57, 73, 76, 111, 146, 147, 148, 149, 155.
David, 146, 147, 148.
Deborah, 31.
Dorothy, 42, 148, 166.
Downing, 149.
Ebenezer, 146, 147.
Eleazar, 11, 128, 141, 148, 149.
Eli, 147, 149.
Elihu, 148, 149.
Elisha, 148, 149.
Elizabeth, 112, 119, 142, 146, 147, 148, 149, 166.
Emily, 166.
Esther, 128, 146, 147, 149.
Eunice, 23, 147, 149.
Gideon, 146, 148, 149.
Giles, 148.
Hannah, 76, 98, 146, 147, 148.
Harriet, 148.
Henry Phelps, 166.
Hester, 149.
Hope. 147.
Ichabod, 146.
Isaac, 13, 32, 101, 146, 147.
Israel, 147, 149.
Jacob, 57, 146, 147, 148.
Jahiel, 99, 149.
Jemima, 57.
Jeremiah Chapin, 149.
Jesse, 120, 147.
Joanna, 99, 149.
John, 13, 100, 146, 147, 148, 149.
Jonathan, 6, 60, 106, 146, 147, 148, 149, 166.
Jonathan C., 42.
Joseph, 74, 146, 147, 148.
Joshua, 147.
Josiah, Jr., 49.
Lemuel, 110, 134, 148, 166.
Lucy, 28, 148, 149.
Lydia, 146, 147, 148, 149.
Marah, 149.

www.ingramcontent.com/pod-product-compliance
Lightning Source LLC
Chambersburg PA
CBHW062027270326
41929CB00014B/2347

9780806346526